# GEORGE WASHINGTON'S
# AMERICA

BOOKS BY *JOHN TEBBEL*

*History:*
George Washington's America
The Battle for North America (editor)

*Biography:*
The Life and Good Times of William Randolph Hearst
George Horace Lorimer and the Saturday Evening Post
The Marshall Fields
An American Dynasty

*Novels:*
The Conqueror
Touched with Fire

*Medical:*
Your Body: How to Keep It Healthy

*Textbook:*
Makers of Modern Journalism (with Kenneth N. Stewart)

E·P·DUTTON & CO. INC
1852  1954
CREATIVE · 102 YEARS · PUBLISHING

# George Washington's
# AMERICA

By

*JOHN TEBBEL*

New York
E. P. Dutton and Company, Inc.

1954

TO THE MEMORY OF
DOUGLAS SOUTHALL FREEMAN
A GENTLEMAN AND A SCHOLAR

# CONTENTS

Introduction

I first met George Washington in the pages of a buff-colored volume titled, *With Washington in Braddock's Campaign*, which I suppose is the place thousands of other boys encountered him, as the literary embodiment of the bland face staring down at them every day from the schoolroom wall.

It was not easy to escape that picture. It followed a boy from school to school, grade to grade, and with it went the legends of the cherry tree, the coin thrown across the Rappahannock, and George's inability to do what all of us did regularly.

A boy with a curious mind could not find out much about Washington. History classes gave him dates and places to remember, and facts to be memorized quickly the day before examinations. If no flesh-and-blood Washington emerged from the standard educational process, there was no living Lincoln, either, and nothing that more than approximated reality in our study of the American past, for it has always been the curse of public-school history teaching that the student is given only two things: facts and attitudes. There were certain facts about Washington to be remembered; there was a certain attitude to be absorbed. Any deviation from either of these norms would get a history teacher into trouble with his school board.

In college, however, curiosity might be partly satisfied, if a boy had a passion for history. By reading the nineteenth-century biographies of Washington, one could see that there was more to the father of his country than appeared on the smooth academic surface. But the picture on the schoolroom wall still lacked reality.

The debunking biographies of the twenties and early thirties were clearly not the answer. From their pages Washington emerged as more than real, so vivid that he appeared in caricature. For one who wanted to believe in Washington as a great

man, these attempts at "humanizing" him raised the suspicion
that the image these authors had created was no more real than
Parson Weems's idealized portrait.

The scholarship of recent years, however, has been a different matter. Curtis Nettels, Carl Van Doren, Thomas Wertenbaker, Alfred Hoyt Bill and other outstanding professional historians have brought the story of Washington and his times into scholarly perspective.

The crowning achievement has been Douglas Southall Freeman's six-volume definitive *Washington,* the completion of which by his own hand was sadly cut short in June 1953, when the nation lost a man who had given it much. It was my privilege to know Dr. Freeman, and to study under him at the School of Journalism, in Columbia University. Afterward, I saw him occasionally, sometimes on the street, or in the classroom, or on a train or plane. He was never too busy to stop and talk, although he worked every waking minute on a fantastic schedule. When I began writing books, he wrote me encouraging notes from time to time, letters that glinted with his characteristic humor, * signed in his minute script.

The present volume would not have been written without Dr. Freeman's teaching and inspiration seventeen years ago, and might not have been attempted without the example he set in his biography, and so I have dedicated it to his memory.

The book is in no sense a formal biography of Washington. It is the story of Washington's travels over the face of America, how he looked to the nation, and how the nation appeared to him. It is about where he slept, what he ate, what he talked about, where he lived, and what his problems were, both emotional and political. It is the story of a great man and his relation to the places and people of his own time, in a period when it was possible for a President of the United States to be as close to his

* He wrote once that he thought I would be able in time to do a history of journalism from "the rise of Hearst until his death, which I hope will not be unduly delayed."

*Introduction*

constituents as a State Representative is today. Inevitably, of course, a biographical portrait emerges, and I have tried to suggest something of the meaning these journeys and experiences of Washington had for him, and may have for us today.

The plan of the book divides it into five sections. In the first of these, I have attempted to define the limits of Washington's America, and to tell of his explorations to these limits, and to describe how his boyhood world expanded from Williamsburg and Mount Vernon until it was as large as the nation and larger, then shrank again at the end into the home country of Virginia. Parts 2, 3 and 4 deal with the journeyings, the places and the people which occupied Washington first as Commander-in-Chief, then as President, in the Middle Atlantic States, and in the cities of New York and Philadelphia. These sections are subdivided chronologically within each chapter, with dates to guide the reader. Part 5 relates Washington to his own region, the South, including his presidential tour and the years at Mount Vernon.

The source materials I have used are the basic ones: J. C. Fitzpatrick's editions of the *Diaries* and the *Writings;* Baker's *Itinerary* and *Washington after the Revolution;* and the five published volumes (as of 1953) of Freeman's *Washington.* With these I have used numerous contemporary sources, all of which are listed in the Reference Notes.

This book is not intended for either scholars or students. My belief is that a vast amount of material which is old hat to such specialists is brand new to most Americans. It is astonishing to discover how little even educated and literate Americans, some with a particular interest in history, know about matters which are almost trite to the scholar. The attempt here has been to take every possible advantage of modern scholarship to authenticate a presentation of Washington intended for the wider audience of the general reader.

I have used, of necessity, the scholar's apparatus to set up the Reference Notes, but not with the specialist's purpose of substantiating every quotation, every piece of evidence. Rather, I

*11*

have tried in them to give the reader an idea of where the facts about Washington come from, and where he can go to find out more about any aspect of Washington's life which happens to interest him. The Notes, I trust, will replace the conventional bibliography in this instance, and prove more helpful because they are keyed to the text.

With the principal sources thus indicated, and the intent of the book clearly stated, I have felt free to correct and modernize the punctuation and spelling in Washington's writings, and in quotations from his contemporaries, except where they illustrate a characteristic or help to make a particular point. In every case, I have been careful not to alter the meaning or the language itself, but only to clarify it for the modern reader.

In sum, *George Washington's America* is my attempt to make the picture on the schoolroom wall come alive within the framework and with the perspective which research in the last decade has provided. How successful I have been must, of course, be left to the judgment of the reader and the critic.

Of the many people who have helped with the production of this book, I want particularly to thank my research assistant, Barbara Ware McBurnett, for her unstinting labor; Earle Walbridge, of the Reference Library, Washington Square College, New York University, for his many favors; and my wife, who has gone over these pages patiently many times.

JOHN TEBBEL

*Brookfield, Connecticut*
*January 30, 1954*

# GEORGE WASHINGTON'S
## AMERICA

# PART 1

# THE WORLD OF WASHINGTON


The center of the world was Williamsburg. For young George Washington it was the place where adventure began and ended, the seat of that authority with which he constantly wrestled for the sake of his "honor," and the true home of gracious Virginia living. There he pursued his mutually uncomfortable friendship with Governor Dinwiddie; from the Governor's Palace he set out on his arduous penetrations of the troubled frontier; and at the inns and splendid houses lying between Palace and Capitol, he played cards, argued, drank a little and danced much.

In his diary he referred to Williamsburg as "the great metropolis," with that affectionate irony peculiar to rural Americans who regard the big city of their region with mixed admiration and fear. Down its principal thoroughfare, the "noble great street six poles wide," named for the Duke of Gloucester, he rode successively as landed gentleman, Colonel of Militia, member of the Assembly and Commander-in-Chief of the Continental Army. He saw Williamsburg at its best, in the brief but glorious flowering it enjoyed from its founding in 1699 to the beginning of its rapid decay in 1779. Its population never exceeded 2000 in all that time, but as the colony's political and social center, the little capital was the most renowned American city south of Philadelphia.

When George first saw it is a matter of doubt. He may have been there as early as July 1748, and possibly again in October 1751, and even a third undetermined time when he was commissioned a surveyor. But his first recorded visit is January 28, 1752, when he alighted from the ship *Industry*, thirty-eight days out of Barbados, fresh from his first and only trip abroad.[1]

[1752]    It had been a brief, eventful excursion. George and his beloved half brother Lawrence had gone down to the island in the autumn of 1751, hopeful the warm climate would alleviate the tuberculosis that was slowly draining the older man's life. But the heat had kept Lawrence indoors during most days, and after a brief flurry of social calls and theatregoing, George had nearly lost his life from the smallpox. His two weeks of struggle with the disease left him permanently pockmarked, but it also gave him an immunity that meant he would be able to travel anywhere, on the frontier or in cities, with safety from the scourge which took an appallingly large percentage of adult lives in his generation.

Barbados had proved so disastrous to the health of both brothers that in December they decided to quit the island and their pleasant house overlooking Carlisle Bay.* Lawrence thought the sun and air of Bermuda might be more helpful to him, but this move would mean a longer absence from Virginia for George than either brother thought desirable. Consequently, Lawrence had prepared to go on alone, and George had sailed for home December 21 on the *Industry*.

Thus young Washington came to Williamsburg from the sea, after a voyage so rough it nearly caused him to miss the traditional roast goose on Christmas Day, and entirely prevented any celebration of the New Year. He had admitted in his diary that he was "very sick." Moreover, someone aboard had slipped a stealthy hand into his sea chest and robbed him of sixteen pistoles, the equivalent of a little more than ten pounds. One must suppose, then, that the sight of the Virginia Capes

---

* The house is preserved today, in altered condition, in the southeastern part of Bridgetown. It belonged to a Captain Crofton, who commanded the island's defenses, Fort James. He asked a good deal for his hospitality: fifteen pounds a month, not including liquors and washing. Presumably he got such high rent because of the splendid location of the house, about a mile from town. Of it George wrote in his diary: "The prospect is extensive by land and pleasant by sea, as we command the prospect of Carlisle Bay and all the shipping in such manner that none can go in or out without being open to our view."

and the York River were more than welcome to the traveler from Barbados. His only journey abroad had failed to make him a potential world traveler.*

Once ashore, he rode toward Williamsburg, having been entrusted with letters for Governor Dinwiddie. Arrived at "the great metropolis," he discovered that Dinwiddie was absent in Green Spring, six miles away, which gave him a few hours to explore the town. Probably he visited the taverns—the Raleigh, the Sign of the Golden Ball, Finnie's Ordinary, among others—and called upon his friends before he walked once more down the broad Palace Green to the Governor's formal brick mansion, where Dinwiddie awaited him. It was the first meeting between the young Virginian and the stubborn Scot whose lives were to be entangled in the making of history, and one of the few happy interviews they enjoyed.

Dinwiddie received his visitor cordially, asked him for dinner, and was solicitous about the health of Lawrence, whom he knew. The evening they spent together was amicable; no questions of command, supply or precedence were involved. They could talk of surveying, if nothing else, because Dinwiddie had been Surveyor General of the Southern Colonies before the Crown gave him a grander title and a Williamsburg palace.

---

* Few men had more distinguished invitations to go abroad than were tendered to Washington in later years. The best homes in England and France would have welcomed him, and he was urged many times by his European friends to come visiting. Sometimes he seemed tempted; often he appeared to regret sincerely that he could not accept. But always something intervened. There were wars to be won, a nation to be launched, and in the short space of time granted to him between these vast endeavors, he could not bring himself to leave the happiness of Mount Vernon.

The truth was that Washington, after the trials and ambitions of his youth were set to rest, wanted nothing more than to be a gentleman farmer. He was not designed to be a member of the international set. Other countries interested him only intellectually. He did not have the world view of a Franklin or a Jefferson, though in his later correspondence he was given to speculation on the vicissitudes of European politics. For the most part he deplored them. To him, Europe seemed a hopeless tangle of plot and counterplot, with war and still more war the inevitable result. It is small wonder that Washington is today the national hero most idolized by isolationist newspapers and politicians.

That was the first of numerous meetings between them. Most of the others were far less felicitous, in the years when Washington was struggling to make a place for himself in the world. The struggle brought him always to Williamsburg. Sometimes he spent hours in gloomy argument with the Governor. At other times he was deeply involved in business, both personal and military.

As a member of the Assembly, he enjoyed those "Publick Times" in the fall and spring when the gathering of the legislators meant a dizzying round of balls, dinners, theatre, racing and hard drinking. The rich planters came up from their river plantations, opened their town houses and entertained lavishly every night. Coaches and chaises thronged Duke of Gloucester Street, and sedan chairs deposited lovely ladies on brick sidewalks before the fine Georgian entrances of the fashionable houses. Washington was an indifferent legislator, but he was enchanted with the social life of the capital. It compensated for the disappointments and frustrations he endured at the Palace.

Outside of Williamsburg, his youthful world centered in the tidewater plantations belonging to the tightly knit Virginia society into which he was born. There were, first of all, the home places. His birthplace, Wakefield, was a gracious but undistinguished house. It possessed—and the impression survives today in the restoration—the half-European, half-colonial feeling of American homes in the early 1700s.

Even less pictorial, but possibly more exciting to George, was his third home place, Ferry Farm, whose 260 acres looked across the Rappahannock to Fredericksburg, a bustling little port with high aspirations, lying on the river's right bank and reached from the left by the ferry that gave the farm its name. As a dweller on a rural Left Bank, George found himself in a comfortable, plain and entirely respectable wooden house of eight medium-sized rooms. It was dark red, and in no way resembled the splendor that would later be his at Mount Vernon, where the Washingtons had lived for four years between Wakefield and Ferry Farm. At that time it bore the homely native place name of Epsewasson.

On Ferry Farm there failed to occur the first of those childhood events by which George is erroneously remembered around the world. It will do no good for scholars to insist that the story about the dollar thrown across the Rappahannock, reverently planted by Parson Weems, has no basis in historical fact. On the contrary, so firmly is the tradition embedded that tourists argue with the caretakers today about the details. Some insist with scorn that any fool knows the historic event occurred at Mount Vernon, and the river was the Potomac, not the Rappahannock. Others dispute as to whether it was a dollar or a Spanish coin. There is similar disagreement on the exact location of the cherry tree George did not chop down.

The traditions will not die, but Ferry Farm itself, rich as it is with associations of both Washington and his mother, has declined steadily in the public interest and now has relatively few visitors. Mount Vernon has overshadowed it.[2]

Aside from the home places, young Washington knew best the houses he visited with his parents, the residences of his numerous relatives, and the plantations of the friends he acquired as he grew up. He must have toddled at an early date across the wide floorboards of Twiford, where the Hedges lived, about nine miles from Wakefield, and it may be hoped that he perpetrated no childish desecrations on the splendid paneling of its gracious rooms, which had a fascinating variation of color among them. George and his parents must also have been frequent guests at Daniel McCarty's place, Longwood, across Pope's Creek and a short distance down the Potomac. Daniel was a Burgess in the Virginia legislature and a Colonel of Militia, offices his small guest would later hold with some distinction.

The house that drew George most strongly, however, for a variety of reasons, lay on "a pleasant tract" just below Mount Vernon, on the river's southern shore. This was Belvoir, home of Colonel Fairfax, and of his cousin, the great landlord of the

*19*

region, Thomas, Lord Fairfax. It was a fine brick structure, sixty by thirty-six feet, with two floors and a full basement; in modern real estate terms it would be classed as a five-bedroom country estate, with the numerous outbuildings (at least five, eventually) typical of large plantations.

The square, thick-fingered nobleman was not often about its precincts. As heir to the 5,200,000 estimated acres of the Northern Neck Proprietary, and the product of a London society that was fashionable if nothing else, he had been expected to create a glittering court on the Potomac. Instead, he took no interest in society and appeared to prefer the down-at-heels, rambling quarters he called Greenway Court, far away in the Shenandoah Valley, where he found the surcease from the company of other people that he seemed to crave. There he indulged himself whenever the weather permitted in the occupation that meant most to him in life: fox hunting.

But George's interest in Belvoir was not its noble landlord, nor even its immediate master, Colonel Fairfax. The attraction (besides the ladies of the house, with whom he was fascinated and abashed, in equal measure) was a young man seven years older, George William Fairfax, the Colonel's eldest son. George William was Washington's boyhood idol, companion on his first penetrations of the frontier, and ultimately his lifelong friend, though in time Fairfax quitted Belvoir for London.

Washington evidently regarded the Colonel's son with respect and intense admiration. He referred to him as "Mr. Fairfax." About George William was the aura of faraway places—he had been born in the Bahamas and educated in England—and with it he had the polish that comes from moving constantly in the best social circles, a polish which took Washington a slow and painful time to acquire. The genuine, unaffected and lasting friendship which sprang up between the two young men was of a kind that Washington was seldom able to enjoy.

It was in the company of "Mr. Fairfax" that George pushed the boundaries of his world beyond the familiar plantations in 1748, and discovered the primitive life of the frontier, where he would soon spend much of his time. The day was to come when he would curse the stubborn mountains and the dangerous valleys to the westward, but at sixteen the prospect of a surveying trip to unknown country, in the company of George William and the veteran surveyor, James Genn, was delightfully exciting.

Washington was not unequipped for the journey, despite his total lack of experience. He was tall and husky, nearly a man, physically able to withstand a trip that would not be easy. He had learned to write, and he was about to try this skill by keeping a diary of his progress. He knew enough mathematics to deal with surveying problems, and he hoped to learn something of that art. Intellectually, he had a grasp of business affairs beyond his years, and he had the good plantation owner's ability to size up land and crops. As a minor but important asset on such a trip, he had already acquired the superb horsemanship for which he was later admired. Finally, he had the eager curiosity that would sustain him through possible hardships. George had heard his elders talk constantly of the frontier. It was a prime conversational topic everywhere, and he had long wanted to find out for himself what the Western lands were like.

[1748]    As he rode away from Belvoir with a light heart that Friday morning in March, George lacked only one thing for the journey, but that was unavoidable and George William was no better off. He was entirely unprepared for the kind of life that awaited him; he was still the young Virginia gentleman, accustomed to good food, good clothes, a watch to tell time by and a comfortable bed to fall into when the day's ride was over. Not that he had been raised in a life of luxury; the Washingtons were not rich. But the difference between living on the frontier and living at home was far greater than he realized.

The two Georges rode out together; they were to meet their

leader, James Genn, at Neville's Ordinary, not far from his house on the Falmouth road, from which he functioned as county surveyor for Prince William County. Neville's was forty miles distant from Belvoir. That was to be the first day's ride.

Crossing the Occoquan Ferry, they struck off down the old road that led from Quantico's head to the newly established second court house of Prince William. Farms were scarce and grew even scarcer as they rode. The country they traveled was woodland, cleared here and there for farming, and only a step or two away from its wilderness state. What had begun as a passable thoroughfare turned quickly into a dim trail, but it led them to an intersection with the Dumfries road, where the court house stood, convenient of access for back-country pioneers as well as tidewater planters. To find the spot today, a traveler would bowl along on Route 508, through the village of Brentsville and two and a half miles farther south. He would then be in Orlando; the court house stood not far to the northeast of this village.

Prince William Court House was halfway to Neville's. Twenty long miles later, the Georges reined in their tired horses at the ordinary so well known to eighteenth-century Virginia travelers. Like the court house, it stood at the intersection of important roads. One led north toward Ashby's Bent, in the Blue Ridge Mountains. That was the surveying party's route. The other road, an ancient Indian trail, was known first as the Shenandoah Hunting Path, later shortened to the more prosaic Carolina Road.

Along both these roads, for nearly two decades, restless tidewater settlers had pushed toward the greener fields of the upper Piedmont. They knew Neville's well.

George Neville was not a man to be impressed by any traveler. As an independent landowner who represented what society there was in his part of the country, he did not run his inn for profit, though he was not averse to taking it. With the free-handed hospitality of the times, he extended his bed and board to those who passed by, at reasonable prices. Presumably he welcomed the young gentlemen from the Potomac and gave them accomodations which were not sufficiently different from those they had left to forewarn them of rigors to come. It was a good, solid ordinary, built to last. It lasted, in fact, near the present village of Auburn, until 1927.

Next morning Genn rode up to join them, and the three cantered off northwestward over the low hills of the land which was to be Fauquier County. Now they began to climb, on rather easy grades, penetrating toward the top of the Blue Ridge at Ashby's Bent, as it was known in the early land surveys—"gap," as it was called by most Virginians. By any name, it was a pass to the wilderness beyond.

From this crest George gazed down into the promised land of the Shenando, as people then usually spelled it. The lovely valley of the Shenandoah was an enormous gray-green carpet spread beneath his feet, the mountains rising in a dark, jagged wall on the other side, west and northwest. The valley floor stretched out to the southern horizon. George wrote about it prosaically enough in his diary, but it is easy to believe he caught his breath at the sight, which still entrances travelers who see it from the disadvantage of paved highways.

It was an easier ride down the slope of the mountain from Ashby's Bent to Ashby's Ferry, where Captain John Ashby, eldest son of Thomas, the pioneer who gave his name to the neighborhood, put them up for the night.

Next morning the Captain took them across the Shenandoah River, at a point where the Winchester road still spans it. Four miles southward and they were in Lord Fairfax territory, upon which the sun never seemed to set. This was the tract of nearly nine thousand acres which Thomas had established the year before, and which would ultimately be Greenway Court when he got around to living on it.

Looking about with fascination, Washington concluded that the Proprietor had made a good selection. Time and again in his diaries George would describe the land he traveled from the viewpoint of the speculator and landowner, and now he wrote (when he got back to Ashby's on Sunday night): "We went through most beautiful groves of sugar trees and spent the best part of the day in admiring the trees and the richness of the land." Trees were one of George's specialties, a subject on which he was becoming an expert, but he had never seen the "sugar" variety before.

The two Georges had spent most of Sunday riding about the Proprietor's acres. Now it was Monday morning and time for Genn to get to work. He had been instructed to survey, first, some tracts which lay about twenty miles north down the river, where small streams flowing out of the foothills of North Mountain to the Shenandoah formed areas known as Cates Marsh and Long Marsh. These places were more convenient to Frederick Town—then the name of the future Winchester —consequently headquarters had been established at Jost Hite's house, near the village. The baggage was sent on there Monday morning, while the party went to work without further preliminary.

Riding to the marsh area along the riverbank, George noted that fertile land was not confined to Greenway Court. The fields where grain, hemp and tobacco had been planted bore a rich testimony.

By Monday night they had gone sixteen miles, to Isaac Pennington's house, where they were given the best beds. Next day, however, Genn had recruited his crew, and after a forenoon of dismal rain which drove the whole party to shelter and an afternoon of hard work, the entire expedition descended, seven men strong now, on Isaac Pennington's hospitality. The host did his best. He put most of the guests into one main room, with George and possibly another man in an adjoining storeroom. It was there young Washington encountered the frontier in a way he had never expected. One could hardly better the young gentleman's shock as he recorded it in his diary (punctuation and spelling modernized):

"We got our supper and was lighted into a room and I, not

24

being so good a woodsman as the rest of my company, stripped myself very orderly and went into the bed, as they called it, when to my surprise I found it to be nothing but a little straw matted together, without sheets or anything else but only one threadbare blanket, with double its weight of vermin, such as lice, fleas, etc. I was glad to get up (as soon as the light was carried from us), I put on my clothes and lay as my companions. Had we not been very tired, I am sure we should not have slept much that night. I made a promise not to sleep so from that time forward, choosing rather to sleep in the open air before a fire, as will appear hereafter."[3]

Fortunately, Genn finished surveying the marshes next day, and before penetrating the real wilderness of the Potomac's upper waters on the south branch, he concluded it would be well to stop overnight in Frederick Town. The happy effect this had on George's spirits is recorded in his diary:

"Wednesday 16th. We set out early and finished about one o'clock and then traveled up to Frederick Town, where our baggage came to us as we cleaned ourselves (to get rid of the game we had catched the night before) and took a review of the town and thence returned to our lodgings, where we had a good dinner prepared for us, wine and rum punch in plenty, and a good feather bed with clean sheets, which was a very agreeable regale."

It was the last "agreeable regale" he was to enjoy for some time. The start next morning was delayed until ten o'clock by rain, but at the day's end they had ridden twenty-five miles and had found a "tolerable good bed [to] lay on" at the home of Andrew Campbell. On the following day they made thirty-five miles, to Thomas Barwick's farm, but there they ran against a wall of frustration. The Potomac was six feet above normal and rising; Genn could not possibly follow his plan of fording it to the trail on the Maryland side. He had a choice of retreating to Frederick Town, waiting for the river to go down (which might be several days), or finding something else to do in the meantime. Being an energetic man, Genn proposed to travel twenty-five miles farther upstream, to the Warm Springs country, now Bath, or Berkeley Springs, in Morgan County.

George was no more impressed with Warm Springs than he was years later, when he visited it often after it became a health resort, first with his ailing brother Lawrence and later with Martha. On this initial visit he looked forward to spending his first night in a tent. But "nothing remarkable happened," he wrote in disappointment.

That was a Friday night. By Sunday, Genn had concluded impatiently that he would take the risk of swimming the horses across to the Maryland side, returning in a canoe, and then bringing over the baggage in the boat. It was a dangerous piece of navigation but carried through without incident. George wrote that they left the horses overnight on the land of Charles Polk, but he contributed no enlargement of the interesting statement made by a Moravian missionary, Brother Matthias Gottschalk, who had stopped there and reported that Mr. Polk kept "a very disorderly house."[4] This house was near what is now the community of Williamsport.

Brother Gottschalk had also traveled the road along which the surveyors struggled the next day through a merciless rain. He described it as "a single narrow path, frequently hardly recognizable, partly because traveling is not very frequent there, and partly because the path is blocked with trees and overgrown with grass and weeds." George called it, succinctly, "The worst road ever trod on by man or beast."

At the end of the journey that day, however, George met a man whose friendship and influence on the frontier would be more valuable than he knew. Thomas Cresap's place was a trading post, a fort and a home, a combination which accurately reflected this remarkable man's personality. He was even then a frontiersman of considerable reputation, to which he added as time went on. His settlement above the junction of the Potomac's north and south branches ultimately came to be the community of Old Town, Maryland.

Cresap gave them accommodations almost luxurious for that

part of the country, but by that time, George was not so particular. He was adapting himself to wilderness life with commendable speed.

The rain fell persistently through the night, all the following day, Tuesday, and on Wednesday morning until noontime, leaving the Potomac in a more turgid condition than before, and making the road beside it virtually impassable. Genn had intended to ride up the river a short distance and cross over again to Virginia. There was nothing to do but wait.

At this juncture George was lifted out of his boredom by the sudden, electrifying appearance of thirty Indian braves, who rode up to Cresap's with friendly yells and told the traders they were a war party, returning somewhat ignominiously with only one scalp. Washington had never seen a war party before, and except for an occasional savage, had probably never seen Indians, at least en masse. Nor had he ever witnessed the grisly sight of a scalp. Doubtless he was relieved to see it was an Indian's.

Whether he learned anything useful from the Indians it is hard to say, but he had the opportunity. Utterly absorbed, he spent the rest of Wednesday and all of Thursday with them. The lessons were there to be learned, and all of them would have been helpful in a few years, when he was compelled to deal with Indians in the reality of war.

He saw, for example, what the gift of a little liquor would do. It caused the war party to forget about its lack of success on the trail and induced the braves to conduct a ceremony, and in this ceremony, George observed the Indians' characteristic love of interminable speechmaking, of ceremony for its own sake, and their ability to amuse themselves with both. Considering the length of the event, George's description of it in his diary is admirably brief.

"They clear a large circle and make a great fire in the middle, then seat themselves around it. The speaker makes a grand speech, telling them in what manner they are to dance. After he has finished, the best dancer jumps up as one awakened out of a sleep, and runs and jumps about the ring in a most comical manner. He is followed by the rest. Then begins their musicians to play. The music is a pot half [full] of water, with a deerskin stretched over it as tight as it can, and a gourd with some shot in it to rattle and a piece of a horse's tail tied to it to make it look fine. The one keeps rattling and the other drumming. All the while the others is dancing."[5]

As an accomplished dancer himself, and one who loved the art, Washington had a connoisseur's appreciation of the sport at Cresap's.

On the following day, Genn put an end to such dalliance by a decision to try the crossing to Virginia, swimming the horses and carrying the supplies by canoe. This was done without trouble, and the party began riding up Patterson Creek, toward the farm of Abram Johnston, fifteen miles away.

Another day's travel brought them to the settlement of Solomon Hedges, a personage thereabouts since he was one of Frederick County's justices. If George expected to be entertained in a style befitting his host's station, he was once more surprised, and at the same time initiated into a frontier custom. When he came to the table and Hedges' servants brought in supper on platters, "there was neither a cloth upon the table nor a knife to eat with, but as good luck would have it, we had knives of [our] own." He learned then what an indispensable instrument a jackknife was considered in the wilderness. Furthermore, Justice Hedges had not enough room to entertain his guests and they had to sleep in the open, or in their tent.

Next day was Sunday and no work was done, but religious principles seldom prevented travel in the colonies, especially in the wilderness, so Hedges guided his guests eastward to the middle stretches of the south branch. There stood the cabins of Henry Van Meter, who represented the third generation of hardy Virginians in his family to make a home on the frontier.

Now the crew went to work in earnest. For the next week or so, property belonging to James Rutledge, thirty miles from Van Meter's, and other tracts were surveyed, and George for the first time on the trip was permitted to run the lines on a job. Meanwhile, there was incident enough to balance the work and make life entertaining for a young man on a jaunt. He went hunting wild turkeys and discovered for himself what elusive targets these "chickens of India," as the early explorers called them, could be. The boisterous spring winds blew their tents down twice, and one night nearly snuffed out the expedition, an episode which George recorded with youthful nonchalance in his diary. On April 2, he wrote: "Last night was a blowing and rainy night. Our straw catched afire that we were laying upon and was luckily preserved by one of our men's awaking when it was in a [blaze]." Then he added without a pause: "We run off four lots this day, which reached below stumps." [6]

By this time the word had got around among the German settlers (immigrants who had come into the Shenandoah from Pennsylvania) that outlanders with strange equipment were tramping through the woods, engaged in no one knew what devil's business. Whole families left their farms to see this visitation for themselves. Their amazement at what they saw was more than equaled by George's impression of these camp followers who appeared so suddenly.

". . . Was attended by a great company of people, men, women and children," he wrote on April 4, "that attended us through the woods as we went, showing their antic tricks. I really think they seemed to be as ignorant a set of people as the Indians. They would never speak English, but when spoken to, they speak all Dutch." And he went on in his usual breathless pace: "This day our tent was blown down by the violentness of the wind."

Every day after that, until they left the territory, the surveyors were accompanied by these forest sidewalk superintendents, who smoked their pipes and stroked their chins, presumably, while they commented on the work in their own language.

On the morning they first appeared, George William borrowed five shillings from Washington and went back toward civilization, probably to procure fresh supplies. Without his friend, George found life on the frontier less fascinating, since he had little in common with Genn and the crewmen, and the weather contributed to his discomfort. It was a mean, perverse spring. One night the air was so oppressive that the tent filled with smoke and drove out its tired occupants. Rain fell so violently late the next day that the party, on its way back to Henry Van Meter's, had to find shelter under a straw shed. Next afternoon, George heard that young Fairfax had returned as far as Peter Casey's, about two miles away from Van Meter's cabins, and went joyfully down to see him, staying the night there—"the first night," the embryo frontiersman reported proudly, "I had slept in a house since I came to the Branch."

When the surveying party struck camp next night, on its return journey, George had a new opportunity to show how well he had adapted himself. "We camped this night in the woods," he wrote, "near a wild meadow where was a large stack of hay. After we had pitched our tent and made a very large fire, we pulled out our knapsack in order to recruit ourselves. Every [one] was his own cook. Our spits was forked sticks, our plates was a large chip. As for dishes, we had none."

Belvoir was never like this!

The contrast was even sharper next day when the man with whom Fairfax had contracted to bring in provisions failed to appear; the larder was empty, and the other men scattered through the countryside on a foraging expedition, while the two Georges sat in the tent and listened to their stomachs growl. Whether they concluded that the adventure had reached the acutely uncomfortable stage, or whether an agreed time of service had expired is not on record, but the young men refreshed themselves late that afternoon with some food brought in by the foragers, and set out together at once for home.

Two days of hard riding, taking short cuts that Genn had avoided, brought them back to the comforts of Frederick Town. Attempting still another short cut on the way home, they lost their road and spent a whole day wandering off as

ar as Ashby's Gap, which they had passed on their route outward. That was the day they saw the first "rattled snake" they
had noticed on the journey, which was remarkable, considering their prevalence in the region.

The final stage of the journey was a route Washington followed many times afterward: over the Blue Ridge at Snicker's
Gap, and then by way of the Shenandoah Hunting Path southward to West's Ordinary, another noted hostelry which was
kept by three generations of Wests until it became Lacy's after
the Revolution; it is still standing at the head of Bull Run Mountain, near the present town of Aldie. From West's the trail led
southeast through the forest, later the track of the Colchester
Road, and so to Belvoir and Mount Vernon, which the Georges
reached on April 13, thirty-three days after they had left home.

[1749]    When he became county surveyor the following
year, George went back over some of the ground he had
covered with young Fairfax. For ten days in the first part of
November 1749, he worked under conditions much more severe
than he had endured on Genn's expedition. For one thing—an
important consideration to him—he was never able to take off
his clothes, except for the few nights he was near enough to
Frederick Town to sleep in an ordinary. He wrote to a friend:
"... I have not slept above three nights or four in a bed, but
after walking a good deal all the day, lay down before the fire
upon a little hay, straw fodder or bearskin, whichever is to be
had, with man, wife and children like a parcel of dogs or cats,
and happy's he that gets the berth nearest the fire. . . ."

[1750]    Sometimes, on his surveying trips, George contrived to make a side excursion for fun. His records of autumn,
1750, for instance, show that he and George William clubbed
a bottle of rum in Mitchell's Tavern at Yorktown, and the
Colonel's son had to borrow a shilling threepence to pay for his

share, a fact Washington dutifully set down in his account book. Then, according to the same record, he set off at once for Frederick Town and further surveys.

[1751]     A year later he went up to Annapolis for the first time, with Lawrence, and this visit cost him three pounds eighteen shillings more than he planned, that being the amount he loaned to his half brother en route to the little Maryland capital.*

In his surveying journeys to the rim of the wilderness, and in family excursions on an ever widening periphery, Washington prepared himself unconsciously for the incredibly difficult journeyings of his mature years. By the spring of 1753, he was ready for the testing.

[1753]     At this juncture he was Adjutant of the Southern District, and he had strong leanings toward a military career. What he hoped for in life was not clear to him, but he often defined it, then and later, by the word "honor." In its simplest terms, "honor" probably meant to him recognition, stature, acclaim. He did not have exactly what has become known in the psychological slang of our time as a power complex, but he yearned to have his merits recognized. He was also something of an opportunist. In the five years since he had last gone to the

* It should be explained that George's meticulous accounts do not brand him as a young money-lender, anxious for every shilling. On the contrary, while he undoubtedly hoped to get the money back, he was simply conforming to social custom, and did a substantial amount of borrowing himself. People borrowed from each other with the utmost freedom, whether the lenders were relatives, friends or acquaintances. Washington was more generous than most, and on at least one occasion offered fifty pounds to a friend's son whom he had never seen. This promiscuous borrowing was, in fact, one of the many curses of the plantation economy. Washington's letters over the years are full of complaints about non-payment of loans, and about his own constant shortages of cash in hand, but he made no attempts to reform either the system or his own generosity.

frontier with George Fairfax, he had changed remarkably. Then he had been unsure of himself, tied still to home and familiar things, sampling frontier life more in the spirit of a lark than anything else. Now he was Major Washington, for his age a person of some distinction in Virginia, and eager to earn himself a higher position. "Honor" pricked him on, and in October, 1753, he volunteered for the dangerous journey that was to lead him at last into the arena of large affairs.

That journey, from Williamsburg to Fort Le Boeuf, undertaken at the worst time of the year, is well known to most Americans. Almost as famous as the message to Garcia is young Washington's carrying of Governor Dinwiddie's warning to the French commander that England would not tolerate invasion of her territory. It was certainly one of the most remarkable journeys in American history, when it is recalled that Washington rode by compass alone through the rugged wilderness from Virginia to a point about twelve miles south of Erie, Pennsylvania.*

In this view of a country he had not yet seen, Washington got his first experience with the rugged terrain that later was General Braddock's despair—"a desolate country uninhabited by anything but wild Indians, bears and rattlesnakes," as one of the General's soldiers put it. He found the unfamiliar route from Wills Creek to the Great Crossing of the Youghiogheny, thirty-four air miles away, an up-and-down affair over successive mountain ridges, climbing steadily on a trail that carried him to a peak elevation of 3,000 feet. By modern reckoning, it would be the equivalent of traveling from a point 115 miles northwest of Washington, D.C., ten miles south of the Pennsylvania boundary, to the site of the present Somerfield, Pennsylvania.

* Yet the map Washington subsequently drew for Dinwiddie, depicting the route he had taken and the position of the French forts, was so accurate that, according to Dr. Freeman, "Even today, with no other paper than this, a traveler who used a compass probably could journey from Cumberland Md., to the site of Fort Le Boeuf." (Freeman, I, 281.)

33

Over such country a man could make fair progress if he had no wheeled vehicles to worry about; he could travel as fast as a strong horse could pick his way around laurel thickets and over the stony mountain streams. Occasional patches of open woodland helped to make up time.

After the Great Crossing, the most formidable obstacle was Laurel Hill, a ridge 2400 feet high with a steep, difficult approach, dropping down on the other side of the crest to a 1700-foot plateau which was flanked on the west and northwest by Chestnut Ridge. As they rode down into this plateau, more open than the terrain around it, George probably heard Christopher Gist speak its name, the Great Meadows. It was a name he would not forget.

As they climbed into the mountains beyond the Great Meadows, they encountered ankle-deep snow, and pushing on toward the junction of the Monongahela with the Allegheny, they forded rain-swollen rivers, the horses swimming through the icy water which was not quite cold enough to freeze.

Then, riding out of the forest late on a November afternoon, George saw for the first time the place where the two great rivers met, a windy, desolate point of land on which the city of Pittsburgh sprawls today. Dinwiddie meant to build a fort there, and so did the French. Whoever succeeded would gain strategic control of the Ohio and Monongahela. Possession of that lonely peninsula, indeed, might control the economic fate of nations.

On the remainder of the journey northward, accompanied by the Indian sachem Half King and the other doubtful allies he had acquired from the village near Pittsburgh called Logstown, George found the country not so precipitous as that he had come through, but nonetheless difficult to negotiate in the miserable weather. He passed the notorious community of Murthering (or Murdering) Town on Great Beaver Creek, a settlement named for some tragedy now forgotten, and today the site of (or at any rate near) Zelienople, in Butler County. Thirty miles farther, in the same county, was the site of the present

34

Branchton, and two days more of travel brought them to the French fort of Venango. The remaining miles were cold, hard traveling, navigating some of the turbid streams on felled trees, fighting off chill and fatigue, but the squire of Mount Vernon nonetheless found occasion to note that they passed "several extensive and very rich meadows."

In the twilight of December 11, they came to their journey's end: Fort Le Boeuf rose dimly before them across a creek. It was twenty-six days since they had left Wills Creek.

The return journey, begun on December 16, was complicated not only by the struggle with the French for the favor of the Indians, but by the drawing in of winter. During the first leg of the trip, made in canoes, they had to stop and pound channels through the ice where slower-running water at the bends had frozen solid, and sometimes portages were necessary. The second leg, on horseback, was begun two days before Christmas. As the horses stumbled along the trail, George could foresee that other measures were necessary; they were able to travel only five miles that day. Consequently the next morning found most of the party walking, and carrying besides the divided load borne by the pack animals. Snow began to fall. The travelers plodded along in a white, silent world, wearily, numbly, wondering how long such misery could be endured. George set down later his own impressions of the terrible journey—matter-of-fact, as usual: "The horses grew less able to travel every day; the cold increased very fast; and the roads were becoming much worse by a deep snow, continually freezing." And it was Christmas.

The intense cold was a terrifying, silent enemy. Three of the party were badly frostbitten, as they discovered when they awoke one morning and it was necessary for them to build a shelter of sorts and wait until the cold lessened. But wait was the one thing George could no longer do. He had already lost valuable, perhaps irreplaceable, time. In his mind was the driving urge to get the French answer back to Dinwiddie with the least delay. He understood that the French not only had no intention of leaving but were intent on consolidating and extending their positions. There was no time to lose if Dinwiddie intended to resist them.

In that state of mind he proposed to Gist a plan the veteran backwoodsman viewed with alarm. Why not leave the horses, George suggested, travel on foot to Murthering Town, then take a short cut to John Frazier's, where they might get fresh horses for the last difficult lap to Wills Creek? For Gist, who was accustomed to walking the woods, it was not a formidable proposition, but he feared that Washington, who had spent most of his traveling time on horses, would not be able to go such a long distance by foot. George insisted, however, and since he was the leader, Gist had to consent.

They dressed for the journey. George described the process this way: "I took my necessary papers, pulled off my clothes, and tied myself up in a match coat. Then with gun in hand and pack at my back, I set out with Mr. Gist, fitted in the same manner."

It did not take George long to find out how right Gist had been. The trail was not difficult, but the cold was "scarcely supportable," and mile by mile the Virginian could feel his unaccustomed muscles chill and tighten. Nevertheless he managed to walk eighteen miles that day until they found overnight shelter in a deserted cabin. With masterly understatement, Gist recorded: "The Major was much fatigued." Still, the Major was able to pull himself to his feet and start out again at two o'clock in the morning, taking advantage of the weird half-light that snow casts in winter darkness. They reached Murthering Town safely.

There was one more major obstacle to surmount, the crossing of the Allegheny. George and Gist reached it at a place now within the corporate limits of Pittsburgh, expecting to find the river solid enough to walk across. But the ice extended only about fifty yards from either shore, and in between was black water, churning with ice floes. There was nothing for it but to build a raft, with only one hatchet between them. They took turns

*36*

using it, while the pale winter sun slid down to the somber hills. Before it had set, working as fast as they could move their chilled arms, they were ready for the crossing.

As they slid off the ice shelf into swift water, the floes began to engulf them. Facing disaster in midstream, George desperately thrust his pole into ten feet of water, hoping that if he could stop the craft momentarily, the ice jam would slip by. Instead, before he could reconsider his error, the rapid current threw pole and raft together so sharply that he was catapulted into the water. He saved himself from sudden death—the second time within two days—by gripping one of the raft's logs, and with those large, strong hands which people often noticed, pulled himself to safety.

Now they were virtually trapped. Unable to reach either shore, they sought shelter on an island, which could be reached only by wading. Of the two, the veteran Gist was the worse off. Ice crusted George's wet clothes, but Gist's fingers were frostbitten. Their only consolation lay in what they had *not* lost: guns, hatchet, packs and George's precious letter.

Providence alone must have saved them—a remark George was to make often in the course of a perilous life. They survived the night, and by morning the river had frozen between island and opposite shore. Ten miles farther, and they were safely at John Frazier's. The remainder of the journey was easy. On January 16, George handed the French commander's reply to Governor Dinwiddie, in his Williamsburg palace. It was exactly a month from the day he left Fort Le Boeuf.

That journey marked the northwestern limit of Washington's world. He traveled the same terrain only three months later, as Colonel in command of the pitiful expedition Dinwiddie sent to fight the French. It led him back to the historic plateau of the Great Meadows, between Laurel Hill and Chestnut Ridge, where he fought and won the "obscure skirmish" which, as the historian Francis Parkman put it, "began the war that set the world on fire," the struggle between France and England for possession of North America.

George came back to Williamsburg from this expedition with his later defeat at Fort Necessity bitter in his mouth. The basis of his failure had been the lack of reinforcement and of supplies, and there Dinwiddie could rightfully charge, as he did, that the colonies of Virginia, New York and North Carolina had been too apathetic, too recalcitrant and too slow-moving in general to provide the wherewithal for their own defense, and to this might be added the rascality of the contractors who had failed to provide the supplies they had pledged.

Americans today may view in this light the intransigence of their forefathers when they drive through the southwestern corner of Pennsylvania and come upon the Fort Necessity National Battlefield Site, eleven miles from Uniontown on U.S. 40, the historic old National Road that meanders from Atlantic City to Oakland, California.

The replica of Fort Necessity erected there in 1931 has been discovered to be in error by National Park Service archaeologists, whose recent diggings have disclosed that it was reconstructed in the wrong place, and was square when it should have been round. On July 4, 1954, these matters were to be set right on the two hundredth anniversary of the battle, with a rededication of the newly restored earthworks and fortification.[7]


[1755]     The frontier was not kind to George. After the hard struggle of the journey to Le Boeuf and the humiliation of Fort Necessity came the disastrous campaign with Braddock in 1755, once more over those forbidding high ridges and tortuous trails between Wills Creek and the future site of Pittsburgh, where now stood the French fort of DuQuesne. The journey forward and back again was a nightmare that haunted George for the rest of his life. Going out, he was seized with those "violent fevers and pains in my head" which signaled the common colonial disease known as "bloody flux." He was so ill that he had to stretch out in one of the wagons, while the long column wound slowly through the dense forest to which the settlers had given

*The World of Washington*

the name "Shades of Death." Doubtless George, tossing about in the wagon, thought it prophetic.

Five days of such travel were too much for Washington, young and strong though he might be, and Braddock ordered him to stay at the rear of the army and rest. Later the General sent back his own prescription for the illness, "absolutely ordering," as George reported, that it be administered. This cure-all was a patent medicine more widely known in England than America. Dr. James's Powders were composed chiefly of phosphate of lime and oxide of antimony, and were the product of Dr. Robert James, an English physician who had been a schoolfellow of Samuel Johnson and had contributed, besides his fever prescription, a three-volume medical dictionary. About the powders, opinion was divided. Dr. Johnson said of his schoolmate's potion: "I never thought well of Dr. James's compounded medicines." But Oliver Goldsmith's publisher was so pleased with their efficacy that he sold them as a sideline. As for George, he offered a fervent testimonial: ". . . the most excellent medicine in the world, for it gave me immediate ease and removed my fevers and other complaints in four days' time. . . ." [8]

Washington was not able to leave his wagon until he caught up with the army again, two miles from the Monongahela's east bank, and then it was the eve of July 9, the Bloody Day, the day of terror and ignominy when Braddock led his army into a trap of ambush and destruction. It was also a day when Washington performed one of the most incredible physical feats of his life. Only a young man of superb physique, and a soldier dedicated to his duty, could have survived it.

He rose that morning in the weak state which follows a long siege of fever. Determined to ride, he had to tie cushions on his saddle so that he could endure the jolting. In that fashion he rode to battle. After the slaughter began, he was deprived of even this much protection (though he probably never thought of it again) when his first horse and then a second was shot out from under him; his third mount survived. A bullet sliced his hat; three others burned a hot track through parts of his uniform without wounding him. Still he moved through the slaughter, trying to carry out Braddock's orders.

The final order from the mortally wounded General came when his force was dissolving in wild, headlong retreat. To cover that retreat, and possibly to hold back a following French attack, Braddock's only hope was Colonel Dunbar's troops, lying nine miles northwest of the Great Meadows. None of Braddock's other aides knew the country, and none in fact could make the journey except Washington.

That was how George, after twelve hours in the saddle and a battle which sickened the imagination, found himself traveling over the same road he had traversed forty-eight hours earlier in so weakened a condition that he had to ride in a wagon. With his two guides, he plunged into a forest of awesome blackness and began the worst journey of his life, the one he could never forget.

To begin with, it was impossible to see in the gloom. George could tell when he was off the trail only by the crackling of bushes under the horses' hoofs. Then the guides would have to dismount and feel along the ground until they touched the loose earth, ruts and stumps of the road.

Worse than this difficulty by far was the weird, melancholy sound that rose from the forest, where the wounded and the fugitives had dragged themselves as far as they could from the carnage. Dead men were a hazard, lying in the road, but it was the living who made the night both pitiful and hideous. They were living, but for most of them, crawling about or lying in agony, death was near. They screamed for help when they heard the horses. Others, near enough to feel the passage of George and his men, shrieked curses after them when they would not stop. And stop he could not; to save one man would further imperil thousands of others.

Thirty years later, Washington wrote: "The shocking scenes are not to be described. The dead, the dying, the groans, lamentations and cries along the road of the wounded for help were enough to pierce a heart of adamant." [9]

Slowly the silence of the forest reasserted itself as they passed the last fugitive, and the blackness gave place to the gray dawn light. He had been in the saddle twenty-four hours; he had miles to go. It was nearly noon before his exhausted horse, whose saddle he gripped with his remaining strength, plodded into Dunbar's camp.

Eight days later he was writing to his brother from the comparative safety of Fort Cumberland, with a trace of grim humor, anticipating Mark Twain by more than a century: "Dear Jack: As I have heard since my arrival at this place a circumstantial account of my death and dying speech, I take this early opportunity of contradicting both, and of assuring you that I now exist and appear in the land of the living by the miraculous care of Providence, that protected me beyond all human expectation; I had four bullets through my coat, and two horses shot under me, and yet escaped unhurt. . . ." [10]


[1756]      Even to an unbeliever it must have seemed that George was indeed under the "miraculous care of Providence" during his years on the frontier. Riding through the wilderness on a tour of Virginia frontier defenses in October 1756, a journey that carried him farther southward than he had ever been, he escaped death once more by the narrowest of margins. Returning from the forts in Halifax, near the North Carolina line, he rode along a trail where Indians were waiting to fall upon another traveler, but their leader, who had left them momentarily to reconnoitre in a different quarter, had given orders not to fire upon anyone who might be passing in the opposite direction, because it would alarm the quarry. The one who passed the other way was Washington. Even if he had escaped the first fire, the carbines of his small party were so wet from rain that they could not have been used. The story of his escape was told to him later by Virginians who were prisoners of the Indians at the time.

At another point in this journey he rode a distance with thirty

41

men, mostly militia officers, who horrified him by their conduct. These were gentlemen adventurers, with whom "order, regularity, circumspection and vigilance were matters of derision and contempt." After seven days of a whooping and hallooing progress, as though they were on a fox hunt, George noted that they reached Augusta Court House without disaster "by the Protection of Providence. . . ." [11] This part of the tour, it may be noted, probably followed the present path of the Chesapeake & Ohio Railroad.

Frontier life was made bearable for Washington by the infrequent trips he was able to make back home to the society of Mount Vernon and Belvoir, and accompanying excursions to Fredericksburg and Williamsburg.

Once Braddock sent him on an errand to Williamsburg to get four thousand pounds from the expedition's paymaster, so that the payroll could be met, and Washington took advantage of his welcome visit to go shopping in the capital. He bought himself a pair of toothbrushes, three pairs of gloves, four pairs of thread stockings, and some other small items. On other occasions, when he spent days at a time in Williamsburg during the endless squabbles with Dinwiddie, he boarded out in such houses as that of the widow of John Coulthard, on the Back Street, and did his entertaining at Finnie's Ordinary.

At home in Mount Vernon he enjoyed the pleasures of plantation society and the company of George William Fairfax's wife, Sally Cary, whom the Colonel's son had married and brought to Belvoir soon after he and Washington returned from their surveying trip. A lively, intelligent girl of warmth and charm, she fascinated George from the first, and there is little doubt that he had unconsciously fallen in love with her. If she was aware of it, no written record exists, but a woman of her perception could hardly have missed the implications of the way Washington probably talked and, on at least one occasion, wrote to her. Fortunately for his career, Sally was by nature as prudent as he and nothing in their long friendship ever caused the slightest scandal.[12]

[1758]     It was during one of these brief respites from the
military life on the frontier that he met and became engaged to
the lovely young widow, Martha Custis, an episode described
elsewhere in these pages. Both Martha and Sally were on his
mind in 1758, his last year of military service in the wilderness,
although the letter to Martha, dated July 20, and supposedly
written at Fort Cumberland, has been shown by modern scholarship to be a forgery. But while George was not the author of this
romantic text beginning, "A courier is starting for Williamsburg, and I embrace the opportunity to send a few words to one
whose life is now inseparable from mine," he unquestionably
did sit down at Cumberland a few weeks later, on September 12,
and pen a remarkable letter to Sally.

It is a long double entendre, this letter, in which Washington,
knowing that it might be read by George William or someone
else before it reached Sally's eyes, nevertheless avowed his love
as much as it could be avowed, and sought to discover before he
began another dangerous journey whether she cared for him—
and this though he was engaged and on the eve of his own marriage. It is a most unusual letter, of a kind not to be found anywhere else in Washington's voluminous correspondence.[13] Sally,
apparently, did not answer.

After he wrote the letter, George set out for the last time on
the long and lonely trail from Fort Cumberland into the Alleghenies, toward DuQuesne and the Ohio, with its heartbreaking Raystown road, which Washington, an expert on the
subject, described as "indescribably bad." But this time the road
led, at the end of 1758, to his resignation from the military life,
with the security of the Virginia frontier in prospect and the
war with the French now become primarily the problem of the
Northern colonies.


[1770]     When he returned to his exploration of the America
that lay beyond the eastern mountains, it was 1770 and he was
the prosperous squire of Mount Vernon, twelve years happily

married to Martha, a man of consequence. Yet it was an echo of his youthful frontier days that sent him westward again. The time had come for a settlement of the claims made by the veterans of 1754, who had been promised, by both colony and Crown, a portion of the Western lands in return for their service. This piece of business, which had become vastly complicated over the years, was more or less thrust into Washington's hands by Governor and Council. By August 1770, George was determined to make an exploring trip of his own, to find out what lands were best and available for his veterans, and to choose his own acreage.[14]

Accompanied by his old friend and physician, Dr. James Craik, Washington left Mount Vernon on October 6 and proceeded in a leisurely fashion to the lower Shenandoah Valley, where his brother Samuel had built a modest but handsome mansion of native limestone a year or two before on the site of what is now Charles Town, West Virginia, thus establishing a community in which more members of the Washington family lived than any other town in the nation. Today it is a place of concentrated Washingtoniana; one out of three residents boasts the name of Washington, or claims to be a descendant; the streets bear such family names as Mildred, Samuel and Lawrence; and a good many of the fine old homes are open to visitors.

Samuel's residence, Harewood, where George and Dr. Craik spent their first night on the way West, is being restored today by one of Samuel's descendants. Whether George designed it, as claimed, remains open to doubt, but its charming drawing room, whose lovely English paneling is intact, is a tribute to the architect, whoever he was. A portrait of Samuel in uniform, presented to him by Lafayette, hangs over the mantel, and before this handsome fireplace, Lucy Washington's sister, Dolly Payne Todd, was married to James Madison.

Outside the house is the outline of what was once a boxwood garden, and a veritable Washington cemetery in which lie Samuel, three of his five wives and numerous relatives.

Charles Washington also settled in the town which bears his

name. His home, which he called Happy Retreat and a later owner renamed Mordington, is preserved today in the spirit, at least, of the time when Charles lived in it. From the hill it occupies, Happy Retreat looks off toward the Blue Ridge Mountains, its two wings constituting the original house and the main structure in between representing the addition Charles did not live to see built, although he planned it. In his day, the wings were connected by a porte-cochere. Washington was often entertained in this house, and one supposes he and his brother performed their business transactions in the west dining room, which was Charles's office.

John Augustine Washington owned land in the district, about a mile and a half from the present town, but he never built on it. That was left to George's nephew, Bushrod, who in 1820 constructed Claymont Court, which survives today in its grove of beautiful oaks as one of the most magnificent remaining architectural examples of the period. The original building was destroyed by fire in 1838, but soon after it was reconstructed. It is a gracious though rather formal house, of three stories, connected by gardens to smaller houses on each side, and surrounded by other gardens and expanses of lawn.

Across the valley from Claymont Court, and facing it, is Blakeley, built the same year by Bushrod's brother, John Augustine II. The brothers married sisters and, in the spirit of duality, erected companion houses.

South of Harewood is Cedar Lawn, the home of another of George's nephews, Thornton Washington, but unfortunately it has not been preserved in the same excellent state as the others, though its restoration is said to be planned.

Still another Charles Town house is Belleair, built by Colonel Lewis Washington sometime before 1830. Its traditions are more nearly related to the Civil War, since one of John Brown's men is said to have stolen from it a sword presented to George by Frederick the Great, and a brace of pistols which had been the gift of Lafayette. Lucy Washington's home, Locust Hill, is nearby, inhabited today by a direct descendant, Lucy Washington Packette, and marred only by the marks of Civil War cannon balls and bullets.

As George paused in these pleasant precincts in 1770, he may have thought that Samuel had a nice situation, but his conversation probably dealt with the Western acres across the Youghiogheny that his land prospector and surveyor, Captain William Crawford, had already selected for Samuel, John Augustine and Lund Washington. He could not foresee that Charles Town, on a sliver of West Virginia real estate between Virginia and Maryland, would soon be dominated by his family, not only in their own time but nearly two centuries later, when the houses they built would still be standing, and tourists would be arranging to visit them at the Thomas Jefferson Hotel, or the Washington Drug Store in Ranson, a mile distant, or Charles Town's own tourist center.[15]

On the way West from Samuel's place, the two travelers from Mount Vernon rode through those Allegheny glades described as "the one bright sunny point in a hundred miles of mountains," and passed the site of Braddock's grave, which Washington tried to find but could not. They descended Laurel Hill, saw the home of Christopher Gist's son Thomas, at a point near the town named for his family in Fayette County, Pennsylvania, and got to Captain Crawford's house about five o'clock on a Saturday afternoon. On Sunday, Washington inspected a nearby coal mine, which "seemed of the very best kind, burning freely, and an abundance of it." [16] Next morning he rode out with Crawford to examine the land selected for himself and the other Washingtons. He was delighted with his own 1600 acres —"as fine land as ever I saw, a great deal of rich meadow"—and he approved the less choice acreage Crawford had picked out for his relatives.

Two days later the party rode down to Fort Pitt, on that windy point of land between the two mighty rivers, which Washington had seen in its desolate, original state. Now he wrote of embryonic Pittsburgh: "We lodged in what is called the town, distant about 300 yards from the Fort at one Mr.

Sample's, who keeps a very good house of public entertainment. These houses, which are built of logs and ranged in streets, are on the Monongahela and I suppose may be about 20 in number and inhabited by Indian traders, etc. The Fort is built in the point between the rivers Allegheny and Monongahela, but not so near the pitch of it as Fort DuQuesne stood. It is 5-sided and regular, two of which (next the land) are of brick; the others stockade. A moat [he spelled it 'mote'] encompasses it. The garrison consists of two companies of Royal Irish, commanded by one Captain Edmonson."

From Fort Pitt, the party, augmented by an interpreter and an Indian guide named the Pheasant, pushed off up the river toward the Ohio country. Travel was primitive, as some of the incidents of the voyage show. About three miles below the mouth of Little Beaver Creek, it was necessary to lighten the canoe, so they hid a barrel of biscuit on Brown's Island. That was on October 22, when they had set out at 7:30 A.M. in a snow-storm, and by evening had passed Wills Creek and reached Mingo Town, now called Mingo Junction, two miles below Steubenville, Ohio. "This place," George wrote, "contains about twenty cabins and seventy inhabitants of the Six Nations." Here they heard the alarming news that two traders had been killed at a place known as the Grape Vine Town, thirty-eight miles below on the river.

There was other evidence that they had reached the limits of civilization. Sixty warriors of the Six Nations were passing through Mingo Town on their way to the Cherokee country, where they intended to attack an old enemy, the Catawbas.

On its guard, the expedition pushed forward cautiously and reached a point near Yorkville, in Jefferson County, Ohio, on the night of the twenty-third. A day later they were at Wheeling Creek, near the site of Wheeling, West Virginia, and went on to Captina Creek, where they found Grape Vine Town, eight miles up this tributary, and there learned that, as often happened, the story of the two traders was based on nothing more substantial than an accidental drowning.

Relieved by this information, the men camped for the night near the middle of the Long Reach, and cast their lines into the river in the hope of snaring a fish. Next morning, George recorded, they found "a catfish of the size of our largest river catfish hooked to one of them . . . though it was one of the smallest kind here."

At the mouth of the Muskingum River, they passed the site on the northern bank where historic Marietta would rise, and beyond it reached the Little Kanawha, although Washington's diary inexplicably fails to mention the foremost attraction on that part of the river, Blennerhassett Island, the largest in the Ohio, whose romantic history has provided generations of writers with gaudy material. The explanation has been made, and it seems reasonable, that Washington failed to note Blennerhassett was an island, by reason of its somewhat puzzling geographic configuration at the time. The tradition which asserts he owned it appears to have no basis in fact.

Farther on, they paddled past the sites of Mason City, Pomeroy and Middleport, Ohio. Reaching the area of present-day Maggie, in Mason County, Washington beached the canoe and got out to look around the country. What he saw was new to him:

"We . . . found many shallow ponds the sides of which abound in grass, inviting innumerable wild fowl, among which I saw a couple of birds in size between a swan and a goose, and color somewhat between the two, being darker than a young swan and of a more sooty color. The cry of these was as unusual as the bird itself, as I never heard any noise resembling it before."

The bird must have been the Great Northern Diver, more commonly known as the loon.

That night the expedition camped below the present York, in Mason County, and next day George sent the canoe on down toward the junction of the Kanawha with the Ohio, while he tramped overland to get a better view of these lands. He walked to the headwaters of Oldtown Creek, then down Crooked Creek to Point Pleasant. That was as far south as Washington ever got

4

*The World of Washington*

in the Ohio Valley. The place was four miles above the little
French settlement they called Gallipolis, and forty miles above
the future city of Huntington, West Virginia. From this point,
George could see for the first time the Great Kanawha, looking
like a placid estuary reflecting the autumnal forest in its smooth,
broad waters.

On the first of November, the party began a short exploration
up the Kanawha, ten miles the first day and four the second,
stopping then to go on a hunt in which they killed five buffalo
and three deer. George was delighted with the wild life: "This
country abounds in buffalo and wild game of all kinds, as also
in all kinds of wild fowl, there being in the bottom a great many
small grassy ponds or lakes which are full of swan, geese and
ducks." Camp that night was below the present town of Ar-
buckle Station, in Mason County, a mile above Fourteen Mile
Creek, forty-six miles from Charleston, West Virginia.

As they turned homeward after this side excursion, Washington surveyed land—eighty square miles which was later subdivided among eight deserving patentees, and two other tracts,
including one for himself.

Three days later, on the voyage back, he stopped to look over
the lush bottomlands on the West Virginia shore that would
later belong to him, and which now go by the homely name of
Washington's Bottom, extending nearly from Newberry Island to Blennerhassett, which George probably passed this time
on the other side. Again leaving the canoe, he explored what is
known today as "the Point" in Parkersburg, West Virginia, and
walked onward as far as the vicinity of Henderson.

Most of the return journey was spent fighting swollen rivers
and enduring autumnal storms, but at a point about two miles
below the mouth of Captina Creek, Washington was able to
disembark again on the Ohio shore and, as he put it, "walked
through a neck of as good land as I ever saw, the land on the hill
sides as rich as the bottom." Next day he left the expedition's
camp near the mouth of Fish Run, West Virginia, and walked
over the land of the Round Bottom, opposite the mouth of Pipe

*49*

Creek, Ohio. This piece he later bought. Most of the subsequent day was spent in similar exploration of the West Virginia side, in the Benwood section of Wheeling Creek.

As he rode the final stage of his journey later that month, stopping to take Sunday dinner with Thomas Gist, he encountered "several families going over the mountain to live," struggling through knee-deep snow that covered the Allegheny crests. The valleys of the Ohio and the Illinois were beginning to fill up, but Washington had no pioneering urge to follow the settlers. His home and his heart were in Mount Vernon, which he reached on December 1, "being absent from it nine weeks and one day."

Summarizing the results of this long and expensive journey, Washington found himself not wholly satisfied. He had seen some "exceeding fine" land, but he had also looked at a quantity of poor soil and other acreage that was not much different from the frontier sections of eastern Virginia. There was a fairly satisfactory amount of land worth patenting, but not the vast, rich territory he had hoped to acquire for his veterans.

[1784]    Washington did not look upon the Western lands again until fourteen years later, in 1784, when he found himself compelled to recoup his fortunes, totally neglected for eight years. He felt it "indispensably necessary," he said, "to visit my landed property west of the Appalachian Mountains, and more especially that part of it which I held [in Fayette County, Pennsylvania] in co-partnership with Mr. Gilbert Simpson. . . ." Along with this private preoccupation, he was once more pressing the dream he had held so long—to find and establish a satisfactory commercial route over the Alleghenies, so that tidewater Virginia would become the outlet of the fertile Ohio Valley.

The westernmost part of his trip had to be canceled, because even at this late date the frontier, if it could still be called that, was not quiet. A party of officers from Fort Pitt visited the General while he paused in Fayette County and advised him against carrying out his plan to go as far west as the Great Kanawha; the Indians were discontented and had been harassing the settlers along the Ohio.

A few days before, Washington had stopped on a Sunday morning at the Great Meadows to view "a tenement I have there ... a very good stand for a tavern...." Not a sentimental man in most respects, he probably did not indulge himself in musing that it was only thirty years since he had marched away from this place in the failure of his first encounter on the field.

His property there, now in Wharton Township of Fayette County, was 234 acres he had bought in 1767, including the site of Fort Necessity. It was, as he noted, a good place for a tavern because it stood on Braddock's Road, between Fort Cumberland and Pittsburgh, surrounded by sweet meadow grass, ripe for the scythe. When Washington died, the tract was sold by his executors to Andrew Parks, of Baltimore; it is now, as noted previously, a national historical site.

In Fayette County, the General also visited a mill and some houses he owned on the tract chosen for him by Crawford, which he had first seen on the journey of 1770. The land in these 1600 acres, he thought, was not "in general equal to my expectations of it." Gilbert Simpson, who had supervised erection of the mill, had been his co-partner in managing the estate, but now they closed out their partnership and Washington auctioned off his holdings at a loss. He could not even obtain a bid for his mill.

However, the accounts were closed at last, and the General rode on into Washington County, Pennsylvania, to tour his land there in what is today Mount Pleasant Township. He held this tract of 2813 acres under a military patent from Lord Dunmore. The families who had settled on it were Scotch-Irish, and when Washington visited their farms, he tried with unusual justice to buy his own land from them. But they refused to sell, and so he brought successful ejectment suits against them. When the property was finally sold in June 1796, it brought $12,000.

Describing the last day of his trip to Fayette County, Washington wrote in his diary on October 4: "Notwithstanding a good deal of rain fell in the night and the continuance of it this morning, which lasted till about 10 o'clock, I breakfasted by candlelight and mounted my horse soon after daybreak, and having Captain Ashby for a guide through the intricate part of the road (which ought, though I missed it, to have been by Prince William old Court House) I arrived at Colchester [ten miles southwest of Mount Vernon], 30 miles to dinner, and reached home before sundown, having traveled on the same horses since the first day of September by the computed distance 680 miles." [17]

Thus, with a sentence nearly as long as the journey, Washington concluded the record of his last expedition to the Western lands, indeed his last trip westward of familiar territory, save for his presidential excursion into western Pennsylvania to quell the Whiskey Rebellion. The man who once wrote wistfully that he wished he might see the Rocky Mountains returned to the circumscribed territory where he was destined to fight his battles both civil and military—and to Mount Vernon, the one place where he was ever to know real happiness.

Somehow circumstances always limited Washington's world. He was the prisoner of his career. It was natural that he should spend his boyhood among the friendly Virginia plantation owners and the bustling little cities they frequented—Williamsburg, Alexandria and Fredericksburg. But then the troubled frontier and the war with the French compelled George to spend his young manhood in the wilderness for the most part. And when the war was over, his family obligations and the business of Mount Vernon held him largely to Westmoreland County and nearby precincts. At the time he took command of the Continental Army, he had traveled no farther south than the North Carolina line, no farther west than Fort DuQuesne, and never north of Philadelphia (not counting the Le Boeuf expedition) except for his journey to Boston in 1756 on behalf of his "honor." *

As Commander-in-Chief, he traveled constantly but nearly always in an arc about New York City—Westchester, West Point, New Jersey, Bucks County, Philadelphia, Delaware, and at last, of course, Virginia again and the final struggle at Yorktown. The battles in the North were affairs that he was compelled to deal with necessarily by remote control. Albany, Saratoga, Schenectady, the towns along the Mohawk—these became for him pieces in the military puzzle which he had to fit in with the aid of his officers who were on the spot.

[1782]     But in June 1782, with Yorktown behind him and the peace nearly achieved, he resolved to see the places from which the desperate business in the Middle Atlantic states had so long detained him. Accompanied by his old friend of the Revolution, Governor George Clinton, he left his headquarters at Newburgh, New York, on the twenty-fourth and embarked in his barge on a leisurely two-day journey up the Hudson to Albany.

The town gave him a hero's welcome. He was, of course, accorded the freedom of the city, and with it addresses and testimonials and banquets. At six o'clock in the evening on his first day there, the church bells everywhere began to ring, filling the air with a happy clamoring until sunset, when the fort thundered out a thirteen-gun salute and the citizens lit their candles in the windows to illuminate the city.[18]

After two days of ceremony, Washington was probably glad to ride out of Albany toward the great battlefield of the North at Saratoga. There, on Saturday the twenty-ninth, he inspected briefly the site of Burgoyne's disaster, sampled Saratoga's noted mineral waters, probably comparing them with the waters of Berkeley Springs in Virginia, and on Sunday rode southwestward from the Saratoga plains toward Schenectady.

* This journey is described in detail in Part 2, Chapter 1.

Here and elsewhere tradition has supplied stories about his progress, since he himself left no memories of the trip except those penned in a letter to the President of Congress written July 9, 1782. These traditions, which depend mainly on the memories of old settlers, have no historical value, but some of them are worth retelling for their own sake.[19]

One relates that Washington was in some doubt about the route between Saratoga and Schenectady, and along the way, stopped to inquire of an "honest countryman" what was the best path to take. The honest countryman gave him those detailed directions which every modern motorist has absorbed from time to time (and which have been the subject of endless jokes), but in Washington he encountered a man — unknown to him, it should be added—who yielded to no one in his absorption with details. The General asked for so many repetitions that the farmer, out of patience at last, concluded: "And after you pass this point, any damned fool could find the way." *

About five miles outside Schenectady, he was met by sixty of the town's principal inhabitants who had come to escort him. He is said to have walked the whole way with his hat under his arm, but it seems doubtful. As they came to the gates of this town which had suffered so many years at the successive hands of Indians, French, Loyalists and British, the ringing of bells, firing of cannon and cheers of the populace were augmented by the whoops of another delegation, a hundred Oneida and Tuscarora warriors, dressed for the war trail and primed for a ceremonial.

Washington received this unexpected homage gravely but, it may be assumed, with some reservations. In Albany he had learned that a renegade coalition of British, Indians and refugee

---

* Telling this story, J. R. Simms (in *Frontiersmen of New York*) appends a moral for the young. It seems that a better-informed neighbor asked the honest countryman if he knew who his questioner had been, and forthwith enlightened him. "As the reader may suppose," says Simms, "he felt that sense of shame which has often mounted the cheek of him who has given a distinguished stranger a rude answer. Young reader, always be sure to answer civilly and keep your temper."

Tories had recently come down the Mohawk on a raiding expedition, and were said to be planning a reconstruction of the old fortifications at Oswego. Hearing that news, he might well have asked himself whether there was ever to be an end to invasion from Canada. This virtually continuous border warfare had been going on in one form or another for nearly a century and a half.

But disregarding the fact that some of the Six Nations tribes had been guilty of bloody and all too recent treachery, Washington took the homage of the Oneidas and Tuscaroras at its face value, and went into the city after he had patiently listened to their ceremonial speeches.

Another tradition says that Brower Banker, a blacksmith who was one of the town's leading citizens, undertook to show the distinguished visitor about the village, and as they walked, an old Negro whom they met took off his hat and bowed to the General, a compliment which Washington politely returned. Banker, says the story, had the bad taste to remark that it was not the custom of the country—and this to a Southerner!—to take such notice of slaves.

"I cannot be less civil than a poor Negro," Washington reproved him.

At the end of the day, which in the social routine of those days meant the middle of the afternoon, came the inevitable public dinner, held at the tavern of Abraham Clinch, who had come to America as a drum-major in Braddock's army. With his customary tact in such matters, Washington inquired particularly for Colonel Frederick Visscher (or Fisher, as he spelled it earlier in life), a colonial officer who had suffered a great deal at the hands of the Indians and Tories, and finding that for some reason he had not been invited to the dinner, asked that a messenger be sent for him. It is said that the Colonel was discovered hard at work in his barn, and consented to leave it only because his appearance was in the nature of a command performance. Washington gave him special attention when he came, at a table filled with such dignitaries as General Schuyler, Colonel Abram

Wemple, Majors Abram Switz, Myndert Wemple and Jelles
Fonda, and the oldest inhabitant, Captain Peter Truax. Among
this company, Visscher was given the chair next to Washington,
at the General's request.

The speeches over, Washington returned to Albany that
night, and next morning boarded his barge and came back down
the Hudson, in time to take part in celebrating the Fourth of
July, at which "The whole army was formed on the banks of
the Hudson on each side of the river. The signal of thirteen cannon being given at West Point, the troops displayed and formed
in a line, when a general *feu de joie* took place throughout the
whole army." [20]

In the midst of this gaiety, Washington found time to add up
carefully the detailed expenses of his first trip to the Northern
frontier. They came to thirty-two pounds, eight shillings.


[1783]    By July of the following year, the General's military
service was nearly at an end. He was restless and bored in his
Newburgh headquarters, waiting for the word of release when
he could ride to Annapolis, resign his commission and hurry to
the joys of Mount Vernon which he had so long anticipated. In
this hiatus, his thoughts turned to the frontier of which he had
enjoyed only a taste the year before. As he put it, ". . . in this
distressing tedium, I have resolved to wear away a little time in
performing a tour to the northward. . . ." He intended not only
to see the country, but, with the instinct of a military man, he
wanted to examine the approaches to the important British outposts in the West.

He set out on his "tour to the northward" July 18, crossing
the Hudson at Kinder Hook and traveling up the east bank,
once more accompanied by Governor Clinton and an undetermined number of officers. At Albany they were joined by
General Philip Schuyler, and rode from there to Stillwater,
where they spent the night at the home of another member of
the numerous Schuyler clan, Harmonus. The only one of the

family at home, says tradition, was a daughter who quite naturally was overwhelmed by the covey of distinguished guests who thus descended on her. She did her best, however, and next morning she was rewarded, so the story goes, when Washington complimented her as he prepared to leave, and raised her hand to his lips. Young Miss Schuyler never forgot it, as successive generations do not forget the chance encounter with celebrity and refuse for a time to wash the hand that has been touched by whoever moves their foolish hearts. When a young nephew, aptly named George, came to visit her as she lay on her deathbed and bent to kiss her when he left, she exclaimed with what may well have been her dying breath, "Not my lips, George, but kiss the hand that long ago was consecrated by the kiss of Washington."[21]

This is the kind of reverential tale, repeated by earlier biographers, which has made Washington into a plaster saint, but nevertheless it is not at all unlikely. The General inspired just such adoration.

From this romantic incident, which must have appeared casual enough to him, Washington rode to the Saratoga battlefields, and there he had the advantage of a guided tour with General Schuyler, who knew every hillock. Today U.S. 4 takes the traveler along the splendid plateau of Bemis Heights, with its breath-taking views to every horizon, through what has been since 1948 the Saratoga National Historical Park.

On the way northward the General stopped to examine Fort Edward and dined at a place which came to be known as the Red House, built by a half-pay officer named Pat Smith in 1765. The Baroness Riedesel had stayed there in 1777, when she arrived with her husband, and had given the house its name, although only the ends and the kitchen were red. The front was yellow. The building was a large two-story affair with a Dutch roof, standing between the barge canal and the Hudson River, about a quarter of a mile southeast of the fort. Washington and his party dined there and stopped again on the way back to have breakfast.[22]

Riding on to Lake George, they secured boats and rowed up the lake to the craggy promontory where Fort Ticonderoga, that much-fought-over guardian of the classic invasion route, stood at last in peace, contemplating the long stretches of water lying north and south. Washington inspected this fortification with more of an eye to its current military value than its exciting history, one supposes, though today thousands of tourists annually reverse this emphasis when they visit the magnificent restoration, certainly one of the finest of its kind anywhere. Then the General moved northward into the lower end of Lake Champlain, to the less celebrated fort at Crown Point, and the defenses of Putnam's Point.

That was the limit of his northern progress. Retracing their route, the party returned down the lakes, and came again to the Saratoga country, pausing at the place called High Rock Spring, where the peaceful beauty of Saratoga Springs would later rise. The place was then only a rugged pine forest sloping down to a marshy valley, but Washington sampled the waters, as he had the year before, and made some shrewd observations of the territory. General Schuyler already had a tent pitched at the Springs which he used for a summer place, having cut a road through the trees from his home at the old Saratoga, now Schuylerville. Discussing the possible future of the Springs with Clinton, Washington and the Governor agreed to buy the spot and a considerable tract of land around it. Unfortunately for their prescience, Clinton discovered later that the idea had occurred to the Livingston family, who had already bought the land. It was a missed opportunity that a land speculator like Washington continued to regret for some time afterward, as his letters show.

From Saratoga, the General's party went on down to Schenectady and then turned west to country that was new to Washington. The route lay down the fertile Mohawk Valley, where the river wound placidly along a plain flanked by gently rolling hills, past the manorial houses of Sir William Johnson, whom George had met in Williamsburg, and his infamous son

John, whose bloody Tory exploits in the Cherry Valley had been one of the Revolution's dark episodes. Along this succession of lovely vistas the party moved by horseback, although the passage would have seemed easier in boats, to Fort Schuyler, then over the portage to Wood Creek and a little farther to Oneida Lake, at a point somewhere northeast of the present city of Syracuse.

Apparently the trip out was made at a rather more rapid pace than the return, which included a side excursion to Otsego Lake (he may have gone as far as the southern, or Cooperstown, end of it), a place Washington particularly wanted to see because, as he explained, the headwaters of the eastern branch of the Susquehanna rose here, and he was perennially fascinated with the river systems he had spent so much time studying, surveying and traveling in his own part of the country.

Just before he made this side trip, Washington came into the vicinity of Fort Plain, in the country settled by the Palatines, and there tradition says he spent a night in the settlement of Palatine (now Palatine Bridge) at the home of Peter Wormuth. By this time the news of his passage had spread by word of mouth up and down the valley, and those who had not been able to catch sight of him on his passage westward came flocking from miles around to see "the world's model man." It would be characteristic of Washington to feel that it was his duty to satisfy their curiosity—he did so often, even at Mount Vernon —and so the story is probably true that he came out and walked awhile in front of the old stone house fronting the river, so that the people, at a respectful distance, could see him.

Peter Wormuth's house was small, and it is probable that most of the General's accompanying officers went that night across the river at Walrath's Ferry and found shelter in Fort Plain. Next morning some of them came back over to escort him to the fort.

As they rode up the hill near the fort, another tradition relates, a pretty scene awaited. The minister's wife had shepherded a few small boys, dressed in their best, to the roadside, where they swung their hats and huzzaed as the General rode by. Washington is said to have lifted his own hat and remarked cheerfully, "Good morning, boys!" It seems a safe story to believe.[23]

At the fort the General was introduced to the officer in command, Colonel James Clyde. Clyde was a New Hampshireman who had commanded a company of bateaumen and rangers, under Lieutenant Colonel John Bradstreet, in the war against the French. This company took part in the assault on Ticonderoga when the beloved General Howe lost his life on the pitiless slopes below the fort. Afterward, Clyde was at the capture of Fort Frontenac. As a Cherry Valley settler in 1762, he had helped develop that delightful spot, and in 1770, he had put up a small church for the Oneidas, equipping it with a bell brought from England which overwhelmed the Indians with joy.

The Colonel may be regarded as typical of the hardy breed of men that Washington met the length and breadth of the Mohawk's winding course. It is said the General implied to Clinton that the Governor ought to reward Clyde for his long and faithful service, which may have been the reason for his later appointment as sheriff of Montgomery County.

After dining at the fort, Washington and his party went on to spend the night in Cherry Valley, where they were the guests of Colonel Campbell, another of the valley's heroes. His original home had been burned during the conflict, but Campbell, who had only recently returned from the wars, had put up a new log house. The accommodations were not elegant, nor were they sufficient, but the General and his suite were soldiers accustomed to rough board. Next morning, a traditional story relates, Governor Clinton watched the Campbell boys at work and play about the house and remarked to Mrs. Campbell, "They will make good soldiers in time."

The Colonel's lady, who had been a prisoner in Canada with her sons during much of the Revolution, answered him fervently: "I hope their services will never be needed." Washington, overhearing the exchange, is said to have sided with his hostess. "I hope so, too, madam," he told her, "for *I* have seen enough of war."*

Again it is a remark wholly characteristic of Washington.

After breakfast at the Campbells', the party rode off on the excursion to Otsego Lake. That night they came back up to Fort Plain, and next morning resumed the journey to Albany. They reached there on August 4, and by the sixth, Washington was in his office at Newburgh. It had been a tour of "at least 750 miles," as he noted, performed in nineteen days.

When the war was over, he welcomed the seclusion and comparative quiet of Mount Vernon, and had no desire to be a traveler again. He would have been content to live in the world of the Potomac.

As President, he was no less limited. When one excepts the presidential tours made to New England, and then South to Charleston and Savannah, Washington's activities as President were confined to the areas of New York City and Philadelphia. The confinement was so stifling to Martha that she complained now and then of its prisonlike quality, but to her husband it was the way of life dictated by duty. He did not complain, except to wish himself back in Mount Vernon, away from the newspapers and politicians who refused to accept him at his own worth.

There was little time remaining when he came home to his "vine and fig tree." But he lived the three years allotted him as he had wanted to live the others: like a Virginia gentleman. He had seen the center of his youthful world, Williamsburg, dwindle away after 1779, when the capital was moved to Rich-

---

* One of the boys, who had spent so much of his boyhood as an Indian captive that he could not speak English when he was exchanged, grew up to be Judge James S. Campbell, a much respected citizen of the valley.

mond. Dinwiddie's "palace" burned down, the splendid estates on the banks of the James fell into neglect and decay, and nearly half the population deserted the old capital, until in 1787 all that remained was a shabby village, kept alive mostly by its farmers' market, the college, and an insane asylum. The Capitol, where Washington and so many other distinguished Virginians had sat as burgesses, was crumbling away, its proud statue of Lord Botetourt disfigured by hoodlums. With its streets unpaved, thick with dust and sand, Williamsburg looked like a great beauty fallen into a shabby and unkempt old age.

But then, the whole of that youthful world had shrunk in the General's eyes. Alexandria, which he had once been certain would become one of the foremost Atlantic ports, was long past its moment of glorious expansion. Fredericksburg, the bustling little town of early days, was no longer bustling. The great cities of the North—Philadelphia, New York and Boston—were a part of his life in the public service, and that life he had put behind him.

There remained Mount Vernon. It was the home place toward which he yearned during the long, heartbreaking years of the Revolution, where he found refuge from the harassments of the presidency. To Mount Vernon he came at last, a traveler who had made the full circle. The endless miles were behind him, the boyhood world had widened until it encompassed the greatest men and the mightiest events of his time, and now it had narrowed once more to its original scope.

Much had vanished from it. Belvoir was in ruins, George Fairfax dead, and Sally far away in London; few of the early companions on his journeys were alive. Yet there was much to remember, and the majestic, unchanging peace of Mount Vernon was the place for an old man to collect his memories.

The Colonel, the General, the President, and plain George Washington, Virginia farmer—they merged in the person of the sober old gentleman who rode about the plantation in 1799, a hickory stick in his hand and an umbrella tied to his saddle-bow to ward off the sun. Here was the traveler at home in the part of America he loved best. In memory, during those last days, he must have journeyed again many times in the other parts of the country where his fortunes had taken him. These journeys, this America, appear in the pages that follow.

PART 2

THE REVOLUTION:

JOURNEYS AND HEADQUARTERS


Chapter 1

New England: Boston Revisited


Judging by the number of places in New England where Washington is alleged to have slept, eaten, watered his horses or simply passed by (a street in Providence, Rhode Island, has a sign boasting that George rode on it), the casual traveler might gather that the great man had spent most of his time there.

The facts are that he visited Boston on just three occasions, saw Vermont not at all, journeyed only to the southeast corner of New Hampshire and no farther into Maine than Kittery, across the border, missing entirely the glories of Cape Cod and its salutary southern islands, Martha's Vineyard and Nantucket. Indeed, when one traces his meager progress across the lovely face of New England, the question arises as to what part of the Washington tradition these original colonies can claim at all.

The answer is: A rich one, and their pride is justified. Two of his Boston visits were historic episodes of a high order—the first, of course, when he took command of the Continental Army and besieged the city until the British evacuated it; and the second, his presidential visit of 1789, when he brought to bear the enormous weight of his prestige by means of a tour through these "Eastern states" in order to solidify public sentiment behind the new government. The following year he made a special trip to reluctant Rhode Island, omitted on the first tour, to confirm that state's support. Hartford and Wethersfield and Newport share an important part of the tradition, because it was in these cities that Washington planned with Rochambeau and the other French officers the grand strategy which brought final victory at Yorktown. On these comings and goings, he stopped at towns and villages, conferred with local leaders, inspected militia and, all told, justified nearly every sign that bears the phrase which has become a national joke: "George Washington slept here."

His associations with New England were hardly pleasant, because most of them had to do with the terrible anxieties of the Revolution, and there is no record that he yearned to embrace its beautiful hills and valleys and settle down. But on the other hand, George showed no particular fondness for any part of the country except Virginia. He was truly at home nowhere but in Mount Vernon. Yet New England must have been often in his thoughts as he rode beside the Potomac in his last years, because it was there that he began the long pilgrimage to immortality, there that he entered upon the journey which could end only in glory or utter disaster.

[1756]   From the beginning, his New England journeys were fateful, although the first trip to Boston in February 1756 was important chiefly to Colonel George Washington, of the Virginia Regiment. The fate of nations did not hang upon it. What was at stake was the troublesome question of command and precedence that dogged Washington personally until he became Commander-in-Chief, and then plagued him anew in respect to his officers. Specifically the problem was whether a certain Captain Dagworthy, a stubborn and arrogant Marylander, should outrank Colonel Washington and command the troops at Fort Cumberland by virtue of what he claimed was a royal commission, superseding George's provincial commission. This question exemplified the problem that created endless command confusion in the years of the war against France, and touched particularly an ambitious young man like Washington, who thought of making the military life a career.

Governor Dinwiddie sided with Washington in the lengthy quarrel, but he had no authority to settle it. The man who could, presumably, was Governor William Shirley of Massachusetts, who was temporarily in command of the British forces in America, following Braddock's death. Pride drove George to make the long trip up to Boston in the hope that Shirley would confirm his authority once and for all.[1]

The extent to which that pride had driven him may be judged by the fact that he planned his journey in the midst of winter. George had no experience with New England winters, but his frontier campaigns had taught him what cold and snow could mean to a traveler. Probably he reasoned that now his way would lie through a civilized, settled country, with no mountains to climb or swollen rivers to ford.

He set out from Alexandria about February 2, 1756, in company with Captain George Mercer, his aide and paymaster; another aide, Captain Robert Stewart; and two servants. With his customary awareness of dress, he was outfitted, if tradition can be depended upon for once, in a handsome buff and blue uniform, a white and scarlet cloak over his shoulder, and all the insignia of his disputed rank. He must have cut a dashing figure.

For the first thirty miles, the path lay along an old familiar route—the road to Annapolis, which was then a sociable, gossipy little town of about a hundred and fifty houses. Beyond, he was in new territory for him, traversing the Patapsco, Gunpowder and Susquehanna ferries, over the Elk River to New Castle, across Brandywine Ferry to Chester, and past well-tilled, rolling farmlands and substantial orchards, then one last ferry over the Schuylkill to Philadelphia, the largest city he had ever been in. It was a passage he would make a great many times in future, under conditions and in states of mind infinitely varied.

George was properly impressed by Philadelphia, the principal city in the colonies, if the claims of New Yorkers were
whittled down to reasonable proportions. Its more than three
thousand houses lined paved streets, equipped with sidewalks
on both sides, and its public buildings were mostly imposing
brick structures. They included eight or ten churches, a college,
a hospital, a State House and two libraries. Patrols walked the
lighted streets at night, in sharp contrast with the dismal gloom
that enveloped most communities after sundown. The spirit
of the city was sober, religious and commercial. Above all,
commercial. Observer after observer, looking upon Philadelphia, confirmed in his reports what was self-evident: the chief
occupation and enjoyment of the populace was making money.

What delighted George most about the city, however, was
its shops. As a Virginia gentleman who loved good clothes but
had not enjoyed the opportunity to buy them during his frontier service in 1754–55, he made the rounds of the tailors and
hatters, outfitting himself in a manner suited to his station. The
process took four or five days, and meanwhile there was considerable speculation in Philadelphia about his mission. French
spies guessed incorrectly that he was plotting a surprise attack
on DuQuesne.

George said nothing to anyone, and on February 13 he rode
out of town toward New York. He might have gone by way of
Trenton, Prince Town and New Brunswick to Newark, whose
main street was nearly two miles long, but he chose instead to
ferry the Delaware at Burlington and follow the route
Allentown–Cranberry Brook (now Cranbury)–Perth Amboy.
There the tired horses got a brief rest as the whole party went
aboard the vessel which would take them to the Narrows, at a
point five miles from Flat Bush and only ten from New York,
into which he rode on the fifteenth, at the end of the day.

Probably he stayed that night at a tavern, but by the next
evening he had found a Virginian to shelter him. The circumstances here are vague. As far as it can be determined, George
had never met Beverly Robinson and would have had no rea-

son to stay at his house except for the all-embracing nature of Virginia hospitality and whatever connection, acquaintance or friendship may have existed between the families. There is not even a record that Robinson had a house in New York at the time, but it appears likely. What is known is that in Robinson's house, wherever it was, George had an experience which produced one of the most romantic and least substantiated legends about his life.

Beverly Robinson had made a most fortunate marriage, to Susannah Philipse, the eldest of Frederick Philipse's two sisters. As the third and last lord of the great country manor overlooking the Hudson at Yonkers, Frederick was the nearest thing to native nobility that the province possessed, and his sisters were among the richest heiresses extant, acknowledged social leaders. However, Mrs. Robinson had not married beneath her: her husband's family equaled the Philipse clan in social status if not in wealth.

Susannah's sister Mary was at the moment living with her. Known to her friends as Polly, she was a handsome girl of twenty-six, with a fine, deep-breasted figure and a neck, Dr. Freeman meticulously notes, which "had some indication of goitre." She was spoiled, one gathers, and the kind of woman who wanted to dominate men, in an era when it was not as customary as it later became. George may well have seen in her some reflection of his mother, another strong-willed, dominant woman, but he also had to regard her, by the realistic code of his time, as a potential match. Though a little old to be unmarried in that day, she was still young, and she possessed 51,000 acres of very valuable property. It was almost his duty to investigate this possibility.

The investigation was enjoyable in itself, because George carried it on by squiring Polly and Susannah around New York. Looking in the papers to see what there was of excitement, he found advertised in the New York *Mercury* of February 16 this attraction: "To be seen at the New Exchange, that elaborate and celebrated piece of mechanism, called the Microcosm, or, the World in Miniature. Built in the form of a Roman Temple, after twenty-two years close study and application by the late ingenious Mr. Henry Bridges of London. . . . It will be shewn every day from six in the morning till six at night, to any select company (not less than six) at six shillings each." The advertisement further promised that "a fire is kept going in the Exhibition Hall during the whole time."

This traveling phenomenon had been shown in Williamsburg the previous autumn, where Washington may possibly have seen it, and had come to New York by way of Philadelphia. It was a curious contraption consisting of numerous mechanical devices, all bobbing up and down at once: Orpheus in the forest, plucking his lyre; men at work in a carpenter's yard; the nine Muses in the midst of a musical concert; birds flying and singing; a procession of coaches, chariots and chaises, "all moving easily and gracefully"; a gunpowder mill in operation; and ships afloat on tossing waves.

It must have been an entrancing spectacle, because George took the ladies twice. Doubtless he took them elsewhere, and otherwise amused himself in the usual manner, going to "Mr. Baron's rout," spending an evening at Willet's Tavern, paying more visits to the tailors (he bought a pair of shoes as well), and playing cards, at which he lost eight shillings. More important, he bought some fresh horses to go the rest of the journey.

In the course of these occupations he probably saw all that was worth seeing in New York, a city even then all color and movement, though it was huddled compactly within a short radius of the Battery. The inhabitants, boastful as always, claimed four thousand buildings, but the count was probably somewhat more than half that figure. Many were of brick. The streets were paved but dirty, and they had no regular pattern, like Philadelphia's. George probably walked up the Broad Way, an impressive thoroughfare even in February, with its gracious rows of shade trees on each side, and he surely admired the churches (Middle Dutch, Trinity and St. George's) and the fort which commanded the harbor as it had since the days of the Dutch. King's College, with a fine view of both North River and the harbor, was a-building not far away.

There were remarkable similarities between the New York of 1756 and the city of today. One of its problems was an adequate water supply; it remains so in our time. There were more Negroes than in any other city in the North, and for some of the same unfounded reasons that persist now they were severely restricted. The difference between rich and poor was nearly as striking as it is today, where the extremes of the East Side sit back to back. Finally, and most remarkable of all, the temper of the people was the same. A visitor in 1765 remarked of them: "People here live to a good old age and very comfortably did they choose to be contented."

But it was still a small town, and people gossiped about George's presence as they had in Philadelphia. It was no longer a secret that he was on his way to see Governor Shirley, but he would not say why. Some thought he wanted Shirley's advice about using the Southern Indians to help the British—an expedient to which the Colonel would certainly have resorted if he could have, with or without Shirley's advice.

After five days in New York, Washington said good-by to Mary and to the Robinsons, and set out on the last leg of his journey. In New London he stopped with an old friend of the family, Joseph Chew, and then boarded a vessel bound for Newport, where he found another Virginian, Godfrey Malbone, to welcome him.

Though by this time the New England winter was smiting him every day, George decided to brave the stormy coast in a man-of-war. He reached his goal on the twenty-seventh, eight days out of New York. Apparently he did not know any Virginians in Boston, because he found quarters at the Cromwell's Head Tavern on School Street, where the Protector's profile exacted tribute from every tall passer-by because the inn's sign hung so low over the sidewalk.

In Boston, George was received with some distinction. The city's liveliest newspaper, the *Gazette*, noted his arrival on

March 1 and termed him "a gentleman who has deservedly a high reputation for military skill and valor, though success has not always attended his undertakings." The Colonel may have considered this an unnecessary reminder of the affair at Fort Necessity. Long before the day of "informed observers," the *Gazette* speculated openly that George was involved in promoting an alliance with the Southern Indians; the report, naturally, came from the paper's New York correspondent.

Until he could see the Governor, Washington inspected the town, as he had Philadelphia and New York. He liked the streets, which seemed spacious to him, and he was impressed with one two miles long, which today bears his name. In the shops were goods he had not seen in the other cities, and to a Virginian they were offered at bargain prices because of the difference in exchange between the two provinces. George was not a man to pass up a bargain. He bought a new hat, patronized one of the best tailors, and acquired some silver lace and two pairs of gloves. The bill came to more than two hundred Boston pounds, but he paid only about twenty-five Virginia pounds.

On his sight-seeing tour about town, George took in Castle William, the fort in the harbor, in which he had a military man's interest; Faneuil Hall ( still a busy tourist attraction); the Court House; King's Chapel (not in use at the time); and other public buildings. Eventually sight-seeing and business converged and he found himself at the head of Milk Street, ready for Province House, where Governor Shirley received guests, though he lived in a splendid house in Roxbury. Province House had a Mussolini-like balcony, from which royal proclamations and those of Shirley were read, and from which the Governor sometimes addressed the people. The house was built of Holland brick, three stories high, equipped with portico and a cupola surmounted by a weather vane which George must have thought singularly apt: an Indian with bow in hand. This Indian, like his real-life counterparts on the frontier, changed direction with the winds.

Young Washington trod briskly through the iron gates (all that survives of Province House today), up the walk that bisected the smooth lawn, shaded by tall trees, and up the twenty red sandstone steps into the presence of the man he had come so far to see.

The interview went smoothly enough. Shirley was an altogether remarkable figure, whom George had no time to get to know. Sir William Johnson could have told him much about the energetic, hustling, ambitious Governor, of whom Francis Parkman observed, "There must have been a fountain of youth in the old man." He fancied himself as a military genius, he was highly successful with the ladies (he married in his late years a girl young enough to be his daughter), and he was not afraid to assume any kind of responsibility or problem. He sincerely felt himself equal to anything, and as royal governors went, he gave Massachusetts good service.

George found that Shirley agreed with him entirely about the presumption of Captain Dagworthy, but the Governor did not tell him that he had only recently dispatched a letter giving Governor Horatio Sharpe of Maryland, whom Dagworthy claimed as a supporter, authority that would make him Washington's superior. As it was, the Governor and the Virginia Colonel came to an amicable understanding, and after the interview, George left Boston immediately. He reached New York on March 10, and there he stopped again with Beverly Robinson. One supposes he found Mary Philipse as enchanting as before, because he spent four days in the city, although he was anxious to be home.*

---

\* That was all, or nearly all, of the Mary Philipse affair. The possibility of a match was certainly discussed, more probably with Robinson than with the lady, but it was not pursued. Yet out of this insubstantial evidence has been woven one of the hardiest Washington traditions. He is represented as having been violently in love with her, being refused because she had given her heart to Roger Morris. The flights of decorative fancy which have grown out of this

Such delays, along with entertaining and visits to the tailor's, had left him short of funds and he had to borrow ninety-one pounds from Robinson to complete his journey. Replenished, he went on to Philadelphia, suffered a short illness which further delayed him, came into Annapolis on the twenty-third, and soon after hurried to Williamsburg. Having discovered his new relationship to Governor Sharpe, which convinced him that the command question was as vexed as before, he was in a mood to resign as he rode into the Virginia capital on March 30.

In this black mood he ended his first excursion to New England, as disturbed in mind as when he began it, and with more knowledge of New York and Philadelphia to show for the trip than of the Northern colonies.

[1775–1776]   It was nearly twenty years before he returned to Boston, years of accomplishment and growth which Washington was sure had prepared him inadequately for the central role in which Congress had cast him as leader of the new army. Dubious of his ability to carry out the task, and fearful to the

---

alleged blighted love of Washington's are innumerable, and some of them have come to be accepted as unquestioned fact.

One of the wildest stories asserts that Polly became a close friend of the unfortunate Major André and tried to save him from execution for his part in Arnold's treachery. She is said to have come to Washington's headquarters in disguise, bearing a flag of truce and accompanied by Beverly Robinson, who pleaded in vain with the stern General to spare André. In a last appeal, Polly is said to have cast aside her veil, but in the words of one account, "finds too late that the face and voice that once charmed him have lost all power to influence the acts of one who only lived for his country. . . ." This story is said to have first appeared about 1848 in a New Jersey newspaper called the *Telegraph*.

The only substance of truth in the entire fabric of tradition is that Polly did give her heart to Washington's former comrade, Roger Morris. She married him. Morris was a Loyalist sympathizer but he would not fight the rebels. Polly may have known André but there is no proof of it. The rest, including George's broken heart, is fantasy.

point of tears that he would lose all his hard-won "honor" in
trying to perform it, he was nonetheless highly resolved on
the morning of June 23, 1775, when he rode out of Philadelphia to take the command at Cambridge.[2]

He began the journey on horseback, but unavoidable ceremony compelled him to change to a light carriage drawn by a
pair of white horses. His companions were the first young men
to become a part of his official "family," a band of "writing"
and "riding" aides who would number thirty-two before eight
years of war were ended. Some were members for a few months,
others for years, and two stayed nearly the duration. Several became historic figures on their own account in later years. "They
wrote long dispatches and they rode on long errands," says one
writer who has studied them, "and when opportunity offered,
they danced and flirted and courted. They were young—young
in their enthusiasm, in their lightheartedness, in their impatient
ambition. . . ."[3]

Those who rode with Washington to Boston were Thomas
Mifflin, thirty-one, and Joseph Reed, thirty-four, both of them
handsome men of good family and manners. Besides these aides,
he was accompanied by a pair of new major generals, forty-
four-year-old Charles Lee and Philip Schuyler, two years
younger, of the rich Albany family. It was ironic that these
subordinates who were by his side at the start of the new adventure should be ones to rise up and challenge him later. The
controversy over these able generals is far from subsiding. Was
Lee an almost psychopathic egocentric whose jealousy and ambition hurt the cause more than it helped, or was he a military
genius whose superior abilities Washington refused to recognize? Was Schuyler's vindication by a court-martial also a reminder that Washington should have sided with him against
Gates, who may or may not have been a part of the intrigue
against the Commander-in-Chief? These questions are still
matters of debate among students of the Revolution.

Whatever might transpire later, it was a serious, dedicated
little band of men that rode out into the rainy countryside on

75

June 23. They had not gone far before they encountered an express, carrying to Congress an account of the battle of Bunker Hill, written by Captain Elijah Hide. A short time later a second express came clattering after the first. His dispatch was a Watertown, Massachusetts, paper which had made a gallant effort to cover the battle secondhand and, after a few generalities, had succeeded in achieving a remarkable sentence. This may have been the origin of the old newspaper anecdote of the cub reporter sent to the scene of a train wreck, who wired back to his editor: "All is confusion, can send nothing." The Watertown editor, similarly harassed, regretted his inability to print a comprehensive story, declaring that "the confusion of the times renders it impractical to give a particular account of what has already occurred but hope to give a good account in our next."

John Adams noted the arrival of these couriers when they reached Philadelphia, confusing the dates when he did it, and out of the notation in his *Autobiography*, Washington Irving created the legend that Washington pressed the couriers to tell him how the militia had behaved and, hearing they had fought like brave men, turned to the others and uttered a most unlikely remark: "The liberties of the country are safe!" It was the kind of utterance calculated to stir applause in a patriotic address, or to be recorded for posterity, but otherwise it is wholly out of character with its supposed author.

The first night's stop was probably at Trenton. Next day they were at Brunswick, where Schuyler and Washington discussed the best way to go into New York City. If they went by the route Washington had traveled on his previous visit, they ran the risk of capture by British warships lying in the harbor. Presumably there was also some danger by the Elizabeth Point road and ferry. Another alternative was the ferry from Newark to Powles Hook.

No immediate decision was reached, and the party pushed on to Newark. "Pushed" may have been the word, as far as Washington's companions were concerned. He was in the habit of getting up before dawn and making a good start without breakfast, to get in as many miles as possible before the heat of the day began to affect the horses. Thus, as he had promised the others, they came into Newark at 9 A.M. on the twenty-fifth. There a committee from the New York Provincial Congress met them, in a state of some perturbation. It appeared that New York's ardently Loyalist governor, William Tryon, was due to arrive in the city that day, returning from a journey of his own. It was Sunday, and the streets were full of people enjoying the air and sunshine. If the Governor and the General arrived at the same time, the partisan passions boiling beneath the surface in the bitterly divided city might explode in riot. Then, too, there was the possibility that any well-advertised entry by Washington might precipitate an attempted capture from one of the British ships.

The committee advised the General to go up the west shore of the Hudson to Hoboken (variously called Hobocken, Hobock and Hocken at the time), past the usual ferry crossing at Powles Hook, and to make his entrance by what was, in effect, the back door. Being a prudent man, Washington agreed.

Before he climbed into the boat that took him across, he did a characteristic thing. With his usual attention to appearance, he dressed for the occasion, wrapping a new purple sash about his blue uniform and putting on a hat with a plume.

How different this entrance from the one of 1756! Then he had arrived unobtrusively during the evening and gone to a tavern, unannounced. Now, as the ferry carried him toward the broad green lawns of Colonel Lispenard's estate, sloping down to the riverbank, with the edge of the town about a mile to the south, Washington could see a huge crowd gathered around the place where he was to alight. It must have been a scene like one of those broad murals that decorate the interiors of banks and public buildings in New York today: the blue band of the river, and beyond it the big house, set square and white in a gently rolling carpet of grass, shaded by majestic trees, and the shifting clusters of people between the house and the ferry landing, the blue uniforms of the city's nine militia companies mingled with the Sunday-best colors of the men and women who had walked out from the city to see the Commander-in-Chief. It was unlike anything Washington had ever faced before, but one whose endless replicas of ceremonial he would contemplate with weary distaste before he died.

About four o'clock, he stepped off the ferry, raised his hat and bowed to the welcoming huzzas that greeted him, and made his way to Lispenard's house, where he was invited for dinner. There have been elaborate descriptions of his progress from dock to house, but as Dr. Freeman observes, "it is difficult to see why hungry men, in something of a hurry, might not have walked across the lawn from the landing while batmen conducted the horses and vehicles along the road and the lane."

The house itself was situated at a point that would now be near the Canal Street approach to the Holland Tunnel, and its seven or eight acres of surrounding land were bounded by the present Canal, Varick, Laight and Hudson streets. Colonel Lispenard gave his name to the street which survived him, a short thoroughfare between Broadway and Sixth Avenue, south of Canal.

As he sat at dinner, the General came face to face with his first dark moment of the war—a premonitory warning of the bitter road ahead. While the cheering, optimistic crowd milled about outside, waiting for their leader to reappear and lead them in a parade, a courier arrived with more news from Boston. Charlestown had been destroyed, and the Continental Army faced a serious shortage of powder almost before it had begun to fight.

Washington conveyed this and other news to Congress in a letter he wrote while the express waited, and then, after taking care of the urgent business that pressed upon him, he went outside and presented a calm, confident face to the citizens.

It was a grand parade—the volunteer companies leading, followed by members of the Provincial Congress, then Lee and Schuyler, the Commander-in-Chief, and the Philadelphia Light

Horse bringing up the rear, with the shouting citizens falling in behind—the largest assemblage of people the town had ever seen.

The marchers wound down Greenwich Road, probably as far as the present Chambers Street, turning into Murray Street and passing the public meeting place known as "The Fields," where City Hall Park is today. Not all who watched had their spirits raised. An old Loyalist like Judge Thomas Jones wrote disgustedly of the "seditious and rebellious multitude." But the Sons of Liberty and their sympathizers raised a loud, seditious cheer as the procession broke up at Hull's Tavern, near Trinity Church, where Washington probably stayed that night.*

Tradition says that Governor Tryon saw the end of the parade and nearly fainted at the sight of Washington's public support, but the tale has no basis either in fact or in Tryon's irascible character. He was not given to fainting spells.

Washington hoped to get started for Boston next morning in his customary good season, but there were the inevitable delays of high office to which he was now compelled to accustom himself. The Provincial Congress sent him an address which had to be answered. There were conferences with Schuyler about his new command in the North. There was even delay in deciding about who was to accompany him as a guard of honor on his departure from the city; prominent citizens and the volunteer companies were clamoring for the honor.

At length, sometime after three o'clock in the afternoon, the guard of honor, made up of everyone who could get in it, and the Philadelphia Light Horse, who had followed their General all the way from home, gathered outside Hull's and the procession got under way. It traveled along what would now be Broadway to the upper end of Central Park, where McGown's

---

* Hull's had gone through two previous incarnations as the Province Arms and as Burns's, and it would subsequently become even more celebrated as the Bunch of Grapes, a name so common that it was the "Joe's Bar and Grill" of its day.

Pass Tavern marked a far northern boundary; then the entourage took a left fork in the road and went on up Broadway by
what was then called the King's Road to King's Bridge, which
spanned Spuyten Duyvil. At this point the New York portion
of the escort turned back, with a final exchange of compliments.

Local historians are not agreed on where Washington spent
his first night out of the city. Some think he slept at Cox's
Tavern, later made a part of the Macomb mansion (or so it is
thought) at the northwest corner of Broadway and 230th
Street. Others say he pulled the covers over himself at Hyatt's
Tavern, sometimes called Kingsbridge Inn, now the corner of
Broadway and 223rd Street. There is also a tradition which
states he stayed at the Van Cortlandt mansion, about a mile
from King's Bridge in what would today be Van Cortlandt
Park.

At any rate he slept, and next morning journeyed onward to
New Rochelle, where the faithful Philadelphians left him at
last. Schuyler had left the company in New York, and now
there were only General Lee and the staff officers.

No argument arises about his New Rochelle lodgings, since
no one appears to know where they were. In the morning the
general traveled to New Haven, where a military company of
Yale students turned out to be reviewed, and two town companies, unable to muster before morning, asked for his critical
eye. That meant another early start delayed, but he could not
very well refuse. He sighed, and agreed.

His lodging that night was the home of the recently deceased
Isaac Beers, at the corner of Chapel and College streets, where
the modern Hotel Taft has replaced the venerable New Haven
House. Next morning the volunteer companies paraded, and
then the General was ushered out of New Haven in style. A
contemporary account describes the departure as "attended by
great numbers of the inhabitants of the town. They were escorted . . . by two companies dressed in their uniform, and by a
company of young gentlemen belonging to the Seminary in

this place, who made a handsome appearance, and whose expertness in the military exercises gained the approbation of the Generals." [4]

The Yale men turned back, so it is said, at Neck Bridge, where Mill River is crossed by State Street, but the older companies, who probably had no classes to worry about, went on for a way.

Taking notice of a country whose delights had not been disclosed to him on the winter journey of 1756, Washington remarked that the Connecticut Valley, on the way to Wethersfield, was "delightful country . . . covered with grass . . . in a very different manner to what our lands in Virginia are."

Passing through New London, he came that night to Wethersfield, then as now a lovely town of wide streets and gracious houses. Nearly all of them in that day had gardens, and were set amid sweeping vistas of lawns and shade trees.

Washington alighted at the home of Silas Deane, his friend and admirer in the Continental Congress. He had a letter for Mrs. Deane, which Silas had given him as he left Philadelphia, but it was not a letter to a lonely wife left at home. It read like a military order: "This will be handed you by his Excellency, General Washington, in company with General Lee, and retinue. Should they lodge a night in Wethersfield, you will accommodate their horses, servants, &c., in the best manner at the tavern, and their retinue will likely go on to Hartford."

Deane's house, afterward occupied for years by Stephen Chester, was the first one south of the Webb house, where Washington would confer with Rochambeau six desperate years later. Mrs. Deane and the members of the family who were there opened the doors of their home to the General, as they would no doubt have done without the letter. The town was not large enough to stage a ceremony, for which Washington must have been thankful, but he was visited by the prominent citizens before he could get off to bed.

For the ride to Springfield next day, Jeremiah Wadsworth gave the General the loan of his horse, to be hitched to the commander's carriage. At Springfield he was confronted anew with pomp and ceremony. A committee from the Massachusetts Provincial Congress informed him that Congress had directed the principal gentlemen of the larger towns from there to Cambridge to meet the Commander-in-Chief and escort him, changing at each stop. That meant Brookfield, Worcester, Marlborough and Watertown, and an additional delay in each one, but it was the kind of attention that could not be refused.

The congressional committee in charge of these arrangements,which had ridden to Springfield, consisted of Moses Gill and Dr. Benjamin Church, who less than four months later was seized as the first traitor to the cause.

In this changing and changeable company, Washington got as far as Marlborough on July 1, and next morning, Sunday, he traveled the short distance to Watertown, accompanied by a troop of horse from Marlborough. In Watertown he received an address from the Provincial Congress, which was meeting there, but to save time he did not answer it until two days later. It was only three more miles to Cambridge, the end of the journey, and he was anxious to press on.

It had been raining all morning, and when the General's company rode into Cambridge from the wet countryside, after miles of ceremony, the moment was oddly anticlimactic: no one appeared to be expecting them. It was a confusion of dates. The troops had turned out on Saturday morning to welcome the General. Disappointed, they had routed themselves from bed on Sunday morning in the rain, but again no Washington. The officers had dismissed them long before two o'clock in the afternoon, when the cavalcade appeared.* Once more contrary to tradition, which asserts that he entered to the noise of cheering throngs and saluting cannon, Washington was ushered without any fanfare to the home of Harvard's president, Samuel Langdon, whose house had been appropriated for the General by the Provincial Congress, leaving only one room for its owner.

* The men may well have been asleep, at least those who were not on duty. The British had murdered slumber, beginning at four that morning, with an artillery assault on Roxbury which went on for three hours.

This, of course, was the Wadsworth house, sometimes called the "President's House," built in 1726 by Harvard for its presidents.

The General wasted no time. Before the afternoon was over, he rode with Lee, Putnam and other officers to get his first view of the fortifications and the general strategic situation. About three quarters of a mile away was a long ridge, at the eastern end of which was Prospect Hill, or "Mount Pisgah," as the natives called it. From this eminence, which today would be in Somerville, north of Union Square, Washington viewed Boston. Before him, only a little distance away, was Cobble Hill, the remains of which lie in the Boston & Maine Railroad yards. From these hills the land sloped away gradually to the marshes and open water. A Bostonian of today would hardly recognize the scene, missing the reclaimed land on which so much of East and South Boston has been built. Bunker Hill was a mile away, and Washington, using his glasses, saw the enemy for the first time. The British sentinels there, looking down over Breed's Hill, could see what remained of Charlestown, and beyond, in the Mystick River, a pair of English floating batteries.

Boston itself was two miles away from Prospect Hill; Washington viewed it from this angle for the first time. He saw that it was about two miles long—that is, north and south—and about a mile and a half wide. Turning southeast, he could observe Roxbury and parts of Dorchester Neck, and looking out over the harbor, he noted the means by which the British held the town helpless: the tall masts of the fleet—like a dry, cedar swamp, as one man had described them—and the fortifications on Castle Island. The new Commander-in-Chief realized that he had his job cut out for him, but he saw in sum what it was—to hold the British forces immobile in Boston until he could get his army ready for larger affairs.

Thus Washington came to the scene of his first task, "after a journey attended with a good deal of fatigue and retarded by necessary attentions to the successive civilities which accompanied me in my whole route," he wrote back to Philadelphia.[5]

On the following morning, at nine o'clock, he took formal

command of the army, although no evidence whatever exists that he took it either under the "Washington elm" or on Cambridge Common. However, the venerable tree became as firmly rooted in tradition as it was in the friendly soil of Cambridge. When it was declared officially dead on August 15, 1923, the tragic news was carried by the wire services to newspapers everywhere in the country, which mourned its demise with appropriate editorials and Sunday features. There were even those who publicly questioned why Senator Martin L. Davey of Ohio, founder of the tree surgeons who bear his name, had not made an attempt to save it, as he had rescued a horse chestnut planted by Washington at Kenmore.

When the elm was cut down the following year, the traditionalists had their day. Dr. J. S. Sargent, of the Arnold Arboretum, examined it and pronounced it at least three centuries old, so it was undoubtedly well grown on the day Washington assumed command. But not a single contemporary description of that day mentions either elm or common.

Nor does any evidence support the old story that a cannon ball passed through the Wadsworth house, suggesting to the General that he would be well advised to move. No one knows why he moved after little more than a week, but the informed guess is that a Virginia gentleman felt awkward about appropriating the house of a man who still lived in it, confined to one room—especially when that man was fifty-two years old, the president of Harvard, and a distinguished personage in his own right. History does not record what happened to the president's wife and five children.

In any case, Washington delicately let the Provincial Congress know that he would like to move, and the forthright colonials obliged by empowering the Committee of Safety to appropriate any other house that suited the General's fancy. He chose the home of John Vassall, a Royalist who had fled the scene. His place was one of seven houses making up "Tory Row," as they came to be called. Washington and Charles Lee occupied it about the middle of July, but Lee, perhaps already uncomfortable in the presence of a man he later professed to despise, took himself on July 26 four miles away to Medford, where he occupied General Royall's house. Characteristically, he renamed it Hobgoblin Hall. Washington stayed in the Vassall house and maintained it as his Cambridge headquarters until he departed for New York on April 4, 1776.

As every Boston tourist knows, Major Vassall's deserted mansion became the Craigie-Longfellow house of a later period, owned and occupied for a long time by the poet, and open to the public today.

In this graceful Georgian house, Washington settled down. He must have noticed, as the proprietor of a large establishment of his own, that his surroundings could be regarded as elegant. Carved woodwork decorated the paneled rooms. There was a drawing room and a dining room for entertaining, on one side of the center hall, and on the other side was the study, opening conveniently into quarters for the aides and secretaries.

Washington took a countryman's pleasure in the Massachusetts countryside, by this time in the lush flowering of full summer. "The village I am in is situated in the midst of a very delightful country," he wrote, "and is a very beautiful place itself, though small. A thousand pities that such a country should become the theater of war. . . ." [6]

And the country welcomed the General. Already he was the hero, the great man, and the devotion of the people about him took the forms they have always taken. A newspaper reported: "Last Sabbath, a child of Colonel Robinson, of Dorchester, Massachusetts, was baptized by the Reverend Mr. [Samuel] Dunbar, of Stoughton, by the name of George Washington." [7]

The legends grew thick as weeds in an unkept field. One of the choicest declared that word was sent to the General one day of a riot on Cambridge Common involving a thousand men, whereupon he leaped to his horse, flew over the fence about the Yard with a fox hunter's ease and, arriving at the heart of the squabble, clutched the ringleaders (fortunately there were only two) in his hands, thus ending the riot. [8]

In his dealings with the men, Washington sometimes got emphatic advice. Colonel Stephen Moylan told him bluntly, on the subject of familiarity between officers and soldiers, a problem that worried Washington, who considered it fatal to discipline: "There is one reason, and I think a substantial one, why a person born in the same town or neighborhood, should not be employed on public affairs of this nature in that town or neighborhood. It is that the spirit of equality which reigns through this country will make him afraid of exerting that authority necessary for the expediting of his business. He must shake every man by the hand, and desire, beg and pray, do brother, do my friend, do such a thing, whereas a few hearty damns from a person who did not care a damn for them would have a much better effect."[9]

In his own correspondence Washington seldom allowed himself a complaint directed against an individual; ordinarily he dwelt on the large questions of discipline and command. But he was irritated enough one November day that year to add this P. S.: "I had just finished my letter when a blundering lieutenant of the blundering Captain Coit, who had just blundered upon two vessels from Nova Scotia, came in with the account of it, and before I could rescue my letter, without knowing what he did, picked up a candle and sprinkled it with grease; but these are the kind of blunders which one can readily excuse. . . ."[10]

Each week Lund Washington wrote to his uncle from Mount Vernon, where he had been left in charge as superintendent, detailing everything that went on, as Washington required of him and future superintendents. Just as faithfully, the master of Mount Vernon took time off from besieging the British to reply, giving directions and advice about the affairs of the plantation, as he did whenever he was away from home. Most of these letters from Cambridge are said to have been destroyed, but one that is preserved is worth quoting.

"Let the hospitality of the house with respect to the poor be kept up," Washington wrote to his nephew. "Let no one go hungry away. If any of these kind of people should be in want of corn, supply their necessities, provided it does not encourage them in idleness, and I have no objection to your giving my money in charity, to the amount of forty or fifty pounds a year, when you think it well bestowed. What I mean by having no objection, is that it is my desire that it should be done. You are to consider that neither myself or wife are now in the way to do these good offices." [11]

By the time he wrote this letter, Martha was on her way to Cambridge. It was apparent that the British and American armies were to spend the winter facing each other, and so Washington and other officers felt free to send for their wives, to cheer the bleak months that lay ahead. Well aware of the dangers of the journey, Washington wrote to his friend Joseph Reed in Philadelphia, asking him to look after the lady when she arrived:

"As she and her conductor (who I expect will be Mr. Custis, her son) are perfect strangers to the road, the stages, and the proper place to cross Hudson's River (by all means avoiding New York), I shall be much obliged in your particular instructions and advice to her. I do imagine, as the roads are bad and the weather cold, her stages must be short, especially as I expect her horses will be pretty much fatigued, as they will, by the time she gets to Philadelphia, have performed a journey of at least four hundred and fifty miles, my express finding . . . her among her friends near Williamsburg, one hundred and fifty miles below my own house." [12]

Reed welcomed Martha to Philadelphia and saw the party on its way, noting slyly that the feminine part of the company was "not a bad supply, I think, in a country where wood is scarce." [13] The supply included not only Martha but Jack's pretty wife Nelly, who accompanied her husband; and General Gates's wife. These people and George Lewis tumbled out of their stage at Cambridge on December 11, after an uneventful journey. Uneventful, that is, as far as incident was concerned, but exciting to Martha because she had never been so far from home, had never before seen the cities her coach passed through after it left familiar Virginia.

At Cambridge she converted headquarters into a different place. Heretofore a drab military establishment, she and Nelly and Mrs. Gates made it a social center, where she entertained as the wife of the Commander-in-Chief was expected to do — "tasteful but never ostentatious," as Freeman puts it. Casual visitors got oranges and a glass of wine. Other guests came to dinner, which was at two o'clock. With Mrs. Gates and Mrs. Mifflin, Martha also returned the social visits of the Cambridge ladies who came to call at the Vassall house.

On Sunday everyone went to church, the "Old Congregational Church," where the Rev. Nathaniel Appleton was minister. Dr. Appleton was aided by such military clergy as Abiel Leonard, once a chaplain to General Putnam's command, the Third Connecticut, now attached to General Knox's artillery regiment. A lady who did not have her mind on the services wrote to a friend in Philadelphia that Mrs. Washington, "our Queen," wore a dress of peach-colored satin one Sunday.

Except for the sound of cannonading, to which she had a hard time adjusting, Martha was quite at home in Cambridge, and the Boston society which had fled to the suburbs accepted her.

Christmas came in on a cold wave that must have seemed nearly intolerable to the Virginians. There was a heavy snowfall on Christmas Eve, followed by a day of bright sunshine. The British ceased fire for the holiday, as did the Americans, while officers called on each other and the soldiers made what cheer they could. Some waded through the snow to country farmhouses, where they could buy fruit and fowl for their dinners.

Thus the first year of war ended, and the second began with a chill that was not of the weather. Sitting gloomily over his correspondence on a quiet Sunday night in January, Washington poured out the personal fears he seldom allowed himself to set down, even to such friends as Joseph Reed.

"The reflection on my situation, and that of this army, produces many an uneasy hour when all around me are wrapped in sleep," he wrote. "Few people know the predicament we are in, on a thousand accounts: fewer still will believe, if any disaster happens to these lines, from what cause it flows. I have often thought how much happier I should have been, if, instead of accepting the command under such circumstances, I had taken my musket on my shoulder and entered the ranks, or, if I could have justified the measure to posterity and my own conscience, had retired to the back country, and lived in a wigwam."

The reasons for his anxiety he went on to enumerate: "We are now without any money in our treasury, powder in our magazines, arms in our stores. We are without a brigadier (the want of which has been twenty times urged), engineers, expresses (though a committee has been appointed these two months to establish them), and by and by, when we shall be called upon to take the field, shall not have a tent to lie in. Apropos, what is doing with mine?" [14] *

Meanwhile the winter months passed, with diversions social and otherwise to enliven them. John Adams, traveling up from Philadelphia to pay the camp a visit, described one that was somewhat different than the polite company he expected to find. He recorded in his diary: "Dined at C [olonel] Mifflin's, at Cambridge, with G. Washington and Gates and their ladies, and half a dozen sachems and warriors of the French Caughnawaga tribe, with their wives and children. Williams is one who was captured in his infancy and adopted. There is a mixture of white blood, French or English, in most of them. Louis, their principal, speaks English and French, as well as Indian. It was a savage feast, carniverous animals devouring their prey; yet they were wondrous polite. The General introduced me to

---

* The tent was being made in Philadelphia by one Plunket Fleeson. It was an elaborate affair, composed of a dining marquee large enough to entertain a considerable company, a living tent with an arched chamber, and an attached baggage tent. The General got it in time to go into the field. Visitors to Valley Forge may see one like it there today.

them as one of the grand council fire at Philadelphia, upon which they made me many bows and a cordial reception."[15]

This occasion had more importance than some of the Indian visitations because the Caughnawagas, though not numerous, inhabited a strategic part of the country, a few miles above Montreal, on the St. Lawrence River, and their friendship was valuable.

Occasionally Washington had some intimations of his fame outside the world of Boston, which absorbed his attention. Alert publishers were having pictures of him drawn, to be engraved and sold to satisfy the demand for those who wished to look upon a Washington bold, a Washington noble, a Washington reassuring or simply an innocuous Washington who could not be distinguished from anyone else. The eminent artists of the day had not yet begun to besiege him for sittings, as they did later, and those who worked at long range let their fancies guide their hands. Joseph Reed sent one of these mezzotints to Martha, depicting the General "in full figure in uniform and cocked hat, on horseback, advancing to the right. A drawn sword in the right hand is held across the body, a battle in the right distance." [16]

Thanking his friend for the gift, George commented on the picture with a flash of his particular brand of humor: "Mr. Campbell, whom I never saw to my knowledge, has made a very formidable figure of the Commander-in-Chief, giving him a sufficient portion of terror in his countenance." [17]

There was a gift of a more notable kind the following month. Phillis Wheatley, the Boston slave girl, whose reputation as a poet was by that time international, had written some verses in praise of the General, which she sent to him. Surveying them today, particularly in comparison with the work of such Revolutionary poets as Philip Freneau, one feels that Phillis's work evoked such extraordinary praise more because she was a young Negro slave girl than because of the poetry's intrinsic quality, though it was no worse than the effulgences of most of her contemporaries.

By the time this poem was written, Phillis had won the distinction of having her poems published in London (in 1773, when she was only nineteen), and she had corresponded with the Earl of Dartmouth and the Countess of Huntingdon, to whom her volume was dedicated.

Her poem to Washington concluded:

> Fix'd are the eyes of nations on the scales,
> For in their hopes Columbia's arm prevails.
> Anon Britannia droops the pensive head,
> While round increase the rising hills of dead.
> Ah! cruel blindness to Columbia's state!
> Lament thy thirst of boundless power too late.
> Proceed, great chief, with virtue on thy side,
> Thy ev'ry action let the goddess guide.
> A crown, a mansion, and a throne that shine,
> With gold unfading, Washington! be thine.

Washington's answer to the poet tells more of him than Phillis could have understood. He wrote on February 28, 1776:

"Mrs. Phillis*: Your favor of the 26th of October did not reach my hands 'till the middle of December. Time enough, you will say, to have given an answer ere this. Granted. But a variety of important occurrences, continually interposing to distract the mind and withdraw the attention, I hope will apologize for the delay, and plead my excuse for the seeming, but not real neglect.

"I thank you most sincerely for your polite notice of me, in the elegant lines you enclose, and however undeserving I may

---

* When Washington wrote the letter, he did not know whether or not Miss Wheatley was married. The salutation is the one used when it was copied in 1781 for Washington's files, and it was known then that she had married. Her choice was romantic but unfortunate: the poor girl married beneath her, a man named John Peters who had no soul for poetry. This event occurred in 1778. She died six years later, at thirty-one. Washington not only preserved her memory with his letter, but her work is included in most standard anthologies of American literature.

be of such encomium and panegyric, the style and manner exhibit a striking proof of your great poetical talents. In honor of which, and as a tribute justly due to you, I would have published the poem, had I not been apprehensive that while I only meant to give the world this new instance of your genius, I might have incurred the imputation of vanity. This and nothing else determined me not to give it place in the public prints.

"If you should ever come to Cambridge, or near headquarters, I shall be happy to see a person so favored by the Muses, and to whom Nature has been so liberal and beneficent in her dispensation."

Phillis never came to call, nor were there to be many more visitors at the Vassall house, because Washington's residence in Boston drew unexpectedly to a close on a Sunday morning, March 17, when the British troops evacuated the city and sailed away with their fleet, leaving the undamaged town behind them.

The General could have made a triumphant entry, but he had much to do, and besides it was Sunday: the Commander-in-Chief must set the example. That afternoon he went to the Old Congregational, where the Rev. Mr. Leonard had found an apt text in Exodus 14:25: "And took off their chariot wheels that they drove them heavily, so that the Egyptians said, Let us flee from the face of Israel, for the Lord fighteth for them against the Egyptians."

Next day and the day after, Washington made examinations of the evacuated city, and found time to send such homely reassurances as this one to John Hancock: "The town, although it has suffered greatly, is not in so bad a state as I expected to find it; and I have a particular pleasure in being able to inform you, sir, that your house has received no damage worth mentioning. Your furniture is in tolerable order, and the family pictures are all left entire and untouched." [18]

On Wednesday he entered the city with the main body of the army. What celebration he permitted occurred on the twenty-eighth, a day he began by writing a letter to the Provincial Congress asking what he should do with the furniture that had been added to his residence since he began living there. He did not know whether it had been charged off to the public account, merely loaned to him, or rented for the occasion. (The legislature responded that there would be no charges, to the public or to the General, but that he should leave the furniture in the hands of someone authorized to give it back to the government.)

Two weeks before, the Washingtons had started house-hunting in New York, where the general now proposed to establish his headquarters, anticipating that the British planned to occupy it next. In letters he had made his wants known—"a large house ready furnished somewhere in or about Bowery Lane." Because his family, including the horses, was large, he would need "a spacious house with large stables," and a housekeeper, cook and steward to run it.

Having taken care of his domestic and other correspondence on the morning of the twenty-eighth, Washington went with his general officers and their suites to the Council Chamber, where they and the councilmen (those, that is, who had had the smallpox), preceded by the sheriff, carrying his wand of office, and followed by a committee from the House of Representatives, and delegations of selectmen, clergy and citizens, marched in solemn procession to the old Brick Meeting House. There a Boston institution was about to be resumed after its interruption by British rule—the Rev. Dr. Andrew Eliot's "Thursday lectures." These lectures, given by prominent divines, had been established with the first settlement of Boston and had continued uninterrupted until 1775.

Dr. Eliot, like the Rev. Mr. Leonard, had found an appropriate text. It was Isaiah 33:20: "Look upon Zion, the city of our solemnities: Thine eyes shall see Jerusalem a quiet habitation, a tabernacle that shall not be taken down; not one of the stakes thereof shall ever be removed, neither shall any of the cords thereof be broken."

After the lecture, the procession wound back to the Council Chamber, from which the dignitaries proceeded more informally to the Bunch of Grapes Tavern (Boston version), where the General Court tendered a testimonial dinner to the General, "an elegant dinner ... provided at public expense," as a contemporary account put it truthfully, adding, ". . . after which many very proper and pertinent toasts were drank. Joy and gratitude sat on every countenance and smiled in every eye." [19]

When the dinner and speeches were over, there was still daylight enough for the General to walk with his staff to Fort Hill and inspect the new fortifications which would guard the city when they were completed.

There was little remaining to do. The usual complimentary addresses were exchanged, and Harvard conferred an honorary Doctor of Laws degree on the departing commander, "who by the most signal smiles of Divine Providence on his military operations, drove the Fleet and Troops of the enemy with disgraceful precipitation from the town of Boston." Dr. Samuel Cooper signed it on April 4 and took it over to the Vassall house himself.

But Dr. Washington had flown; that morning he had set out for New York. He lingered in Providence, leaving there on Sunday, April 7; dined with Governor Trumbull in Norwich next day, reached New London that night; breakfasted in the morning at Caulkins's Tavern, between New London and Lyme; passed the night in Lyme at the McCurdy house; arrived in New Haven on Thursday morning, and entered New York on Saturday. General Gates and other officers accompanied him on the journey; Martha came down a few days later by way of Hartford.

The second journey to Boston was ended. Like the first, it had begun in doubt, but this time it ended in triumph.

Chapter 2

New England: Excursions and the Grand Tour


After he left Boston in 1776, Washington made only
three other excursions into New England during the Revolution. They were anxious journeys, undertaken in the hope—now
so near realization, then snatched away—that the French commanders could provide the means to final victory. The hope
was well founded, as it proved, but the wait was agonizing.


[1780]     The first journey, in September 1780, was an ex-
ploratory conference with Rochambeau in Hartford.[1] It ended
in the shock of Arnold's treachery, an event that might have
affected the General even more if he had not just glimpsed the
possible end of conflict. Nothing could be more important than
sighting, even distantly, the hard-won goal.

Washington left his headquarters at the Hopper house, in
Bergen County, New Jersey, on Monday, September 18, crossing the Hudson at King's Ferry. Arnold met him and rode along
to Peekskill, where they passed the night. In the morning, Arnold went on to his headquarters at the Robinson house, and
Washington resumed his journey in the company of the officers
who were traveling with him.

When they reached Hartford on Wednesday, they were met
with elaborate ceremony. There was a thirteen-gun salute by a
company of artillery, and the Governor's Guards were drawn
up to receive them. As the General advanced into the city, he
was met by Governor Jonathan Trumbull and their mutual
friend, Colonel Jeremiah Wadsworth, Commissary General in
charge of supply for the French troops, along with every local
politician who could manage to squeeze himself into the welcoming party, as has been the custom with such affairs from that

day to this. Everyone in Hartford who was not restrained by illness or essential labor crowded and pushed to get a glimpse of Washington.

The principals of the occasion smiled and bowed their way through the populace until they reached Colonel Wadsworth's house, afterward moved from this site where the Connecticut Historical Society erected its building.

Count de Rochambeau and Admiral de Ternay had not yet arrived from Newport, but a little later they were ferried across the river to the City Landing, and the ceremony of arrival was enacted all over again. The French commanders and their suites were conducted to a space before the Capitol, where Washington and his officers were drawn up. After the formalities had been exchanged, no doubt everyone was more than ready to retire to Colonel Wadsworth's house and get to the business of the conference.

One of Rochambeau's aides, the Count de Fersen, later set down his impression of Washington: "His handsome and majestic, while at the same time mild and open countenance perfectly reflects his moral qualities; he looks the hero; he is very cold; speaks little, but is courteous and frank. A shade of sadness overshadows his countenance, which is not unbecoming and gives him an interesting air...." To this Gallic touch, the Count added that "his suite was more numerous than ours. The Marquis de Lafayette, General Knox, Chief of Artillery, M. de Gouvion, a Frenchman, Chief of Engineers, and six aides-de-camp [among whom were McHenry and Hamilton] accompanied him. He had besides an escort of 22 dragoons." *

---

* The horses ridden by these men have given Hartford a historical association not shared by less fortunate cities. Where these mounts were quartered is not known, except that Washington's were bedded down in the stable behind the Wadsworth house. This stable is the only remaining one where Washington's horse slept. Built in 1730, it has been described as "a rare and handsome structure, beautiful in the forthright simplicity and strength of its design...." [2]

*96*

With this entourage, Washington left Hartford on Saturday the twenty-third, and rode that day to Litchfield, whose broad street lined with magnificent homes looks much the same today as it did to Washington. It is one of the few remaining authentic, unrestored glories of the American past. The house Washington slept in, General Oliver Wolcott's on South Street, stands today in admirable preservation and is still occupied as a private residence.[3]

As Washington rode out of Fishkill next day, Sunday, on his way home, he encountered Monsieur de la Luzerne, the French minister, en route to Newport to visit Rochambeau. Luzerne, exerting what must have been the most diplomatic pressure to influence Washington in a matter of this kind, induced him to go back to Fishkill and spend the night. However, the General got his customary daybreak start the next day, and by noon was at the Robinson house, only an hour after Arnold had fled from it to the protection of his British friends.[4]

At the Hartford conference the groundwork was laid for the collaboration of French seapower with the American army, but the arrangement was hedged about with "ifs" and speculations. As Washington wrote to a friend in Congress, "We could only combine possible plans, on the supposition of possible events and engage mutually to do everything in our powers against the next campaign." [5] At least the American commander and the French officers had met and admired each other; the will to combine for victory was there, and the timing of their joint effort depended now on the outcome of land operations in North Carolina, and the balance of power between Admiral Des-

---

Today it is surrounded by downtown Hartford, and the real estate it occupies is so valuable that it cannot be set aside as a historical site. As this was written, the Connecticut D. A. R. had agreed to provide for the stable's upkeep, but the $20,000 needed to remove and restore it at nearby Lebanon had not been forthcoming.

*97*

touches' French fleet in Newport and Admiral Arbuthnot's British ships, sheltering in the lee of Gardiner's Island, off the tip of Long Island.

[1781]     On March 1, at his headquarters in New Windsor, New York, near West Point, Washington read the dispatches from Newport for which he had been waiting so long. Admiral Destouches had decided the time was ripe to carry out the plan Washington had previously discussed with the French; he was preparing to sail southward and begin the operations in Chesapeake Bay that, it was hoped, would succeed in bottling up the British.

When he read this welcome news, Washington set out for Newport the next day—Friday, March 2—at a killing pace, determined to get there before Destouches sailed, so he could perfect on the spot the details of a strategy that might mean the end of the war. The roads were muddy and his horses struggled in the mire, but the General urged them to the utmost. Yet, on the second day, when one of them fell through a wooden bridge and hurt a leg, the Virginia gentleman who had grown up with horseflesh did not swear impatiently and abandon the animal on the spot. Though he had to leave it behind, he ordered it to be cared for properly.

The human delays, as usual, were more irritating. In Hartford, which he reached on Sunday, he had military matters in his own army to take care of; Governor Trumbull rode on with him next day to Lebanon, where he was again delayed while he reviewed the Legion of the Duke de Lauzun, which was quartered there.

On Tuesday, March 6, about two o'clock, he arrived at Newport by the Jamestown ferry, and went at once in the Admiral's barge to the French flagship the *Duc de Bourgogne*, eighty guns, lying at anchor in the harbor. There he found Admiral Destouches, Rochambeau and the senior officers of the fleet and army waiting for him. He had met some of them at the Hartford conference but most were unknown to him, nor could he do much more by way of making their acquaintance than smile, shake hands and exchange greetings through an interpreter, since neither spoke the other's language.

When the introductions were over, Washington went ashore, while the guns sounded a grand salute. He landed at Barney's Ferry, at the corner of the Long Wharf and Washington Street. Although it was a bitterly cold day, with a sharp wind whipping off the harbor, he found the French troops lined up three deep on both sides of the route leading from the ferry house to Clarke Street, then right to Rochambeau's headquarters, which was the house of William Vernon, in New Lane, now the northeast corner of Mary and Clarke streets.*

Washington is said to have been touched by this reception. Possibly he remembered the last time he had been in Newport, when he paused there in 1756 on his way to plead the cause of a colonial commission before Governor Shirley; now he was a great man, in whose honor soldiers of a foreign country mustered in the cold, and a town which had scarcely noticed his coming a quarter century ago now was ready to turn itself inside out for him.

Newport, in fact, was prepared to make a real sacrifice. Its citizens were so impoverished by the war that when the town was ordered to be illuminated on the night after the General's

---

* This splendid old house, with its charming brick-paved garden and magnificent palladian window at the rear, is now occupied by one of Newport's social agencies, but a plaque outside identifies it.

No mention of Newport could be made without noting the admirable work of the Newport County Preservation Society in restoring the old houses of the city and preparing them for public view. Several of the city's 400 houses which date before 1800 are available to the visitor (though most are in private use), and the Society is now engaged on a major project which will restore the splendid row of waterfront houses along Washington Street. At number 54, one of the best of these is already open: the Hunter house, which Admiral de Ternay used as his headquarters when he was in Newport as commander of the French fleet. Some experts say it is the best Georgian house of its period still surviving. Certainly it more nearly re-creates the atmosphere of Washington's time in Newport than any amount of verbiage could do.

*99*

arrival, the Town Council took note of the many unfortunate inhabitants who would not be able to join the celebration and voted to buy candles for anyone who was without, so that every house in town might be illuminated.

The night was clear and still, after the cruel wind of the day before, and a brilliant procession moved through the streets after darkness fell. First came thirty boys, with candles fixed to the ends of long staffs, and behind them walked Washington, Rochambeau and other officers, both French and American, with their aides and a concourse of Newport's ranking citizens and politicians. The parade wound through the main streets of the town and returned to its starting point, Rochambeau's headquarters. Then, with the grace which came naturally to him, Washington waited on the steps until everyone else had entered the house, after which he addressed the torch-bearing young men and thanked them for their services.[6]

As usual, the General had captivated everyone. What the meeting meant to one French officer, who would see considerably more of Washington, was recorded by Claude Blanchard, Commissary of the French army, who was presented to him, probably at Newport headquarters. "His face is handsome, noble and mild," Blanchard wrote. "He is tall (at least five feet, eight inches).* In the evening I was at supper with him. . . . I mark, as a fortunate day, that in which I have been able to behold a man so truly great." [7]

As usual, too, Washington captivated the ladies particularly. After the parade through the streets, he attended a ball given by Rochambeau at Mrs. Cowley's Assembly Room and according to social usage, he was requested to open it. With his unerring eye in these affairs, he chose for his partner "one of the most

* A very bad guess. A good many of the people who met Washington for the first time recorded their estimate of his height, and nearly without exception they were wrong. Blanchard, accustomed to being among men of smaller stature, was farther off than most; undoubtedly five feet, eight inches seemed tall to him. Not until Washington was measured in his coffin was his exact height recorded for posterity, and even that did not settle the matter, as the varying figures in current articles and books about him indicate.

beautiful and fascinating of Newport's many belles," Miss Margaret Champlin, who afterward married Dr. Benjamin Mason. It was Miss Champlin's privilege to select the dance, and she graciously chose "A Successful Campaign," then at the top of the Newport hit parade. As a final, abandoned gesture of sheer gallantry, it is said that the French officers seized the instruments from the musicians (a violation of union rules that would not be tolerated today in a town with a strong local) and played the music for this dance themselves.[8]

With the welcoming out of the way, Washington returned to military realities on the morning of the eighth. In fact the previous day, despite all its pageantry, had been one of the utmost anxiety and frustration. Speed was essential if the French fleet was to get past the British ships, lurking in Gardiner's Bay, before British intelligence discovered the movement. An interception might be fatal; the balance of seapower was too nearly even to risk an engagement. On the seventh the ships were loaded and everything was ready; the wind favored the French and hampered the British—yet Destouches did not sail. (The failure to do so has never been satisfactorily explained, and Washington's careless complaint about it, in a letter which was captured by the British and printed, later got him into momentary hot water with the French commanders.)

Nor did the eighth, with the wind again favorable, induce any morning action on the part of the fleet, except that one of its ships ran aground and could not be floated all day. The sun was setting before Destouches took his men-of-war triumphantly to sea. Washington watched them go with a troubled heart, wondering what consequence might follow the delay.

He was not long in hearing the news he dreaded. Three days later, American lookouts observing the British fleet reported that it had put to sea on the tenth. That removed all but the slimmest possibility that the French could get down to Virginia waters, relieve the Americans and trap the British, and get safely away before Arbuthnot could stop the movement.

Meanwhile, there was nothing to do but wait for further news

—and, of course, spend the time attending the receptions and dinners and listening to the addresses offered by the town's principal citizens and by the French officers who remained. Washington concluded these as speedily as possible, and prepared to leave.

He departed on the morning of March 13, passing through Bristol, Rhode Island, and arriving at Providence in the evening. His reception in Bristol was typical of the kind of welcome he was accorded in every town of any size through which he passed.

"When the news of his approach was received, a company of inhabitants, mounted on horseback, went down to the ferry to meet him and to escort him to the village. Accompanied by his aides, he passed directly through the town, riding the entire length of Hope Street. As he passed State Street, a salute was fired in front of the Court House, which then stood in the middle of the street. When he passed Bradford Street, the inhabitants, clad in their best apparel, stood upon either side of the street, being divided according to their sexes, and as he passed, showed their respect for him by strewing his path with flowers, evergreens, etc. accompanied with the highest marks of civility. When Washington reached the Bridge he turned to the inhabitants, and addressed them in brief but eloquent manner, returning the kindness and civility which had been shown him."[9]

His welcome in Providence that night was, of course, far more tumultuous, as the people of the busy and contentious capital turned out to pay honor to a cause and a leader they had not always wholeheartedly supported. In his memoirs, Count Dumas, a French officer assigned to accompany the General this far on his journey home, relates that the crowds met them far out in the suburbs, and soon the party was surrounded by shouting children carrying torches, an advance guard for the adult population. "All were eager to approach the person of him whom they called their father," the Count recalled, "and pressed so closely around us that they hindered us from proceeding."

Washington was "much affected," as he occasionally was by

these demonstrations of public affection, especially those that were not planned ceremonials. Taking the Count's hand, says the memoir, he declared fervently, "We may be beaten by the English; it is the chance of war; but behold an army which they can never conquer."*

He spent the night at Providence, in the house of Jabez Bowen, and the next morning, escorted by the usual civil and military cavalcade, rode out by way of Lebanon, over execrable roads and in bad weather to Hartford, where he arrived on Friday night, the sixteenth. He spent all of Saturday in the city, answering correspondence, conferring with Governor Trumbull and others, and Sunday morning resumed the journey. He was back at headquarters in New Windsor on the afternoon of March 20.

[May 1781]    There followed a tense period of nearly two months before he could arrange a final conference with the French. Ten days after his return from Newport, Washington learned what had happened to Destouches and the fleet. The Admiral had encountered the British off the Virginia Capes on March 16, and after an hour's indecisive engagement the action had been broken off with two ships damaged on each side and neither admiral, apparently, anxious to press for victory. But Destouches was discouraged; he had concluded that it was best to return to Newport.

The news plunged Washington into gloom. It seemed to

* Irving and Bancroft place this incident at Washington's headquarters after he returned from the Hartford interview with Rochambeau in September 1780, and Baker, in his *Itinerary*, appears to agree, pointing out that Dumas did not write his memoirs until he was an old man, and likely to confuse dates. The question is not important, but it may be added that there is no more evidence to support it in one place than another. Like the words of other great men reported by someone else, Washington's remark sounds more like something Dumas intended for posterity than anything the General might really have said.

him now that Virginia would shortly be plundered and North Carolina could expect the same fate. His own army was in its customary precarious condition as to food, clothing and pay. The victory that had seemed possible when he first met Rochambeau at Hartford now appeared to be one more missed opportunity.

But sometime about the middle of May an express arrived at New Windsor with dispatches which again reversed the gloomy outlook and provided fresh hope. The *Concorde*, a French frigate, had landed at Boston on May 6, carrying passengers who could change the course of the war. One was the Count de Barras, who had been sent to replace the Chevalier Destouches in command of the French fleet. Another was the Vicomte de Rochambeau, the General's son, who carried important messages from France. Both these gentlemen, and the commanders in Newport, desired an immediate conference with General Washington. Would he come?

Never was an invitation accepted more readily. He would come at once, if the twenty-first of May was acceptable, and since the Connecticut legislature would then be meeting in Hartford, he suggested nearby Wethersfield.

It was so arranged. Washington made his preparations by letter and otherwise, and set out on Friday, May 18. His eagerness for the meeting carried him forty-three miles from Fishkill Landing the first day. As he rode on the thoroughfare which then connected Newburgh with Hartford, he came to the west bank of the Housatonic River and there encountered, in process of construction, the first covered bridge in Connecticut. The site today is just off U.S. 7, near the village of Gaylordsville, north of New Milford, in the town of Kent, and the tiny crossroads settlement around it is appropriately named Bull's Bridge. Washington found Jacob Bull, the pioneer settler there, in the act of building his 110-foot, single-span structure, more than sixty feet above the river. No floor planks had been laid. The General explained his urgent mission, and Bull promptly and patriotically laid some planks over the supports so that

Washington could lead his horse across. Rebuilt several times, most recently in 1949, this bridge is still in service.[10] *

Resting that night at Morgan's Tavern, he breakfasted next morning at Litchfield, dined in the afternoon at Farmington and as the long Saturday came to an end, he met his escort from Wethersfield, a company of gentlemen who ushered him to Joseph Webb's house, which an anonymous French diarist, probably Cromot du Bourg, described as "a charming spot," in a town where, he added enthusiastically, "it would be impossible to find prettier houses and a more beautiful view." As the General dismounted, he was given a thirteen-gun salute from the battery under Captain Frederick Bull, undoubtedly a relative of the Bull at the bridge. The French had not yet arrived.

The traveler today is able to see for himself "this charming spot" where Washington devised with Rochambeau and the others the plan for the siege of Yorktown. The Webb house is open to visitors, in the town of Wethersfield, and the council room itself has been preserved, along with the General's bedchamber, which has the original wallpaper if not the original bed. Mrs. Webb had the paper, a dark red flock, put up especially for the General's coming.

Governor Trumbull came over from Hartford on Sunday morning and went to church with George. Their diary entries for the day reflect their respective states of mind. Washington's thoughts were all on the vital matter before him. His entry is dated simply May 20, and relates: "Had a good deal of private conversation with Governor Trumbull, who gave it to me as his opinion that if any important offensive operation should be undertaken he had little doubt of our obtaining men and provisions adequate to our wants."

Trumbull's entry is pious, headed "Lord's Day, May twentieth," with a learned note of patience, in Latin: "Went with Capt. Fred Bull in a carriage to Wethersfield—attended divine

* This story has been challenged recently by a bridge expert who says Bull's Bridge was not a covered bridge at this time.

service with Gen. Washington per tot diem. Mr. Marsh
preached. Mat. 7:8—blessed are the poor of spirit for theirs is
the kingdom of Heaven." Dr. Freeman notes that "the application of these cherished words to the continental cause seemed
too obvious for the pious Governor to dwell on it."

The French were expected to arrive in Hartford next morning, and Washington and his officers rode up to receive them.
Count Rochambeau, General de Chastellux and their "families"
were there, but the new Admiral, Count de Barras, was not.
Rochambeau explained that the Admiral had been detained in
Newport by the sudden appearance offshore of what he presumed to be Arbuthnot's fleet. Washington had much desired
to meet Barras, not only for the sake of politeness, but because
this was a man with whom he would have to deal. However,
General Chastellux reassured him privately that the Admiral
was "a good, plain dealing gentleman who will give no difficulty."

The conference continued for the next two days, during
which plans were worked out to the general satisfaction of both
sides. The gentlemen took turns entertaining each other, and
when the Governor was a guest of the officers on Wednesday
night, he was careful to note in his diary that it was "supra
public expense."

By Thursday the twenty-fourth, Washington was ready to
leave Wethersfield. He rode home at the same breakneck pace
he had come, and by the same route, reaching his headquarters
about sunset on May 25. There were enormous difficulties
ahead, and the issue was still far from settled—but Yorktown
and victory were in sight.

[1789]     That was the last Washington was to see of New
England for eight years. Then, once more, he returned under
circumstances as different from those of the war years as these
had been different from the first lonely trip to Boston. Now,
in the fall of 1789, the Revolution and the short interval of

peaceful recuperation at Mount Vernon were behind him. The new nation had given him its highest honor: he was first President of the United States.

Yet, as always, there were difficulties. Being a nation was an entirely new experience for the colonies and there were many, individuals and states, who were not certain they liked it. The General, in effect, had been given a different title and another command. Instead of balky, inconstant and sometimes treacherous generals, he now had to contend with jealous and disparate elements in the states. Rhode Island and Vermont, in fact, had not accepted the federal Constitution.

Before Congress adjourned on the twenty-ninth of September, to meet again January 4, 1790, Washington had consulted with the members, particularly those from New England, about the advisability of making a tour through the "Eastern States" for purposes of unification. The new President was well aware of his overwhelming prestige, and in this instance he sought to turn it to a useful political purpose. Those he consulted were enthusiastic about the idea, but they warned him that he had better plan to make a Southern tour, if he wanted to avoid trouble. This Washington promised to do later (see Part 5, Chapter 2). Vermont and Rhode Island were to be diplomatically omitted on the Eastern tour.

He could not have picked a better time to go. It was October, and New England would be in its full autumnal beauty. Besides, he was recovering from a serious illness, and as he wrote to his sister, "a sort of epidemical cold" had been going the rounds in New York, making the proposed trip a "way of relaxation from business and reestablishment of my health. . . ."[11]

Like so many of Washington's journeys, however, it began in foul weather.[12] As he rolled away from the presidential mansion at nine in the morning of October 15, with four horses drawing his coach and his two secretaries, Tobias Lear and Major Jackson, riding along outside, the skies were threatening; in another hour it began to rain. Chief Justice John Jay, Secretary of the Treasury Alexander Hamilton and General

Henry Knox, Secretary of War, had ridden out of the city as an escort, but it was probably at this point that they turned back.

The rain fell steadily until eleven o'clock. By that time the party had reached Hyatt's Tavern at King's Bridge, and it seemed a good place to get Lear and Jackson and the six servants out of the weather. They had an early dinner there, proceeding after it through "frequent light showers" to the first night's stop, the "very neat and decent inn" kept by the Widow Haviland at Rye.

Now that he was relieved of his constant anxieties as Commander-in-Chief, and the cares of the presidency had not yet begun to weigh on him, Washington was able really to look at the country through which he traveled, in a way that had not been possible since his youth. It was the master of Mount Vernon, not the General or the President, who wrote:

"The road for the greater part was stony but the land strong, well covered with grass and a luxuriant crop of Indian corn intermixed with pompions (which were yet ungathered) in the fields. We met four droves of beef cattle for the New York market (about 30 in a drove), some of which were very fine, also a flock of sheep for the same place. We scarcely passed a farmhouse that did not abound in geese.

"The distance of this day's travel was 31 miles, in which we passed through (after leaving the Bridge) East Chester, New Rochelle and Mamaroneck, but as these places (though they have houses of worship in them) are not regularly laid out, they are scarcely to be distinguished from the intermediate farms, which are very close together and separated as one enclosure from another also is, by fences of stone, which are indeed easily made, as the country is immensely stony. Upon inquiry we find their crops of wheat and rye have been abundant though of the first they had sown rather sparingly, on account of the destruction which had of late years been made of that grain by what is called the Hessian fly."

They were off from the Widow Haviland's at seven o'clock

on Friday morning, and immediately ran into a "hilly and immensely stony" passage through Horse Neck, six miles from Rye. Following his custom, Washington did not pause for breakfast until they were a good six miles farther, in Stamford, where they stopped to eat at one Webb's, "a tolerably good house but not equal in appearance or reality to Mrs. Haviland's." He admired Stamford's Episcopal church and meetinghouse, then rode ten miles farther to Norwalk, where they stopped to feed the horses—or "baited," as it was usually expressed in those days. While the horses refreshed themselves, the party made a brief examination of the town, apparently finding little to admire. Sea vessels stopped at one end of the village, Washington noted, and at the other end were mills, stores and two churches, Episcopal and Presbyterian.

There were twelve more miles to travel before they could lodge for the night at Fairfield, much of it over a rough road, though not as bad as the one through Horse Neck. While he jolted along, the President gazed out the coach windows and observed the farmers busy gathering, grinding and pressing apples. He saw reminders, too, of the ordeal only six years ended: "The destructive evidences of British cruelty are yet visible both in Norwalk and Fairfield, as there are the chimneys of many burnt houses standing in them yet." And again the Virginia landowner assessed the economic assets of what he saw: "The principal export from Norwalk and Fairfield is horses and cattle, salted beef and pork, lumber and Indian corn to the West Indies, and in a small degree wheat and flour."

No record exists of where Washington spent the night in Fairfield, but his diary establishes that he routed out Lear and Jackson while it was still dark on Saturday morning and had his entourage rolling out of the village a little after sunrise. Ten miles away, over a road which George admitted grudgingly was "not on the whole bad (for this country)," they stopped for breakfast at Stratford, "a pretty village" on or near the Stratford River.

Here Washington met the first of his official receptions. He was prepared this time for a journey which would necessarily become a round of ceremonies, but the first one at Stratford was apparently unimpressive—"an effort of military parade," he called it. The newly elected Senator from Connecticut, William Samuel Johnson, who was also president of Columbia College (just reorganized from its King's College days), came to visit the President as he paused to receive the dignitaries. It was Dr. Johnson's home town, and he had come there with his wife to spend a few quiet days after the adjournment of Congress.

The reception committee, "several gentlemen on horseback," escorted Washington to the ferry, nearly a mile from the town, and after crossing it, he was then three miles from Milford, a village the traveler summed up in a succinct sentence: "In this place there is but one church, or in other words but one steeple, but there are grist and saw mills, and a handsome cascade over a tumbling dam."

Taking the lower road through West Haven, the President's party came into New Haven before two o'clock that Saturday afternoon, in time for Washington to take a walk through the city and admire its buildings. By taking the West Haven route, he discovered, he had missed the committee sent out to welcome him on the other road and escort him to the city. The frustrated welcomers presented their address at seven o'clock that night, and the early evening was spent in receiving other addresses and the respects of officials, including Governor Samuel Huntington, Lieutenant Governor Oliver Wolcott and Mayor Roger Sherman.

At this stage of his career, Washington was adept in the political art of not offending anyone if possible, and so on Sunday he went in the morning to the Episcopal church and in the afternoon to one of the Congregational meetinghouses. At Brown's Tavern, where he was stopping, he entertained a tableful of politicians for dinner and finished the afternoon by drinking tea with Mayor Sherman. In the evening, Connecticut officers who had fought in the Revolution came to Brown's and paid their respects to the General.

A citizen had to get up early in the morning to see Washington off, but most of New Haven's residents tumbled out to watch his state coach roll away from the city at six o'clock, accompanied by a troop of cavalry and the inevitable committee on horseback.

By half past eight he had covered the thirteen miles to Wallingford, where the party had breakfast, took a walk through the town, and Washington discovered a new industry: "At this place we see the white mulberry growing, raised from the seed, to feed the silkworm. We also saw samples of lustring (exceedingly good) which had been manufactured from the cocoon raised in this town, and silk thread very fine. This, except the weaving, is the work of private families."

Starting off again at ten, the presidential chariot clattered through Durham and came to rest in Middletown, on the Connecticut River, at one o'clock. While dinner was being cooked —the President had apparently caught some tavern unprepared —he made his usual circuit of the town, "from the heights of which the prospect is beautiful." At three he was ready for the final lap of the day, this time to familiar Hartford by way of the memorable village of Wethersfield. In that "charming spot," where he had plotted with Rochambeau, he was met by another old friend of the conference days, Colonel Wadsworth, who was there with a party to escort him into Hartford, which they reached at sunset. He lodged for the night at Bull's Tavern.

After breakfast Tuesday morning, Washington set about his presidential duties of examining the local manufactures. "I viewed the woolen manufacturing," he says, ". . . which seems to be going on with spirit. Their broadcloths are not of the first quality as yet, but they are good; as are their coatings, cassimeres, serges and everlastings. Of the first, that is, broadcloth, I ordered a suit to be sent to me at New York; and of the latter a whole piece, to make breeches for my servants. . . ."

As President, Washington had already initiated a "Buy American" movement that would have done credit to later high-tariff protectionists. The man who had once taken a gentleman's pleasure in fine clothes from London had been inaugurated in an American suit, and often made a public point, as he did in Hartford, of buying the new nation's products.

Although he did not mention it, he must have been enjoying the autumn foliage and good weather since the rainy start from New York, but now, as he prepared to leave Hartford on Wednesday, October 21, the rains came down so heavily that he could not depart until after ten o'clock, thus missing a breakfast engagement with Senator Oliver Ellsworth at his home in Windsor, seven miles above Hartford. The President, however, stopped for an hour's chat with the Senator when he did pass by; as an old hand at dealing with legislators, he knew what might result from even an unintentional snub.

By four o'clock the party arrived in Springfield, Massachusetts, and once more dinner was not yet ready, leaving time for a tour of the town. The view of it inspired Washington to a social commentary in his journal: "There is great equality in the people of this state. Few or no opulent men—and no poor—great similitude in their buildings, the general fashion of which is a chimney (always of stone or brick) and door in the middle, with a staircase fronting the latter . . . two flush stories with a very good show of sash and glass windows. The size generally is from 30 to 50 feet in length, and from 20 to 30 feet in width, exclusive of a back shed, which seems to be added as the family increases."

In the evening, the Springfield dignitaries came to Parson's Tavern, where the President was stopping, and sat for a sociable hour or two with him. Washington, a connoisseur in these matters, thought the tavern "a good house."

As he stopped to feed the horses next morning, an express brought a letter from Governor John Hancock, telling of the elaborate plans made for his visit to Boston and inviting him to stay at the Governor's house. Patiently, Washington sat down and wrote a reply to be sent back by the express, in which he set forth the rules he had laid down for himself about lodgings, and pleading (in vain, as it proved) for some moderation in his reception.

"I am highly sensible of the honor intended me," he wrote, "but could my wish prevail, I should desire to visit your metropolis without any parade or extraordinary ceremony. From a wish to avoid giving trouble to private families I determined, on leaving New York, to decline the honor of any invitation to quarters which I might receive while on my journey, and with a view to this rule, I had requested a gentleman to engage lodgings for me during my stay at Boston. I beg Your Excellency to be persuaded of the grateful sense which I entertain of the honor you intended to confer on me, and I desire to assure you of the respectful regard with which I am, etc." [13]

Washington stopped that night at Isaac Jenks's tavern, ten miles from Brookfield, at Spencer, but if the traditional story is true, he intended to stay elsewhere. True or not, the story represents a small domestic tragedy. Late in the afternoon he is supposed to have sent a messenger ahead to secure accommodations at an inn but the emissary found the proprietor absent. His wife did not understand that it was the President of the United States who sought room and board, thinking instead it was the president of Rhode Island College and his wife, who frequently stayed with them. Being indisposed that day, she sent back word that she was not feeling well enough to entertain the travelers and the president must go on to the next tavern. Told when it was too late that it was Washington who had intended to honor her establishment, she is said to have burst out in patriotic disappointment, "Bless me, the sight of him would have cured my illness." [14]

As the party approached Boston, the ceremony along the way increased, and one supposes Washington understood resignedly that his plea to Governor Hancock would be put down to modesty, if it was considered seriously at all. In Worcester, he was greeted with an elaborate welcome and the thunder of salutes. To satisfy the great throng that had gathered to see him, he got out of his coach and rode through the streets on horseback. In spite of this delay, he went sixteen miles to Marlborough for dinner, and fourteen more to Weston, where he lodged.

Saturday, the twenty-fourth, was to be the great occasion—the triumphal entry into Boston. If Washington really imagined that he would be able to do it "without any parade or extraordinary ceremony," he must have been finally disillusioned when he reached Cambridge and began to see the preparations that had been made. The village was in a state of confusion and high excitement. Washington had made a ten o'clock appointment to meet the company of militia that was to escort him to the Boston town line, but the men were still putting on their dress uniforms—at least they were not ready. Meanwhile, the President stopped in at his old headquarters in Vassall's house, and the memories must have overwhelmed him as he sat down in the rooms where he had first commanded the Continental Army.

By eleven o'clock the militia was ready. Washington had dressed at seven o'clock that morning, putting on his best uniform for the occasion. Now he had brought to him what might have been called his ceremonial horse, a handsome white charger. Thus equipped and bedecked, he rode toward Boston.

At the town line one of those amusing contretemps occurred which regularly bedeviled authorities—and often do today, for that matter. Hancock had sent Lieutenant Governor Samuel Adams out to the town line to welcome Washington officially to Boston; the Governor himself was supposedly in bed with the gout. But at the city limits, Adams found the officials of Boston, who claimed heatedly that the state was trying to take away a right which properly belonged to the city. If any welcoming was to be done, said the city politicians, they were going to do it. Sam Adams, who had successfully defied the King of England, found he could not prevail upon his fellow officeholders with reason or threats; he had to give in. Consequently, while Adams and the members of the state Executive Council stood by, the Mayor and his men conducted the speechmaking and ceremony, to which Washington, Vice-President John Adams, ex-Governor James Bowdoin, a Senator or two, distinguished citizens, several committees, representatives of forty or fifty societies, and platoons of mechanics and tradesmen with banners listened with as much patience as they could muster.

Then the whole procession moved off toward the waiting city, in a parade which the honored guest described as "in every degree flattering and honorable." By this time it was nearly one o'clock and the crowds had been waiting all morning. They were left in no doubt that the President was approaching. As one contemporary account describes it: "At one o'clock, the President's approach was announced by federal discharges from Capt. Warner's artillery at Roxbury—from the Dorchester artillery posted on the celebrated heights of that town —from Capt. Johnson's artillery at the entrance of the town— and from Castle William; by a royal salute from the ships of His Most Christian Majesty's squadron, and by the ringing of all the bells."[15]

In the midst of this din, Washington entered the city and his procession moved toward the State House. The best description of its progress and the welcome prepared was written by Washington himself, who noted it down in his diary as though he were an observer of the event instead of its object:

"Then following the Lieut.-Gov. and Council in the order we came from Cambridge (preceded by the Town Corps, very handsomely dressed), we passed through the citizens classed in their different professions and under their own banners, till we came to the State House, from which across the street an arch was thrown, in the front of which was this inscription— 'To the man who unites all hearts'— and on the other— 'To Columbia's favorite Son'—and on one side thereof next the State House, in a panel decorated with a trophy composed of the Arms of the United States, of the Commonwealth of

Massachusetts and our French allies, crowned with a wreath
of laurel, was this inscription: 'Boston relieved March 17, 1776.'
This arch was handsomely ornamented, and over the center of
it a canopy was erected 20 feet high, with the American Eagle
perched on the top. After passing through the arch and entering the State House at the south end and ascending to the upper
floor and returning to a balcony at the north end, three cheers
was given by a vast concourse of people who by this time had
assembled at the arch. Then followed an ode composed in
honor of the President (sung by the Independent Musical Society) after this three cheers, followed by the different professions and mechanics in the order they were drawn up with
their colors, through a lane of the people, which had thronged
about the arch under which they passed. The streets, the doors,
windows and tops of the houses were crowded with well-
dressed ladies and gentlemen. The procession being over, I
was conducted to my lodgings at a Widow Ingersoll's (which
is a very decent and good house) by the Lieut.-Gov. and Council, accompanied by the Vice President, where they took leave
of me. . . ."

Washington noted parenthetically at the end of this entry
that he "was to have had dinner with Gov. John Hancock, who
sent word he was indisposed." Thus he passed over tactfully
a small incident of ruffled feelings in high places. Apparently
he was not convinced that the Governor was really ill, or perhaps he accepted the proposition that Hancock was not well
enough to come out to the town line, but when the Governor
made no move to come to the Widow Ingersoll's and pay the
first visit, as protocol demanded, there was nothing for Washington to do, if he followed strict social usage (and he usually
did), but to cancel the dinner engagement at the Governor's
house that night, which had been made in advance. This he
did, dining with John Adams instead.

Next day at one o'clock Washington dispatched to Hancock a note in which irony was mingled with polite address:
"The President of the United States presents his best respects

to the Governor, and has the honor to inform him that he shall be at home till 2 o'clock.

"The President of the United States need not express the pleasure it will give him to see the Governor; but, at the same time, he most earnestly begs that the Governor will not hazard his health on the occasion."

Whatever had motivated Hancock's reluctance — his jealousy of Washington, dating from the time the General was given the command of the Continental Army that he wanted for himself, or possibly the state of internal politics in Massachusetts, or whether he actually felt too ill to go—the note with its overtones brought him quickly to account, Hancock's reply is dated half past twelve, indicating that the clocks of the President and the Governor were not running in harmony. It was an answer at once polite, plaintive and heroic:

"The Governor's best respects to the President; if at home and at leisure, the Governor will do himself the honor to pay his respects in half an hour. This would have been done much sooner, had his health in any degree permitted. He now hazards everything as it respects his health, for the desirable purpose."

When he appeared at last, Hancock managed to put on a most convincing show. He was carried into Washington's presence by retainers, with his gouty foot bandaged.

In the four days he remained in Boston, Washington had scarcely a moment when he was not being honored by someone. Those who could not do it in person demonstrated their devotion in other ways. For the duration of his visit, the ladies of Boston encircled their middles with broad white ribbon sashes, imprinted in golden letters with the initials G.W. woven about with a laurel wreath. The ladies in society, quite naturally, found means of improving on this decoration which anyone could wear. At the grand ball in the Concert Hall on the twenty-eighth, attended by every person of consequence in the city, the Marchioness Traversay appeared with the conventional sash, but with G.W. also woven into the bandeau of her hat, and as an extra added attraction, an eagle set in brilliants on a black velvet background. The more than one hundred other ladies who attended had also endeavored to outdo each other, so it was no wonder that Washington, who always wrote appreciatively of female company, remarked in his diary that their appearance "was elegant, and many of them very handsome."

The public adoration of Washington went to ludicrous lengths. During his stay there was a wave of influenza cases in the Boston area, and the story went about that the President had been the first one to have it. It was instantly fashionable to be taken with "the Washington influenza." The rumor was based on nothing more substantial than a rainy, stormy day that the President spent at home, when he was, as he said, "myself much disordered by a cold, and inflammation in the left eye." The cold did not prevent him from receiving visitors, dining with guests, drinking tea with the Governor, and making a call himself in the evening.

The days were filled with events. He attended the Episcopal and Congregational churches, went to a "large and elegant" dinner given by the Governor and Council at Faneuil Hall, heard an oratorio, received innumerable addresses, visited schools and public places. One day he paid a visit to the *Illustrious*, flagship of the French squadron that lay in the harbor, as guest of its commander, and went on to inspect another 74-gun ship in the fleet, the *Superb*. The harbor rang with salutes. "Going and coming," Washington noted, "I was saluted by the two frigates which lie near the wharves, and by the 74s after I had been on board of them, as also by the 40-gun ship which lay in the same range with them. I was also saluted going and coming by the fort on Castle Island."

Everywhere he went in Boston, he was struck by the progress that had been made since he left the city in 1776. A good many public buildings had been erected, the wharves had been repaired and the bridges to Charlestown and Cambridge rebuilt. Hardly a trace of war remained. Factories had sprung up in and about the town, and the fields outside it, which had been only pleasant meadows when he last saw them, were now heavy with crops and houses.

On October 29, he was ready to resume his tour. He left Boston by way of Lynn, which he described as "only a row of houses, and not very thick, on each side of the road." But he added with a note of commendation: "It is said 175,000 pair of shoes (women's chiefly) have been made in a year by about 400 workmen."

He had heard of Marblehead, and went out of his way to see it, particularly the fishing industry, which interested him because of his own pursuit of it on the Potomac, where it was a part of the economy of Mount Vernon. The fish of Marblehead he admired; the inhabitants he did not. The town appeared to him as it does today, as having "an appearance of antiquity; the houses are old," but he thought the streets were dirty and "the common people are not very clean."

He stayed that Thursday night in Salem, where he was conducted in another parade to the Court House. There he heard an ode sung in his honor. By way of compensation for more ceremony, he enjoyed one of his favorite recreations that night, attending an assembly where "there was at least an hundred handsome and well dressed ladies." He removed himself from their charming company at his usual hour, however, and returned to his lodgings at nine.

As he passed two miles beyond the little village of Beverly next day, he came upon New England's first cotton mill and stopped to inspect it. "The whole seemed perfect," he wrote of his visit, "and the cotton stuffs that they turn out excellent of their kind; warp and filling both are now of cotton." The Cabots, who owned the mill, seemed to be "carrying on with spirit," he added.

Ten miles farther he paused at Ipswich, to be met by the local officials and a delegation from Newburyport, where he intended to lodge that night. The speechmaking was relieved by the serving of "a cold collation." In Ipswich he was pleased to see once more a wartime friend, that altogether remarkable "patriotic parson," the Rev. John Cleaveland, of Essex, Massachusetts. Born in Canterbury, Connecticut, he had fought in the French and Indian War as well as the Revolution, in which he had been chaplain with Colonel Little's regiment, the 17th Foot. He had enlisted at Cambridge on July 1, 1775, and it was said that he had "preached all the men of his parish into the army," and then went himself.

Parson Cleaveland's exploits in the Revolution were told and retold for years after. Once, it was said, he was engaged in prayer before a newly drafted company of militia, invoking the Deity for their protection in his customary stentorian tones.

"I pray, Oh Lord," he shouted, "that the enemy may be blown—"

"—to hell and damnation," cried a soldier, filled with evangelistic patriotism.

Parson Cleaveland scarcely paused, nor did he lower his voice from a bellow.

"—to the land of tyranny from whence they came," he concluded.

It was this beloved and legendary character, so the traditional story goes, who came up to Washington in Ipswich, with his cocked hat tucked respectfully under his arm.

"Put on your hat, Parson, and I will shake hands with you," said Washington. This was a major concession in itself, because he seldom shook hands after he became President, at least not at public affairs.

"I cannot wear my hat in your presence, General, when I think of what you have done for this country," Cleaveland replied.

"You did as much as I," the General returned politely.

"No, no!" the parson protested.

The General found the right note on which to end this impasse of mutual modesty.

"You did what you could, and I've done no more," he said.[16]

Bidding the parson and the others farewell, Washington

went on to Newburyport, where he was received with military honors, a parade, and fireworks in the evening.

Next morning he passed into New Hampshire, accompanied by its President, John Sullivan, and its two Senators, John Langdon and Paine Wingate. By the time he reached Portsmouth the endless receptions must have become burdensome, flattering though they were. There is a note of weariness in his description of the arrival at Portsmouth that afternoon:

". . . The streets, doors and windows were crowded here, as at all the other places; and alighting at the Town House, odes were sung and played in honor of the President. The same happened yesterday at my entrance into Newburyport, being stopped at my entrance to hear it. . . ."

Hear it he did, however, and came at last to the shelter of Colonel Brewster's tavern, where the dignitaries dined with him.

Here he stayed until Wednesday, November 4, relaxing more than he had done anywhere along the route. Once, exploring the harbor in a barge, he landed briefly at Kittery, "in the Province of Maine." That was the northernmost point he ever reached in New England.

On this jaunt around the harbor defenses, it was natural that Washington, an inveterate fisherman whenever he got the opportunity, should welcome the chance to go outside the harbor limits to the fishing banks, where he dropped over his line. "It not being a proper time of tide," he wrote, "we only caught two," but whether he or another member of the party caught them he was too modest to say.

He was not enthusiastic about the city of Portsmouth. He wrote of it: "There are some good houses (among which Colonel Langdon's may be esteemed the first), but in general they are indifferent, and almost entirely of wood. On wondering at this, as the country is full of stone and good clay for bricks, I was told that on account of the fogs and damp, they deemed them wholesomer, and for that reason preferred wood buildings."

Concerning the ladies and the dancing facilities in town, he was much more enthusiastic. He thought the assembly room "one of the best I have seen anywhere in the United States." His observation of the ladies was more than ordinarily acute: ". . . There were about 75 well dressed, and many of them very handsome ladies, among whom (as was also the case at the Salem and Boston assemblies) were a greater proportion with much blacker hair than are usually seen in the Southern States. . . ."

By comparison with what had gone before, he virtually sneaked out of Portsmouth on Wednesday morning, "quietly, and without any attendance, having earnestly entreated that all parade and ceremony might be avoided on my return." Before ten o'clock he was fourteen miles away at Exeter. "This is considered the second town in New Hampshire," he wrote, "and stands at the head of the tidewater of Piscataqua River. It is a place of some consequence, but does not contain more than 1,000 inhabitants. A jealousy subsists between this town (where the legislature alternately sits) and Portsmouth, which, had I known it in time, would have made it necessary to have accepted an invitation to a public dinner, but my arrangements having been otherwise made, I could not. . . ."

Presumably giving silent thanks that he had not heard of the rivalry, he went on to Kingstown and thence to Haverhill, where he stayed the night in that "beautiful part of the country." On this return journey by a different and quieter route through open country and small towns, Washington stopped often to talk with the farmers in the fields about their crops, in the manner of Presidents ever since, though it must be said that Washington was not campaigning and had an honest and absorbing interest in agriculture.

On the night of November 6, so the tradition declares, he was supposed to have stayed with an old friend in Mendon, Colonel Amidon, but he was turned away by a dull-witted maid who failed to recognize him. It is said, probably without much truth, that when the Colonel found out about it, he and his daughter rode to Uxbridge, where Washington had finally stopped at

Samuel Taft's tavern, to try to persuade the President to return. The General, in dressing gown, nightcap and slippers, received his apologetic callers but refused to return. This story is highly unlikely, though it makes a pretty picture.

When he got to Hartford two days later, Washington wrote an unusual but not untypical bread-and-butter letter to Taft: "Being informed that you have given my name to one of your sons, and called another after Mrs. Washington's family, and being moreover very much pleased with the modest and innocent looks of your two daughters, Patty and Polly, I do for these reasons send each of these girls a piece of chintz. And to Patty, who bears the name of Mrs. Washington, and who waited more upon us than Polly did, I send five guineas, with which she may buy herself any little ornaments she may want, or she may dispose of them in any other manner more agreeable to herself.

"As I do not give these things with a view to having it talked of, or even to its being known, the less there is said about the matter, the better you will please me, but that I may be sure the chintz and money have got safe to hand, let Patty, who I dare say is equal to it, write me a line informing me thereof, directed to 'The President of the United States at New York.' "

This agreeable piece of sentiment was marred only by the fact that Washington's memory or his hearing was faulty. Patty's name was Mercy, not Martha.

He bore on rapidly for New York. On the way to Uxbridge, he had passed through Watertown, breakfasted at Abbot's Tavern in Andover with Samuel Phillips, President of the Massachusetts Senate; paused in Lexington, where he "viewed the spot on which the first blood was spilt in the dispute with Great Britain"; lodged a night in Watertown with a Widow Coolidge, whose house he thought "very indifferent"; and then went on down through Sherburn, Holliston, Milford and Mendon. Now he traveled through Connecticut by way of Thompson, Pomfret and Ashford. He would have continued on Sunday, the eighth, except that the Connecticut legislature, in an excess of piety, had passed a law forbidding Sunday travel, Washington noting in his diary that it was not only "contrary to law" but "disagreeable to the people of this state."

An old Connecticut story declares that Washington had missed his way on Saturday and on Sunday morning started to ride a few miles to the town where he had previously intended to go to church. On the way, it is said, he met a tithingman who did not recognize him, ordered him to stop and state his business, and finally agreed to let him travel the remaining distance if he promised to go no farther.[17]

This tradition is contradicted by Washington's diary, which records that he stopped at Squire Perkins's tavern in Ashford on Saturday night and stayed there all of Sunday, though the inn was not a good one, because the horses needed rest "after passing through such intolerable roads." As for attending church, he says, "a meeting house being within a few rods of the door I attended morning and evening service, and heard very lame discourses from Mr. [Enoch] Pond."

Leaving the dubious hospitality of Squire Perkins on the ninth, he rocked and swayed over twenty-four miles of "hilly, rocky and disagreeable roads," passing through Mansfield, which was making more silk than any other town in the state, and over a final ten miles of good roads reached Hartford a little after four o'clock. From Hartford, the road led through Worthington and across the plains of Wallingford, down to the shore at New Haven, which he reached about half an hour before sundown. There he found Elbridge Gerry, who had just arrived from New York and was able to give him news of Martha.

The final lap of the journey went rapidly, over more familiar roads and without incident, except for some lame horses which delayed him overnight at the Widow Haviland's, twelve miles from Stamford. On Friday, November 13 (probably he had never heard of the superstition) he made an easy passage into New York, arriving between two and three o'clock. He had left ceremony behind him only to find more. "It being Mrs. Washington's night to receive visits, a pretty large company of ladies and gentlemen were present," his diary concludes.

To all intents, his tour had been politically successful. He returned impressed with the progress of the country, gratified by the adulation of its citizens, and in possession of a journal which contains one of the best descriptions available of New England in that period. The quotations from it here only suggest its fascinating detail. Washington described the average farm and how it was worked; he noted the state of the roads, the style of the fences, the condition of agriculture, the exact number of churches, and gave detailed descriptions of all the principal towns. It is a document worth anyone's study.

[1790]  By way of a postscript to this journey, he made the delayed visit to Rhode Island in August of 1790. It is not known why he failed to visit Vermont; her quarrel with New York which delayed her entry into the Union had been settled the same year.

Rhode Island had ratified the Constitution on May 29, 1790, and Washington decided soon after to make his trip, reasoning that there would be less opportunity to do it later, because Congress on July 9 had approved a bill authorizing the creation of the District of Columbia for a permanent capital, meanwhile deciding to remove to Philadelphia for the next session.

Congress had approved this New England postscript, but there was some fear among the Senators, and in Rhode Island as well, that unreconstructed advocates of independence might make a disturbance against the man who represented union, though he was the nation's hero. Rhode Islanders were not celebrated for their tactfulness in political affairs.

Perhaps to avoid the bad Connecticut roads, or perhaps simply for a change, the President went by ship, in the packet *Hancock*, Captain Brown. He was accompanied by Governor Clinton, Thomas Jefferson and an assortment of lesser dignitaries, along with three gentlemen of his official family.

He came first to Newport on Tuesday, August 17, where his reception was cordial but nothing to compare with his wartime visit. He walked about town, surveying "the various beautiful prospects from the eminences above it," and attended the usual "elegant dinner" at the Town Hall. Next morning he sailed up Narragansett Bay to Providence, arriving about four o'clock. A contemporary account sums up his reception neatly in a single paragraph:

"A procession (civil and military) was formed agreeable to a previous arrangement, and the President escorted to his lodgings at Mr. Daggett's. On the President's landing a federal salute was fired, and the bells in town rang a joyful peal. The salute was reiterated on his arrival at Mr. Daggett's. The general attendance of almost every inhabitant of the town in the procession, together with the brilliant appearance of the ladies at the windows and doors of the houses, evinced in the most sensible manner their pleasure on this happy occasion. In the evening the college edifice was splendidly illuminated." [18]

Apparently there would be no trouble. Next day he "walked through the principal streets to view the town," and on the excursion was "escorted to the college by the students, and by Dr. [James] Manning introduced into the college library and museum, and afterwards went on board a large Indiaman on the stocks, belonging to Messrs. Browne and Francis." [19]

At three o'clock he sat down with three hundred people to a dinner in the Court House, where thirteen toasts were drunk in conjunction with salutes from cannon. When these toasts were concluded, Washington stood up and offered one of his own: "The town of Providence!" Then he rose from the table and went down the hill to his packet, followed by "a numerous procession."

To dispel any further idea of revolt, the paraders went back up to the hill to Governor Arthur Fenner's home, gave three cheers, and dispersed in good order.

On this note of sweetness and light, and with best wishes from the hitherto most recalcitrant of its citizens, Washington said good-by to New England for the last time. He never returned.

Chapter 3

New Jersey

Nowhere in America, outside of his native Virginia, has the memory of Washington been kept so green as in New Jersey. The Jerseymen (and more particularly, the Jersey-women) take a proprietary interest in him. Anyone who lives or lectures or travels in New Jersey for a time gets the distinct impression that Virginia and Mount Vernon are some kind of historical mistake and that George Washington is really a native son. This impression is reinforced by the number of houses, inns, roads, stables, dinnerware and eighteenth-century knickknacks said to have associations with the General, and by the time that is devoted to his memory in one way or another at club meetings of every kind.*

By all these ties, both real and imaginary, the drama of the Revolution and Washington's role in it are bound to the hills and plains of New Jersey. Geography made it a focal point of the war, and the Commander-in-Chief did in fact spend a good part of his time there. After the siege of Boston at the start of the conflict (except for the Northern campaign, in which he had no direct part), the war from Washington's view of it consisted in maneuver and battle around the perimeter of a wide arc extending roughly from Newport on the north to North Carolina

* A story from Wood-Ridge, New Jersey, in the New York *Times* of August 2, 1953, reported that the old Brinkerhoff house in that town, a pre-Revolutionary landmark, was about to be converted into a library. Well illustrating the affinity between such projects and Washington's memory, however tenuous, the *Times* correspondent wrote: "George Washington took notice of the Brinkerhoff house at the height of the Revolution, but he had no time to stop there, because at the time his army marched along Polifly Road it was in the great retreat from Fort Lee. . . ."

on the south, with New York at the center. The segment of the arc in which the General spent most time was the central part, running the length of New Jersey. Here he retreated from battles elsewhere and spent grim winters trying to hold his army together, and from it he hopefully launched spring campaigns. On this ground, the British challenged him, and in the challenge helped the Continental Army to find itself.

[1776–1777]     The first winter of the war after the British evacuation of Boston found the seeming triumph of March 1776 reversed. One might question whether the British had fled from Boston, but there was no doubt about Washington's retreat through the Jerseys. He was only a breath away from annihilation.

It had begun innocently enough on November 15, 1776, when the main army was in camp at Hackensack, five miles northwest of Fort Lee, and Washington had established headquarters at the home of Peter Zabriskie. A messenger brought the news that the British had begun an attack on Fort Washington, across the river, where American troops were presumed to be holding the British in New York. Washington went at once to Fort Lee and was halfway across the river when he met Generals Greene and Putnam, who had just come from Fort Washington and who assured him the Americans could and would defend it. Because it was late in the evening, the General decided to turn back, but next day he crossed the river to the Roger Morris house, the headquarters from which he had already precipitately retreated. There he examined the strategic situation and, convinced that it was deteriorating rapidly, returned to Jersey. Fifteen minutes after he had left it, the British were in possession of the Morris house.

Obviously the British had burst out of New York and were intent on following up their advantage. Fearing that he would be trapped between the Hackensack and Passaic rivers, Washington took his army across the Acquackanoc bridge to the west side of the Passaic on November 21, and there began the famous but ignoble retreat in which, it was said, "often the music of the pursued and the pursuers would be heard by each other, yet no action occurred." So close was the pursuit that the advance guard of the British army entered Newark on the twenty-third as the American rear guard left it.

One of the desperate men in retreat, though not one of the fearful ones, was Thomas Paine, who had been with the troops at Fort Lee. His desperation increased as he observed the fear and apathy of the civilians, who saw the rebellion collapsing, the troops in headlong retreat—and made no move to save themselves. Out of his shame and anger came the first paper of the *American Crisis* published in Philadephia that December, whose opening words generations of Americans would remember: "These are the times that try men's souls . . ." The noble words are remembered, but much of what followed them has been forgotten.

"Both officers and men," Paine said, describing the situation, "though greatly harassed and fatigued, frequently without rest, covering, or provision, the inevitable consequences of a long retreat, bore it with a manly and a martial spirit. All their wishes were one; which was, that the country would turn out, and help them to drive the enemy back. Voltaire has remarked that King William never appeared to full advantage but in difficulties and in action. The same remark may be made on General Washington, for the character fits him. . . ."

With the enemy sweeping down through New Jersey toward the probable objective of Philadelphia, Washington withdrew his army ahead of them, skillfully saving it from panicky flight, and coming to a stop at last on the Pennsylvania side of the Delaware, where he set up his headquarters at the house of Thomas Barclay, who called it "Summer Seat." (It was later the property of Robert Morris, the financier of the Revolution.) Barclay, a prominent Irish Philadelphian, was one of the original members of the Society of the Friendly Sons of St. Patrick. Summer Seat, on a 221-acre tract, was about half a mile from the river, in what subsequently became Morrisville, opposite Trenton.

There Washington stayed until December 14, when he moved to William Keith's farmhouse, on the road from Brownsburg to the Eagle Tavern. It was in these quarters that he planned the Christmas recrossing of the Delaware, an action immortalized in the minds of millions of Americans by virtue of one highly inaccurate painting of the event hanging in schools across the nation.

Fanciful as the painting may be, the maneuver itself was daring, imaginative, and illustrated perfectly what Paine said of Washington's character. As every schoolboy knows, the Commander-in-Chief got his army across the river on Christmas night, completing the job about three o'clock. The take-off point was McKonkey's Ferry, now Taylorsville; he landed at a point about nine miles above Trenton. Then, early in the morning of the twenty-sixth, he descended upon the startled Hessian troops at Trenton and compelled them to surrender after a brief struggle. Taking his prisoners and captured arms with him, he retreated to Pennsylvania and set up headquarters at Newtown, then the county seat of Bucks County, in the house of John Harris.

Three days later, following up his victory, he again crossed the Delaware into New Jersey and proceeded with the army to Trenton, where his headquarters were in the house of Major John Barnes, a Loyalist who had fled it, on the west side of Queen (later Greene) Street. He stayed there only three days, however, then moved to the True American Inn, on the south side of Assunpink Creek.

Down to this hitherto unimportant stream came Lord Cornwallis from Princeton, with what Washington shortly discovered was a much superior force. Again "in difficulties and in action," as Paine had said it so well, Washington appeared "to full advantage" and executed another fine maneuver that had no painting to immortalize it but was quite as daringly successful. His army, leaving its fires alight to deceive the British, stole silently away at midnight, circled the enemy, marched the ten miles to Princeton by sunrise of January 3, 1777, and again won a decisive victory—and against not German mercenaries but two regiments of British regulars. It was of this night's work that Horace Walpole said: "Washington the dictator has shown himself both a Fabius and a Camillus. His march through our lines is allowed to have been a prodigy of generalship." *

After the battle, Washington and some of his officers spent the night of the third at John Van Doren's house, south of Princeton. Next morning the army marched off to winter quarters at Morristown, reaching there on January 6.

Morristown was a place Washington would get to know well before the war was over. On this first visitation he made his headquarters at Colonel Jacob Arnold's tavern, on the northwest side of the public square, a substantial frame building which existed until 1886, and then became the United States Hotel.

With the enemy smarting from his New Jersey wounds, Washington spent a comparatively peaceful winter at Morristown, although the wretched condition of the men caused him daily concern. Martha came to join him in March, and except for a short illness in the same month, there was nothing of unusual moment to report. Martha, as usual, quickly established a

---

* The march may be worth summarizing briefly. According to Fitzpatrick, the route was by way of Sandtown Road, near the present Hamilton Avenue, across Miry Run near Mercersville, then by Quaker Bridge, Clarksville and Stony Brook to Princeton.

Cornwallis, the day before, had marched from Princeton until he struck the American skirmish line near Maidenhead, where the strength of the resistance delayed him in reaching Trenton until four o'clock in the afternoon. Before the day was over, the British tried unsuccessfully to cross Assunpink Creek by the Queen Street bridge.

Washington's subsequent decision to attempt the night march was made in a council of war at Alexander Douglass' house, where the red brick German Lutheran church on South Broad Street was to rise later, only to be transported to Stacy Park, near the old Hessian Barracks.

social order, entertaining the ladies of quality in the vicinity and the officers' wives who had come to the camp. In this social circle, Washington's aides, his ambitious and amiable young men, were always figuratively at Mrs. Washington's elbow.

The routine of the days was more or less regular. Washington was up early in the morning, his habit, and by dinnertime, which was at two or three o'clock, depending on circumstance, the day's military business had been transacted. Sometime in the early spring, the General started serving rum and water at his table instead of wine, which pleased John Adams but was probably no joy to the young aides, most of whom were accustomed to better living.

Mrs. Theodorick Bland, wife of the Colonel, a frequent visitor to the camp in April and May, shrewdly characterized these aides in a letter to her sister: ". . . Col. [John] Fitzgerald, an agreeable, broad-shouldered Irishman — Col. [George] Johnston . . . who is exceedingly witty at everybody's expense but can't allow other people to be so at his own, though they often take the liberty—Col. [Alexander] Hamilton, a sensible, genteel, polite young fellow, a West Indian—Col. [Richard] Meade —Col. [Tench] Tilghman, a modest, worthy man who, from his attachment to the General lives in his family and acts in any capacity that is uppermost, without fee or reward — Col. [Robert] Harrison, brother of Billy Harrison that kept store in Petersburg and as much like him as possible, a worthy man— Capt. [Caleb] Gibbs of the General's Guard, a good-natured Yankee who makes a thousand blunders in the Yankee style and keeps the dinner table in constant laugh."

They were all, Mrs. Bland concluded, "polite, sociable gentlemen who make the day pass with a great deal of satisfaction to the visitors."

After dinner, this gossipy lady reported, came the high point of the day, when there were riding parties, in which the General joined if the pressure of affairs did not keep him indoors. On these rides, she disclosed, with the suggestion of a titter, the General threw off the hero and became "the chatty, agreeable companion—he can be downright impudent sometimes—such impudence, Fanny, as you and I like. . . ."

This must have been exactly the kind of recreation that pleased him most—riding through the burgeoning New Jersey countryside in the early spring, with agreeable female company, which he always enjoyed, by his side. On other days, he sometimes played ball in a field near headquarters, with some of the junior officers. It was a little of Mount Vernon transferred to these alien hills, in the midst of an ordeal which, if he allowed himself to dwell on it without relief, must surely have driven even him to absolute despair.

Late in May, as the British stirred from their own winter nap, and Washington tried to guess which way they would go, he concluded that it would be best to move the army nearer to Brunswick. Whether the enemy chose to go south toward Philadelphia or the other way, toward the eastern states, he would be in a strategic position to follow, and so he advanced to the left bank of the Raritan, at Middlebrook, seven miles northwest of Brunswick. Three days later most of the army followed him.

The troops viewed the new situation with somewhat mixed feelings. All were relieved to be out of winter quarters, where many had undergone constant suffering. Some of the officers were far more optimistic than the circumstances justified. Brigadier General George Weedon, rejoining the army after a long leave, wrote: "The whole of [the army is] now encamped in comfortable tents on a valley covered in front and rear by ridges which affords [sic] us security; His Excellency, our good old General has also spread his tent and lives amongst us. . . . Our men all happily over the smallpox and remarkable healthy, well armed and well clothed . . . and in the highest spirits. . . ."

But another officer, Adam Stephen, wrote ruefully to a friend: "The enemy are in possession of a fine country, well supplied with green lamb, veal, beef, mutton and pretty girls." (By "green lamb," Stephen meant simply "young and tender," a not uncommon eighteenth-century usage.)

In June the opposing armies flirted with each other but did not bring on an engagement. On June 25, Washington moved his camp to Quibbletown, now New Market, in Middlesex County, about six miles from Middlebrook on the road to Amboy. General Howe countered the next day by advancing his army from Amboy as far as Westfield, whereupon Washington pulled back to Middlebrook. There was a brief skirmishing as the armies almost touched each other, then Howe fell back to Amboy on the twenty-seventh. Three days later the British general unexpectedly loaded his army onto their supporting ships and evacuated New Jersey entirely, moving over to Staten Island.

As so often happened during the war, Washington was perplexed about what the British intended to do next; at times their moves were inexplicable to him. Howe might sail up the Hudson and collaborate with Burgoyne in the anticipated attack on the Northern posts, or might turn on Philadelphia. Washington supposed he would go north. In any event, it would be best to move his own army back to Morristown, where it would be free to go in either direction.

But after consulting with his officers, Washington was so confident that Howe intended to move up the Hudson that he began to march his own army northward on July 12. For two days he was delayed at Pompton Plains by a heavy downpour of rain. The Plains, which were useful to him as a quartering place, lie between the Pompton Mountains and the Preakness hills, constituting a plateau nearly twenty miles around and nowhere wider than four miles. The Pompton River flows along its eastern side to the Passaic; marshy peat bogs occupy the southern and western sides. At the head of the Plains, eighteen miles from Morristown, is Pompton. Today, of course, this is settled terrain, one of New Jersey's beauty spots.*

* Whenever Washington stopped at Pompton he is presumed to have stayed at a place called the Yellow House, later the Old Yellow Cottage, which Judge Ryerson had occupied at the beginning of the war and then turned over to a

Though he did not know it, Washington had an able recruiter in the Pompton Plains country, an eccentric preacher, the Rev. Dr. Gano, who sternly commanded his parishioners to enlist by reminding them that the Lord had "no nine- or six-months men in his service."

The rain stopped at last and the army marched on, but at the northern limits of New Jersey, Washington hesitated. Howe still lay quiet at Staten Island. What did he intend to do? On July 24, it was certain that he had sailed from New York Harbor—not north, as the Commander-in-Chief had anticipated, since Ticonderoga had already fallen to Burgoyne, but southward toward Philadelphia. There was nothing to do but reverse the army and that as rapidly as possible—back through Pompton, Morristown, Reading, and out of New Jersey. Out toward the defeat at the Brandywine, a second defeat at Germantown—and then the lowest point of all, the winter of 1777-78 at Valley Forge.

[1778]     After that experience, which left a lasting mark on the General, his men and the nation's history, it seemed impossible that the army could pull its tattered self together and move again. Yet here it was June 1778, the British had evacuated Philadelphia, where they had spent a pleasant winter, and were

---

Mr. Curtis, who kept it as a tavern. Curtis is said to have had a tavern sign painted bearing pictures of a horse, a fish and a bird, with this legend beneath:

> This is the Horse that never ran.
> This is the Fish that never swam.
> This is the Bird that never flew.

All this is disputed by New Jersey historians, who say that the Yellow Cottage was about a quarter of a mile above the Pompton Steel Works, off the old Hamburg Turnpike, a yellow frame house two stories high in front with a roof sloping off sharply at the back and a covered veranda in front. This version asserts that it was occupied during the Revolution by Caspar (or perhaps Arent) Schuyler, whose beautiful daughter Hester delighted Washington and his aides and married General Colfax, leader of the Guards, as soon as the war was over.

marching up toward Trenton – and here was Washington, marching with them into New Jersey, crossing the Delaware at Coryell's Ferry, now Lambertville. Impeded by rain, the Americans advanced slowly and reached Hopewell on June 24. Here Washington stopped overnight for a council of war at his quarters in the Hunt residence, about a mile from the Baptist Meeting House. Both these buildings are still standing, and the Meeting House, as Dr. Freeman notes, is "a cherished memorial in the village."

These movements of the armies were a prelude to their meeting on June 28 at the Battle of Monmouth Courthouse, which, as Washington wrote, "from an unfortunate and bad beginning, turned out a glorious and happy day." [1] Here two significant events occurred. One was that "unfortunate and bad beginning," when Washington met General Charles Lee and the advance corps in full retreat, the enemy at his heels.

The other significant event of June 28 was the Continental Army's rise from defeat and despair. The victory at Monmouth was a major turning point. Another disastrous defeat might have broken its spirit entirely; the victory gave it new hope.

Summing up the events of that day, Lafayette wrote: "During this affair, which ended so well, although begun so ill, General Washington appeared to arrest fortune by one glance, and his presence of mind, valor, and decision of character, were never displayed to greater advantage than at that moment. The General and he [Lafayette] passed the night lying on the same mantle, talking over the conduct of Lee, who wrote the next morning a very improper letter, and was placed under arrest. He was afterwards suspended by a council of war, quitted the service, and was not regretted by the army."

While this partisan view may not have been wholly accurate, it was unquestionably a glorious day and it is no wonder that Washington and his staff were in a good humor as they journeyed to Paramus, the next camp, on July 11. At noontime they visited the falls of the Passaic, and as James McHenry relates the subsequent pastoral interlude: "After viewing these falls we seated ourselves around the General under a large spreading oak within view of the spray in hearing of the noise. A fine cool spring bubbled out most charmingly from the bottom of the tree. The traveling canteens were immediately emptied and a modest repast spread before us of cold ham, tongue and some biscuit. With the assistance of a little spirit we composed some excellent grog. Then we chatted away a very cheerful half hour and then took our leave of the friendly oak and its refreshing spring."*

At Paramus they lingered four more cheerful days, the cheer being provided by the hospitality of the lovely Theodosia Prevost, a widow who later achieved a more dubious fame by marrying Aaron Burr. At her house, which she called the Hermitage, Washington's young aides found "some fair refugees from New York," with whom, as McHenry put it, "we talked and walked and laughed and danced and gallanted away the leisure hours...."

By this time Washington had learned that the British had removed themselves from New Jersey and spread themselves over Staten Island, Long Island and Manhattan (New York Island, as it was called then). In the face of this new situation, Washington, too, left New Jersey for a strategic line above New York in Westchester County.

It was November before he returned. Another winter of in-

---

* On this day, or later, or perhaps not at all (though Thacher and the Marquis de Chastellux both tell the story), Washington paid a visit to Peter Van Winkle, a human curiosity who lived near Passaic Falls. Van Winkle, who was probably a hydrocephalic case, had a head so enormous that it needed a framework on the back of his chair to support it, and he could not be moved without help. In the course of the conversation (which, it must be repeated, seems most unlikely) Washington is said to have asked Van Winkle whether he was a Whig or a Tory.

"Well, it do not take an *active* part on either side," Van Winkle said, apparently meaning his head.

This unfortunate man was the uncle of United States Senator Peter G. Van Winkle, of West Virginia, whose family lived for years in a stone house at the foot of Bank Street, in Paterson, New Jersey, a house that was later the Passaic Hotel.[2]

action appeared in prospect, and Washington had arranged his
troops for their hibernation, nine brigades on the west side of
the Hudson, from West Point down to Middlebrook, and five
on the east side, from Fishkill to Danbury. He chose Middlebrook as his headquarters, with seven brigades quartered around
it and the Jersey Brigade in Elizabethtown as an outpost.

[1779]    On his way to these quarters, as he paused at Fishkill, the General observed the German troops of Burgoyne's
army, who as prisoners were being marched off to Virginia
cantonments. The military courtesy of the times suggested,
though it did not demand, that he invite the senior officers to
dinner. They were naturally extremely curious to see him and
accepted at once, but when they came, they drank toddy and
examined him carefully, clicked their heels politely and would
not stay to dine. One of the officers wrote later his impressions
of the conqueror:

"[Washington] speaks very distinctly and expressed himself
rather more sincerely than complimentary; however, is quite
polite. In short, he impresses you as a good man, who can be
trusted. He has nothing extraordinary about him, which I had
expected."

The General did not know he had failed to make an impression. He went on more or less serenely to Middlebrook, where
on the eleventh of December he established his winter headquarters four miles from the town at John Wallace's house, a
comfortable enough place but crowded. The Wallace house is
today a New Jersey Historical Site, open to the public, but the
geography has changed somewhat since Washington's time.
Middlebrook is now Boundbrook, and the house is in Somerville, the county seat of Somerset County, between that city and
Raritan, about where the highway crosses the tracks of the
Central Railroad of New Jersey.

By comparison with the horrors of Valley Forge the year
before, the winter at Middlebrook proved to be almost an idyll.

Washington was called to Philadelphia to consult with Congress in December, just before Christmas, and spent more than a month there. As one of the town's newspapers noted, it was "the only relief he has enjoyed from service since he first entered into it."[3] Martha joined him, and he enjoyed both his "domestic retirement," as the paper delicately put it, and the entertainments everyone was anxious to provide him.

When he returned to Middlebrook in February, taking Martha with him, he found a gay social life going on in and about headquarters. He could find more enjoyment in it this winter, knowing that the men were better off. They were "again in huts," he wrote to Lafayette in Paris, "but in a more agreeable and fertile country than they were in last winter at Valley Forge; and they are better clad and more healthy than they have been since the formation of the army...."[4]

Martha entertained in the Wallace house, small as it was, but the social obligations were better distributed. Quartered in houses nearby were several of the other generals, most of whom had their wives with them.

One of the busiest places was the headquarters of General Knox, in Pluckamin, where the artillery was quartered. Knox and his wife lived in the home of Jacobus Van der Veer, on what was later the Ludlow farm, near the Bedminster church. There, on February 18, Knox and his lady, with the officers of the artillery, gave an entertainment in honor of the alliance with France. George and Martha Washington, and the other officers and their wives, along with prominent citizens from far and wide, were invited.

At four in the afternoon there was a discharge of sixteen cannon, after which the company sat down to dinner in a large public building. Fireworks lighted the evening sky, and the celebration concluded with a ball, which Washington and Mrs. Knox opened. This affair, which should have been held on the sixth but was postponed to the eighteenth because of Washington's absence, was described afterward with considerable satisfaction by the host.

"We had . . . a most genteel entertainment given by self and officers," Knox wrote in a letter. "Everybody allows it to be the first of the kind ever exhibited in this state at least. We had above seventy ladies, all of the first *ton* in the state, and between three and four hundred gentlemen. We danced all night—an elegant room, the illuminating fireworks, &c. were more than pretty. . . ."

Another memorable party occurred at the quarters of Nathanael Greene, then Quartermaster General. If this was the gayest of the generals' houses, it was owing to Greene's lovely wife Catherine. She was only twenty-five, but she had an intelligence, a poise, almost a worldliness that were far beyond her years. With this intelligence she possessed a soft, dark-eyed kind of beauty, and it is understandable that there was never a lack of admiring though highly respectful, men about the house. Women liked her, too, for her vivacity and social charm.

The Greenes lived in a house already mellowed by age, a venerable two-story, Holland-brick Dutch farmhouse occupied by old Derrick Van Veghten, an ardent patriot, whose Netherlands forebears had settled the Raritan Valley. The house was halfway between Middlebrook and Somerville, on the Raritan River.

To this establishment on the evening of March 19 came Washington and some of the other officers for an evening that was celebrated because of the General's obvious enchantment with Catherine Greene, and her husband's apt description of the affair. "We had a little dance at my quarters a few evenings past," the able Rhode Islander confided to his friend Colonel Wadsworth. "His Excellency and Mrs. Greene danced upwards of three hours without once sitting down." Where Martha was during this interval history does not record; knowing her husband's rockbound moral character, she probably was not greatly worried, though it would be interesting to know whether she was human enough to be annoyed. Apparently the Quartermaster was not disturbed. He concluded his description: "Upon the whole, we had a pretty little frisk."

There were a few of the younger officers, including Light Horse Harry Lee, who struck it rich in the apportioning of quarters. In the language of five or six wars later, it could truly be said of them that they had never had it so good. They lived in a large house above Middlebrook on an eminence known as "Phil's Hill," owned by Philip Van Horn. The architecture of the place was negligible, but it was otherwise glorified by the presence of the five Van Horn daughters, all of them good-looking, polite and accomplished, all of them madly pursued from every quarter of the compass by Washington's young aides and officers. They were pursued with equal fervor by the young British officers when *they* were quartered there, and it was said that the Van Horn girls were not inclined to quibble about a man's politics. A writer years later spoke of them truly when he said that they were "often the means of mitigating the ferocities of war."[5]

These girls and others of the neighborhood helped to contribute to the gaiety of nations that winter. There was a constant round of activity. The Mesdames Washington, Greene and Knox often entertained visitors from Virginia, Philadelphia and New England. Lady Stirling and her daughter Kitty often drove over from Basking Ridge to call. Catherine Greene's close friend, Mrs. Lott, and her daughter Cornelia came from as far away as the other side of Morristown. General Livingston's daughters arrived for a stay of several weeks at headquarters, and the wives and daughters of a good many other generals and colonels were much in evidence. There were ceremonies, reunions, dances, teas, dinners and assemblies. Never had the horrors of war been so enjoyable.

Washington always had several of his officers at dinner, and on some days as many as thirty people sat down at his table, including visitors. Dr. Thacher, who was with Washington much of the time during the war, describes one of these dinners in February, at which there were, besides himself and another visitor, "two young ladies from Virginia, the gentlemen who compose his family, and several other officers." Watching the

General at table that day, Thacher set down these observations in his journal:

". . . In conversation His Excellency's expressive countenance is peculiarly interesting and pleasing; a placid smile is frequently observed on his lips, but a loud laugh, it is said, seldom if ever escapes him. He is polite and attentive to each individual at table, and retires after the compliment of a few glasses. Mrs. Washington combines in an uncommon degree great dignity of manner with the most pleasing affability, but possesses no striking marks of beauty."

So the winter passed away, a winter that was, as Thacher noted in April, "remarkably mild and moderate; since the 10th of January we have scarcely had a fall of snow, or a frost, and no severe weather." On a warm, bright Sunday in May, the second, the social season came to a brilliant close with a grand review of the army, held in honor of the French minister, Monsieur Gerard, and Don Juan de Mirailles, a somewhat mysterious and unfortunate (by the next year he was dead) emissary from the Spanish court. Monsieur Gerard had come to consult with Washington on the operations of Count d'Estaing's fleet; it was not clear why Mirailles had come.

Either before or after the grand review, General Steuben entertained the distinguished visitors at his headquarters about a mile south of the Raritan, on the farm of Abraham Staats, which was situated at the end of a long, grassy lane running in from the New Brunswick road. The Baron had erected a marquee in a nearby grove, and under it he gathered sixty guests, including Washington, the visitors and his fellow officers.

In his *Military Journal*, Dr. Thacher has left us an admiring report of the grand review itself. He wrote: "The whole of our army in this quarter was paraded in martial array in a spacious field, and a stage was erected for the accommodation of the ladies and gentlemen spectators. At the signal of thirteen cannon, the great and splendid cavalcade approached in martial pomp and style. A very beautiful troop of light horse, commanded by Major Lee, a Virginian, marched in front, then followed His Excellency the Commander-in-Chief, and his aides-de-camp, next the foreign ministers and their retinue, and the general officers of our army and their aides closed the procession. Having arrived on the field of parade, the Commander-in-Chief, with the foreign ministers and general officers, passed in front of the line of the army, from right to left, in review, and received the military honors due to their rank, after which the gentlemen dismounted and retired to the stage and took seats with Mrs. Washington, Mrs. Greene, Mrs. Knox and a number of other ladies who had arrived in their carriages. The army then performed the field maneuvers and evolutions, with firing of cannon and musketry."

Thacher was at another review on May 14, when his brigade was paraded for the benefit of several Indian chiefs who were visiting Washington. This must have been something of an anticlimax, but the General conducted the review with his usual dignity. On a fine gray horse, and followed by his mulatto servant Bill, he rode before the line and took the salute. Behind him, wrote the mildly horrified doctor, came "a singular group of savages, whose appearance was beyond description ludicrous."

It was a winter and spring set like an island in this strangest of wars, judged by modern standards. Armies swept up and down, men died horribly, often they suffered from cold and hunger, momentous issues were being decided—yet a good part of the population ignored the conflict under their noses when they could. Some were bored by it, some had no strong feelings for either side, others resented the interruption of their work in the fields and villages, and the largest proportion of the Continental Army performed its service unwillingly and departed at the hour that service was ended, no matter what the military situation might be. And there were those winters in which the privileged part of the army conducted its social life much as usual, and the amenities between the opposing armies, and between the populace and these armies, were nearly always observed. Only on the frontiers, in such places as the Cherry

Valley, was there real pillage and constant terror and a deadly bitterness. The war was civilized, for the most part, elsewhere.

But after this winter, during which it seemed for a time as though the war had stopped entirely (except, of course, to Washington and his staff officers, who knew better), the business had to be resumed. The army moved out of Middlebrook early in June, heading north toward Smith's Clove, in Orange County, New York, a rich, level plain at the foot of high mountains, fourteen miles distant from West Point. There it encamped on June 7.

After a quiet summer and autumn, during which Washington maintained his headquarters mainly at West Point, watching the consolidation of British forces in New York, preparing (though he did not know it) for a southern campaign, he concluded that it would be necessary to winter again in New Jersey. Accordingly he settled anew with the army at Morristown, and on December 7, 1779, took up his headquarters at the home of Theodosia Ford, whose late husband, Colonel Jacob Ford, had commanded a regiment of Morris County militia in the painful retreat through New Jersey in 1776. This house, open to the public today, has been described as ranking "second only to Mount Vernon as a storehouse of Washington relics and associations, although it was looked upon for almost a century as just another place where Washington slept."[6] It stands at 230 Morris Avenue, in Morristown.

Washington's associations with the Ford house must have been grim ones after that winter. It was as difficult as the one before had been easy, gloomy where the other had been gay. At the beginning of it, the General had been able to enjoy one experience in the Morris Hotel, which was then used as a commissary's storehouse, when he saw his friend Lafayette initiated at a Masonic rite, the celebration of the festival of St. John the Evangelist. A room in the second floor of the building was reserved as a ballroom and for Masonic lodge meetings, and whenever he could, the General dropped in to practice the rites, as he did in other places at which he was stopping.

[1780]     But the winter of 1779–80 did not lend itself to sociability. By the third of January the snow was at least four feet deep in the Hudson Valley, and the ice so thick that it was possible to walk across the river at King's Ferry. From the third to the eighth a violent storm raged intermittently, beginning with an enveloping snow. Dr. Thacher reported: "On the 3rd instant we experienced one of the most tremendous snowstorms ever remembered; no man could endure its violence many minutes without danger of his life. Several marquees were torn asunder and blown down over the officers' heads in the night, and some of the soldiers were actually covered while in their tents, and buried like sheep under the snow. . . . The snow is now [this was written on the eighth] from four to six feet deep, which so obstructs the roads as to prevent our receiving a supply of provisions. For the last ten days we have received but two pounds of meat a man, and we are frequently for six or eight days entirely destitute of meat, and then as long without bread. The consequence is, the soldiers are so enfeebled from hunger and cold, as to be almost unable to perform their military duty, or labor in constructing their huts."

Even before the severe January weather had set in, Washington was deeply disturbed about the plight of his soldiers. He had written to Joseph Reed on December 16: "The situation of the army with respect to supplies is beyond description alarming. It has been five or six weeks past on half-allowance, and we have not more than three days bread at a third allowance on hand, nor anywhere within reach. When this is exhausted, we must depend on the precarious gleanings of the neighboring country. Our magazines are absolutely empty everywhere, and our commissaries entirely destitute of money or credit to replenish them. We have never experienced a like extremity at any period of the war. . . ."

The weather was, ironically, a help to the British. The January storm froze New York Harbor so solidly that Staten Island could be supplied by sleighs from New York, and once a cavalry troop rode over from the island to the Battery. The

North River was frozen thickly enough to support heavy cannon, and the East River was clogged for days with huge, jagged chunks of ice.*

But in Morristown the soldiers huddled together in their tents while they waited for the huts to be completed, and the junior officers slept five and six together, their feet to the fire.

At headquarters life was far from happy. On January 22, Washington wrote to General Greene what was, for him, a complaining letter, although his discomforts were relative. They had not, he said, "a kitchen to cook a dinner in, although the logs have been put together some considerable time by my own Guard. Nor is there a place at this moment in which a servant can lodge with the smallest degree of comfort. Eighteen belonging to my family, and all Mrs. Ford's are crowded together in her kitchen, and scarce one of them able to speak for the colds they have caught." ı↑

Yet, incredibly, the younger men contrived to create some diversion out of adversity. When the storm subsided, they went on sleighing parties, and Washington and thirty-four

* While the Americans were suffering, the British, amid the comforts of New York, were taunting them with words, in newspapers and broadsides. One of the most elaborate of these literary efforts declared:

"Thirteen is a number peculiarly belonging to the rebels. A party of naval prisoners lately returned from Jersey say that the rations among the rebels are thirteen dried clams per day; that the titular Lord Stirling takes thirteen glasses of grog every morning, has thirteen enormous rum-bunches on his nose, and that (when duly impregnated) he always makes thirteen attempts before he can walk; that Mr. Washington has thirteen toes on his feet (the extra ones having grown since the Declaration of Independence), and the same number of teeth in each jaw; that the Sachem Schuyler has a topknot of thirteen stiff hairs, which erect themselves on the crown of his head when he grows mad; that Old Putnam had thirteen pounds of his posteriors bit off in an encounter with a Connecticut bear ('twas then he lost the *balance* of his mind); that it takes thirteen children, all of whom expect to be generals and members of the High and Mighty Congress of the 'thirteen United States' when they attain thirteen years; that Mrs. Washington has a mottled tom-cat (which she calls, in a complimentary way, 'Hamilton') with thirteen yellow rings around his tail, and that his flaunting it suggested to the Congress the adoption of the same number of stripes for the rebel flag."[7]

End of British sentence.

others subscribed to form a dancing assembly in Morristown. [12] A few attractive girls managed to get through the snowdrifts for a party, including Elizabeth Schuyler, a beauty who was admired by Tench Tilghman and Alexander Hamilton.

But after the party-makers had gone home and headquarters had settled down for the night in its crowded, uneasy rooms, there were often alarms in the late hours. The frozen river made an easy passage for raiding parties from New York, and sometimes the Headquarters Guard had to tumble out of their huts across the roads, come into the house and stand with their muskets at the windows. [

And the winter continued its relentless grip week after week, with no respite. There had never been such a season. "The oldest people now living in this country do not remember so hard a winter as the one we are now emerging from," Washington wrote Lafayette in Paris on March 18. [7] The severity of the frost, he added, had exceeded "anything of the kind that had ever been experienced in this climate before." Dr. Thacher echoed this verdict at about the same date. "The present winter is the most severe and distressing which we have ever experienced," he wrote in his journal. "An immense body of snow remains on the ground. Our soldiers are in a wretched condition for the want of clothes, blankets and shoes; and these calamitous circumstances are accompanied by a want of provisions. . . ." [14]

Valley Forge has gone down in history as the apotheosis of the army's privations, but Morristown was as bad, and in some respects worse. Washington may not have seen a soldier covered only with a blanket running from one hut to the next, a sight at Valley Forge that haunted him for years, but he did see half-naked men, some of them without shoes, standing in the bitter weather and hacking at tough oak and walnut trees to get wood for the huts.

By April the weather had moderated considerably, and the signs of an early spring appeared. The new French minister, the Chevalier de la Luzerne, and the mysterious Spanish agent,

Don Juan de Mirailles, appeared at headquarters and viewed from the New Jersey hills the entrenchments of the enemy on York and Staten islands. For these honored guests, the indefatigable drillmaster, Baron Steuben, paraded four battalions of the ragged army on April 24.

That night the chief officers entertained Washington and the Chevalier at a ball in the Morris Hotel, at which there were "a numerous collection of ladies and gentlemen of distinguished character." The Spanish agent could not attend; he was lying ill with the "pulmonic fever" (it might have been almost anything, from this description) which took his life four days later in the General's headquarters.

There was another parade of the troops on May 29 for the benefit of a congressional committee, come to inspect the army at first hand and make a report on its needs. This committee confirmed everything that Washington had been trying to beat into the impenetrable skulls of the lawmakers for six months. Now they heard from three of their ablest members —Philip Schuyler, John Mathews and Nathaniel Peabody— that "the army was five months unpaid; that it seldom had more than six days provisions in advance, and was on several occasions, for sundry successive days, without meat; that the army was destitute of forage; that the medical department had neither sugar, tea, chocolate, wine nor spirits; and that every department was without money, or even the shadow of credit."

Yet this was the same army that had been paraded for inspection and review by Washington on May 9, in which the troops had "appeared to much advantage," and Baron Steuben, who had been laboring tirelessly to prepare them for the summer campaigns, thanked their officers "for the military and soldierly appearance of the men." [8]

It looked as though the first test of the new fighting season would begin on the night of June 6, when the British landed at Elizabethtown Point from New York and advanced in the morning to a point just short of Springfield. Washington countered by moving his army to the heights above Springfield, ten miles southeast of Morristown, during the afternoon. There was some desultory skirmishing, and then at night the enemy pulled back to Elizabethtown Point. For two weeks nothing further happened, each side apparently waiting for the other to move. Washington fancied that the British might be planning a quick movement up the river to attack West Point, and consequently began moving his troops slowly northward on the twenty-first, but instead the British contented themselves with burning Springfield, after which they retired under cover of darkness on the twenty-third to their base on Staten Island.

Washington moved his headquarters up to Ramapo on June 27, about seven miles below the present Ramapo, New York. The New Jersey Ramapo was a small settlement on the river of the same name, in Bergen County. At the moment it represented only a stopping-off place for three days, until the General could establish himself for a longer period at Preakness, about five miles northwest of Passaic Falls (now a part of Paterson), where he arrived on July 1.

There he made his headquarters at the home of Colonel Theunis Dey, in one of the finest houses in New Jersey; a century later it was termed "remarkable for its architectural symmetry and the artistic finish of the masonry."[9] It was probably built by Derick Dey, the Colonel's father, in 1720, and its situation in the valley beyond the Preakness hills was beautiful. There were vistas in every direction, and the network of roads around it linked the place, from a military standpoint, to Newark, Elizabethtown, Springfield, Middletown and southern New Jersey; on the southeast to Totowa, Acquackanoc and Hackensack; and on the northeast to Paramus, Pompton and Ringwood.

The house stood about a hundred yards off the main road and faced south. Two stories high, with a double-pitch roof, it was constructed of brick, trimmed at the doorway and windows with polished brown sandstone. The timbers inside were of hewn oak, in the best construction style of the day, joined with wooden pins. A center hall twelve feet wide bisected the first floor from north to south, with two rooms on each side of it and in each of them a fireplace faced with rubbed brown sandstone. The ceilings were nine feet high in this first floor, and only a foot less on the second.

Washington occupied four of the rooms in the house, probably two on each floor. One on the first floor he used as an "audience chamber" and dining room for private meals; the family dined in the great hall. In his office, Washington is said to have had the walls papered at his own expense.

Apparently the General was fond of this house. The war that summer took him across the Hudson to Westchester County, and for a time to Teaneck, where his headquarters were at the Liberty Pole Tavern, on Palisade Avenue in the present town of Englewood; "Teaneck" was a name given at that time to an entire ridge of land. In September he was quartered for a time in the Hopper house, on the road to Morristown, only two miles from the New York line and four south of Ramapo Pass. It was there he heard of Gates's defeat in the Battle of Camden, South Carolina, and from there he set out for his Hartford conference with Rochambeau.*

But on October 8, with the French strategy negotiations under way, and the sad business of Arnold's treachery and André's execution behind him, he re-established himself at the Dey house in Preakness, where he remained until November 27.

* While Washington was moving up and down the Jerseys in August and early September, the British in New York wondered what he was up to. Their doubt and outward scorn are reflected in a paragraph from the best Tory newspaper (perhaps the best of any stripe) in the city. James ("Jemmy") Rivington, the remarkable proprietor of the *Royal Gazette*, undoubtedly wrote this himself, with the acid pen which so irritated General Putnam that he had it first on his list of postwar business to come down to New York and lick Jemmy Rivington. On August 6, 1780, the *Gazette* declared:

"Our old acquaintance Mr. Washington we learn is approaching us Polyphemus-like, with hasty and ample strides, his dire intents (supported by myriads of heroes and in his train a thirteen-inch mortar drawn by eight charming lively oxen) are given out to be another coup upon Powles Hook. His last halt was at Paramus, some thirty miles off."

There, in November, he was visited by the Marquis de Chastellux, the French major general whose *Travels in North America* is one of the travel classics written about this country. The Count described his arrival:

"After riding two miles along the right flank of the army, and after passing thick woods on the right, I found myself in a small plain, where I saw a handsome farm; a small camp which seemed to cover it, a large tent extended in the court, and several waggons round it, convinced me that this was His Excellency's quarters; for it is thus Mr. Washington is called in the army, and throughout America. M. de la Fayette was in conversation with a tall man, five foot nine inches high (about five foot ten inches and a half English), of a noble and mild countenance. It was the General himself. I was soon off horseback, and near him. The compliments were short; the sentiments with which I was animated, and the good wishes he testified for me were not equivocal. He conducted me to his house, where I found the company still at table, although the dinner had been long over. He presented me to the Generals Knox, Wayne, Howe, &c., and to his family, then composed of Colonels Hamilton and Tilghman, his secretaries and his aides-de-camp, and of Major Gibbs, commander of his Guards; for in England and America, the aides-de-camp, adjutants and other officers attached to the General, form what is called his family. A fresh dinner was prepared for me and mine; and the present was prolonged to keep me company." [10]

Next day Washington took his guest on a review of the army at the various camps it occupied, and on the following day De Chastellux participated in the decisions made concerning the disposition of the troops to winter quarters.

"At our return we found a good dinner ready," he writes, "and about twenty guests, among whom were Generals Howe and Sinclair. . . . The conversation was calm and agreeable; His Excellency was pleased to enter with me into the particulars of some of the principal operations of the war, but always with a modesty and conciseness which proved that it was from pure complaisance he mentioned it. . . . The weather was so bad on the twenty-fifth that it was impossible for me to stir, even to wait on the generals, to whom M. de la Fayette was to conduct me. I easily consoled myself for this, finding it a great luxury to pass a whole day with General Washington, as if he were at his house in the country, and had nothing to do. The Generals Glover, Huntington and some others dined with us, and the Colonels Stewart and Butler, two officers distinguished in the army. The intelligence received this day occasioned the proposed attack on Staten Island to be laid aside. . . . It was determined therefore that the army should march the next day to winter quarters, and that I should continue my route to Philadelphia." [11]

De Chastellux was leaving not only distinguished company but a good table. The "good dinner" he came back to after his review of the troops included about ten dishes of butchers' meat and poultry, accompanied by vegetables and the accepted claret and madeira, followed by various pastries. Besides the General and his family, there were twenty guests that night, and the table had to be turned diagonally in the room to seat everybody.

The suppers they enjoyed in the evening were light, only a few dishes, after which the cloth was taken away and the servants brought on apples, wine and a bowl of cracked hickory nuts. For Washington this was the best part of the meal, to sit and talk, sipping a little wine and eating nuts with a methodical solemnity which depressed some of his visitors in later years. Occasionally someone would rise and propose a toast—noble and patriotic ones at first, and finally the names of charming ladies.

An amusing piece of dinner-table conversation was reported by Major Theodore Woodbridge, of the Connecticut line, who tells of an incident at Sunday dinner on August 26, while Washington was at Teaneck on his way to Preakness. Major Leavenworth appeared at headquarters about dinnertime with a branch bearing thirteen apples, set curiously together in a cluster. Washington sent the Major a bottle of rum with his compliments for the gift, examined the branch with interest and handed it to Lafayette. While the Marquis was looking at it, two of the apples dropped off.

"You have ruined two of our states," Washington remarked amiably to Lafayette.

Lafayette passed the branch around the table, and by the time it reached General Greene, all but four had dropped off.

"They're all gone except the four New England states," Greene said, keeping up the jest. "Here's one smaller than the others. That must be Rhode Island."

Lafayette pointed to a withered apple, clinging to the branch at a distance from the four hardy survivors.

"There is one dried up before it was grown," he laughed. "It must be Vermont." [12]


[1783]     Washington left New Jersey for winter quarters at New Windsor, New York, in November 1780, and did not return to the state (long enough to establish a headquarters, that is) until the end of the Revolution. Then, at the request of Congress, in session at Princeton, he issued his last orders at Newburgh on August 17, 1783, and the day after came down to Rocky Hill, New Jersey, four miles from Princeton. It was to be the last headquarters of the Revolution.

On the way, he stopped at West Point and, among other activities, got himself weighed—209 pounds. By the twenty-fourth he was at Rocky Point, establishing himself in the home of Judge Berrien, thoughtfully engaged by Congress for his purposes. It was a two-story frame building with piazzas, on a hill a little way from the Millstone River. His situation there was described by an eighteen-year-old artist, William Dunlap, who came to paint the General's portrait. Dunlap wrote of his frequent visits:

"The only military in the neighborhood were the General's suite and a captain's guard, whose tents were on the green before the Berrien house, and the Captain's marquee nearly in front. The soldiers were New England yeomen's sons, none older than twenty; their commander was Captain Howe, in after times long a resident of New York. . . . I was quite at home in every respect at headquarters; to breakfast and dine day after day with the General and Mrs. Washington, and members of Congress, and noticed as the young painter, was delicious."

Unfortunately young Mr. Dunlap's effort, a crayon drawing, has "no particular significance in the history of Washington portraiture," according to Fitzpatrick.

Other odd mementos are left from the Berrien house days. There is, for example, a description of the horse—a small roan four-year-old—on which the General rode the five miles into Princeton in forty minutes to attend Congress. He sat in an "old crooked saddle" placed on a deep blue flowered saddle cloth, trimmed with buff cloth at the edge.

And there are, too, the memories of old inhabitants, which of course can only be taken for what they are worth—memories repeated many years after the event, and copied two or three times thereafter. A charming one, and not unlikely, concerns a Cooperstown, New York, lady who recalls that in these days, or shortly before, she sat as a child of three on the General's lap. In the immemorial way, he placed her on his knee, waiting until her mother was out of the room (which would be consistent with his dignity), and sang this song while he trotted her:

> *"There was an old, old man, and an old, old woman.*
> *They lived in a vinegar bottle together*
> *Sheltered alike from wind and from weather,*
> *They lived in a vinegar bottle together."*

The last line was repeated several times as a chorus. When the mother returned, the General is supposed to have said to her: "The little jade wished to know how the old people escaped from the bottle, and before I had time to reply to her question, she anticipated me by saying, 'I guess, General, they knocked off the neck.' "

The same old lady recalled that a German woman living nearby had been an inveterate Tory, referring to the General as "George the rebel" until she caught sight of him on this visit, whereupon she burst into tears and crying, "Godlike, godlike," in her own language, from that moment became a Whig.[13]

Another story told of the General in these last, relaxed days of his service at Rocky Hill declares that one day when he went to the wine chest, seeking to send away a guest with a small nip under his belt, he discovered that it was empty of the proper wine. He saw three or four glasses with cheer from the night before left in them, and, pouring them into a clean tumbler, is said to have stirred them up with a rooster's feather, meanwhile remarking, "At least I have a cocktail to offer my friend."[14]

This, one might say, is the acme of the fortuitous anecdote.

On September 5, Washington entertained Congress, and with a nice gesture sat them down to dinner in a captured British marquee. His guests could not help noticing how different he looked now that the war was over and its burdens were no longer oppressing him every waking moment. One of those present recorded that his "front" was "uncommonly open and pleasant, the contracted, pensive phiz, betokening deep thought and much care, which I noted on Prospect Hill in 1775 is done away." He even expanded a little at the table, making the kind of small jokes before this large and distinguished gathering that formerly he had only ventured to those nearest him. Someone at the table remarked that the "Superintendent of Finance has his hands full," and the General quipped, "I wish he had his pockets full, too." Another guest informed him that the silver wine goblets on the table had been fashioned by a man who had "turned Quaker preacher."

"I wish he had been a Quaker preacher before he made the cups," Washington sighed.

If he had not known it before, in these last hours of his command Washington must have begun to realize that in the process of winning the war he had become a national hero. Reading the newspapers, letters and reports that formerly he had not the time to scan, he saw the evidence. Celebrations of his birthday that year had taken place in Boston, Richmond and numerous other places. Peace observances had glorified his name—"the loved name of Washington," one newspaper called it—and everyone was anxious to confer new honors on him. Philadelphia declared he was to be the Grand Master of a "new order of knighthood, called the Order of Freedom. . . ." In that city, on the banks of the Schuylkill, there had been a St. Tammany's Day Celebration at which the band played a march called "Great Washington." A woman who owned a tavern in New Haven changed its name from the Sign of the New Moon to the Sign of General Washington.

There were innumerable others, enough to keep a modern celebrity reading his scrapbook for hours. But Washington was anxious to be off to Mount Vernon. Already he was planning how to transport the huge load of his papers. Discussing the matter by letter with Colonel Timothy Pickering, he estimated that it would take four or five wagons to transport them to Virginia.

As his mind turned from war to peace, suppressed desires came to the surface; large plans thrust into the background reasserted themselves. On October 12 he wrote to Lafayette:

"I have it in contemplation . . . to make a tour through all the Eastern states, thence into Canada, thence up the St. Lawrence, and through the Lakes to Detroit; thence to Lake Michigan by land or water, thence through the Western country by the river Illinois to the river Mississippi, and down the same to New Orleans; thence into Georgia by the way of Pensacola; and thence through the new Carolinas home.

"A great tour this, you will say, probably it may take place nowhere but in imagination, though it is my wish to begin it in the latter end of April of next year; if it should be realized, there would be nothing wanting to make it perfectly agreeable but your company."

On the same day he wrote in a similar vein to the Marquis de Chastellux, recounting his trip up the Mohawk Valley and how it had opened his eyes to the immense possibilities of the "vast inland navigation of these United States," and praying, "Would to God we may have wisdom enough to improve them." Then he went on, "I shall not rest contented till I have explored the Western country, and traversed those lines (or a great part of them) which have given bounds to a new empire."

But even as he wrote the words he must have known how unlikely they were of fulfillment, for he added that "when it may, if it ever shall happen, I dare not say, as my first attention must be given to the deranged situation of my private concerns, which are not a little injured by almost nine years absence and total disregard of them."

For these private concerns he left the scenes of his New Jersey tribulations and successes. There was still the ceremony of taking formal possession of New York, in preparation for which he went up to West Point on November 14. There were other chores to be done, too, before he would be riding hard to reach Mount Vernon by Christmas Day, but for the General, basking in the last few days at Rocky Hill in the warmth of public approval, the war was over.

Chapter 4

Pennsylvania

Pennsylvania means Valley Forge. The connection is automatic in the minds of most people, and Washington's movements on the face of that commonwealth show that, whatever else he did there, outside of Philadelphia, the winter at Valley Forge overshadowed everything else.

He had other headquarters, of course; some of them have been mentioned briefly in the New Jersey pages of this volume. These were the Bucks County residences he occupied after the retreat to the Delaware in November–December 1776. The first was Thomas Barclay's (George spelled it Berkeley) "Summer Seat," where he came to rest after the retreat. Then came his residence at the William Keith place, on the Brownsburg-Eagle Tavern road, with the remainder of his generals scattered through Upper Makefield Township in farmhouses within easy communication distance. Washington had chosen the Keith house because it was sheltered, near the river and close to Jericho Mountain, from whose summit in wintertime an observer could spot signals far up and down the river. He was also near the Delaware's upper fords, where the enemy might be expected to cross, if the attempt was made, and in another direction lay the vital depot of supplies at Newtown, a half hour's ride away. In the yellow pine interior of this farmhouse, Washington planned his recrossing of the Delaware.[1]

That event deserves some further observation from the Pennsylvania side. McKonkey's Ferry, where the crossing occurred, must have reminded Washington of his boyhood; it was so like the apparatus at Ferry Farm which had borne him many times across the Rappahannock to Fredericksburg. The

McKonkeys operated it winter and summer. In the taproom
of their ferry house, the General is supposed to have drunk
hot coffee before he set out that historic Christmas night,
though it is doubtful if this tradition has a word of truth in it.

They were Marblehead men for the most part who rowed
Washington and his army across the Delaware—the same
strong-backed Massachusetts fishermen who had carried the
General across the East River in the retreat from Brooklyn.
They had now to negotiate a crossing of 1050 feet, against a
strong, choppy current filled with drifting ice.

This kind of hardship was training of a sort for the following winter, when the crossing and the campaign that followed
it would seem a holiday by comparison.

Of the millions of words written about the Valley Forge
winter, a good part is tradition, and another substantial percentage is the ornamental embellishment of politicians and in-
spirational writers who have used the sufferings of the Continental Army for every kind of purpose, noble and ignoble. But
even when the false sentimentality, the patriotic exaggeration
and the rest of it are stripped away, the facts alone disclose
what an emotional experience the winter must have been for
everyone from Washington down to the lowliest private.


[1777–1778]     After the battles of Trenton and Princeton,
the year 1777 had begun well enough, and the first winter at
Morristown had not been difficult, but the summer had been
filled with doubt and uncertainty. Affairs in the Northern Department went badly, and Washington had been compelled to
keep the army inactive during the good fighting months while
he waited to see where the British would attack. Since he surmised it would be Philadelphia, the troops had come to rest
on August 1 at Schuylkill Falls, between Germantown and
the Schuylkill River, five miles north of the city.

Washington, who had been in Philadelphia, joined his army

159

there on the afternoon of the fourth, establishing himself at Henry Hill's country place on Indian Queen Lane, a mile or so east of the Falls. On the morning of the eighth, the troops were reviewed. The most interested spectator at this occasion was Lafayette, just commissioned a major general. He had met Washington only six days before and had been instantly captivated by him, but even with his quick devotion to the man and the cause, he had a hard time finding anything to stir his enthusiasm in his first view of the American army.

Accustomed to the splendid battalions of the Continent, his dismay is apparent even in the discreet lines of his third-person memoirs:

"About eleven thousand men, ill armed and still worse clothed, presented a strange spectacle to the eye of the young Frenchman: their clothes were parti-colored, and many of them were almost naked; the best clad wore hunting shirts, large gray linen coats which were much used in Carolina. As to their military tactics, it will be sufficient to say that, for a regiment ranged in order of battle to move forward on the right of its line, it was necessary for the left to make a continued countermarch. They were always arranged in two lines, the smallest men in the first line; no other distinction as to height was ever observed. In spite of these disadvantages, the soldiers were fine, and the officers zealous; virtue stood in place of science, and each day added both to experience and discipline."

Where these strangely assorted troops would meet their next test was still a matter of doubt. On the afternoon of the review, Washington concluded that Howe's fleet, maneuvering off the coast, had decided not to land after all and was sailing back up toward New York; consequently the army was put in a slow northward movement until more definite intelligence could be obtained. That decision was made on Friday. By Sunday the army was twenty miles north of Philadelphia at what was called the Neshaminy Camp, in Bucks County. Headquarters was in a stone house typical of the country, on the Old York Road and near a bridge spanning the Little Neshaminy Creek. A place called the Cross Roads, later Hartsville, was about half a mile away.

There the Americans rested while their General tried to read Howe's mind at long distance, and on the basis of conflicting intelligence. At first it seemed that he had turned south and was headed for Charleston, in which case there would be no military virtue in a southern pursuit, and the army would go back to its posts on the Hudson. Then, on the twenty-second, on the heels of the good news of Stark's victory at the Battle of Bennington, came the intelligence that Howe's fleet had moved into Chesapeake Bay and that Philadelphia must indeed be their objective, as Washington had surmised in the first instance.

Next day the troops began marching back southward to meet this threat. On Sunday, August 24, they paraded through Philadelphia, some ten thousand men with Washington at their head, crossed the Schuylkill by the Middle Ferry at Market Street, and strode away from the threatened city toward the eastern shore of Maryland.

While Washington was establishing his headquarters on Quaker Hill in Wilmington, with most of the army on the high land west of town, Howe was landing 18,000 men at Turkey Point, at the head of Chesapeake Bay. Two days later he marched them to the Head of Elk, eighteen miles from Wilmington, and there issued his "Declaration," which promised pardon to those rebels who were willing to recant. It was, said Washington when he read it, "what we might reasonably expect." It was no different than Howe's previous proclamations, he pointed out, and represented only "another effort to seduce the people to give up their rights, and to encourage our soldiers to desert." [2]

The day before this Declaration was issued, Washington had gone out with a body of cavalry to reconnoiter the British positions, and had encountered a storm so violent that he had to seek shelter overnight at a farmhouse near Gray's Hill—an uneasy residence since he was within range of the enemy's scouts. Gen-

erals Greene, Weedon and Lafayette were with him—a fine bag
of brass if any enterprising British patrol had happened to wan-
der in that direction. It was a circumstance for the "might-have-
been" historians to cherish. Only a mile or two separated the
Commander from capture, an event that might well have meant
the end of the Revolution, for it is inconceivable that the war
could have been won without Washington.

These preliminary maneuvers were followed shortly by the
disastrous Battle of the Brandywine on September 10. Before
the battle, Washington had been staying at the house of Benjamin Ring, a mile east of Chadd's Ford, on Brandywine Creek.
After the defeat, which was decided about three miles to the
north near Birmingham Meeting House, the General, who was
"happy to find the troops in good spirits" and hopeful of com-
pensating another time "for the losses now sustained," lodged
in the stone house of John McIlvain, while his beaten troops
assembled along the Queen's Highway, east of Chester. Next
day they began a short retreat back up to the former camp at
Schuylkill Falls, which they reached on the thirteenth.

Having cleaned their arms and equipped themselves with ammunition, the men waded back across the Schuylkill at Matson's
Ford, now Conshohocken, in water up to their waists, and began moving up the old Lancaster road in an effort to prevent
the British from turning their right flank.

On the way, Washington stopped at the Buck Tavern, nine
miles northwest of Philadelphia, one of the best-known inns of
its day, and later a private house. He moved from there to the
home of Joseph Malin. Two other hostelries noted in Pennsylvania history stood nearby, the Warren and White Horse
taverns.

It was near the latter, on the morning of the sixteenth, that
adversity began to settle down on the Americans once more.
The advancing British ran against the Continental picket line,
300 strong, and sent them flying at the first fire. Then Washington's old enemy, the rain, began to descend, and as it had so

many years ago at Fort Necessity, became such a calamitous downpour that firearms were useless and there was no alternative but retreat. The troops marched five miles north to Yellow Springs; the General lodged three miles away at the Red Lion Tavern, now Lionville. In the retreat, the tents and baggage became separated from the army and the men spent a miserable night. Next day they managed to get eight miles farther—to Warwick Furnace, where guns had been manufactured and repaired (sixty of the army's cannon were cast there in 1776), but now they had to be allowed to rest a day; they could not go on.

It was as far as Washington intended to retreat. On the nineteenth he turned the main body southward again and marched it by way of a village on the Reading road called the Trappe to a camp at Perkiomen Creek. The horrors of that march were reported by one observer en route: "The procession lasted the whole night, and we had numerous visits from officers, wet breast high, who had to march in this condition during the whole night, cold and damp as it was, and to bear hunger and thirst at the same time." [3]

In spite of such forced marching, the British were moving with alarming speed toward the supply depot at Reading, so Washington had to push his men forward once more on the twenty-first to a place four miles from Pottsgrove, later Pottstown, where he made his headquarters in the Potts mansion, which the town's founder, John Potts, had built in 1753. (It afterward became a hotel.) Washington was as much disturbed by his own army's condition as he was by British enterprise. The men were desperately in need of blankets and clothing; Valley Forge was beginning to cast its black shadow.

An exasperating difficulty was added to his woes as he waited at Pottsgrove. It had never been easy for him to obtain proper intelligence of the enemy's movements, but among these Pennsylvanians, "being to a man disaffected" as he put it, he could get none at all. Thus the British managed to get by him on the night of the twenty-third, and immediately began the march on

Philadelphia which he had pushed his troops so hard to prevent. Informing Congress of this melancholy event, he added grimly: "At least one thousand men are barefooted, and have performed the marches in that condition." [4]

Nevertheless, he was determined not to let the enemy have their objective without a fight. He marched on in pursuit, with the aid of Jersey militia reinforcements and the impressment of blankets, shoes, stockings and other clothing from the reluctant residents of Lancaster County. On September 26 he was at Pennybacker's Mills, later Schwenksville, in Montgomery County, where he lodged at the two-story stone house of the owner, Samuel Pennybacker. A week later he had gone as far as Methacton Hill, and from that point on the evening of October 3 his army began its attack on the enemy at Germantown, where, as he wrote in bewilderment, "In the midst of the most promising appearances, when everything gave the most flattering hopes of victory, the troops began suddenly to retreat, and entirely left the field, in spite of every effort that could be made to rally them." [5]

The flight of the Continentals has never been satisfactorily explained, although any number of explanations have been offered. Their terror may be judged by the fact that these men, who had marched all the preceding night with no sleep, and ten miles more on the day of battle, did not stop until they had put twenty miles between them and the British, although they could have halted safely at half that distance.

To enable them to recover from the effects of their panic, Washington decided to "rest and refresh" his men at a temporary camp. As they rested, first at Pennybacker's Mills, General Knox was certain that they were "in the highest spirits, and ardently desire another trial." They marched on October 8 to the Baptist Meeting House in Towamencin Township, on the Sumneytown road near Kulpsville, about twenty-six miles from Philadelphia. In the burial ground of this church were laid to rest General Nash, of North Carolina, and other officers who had been wounded at Germantown and died after the retreat. The General was buried with full military honors on

Thursday morning, the tenth, and afterward Washington returned to his headquarters at the farmhouse of Frederick Wampole, a half mile away.

The march was resumed on October 16, after the pause at Towamencin, and that night the army camped at Worcester, where the Commander-in-Chief established himself at the house of Peter Wentz—like the other Pennsylvania houses, a sturdy, two-story stone building. Here he heard the exhilarating news from the north of Burgoyne's surrender at Saratoga, a stroke of fortune so unexpected that momentarily he came to believe, as he wrote Putnam, that one more such victory would complete the defeat of the British, a belief that was correct except that it was four years from fulfillment.

Meanwhile, he learned that the British had evacuated Germantown and moved their defenses to the perimeter of Philadelphia itself, which emboldened him to take his own forces down to Whitpain Township, within fifteen miles of the city. He lived here at James Morris' house, a mile west of the present town of Ambler. This house had been built in 1736 by Abraham Dawes, Mrs. Morris' father, and later came to be called Dawesfield.

After a week and a half at Whitpain, he moved two miles closer to the city, to Whitemarsh. His headquarters here was a baronial hall belonging to George Emlen, at the edge of a wet meadow, with a splendid valley stretching away at one side and Camp Hill on the other. The meadow was so wet at the time that, when the guards retired, the men had to march almost breast-high in water.

Three days after he was installed here, on November 5, Washington was startled from his morning's work by a cannonading below on the Delaware. With some of his staff officers, he rode to Germantown and climbed to the top of a house there, but when he tried to discover the source of the pounding guns which banged away until afternoon, a haze and thick clouds of smoke hid everything except the masts of two unidentified vessels. If he could have seen, it would not have cheered him. The cannonade was a grossly unequal battle be-

tween a 64-gun British warship, the *Somerset,* with a smaller
companion, pitted against some Continental row-gallies, aided
by a two-gun battery.

At Whitemarsh, Washington was somewhat embarrassed by
the lack of his baggage, which had not caught up since the army
left Schuylkill Falls in September, but he contrived to entertain some of his officers every day at three o'clock dinner. When
he was not entertaining, he had some melancholy reflections to
dwell upon in the dreary November days. The first intimation
of the Conway affair had reached him, placing him in possession of the humiliating knowledge that there were high-ranking
officers in his own army who were anxious to displace him. He
had no doubt that there were others—undoubtedly some in Congress and God knew how many among the civilian population
—who were drawing unflattering comparisons between General
Gates's successes in the North and his own defeats in Delaware
and Pennsylvania. They would not know, or care, that at no
time since Howe's landing had he been able to muster an equal
force, while at the same time, as he pointed out in a letter to
Patrick Henry, the New England states and New York had
been so anxious to defeat Burgoyne that they had poured in to
Gates's support fourteen thousand militia, all well armed and
provisioned. The contrast was a sorry one. In his case, his men
were too few and too destitute, and too handicapped by a hostile countryside which gave every advantage to the already
overwhelming superiority of the enemy. While Gates was enjoying his triumph, Washington was offering a reward of ten
dollars to any soldier who could produce the best substitute
for shoes made from rawhides.

This was the prelude, the state of mind, in which Washington and his army approached the ordeal of Valley Forge. It
could scarcely have been a worse preparation. But as late as
November 24 Washington still contemplated an attack on Philadelphia; however, his officers voted eleven to four against it in
a council of war. He knew that he was expected by everyone
to make the attack, and his popularity would not be enhanced

by a withdrawal, but another defeat would be far more damaging. He surveyed the enemy's fortifications for himself, and realized that they were even stronger than he had been led to believe. One of the engineers remarked that, in his opinion, a force of only five thousand men behind those works could hold off an army of any size. Clearly it would be suicidal to attempt an attack. On November 30, he called a council of war to decide on a place for winter quarters, and when the officers could not arrive at a decision, he decided for them: Valley Forge.

Howe gave them a parting salute. He moved his army out of the city on the night of December 4 and arrayed them on Chestnut Hill the following morning. For three days there was marching and countermarching, and a few hot skirmishes between advanced lines and flanking parties, but in the end Howe evidently concluded that the pleasures of the winter in Philadelphia were preferable to doubtful adventures in the hills outside it, and he marched back to the city again on the afternoon of December 8.

As the American army proceeded toward its winter quarters, it had still another brush with the enemy: it encountered a British foraging party four thousand strong under Cornwallis, which momentarily prevented the army from crossing the Schuylkill at Matson's Ford and compelled the soldiers to go over instead at Swede's Ford, now Morristown, three miles farther up the river.

With this hazard behind it, the army reached a place called Gulf Mill on December 13. The mill itself, a large stone structure, stood at the intersection of the Gulf road with Gulf Creek. Where this creek had cut through Gulf Hill, a deep and gloomy depression, it was known as "the Gulf." The soldiers were not overjoyed by it. One of them wrote that the place seemed "well adapted by its situation to keep us from the pleasure and enjoyments of this world, or being conversant with anybody in it." [6]

According to tradition, Washington made his headquarters about a mile north of the mill in a house which was one of the notable buildings of its time, Walnut Grove, the home of Lieutenant Colonel Isaac Hughes, of the Pennsylvania militia. It had been built by his father, who had had the misfortune to be a stamp officer.

The army camped at the Gulf for nearly a week while the exact location of the quarters was being determined at Valley Forge, six or seven miles way. John Laurens wrote to his brother Henry: "Our truly republican General has declared to his officers that he will set the example of passing the winter in a hut himself. . . ." But this was probably camp gossip. No one expected Washington to share the lot of the soldiers, truly republican or not, and it would have been impractical for him to do so. The General had his "family" to think of; it was essential to the business of conducting a headquarters to have them at hand. Some of the wives could be expected, too, including Martha. No hut could properly have contained so many people of both sexes, and left room for the work of running a war, which Washington had to perform every day.

The day before the army left the Gulf was the one set apart by Congress that year as Thanksgiving. It could not have come at a more apt time. On the eve of entering Valley Forge, the army stayed in its quarters and the chaplains went among the corps and brigades, leading them in prayer.* Next day they began the march, and on the day after, December 20, they were at their winter destination.

Washington did everything for his soldiers that careful advance planning could provide, and one must admire the resourceful way he approached so formidable a problem. The site itself was the best available under the circumstances. It was a triangular piece of ground, bounded by Valley Creek, the Schuylkill and an irregular range of hills. A minimum amount of fortifying on the hills and on the bluffs overlooking the rivers

---

* There were some who felt the need of it. Lieutenant Colonel Henry Dearborn wrote in his diary that December 18: "This is Thanksgiving Day, but God knows we have very little to keep it with, this being the third day we have been without flour or bread, and are living on a high, uncultivated hill, in huts and tents, lying on the cold ground. Upon the whole I think all we have to be thankful for is that we are alive and not in the grave with many of our friends."

would make his position strong defensively; heavy timber surrounding the site would produce both fuel and logs to build huts; and the two streams assured him of a plentiful water supply. The major disadvantage was the result of British maneuvering in September: in their operations along the Schuylkill, they had done away with everything useful in sight. A few dwellings and farmhouses remained; everything the troops needed except for the natural facilities noted would have to be supplied, and supply was the rock on which the Continental Army was constantly foundering.

The first and most pressing need was shelter. The General had planned this operation too. The troops were given exact directions for building the huts; every regiment was divided into units of twelve, each equipped with the proper tools to build a hut for that number of men. To spur the lazy and the laggards, Washington offered a prize of twelve dollars to the unit in each regiment which built its hut quickest and best, and another hundred to the man, whether officer or soldier, who could devise a cheaper and more quickly produced covering for the huts.

While the huts were building, the "truly republican General" did live among the men in his marquee, but soon he found a house for his headquarters in the village. It was a two-story stone affair belonging to Isaac Potts. One day it would be a national shrine, visited by generations of reverent Americans. At the moment it was the best of a bad bargain, being much too small to accommodate the General and his staff as it was accustomed to being accommodated. The household was large that winter—nine aides to begin with, including Major Gibbs, and ten before the season was over, with the arrival of Dr. James McHenry.

In the conventional pictures of Valley Forge evoked by imaginative paintings and uninformed politicians, the impression is of men huddled about fires in deep snow driven by blustering winds. The reality was bad enough, but it took a somewhat different form. There was little snow that winter—no more than four inches in the first weeks—and the army had endured, and would endure, much harder weather. Rain was the worst part of the climate. It was cold and persistent, so persistent that it became a grim joke. Two soldiers meeting in it would say:

"Good morning, brother soldier, how are you?"

"All wet, thank'e; hope you are so." [7]

Otherwise the discomforts, if so mild a word could be used, were familiar states of wretchedness to most of the men. They were more or less used to ragged, inadequate clothing, sleeping without blankets on the cold, hard floors of huts, and foul weather. At Valley Forge there were exaggerations of these conditions—more actual nakedness, and often no sleeping protection whatever. But the one lack that would be remembered most by the Continentals when they looked back on Valley Forge was their gnawing hunger and the daily threat of starvation. It was their chief complaint; everything else could be endured. It was their General's chief complaint, too, in nearly every letter he wrote to Congress, but the situation never improved to a point of comfort, and most of the time it bordered on desperation.

Provisions ran out entirely just before Christmas, and for a time there was no food at all for some of the men. Washington heard a miserable chant sounding from tent to tent, beating in the still December air with a sullen cadence: "No meat, no meat."

Anyone who may still doubt the incredible strength of Washington's character has only to consider a commander in such a situation, with such cries in his ears, convinced that unless something were not done immediately his army could only "starve, dissolve or disperse"—and then to be handed a memorial from the Pennsylvania Assembly, which had contributed as much to these conditions as any political agency, complaining about his retirement to winter quarters and insisting on a campaign.

"I can assure those gentlemen," Washington wrote to Congress with infinite patience, "that it is a much easier and less distressing thing to draw remonstrances in a comfortable room by a good fireside, than to occupy a cold, bleak hill, and sleep under frost and snow, without clothes or blankets. However, although they seem to have little feeling for the naked and distressed soldiers, I feel superabundantly for them, and from my soul I pity those miseries which it is neither in my power to relieve or prevent."

That was the worst of the matter from Washington's standpoint—that he could not relieve or prevent the suffering about him, beyond his exhortations to Congress. But whatever it cost him in terrible daily anxiety, the General presented his customary austere, unruffled front to the world. In the middle of February, when the ordeal was at its worst, and Washington had written to Governor Clinton that his troops were "naked and starving," a visitor from abroad found the Commander an inspiring sight.

Peter S. du Ponceau, the secretary of Baron Steuben, who had arrived on February 23 with that gentleman, recorded his first impression: "I could not keep my eyes from that imposing countenance—grave, yet not severe; affable, without familiarity. Its predominant expression was calm dignity, through which you could trace the strong feelings of the patriot, and discern the father as well as the commander of his soldiers. I have never seen a picture that represents him to me as I saw him at Valley Forge, and during the campaigns in which I had the honor to follow him. Perhaps that expression was beyond the skill of the painter; but while I live it will remain impressed on my memory. . . ."

To the Baron, a Prussian officer called in to be Inspector General of the army, the appearance of the troops he was supposed to discipline was shocking. "The arms at Valley Forge were in a horrible condition, covered with rust, half of them without bayonets, many from which a single shot could not be fired," he wrote soon after his arrival. "The pouches were quite as bad as the arms. A great many of the men had tin boxes instead of pouches, others had cow-horns; and muskets, carbines, fowling-pieces and rifles were to be seen in the same company. The description of the dress is most easily given. The men were literally naked, some of them in the fullest extent of the word. The officers who had coats, had them of every color and make. I saw officers, at a grand parade at Valley Forge, mounting guard in a sort of dressing gown, made of an old blanket or woolen bedcover. With regard to their military discipline, I may safely say no such thing existed."

Yet here was Martha, arriving in camp on February 10, and reporting cheerfully to Mrs. Mercy Warren that she had found the General very well. "Officers and men are chiefly in huts," she wrote, "which they say is tolerably comfortable; the army are as healthy as can well be expected in general. The General's apartment is very small; he has had a log cabin built to dine in, which has made our quarters much more tolerable than they were at first."

The entertainments began at once, and though they may have been spartan by comparison with those in other headquarters, they were far from the misery in the valley. Lady Stirling and her daughter were there, so were the wives of some of the other generals; and social life was so much as usual that General Knox and his wife were gossiping in their letters about whether Nathanael Greene and his lady were really getting on. A few young ladies were bold enough to visit the camp and enjoy the company of the aides. There were dinners and tea drinkings and frequent evening affairs, and if the house was so crowded that Alexander Hamilton had to sleep in a hall bedroom and the Potts family were probably quartered in the attic over the kitchen, it was still a comfortable and well-appointed dwelling for the times. The one-story log addition to the kitchen, which was used as an extra dining room and is said to have been Martha's suggestion, helped greatly to relieve that portion of the household's hospitality.

In the little room he used for an office, Washington drew up a detailed fifty-page plan for a new system of administering the army. It described the deplorable condition of the troops in detail and outlined the changes and improvements he thought essential. For three months a six-man committee from Congress stayed in camp and worked on this plan with Washington, holding its sessions two and a half miles away at William Moore's house, Moore Hall. By the time the committee had satisfied itself, and the plan had been approved by Congress, the Valley Forge crisis was over. Valuable as the committee's work may have been for the future, it still appears inexplicable that men of their ability and discernment (the committee included such members as Gouverneur Morris and Joseph Reed) could not have done more to meet the present crisis.

When he was not meeting with this committee, or dealing with the daily problem of keeping the army together, Washington received visitors and found what satisfactions he could in the social life Martha arranged for him. A glimpse of his daily routine in early April is provided by one of four Quaker ladies who waited on him April 6 for permission to pass to Yorktown, Pennsylvania, where they were seeking the release of some imprisoned friends.

"Arrived at headquarters at about half past one," the lady records. "We requested an audience with the General, and sat with his wife (a sociable, pretty kind of woman) until he came in. A number of officers were there who were very complaisant, Tench Tilghman among the rest. It was not long before G. Washington came, and discoursed with us freely, but not so long as we could have wished, as dinner was served, to which he invited us. There were fifteen officers, besides the General and his wife, General Greene and General Lee. We had an elegant dinner, which was soon over, when we went out with the General's wife, up to her chamber—and saw no more of him. He told us he could do nothing in our business further than granting us a pass to Lancaster, which he did. . . ."[8]

Another visitor, arriving for the day on the morning of April 16, had some more pointed observations to make: "I spent a day in the camp, attending the reviews and examining the condition and situation of the army. My heart bled at the recital of their sufferings and privations the past winter. Exalted virtue and patriotism, and the strong attachment of the officers to General Washington, only held the army together. The poor soldiers were half naked, and had been half starved, having been compelled for weeks to subsist on simple flour alone, and this too in a land almost literally flowing with milk and honey. Oh, these detestable Tories! I saw Washington on horseback, attended by his aides passing through the camp." [9]

By that time, however, the nightmare of the winter was over and even this tattered army had begun to bloom again. The General found shad and sprouts on his table, and he was busy with plans for a new campaign. The last day of April may have found him thinking nostalgically of the green beauty of Mount Vernon, where only four years before, to the day, he had sat down to dinner without a single guest present, and enjoyed the sunset from the portico with Martha. This April 30 of 1778 had begun as drably as the other days of that winter and spring when the glorious news came: France had recognized the independence of the colonies, and the prospective alliance between the two countries meant that Americans would not have to fight for freedom alone.

A wave of hope and rejoicing swept over the Valley Forge camp. Washington immediately authorized a celebration for May 7, then went out in a nearby field and played a game of wickets with some of the younger officers.

The festivities on the seventh were in vivid contrast to every other occurrence in that miserable camp. At nine in the morning, Washington, his officers and their wives and suites went to the religious services of the Jersey Brigade. At half past eleven, they reviewed the army, after which Washington entertained at a huge dinner for, by one estimate, as many as 1500 people. This "collation" was preceded by an elaborate *feu de joie*, "conducted with great judgment and regularity," as one observer wrote home to a friend, continuing his description: "The gradual progression of the sound from the discharge of cannon and musketry, swelling and rebounding from the neighboring hills and gently sweeping along the Schuylkill, with the intermingled huzzas—to long live the King of France—long live the friendly European powers, and long live the American states, composed a military music more agreeable to a soldier's ear than the most finished pieces of your favorite Handel. The *feu de joie* being over, and the troops marched back to their different quarters, the officers came forward to the entertainment provided by His Excellency.

". . . The amphitheatre looked elegant. The outer seats for the officers were covered with tent canvas stretched out upon poles; and the tables in the center shaded by elegant markees [sic], raised high, and arranged in a very striking and agreeable style. An excellent band of music attended during the entertainment, but the feast was still more animated by the discourse and behavior of His Excellency to the officers and the gentlemen in the country who were present. . . . Mrs. Washington, the Countess of Stirling, Lady Kitty her daughter, Mrs. Greene and a number of other ladies favored the feast with their company, among whom good humor and the graces were contending for pre-eminence. The wine circulated in the most genial manner—to the King of France—the friendly European powers—the American states—the Honorable Congress, and other toasts of a similar nature, descriptive of the spirit of freemen."[10]

One guest described the menu as a "profusion of fat meat, strong wine and other liquors," but it must have been relished by a good many who had not recently been in the habit of feasting. The company did not break up until six o'clock in the evening, when Washington got up to return to his headquarters. "When the General took his leave," another guest reported, "there was a universal clap, with loud huzzas, which continued till he had proceeded a quarter of a mile, during which time there were a thousand hats tossed in the air. His

Excellency turned round with his retinue, and huzzaed several times."

The winter at Valley Forge ended officially on Friday, June 19. The British had evacuated Philadelphia the day before and marched northward; now Washington prepared to follow them. There were several stops before they left Pennsylvania behind, notably at Doylestown, which was then hardly more than a crossroads, about ten miles from Coryell's Ferry on the Delaware, later Newhope. Rain, the perennial companion, fell on the troops here and during the march to the Ferry, but one supposes they did not mind it as much as usual, because they were leaving Valley Forge behind them at last.

Except for the time he spent in Philadelphia, and quick marches through the state, notably to Yorktown, Virginia, Washington spent little more time in Pennsylvania. One other visit, however, is worth recording.

[1782]    In July 1782, having spent the winter in Philadelphia after the decision at Yorktown, Washington was on his way back to headquarters at Newburgh when he deviated somewhat from his usual course to stop at the Moravian town of Bethlehem, whose Bach festival is now one of the glories of the American musical scene. He had stayed overnight on the twenty-fourth in Pottsgrove, with its memories of the prelude to Valley Forge; the next day he arrived quietly in Bethlehem, accompanied only by two aides, and stopped at the Sun Inn. There Brother Ettwein, the Moravian leader, and others of the brethren came to pay their respects. After dinner Washington inspected the choir houses and points of interest, and in the evening went to the services, which Brother Ettwein conducted in English for the General's benefit. The text was from II Corinthians 6:4: "In all things approving ourselves as the ministers of God," and as the old Moravian Archives tell this story, "the choir rendered some fine music both at the beginning and at the close. The General manifested much friend-liness, and the pleasure and satisfaction which the visit afforded him were clearly to be inferred from his utterances." *

Early the next day he journeyed to Easton, accompanied by Brother Ettwein, who went on ahead to Hope, the next stop, to make preparations for his entertainment. At Hope, twenty miles northeast of Easton, Washington and his aides dined on the twenty-sixth, and then walked about this village which the Moravians had founded in 1769. That day they rode eighteen miles farther, probably to Sussex Court House, now Newton.

Where else he may have stopped before he left the state is not recorded, and what his thoughts may have been as he passed near his Valley Forge quarters on the way to Bethlehem, he did not disclose. He visited Valley Forge later, in happier times, but he did not dwell on the memories it must have brought back. That was not his habit.

He could not erase those memories, however, and the images they evoked appeared in his correspondence long after the war was over—the soldier running from hut to hut with a ragged blanket to cover his nakedness, the six days when there was no meat, and the other days when there was no food at all. These things he could not forget.

---

* Lafayette also had reason to recall Bethlehem with pleasure. It was there, in the autumn of 1777, that Liesel Beckel, "the fair Moravian sister," nursed him back to health from the wound he sustained on the Brandywine.

Chapter 5

Maryland and Virginia


"About noon," wrote General Heath on Sunday, August 19, 1781, "His Excellency Gen. Washington left the army, setting his face towards his native State, in full confidence, to use his own words, 'with a common blessing,' of capturing Lord Cornwallis and his army."

Thus began the story of a march and a battle, the military climax of the Revolution, in which Washington began by retracing many of the roads he had traveled earlier, and ended by returning for the first time to the tidewater country he loved.

There had been no lack of warfare in the Southern Department, but other Continental commanders had fought it. Washington had entrusted the task of defending Virginia and her neighbors to other men, while he confined his part of the grand operations to the arc encompassing vital New York and Philadelphia. Important as those maneuvers had been in contributing to the war's final outcome, it was nevertheless ironic that the two decisive battles occurred elsewhere, at Saratoga and Yorktown.


[1781]    It is unlikely that the General was concerned with where on the map the struggle would be ended. But there may have been some human considerations in his mind that autumn of 1781, as he turned his face toward home. It must have meant something to him, as Commander-in-Chief, to confront the main body of the enemy at last with an army more nearly equal in numbers and equipment. To this could be added the belated fulfillment of a hope long deferred. The plans conceived with the French at Hartford and Wethersfield and Newport, the tantalizing months of agonized waiting to be certain of the

178

French fleet, the kingpin in the joint plan—these anxieties could now be put aside. The French and American armies had joined at Phillipsburg, New York, twelve miles from Kingsbridge; the French fleet was on its way to the Chesapeake. The jaws of the trap were ready to close by land and sea on Cornwallis. All that remained was to spring it.

On the day Washington set his face toward Virginia "in full confidence," both armies began to move toward the Hudson and the crossing at King's Ferry. The American column marched by way of Sing Sing, through the neighborhood of the present Ossining and Harmon, while the French traveled by way of Northcastle, Crompond and Pinesbridge.

The eastern terminus of King's Ferry was Verplanck's Point, eight miles below Peekskill. The Americans arrived first about ten o'clock on the morning of August 20, and began to cross at once. The General himself crossed and made his headquarters about two and a half miles below Stony Point, the ferry's western terminus, in the house of Joshua Hett Smith. It was a place of painful associations for him, because it was in these rooms that Arnold and Major André had spun their disastrous plot. If the memory disturbed him, however, Washington made no mention of it in his journal or letters. Rather, it appeared, he enjoyed the comforts of this elegant mansion, formally Belmont, better known in the neighborhood as "Smith's White House."[1] Before Arnold's exposure, Washington had often enjoyed the hospitality of its owner.

It was a location ideal for supervising the long, complicated task of getting the armies across the river, and for sheer scenic splendor it could hardly be improved upon. The house, a square, two-story affair with wooden wings, stood on a ridge overlooking the Hudson, on the west side of the road. To the south, across the village of Haverstraw, three miles below, Washington could see High Tor. A later generation would think of it as the place where Burgess Meredith sat on a steam shovel and tossed off Maxwell Anderson's poetry in the play named for the mountain; to Washington it was the eminence at whose foot Arnold met André. He could see, too, the slim reach of Teller's Point, off which the British ship *Vulture* had lain to receive the plotters. There was the rounded cup of Haverstraw Bay, and the long sweep of the river north to Seylmaker's Reach. By a peculiarity of the terrain, Washington could look northward and see the river apparently flow out of sight into the mountains, and leave no trace of its course among the peaks.

Inside, Joshua Smith's house had a spacious air, though the place had lost some of its grandeur during the war. One of its marble mantelpieces was in the style of the costly trimmings in the Philipse manor house, and as in that noteworthy residence, it had high ceilings of a kind not common in colonial architecture. Everywhere the visitor gazed he saw evidences of good taste. To Washington, it must have been a reminder of the Virginia mansions, although these Northern establishments could hardly be compared with the stately Georgian dwellings of the James River planters.

Claude Blanchard, the French Commissary, came to the Smith house headquarters on August 21 and had tea with the General. Four days later he saw Washington again at the ferry, where a pavilion had been provided for him so that he could watch the progress of the crossing. "He seemed," so Blanchard surmised, ". . . to see a better destiny arise, when at this period of the war, exhausted, destitute of resources, he needed a great success which might revive courage and hope."

The pavilion or marquee, from which the General watched his troops flowing across the stream, had been built for him by the French officers at Verplanck's Point, on the eastern side. Gazing westward, he could see the rude thrust of Stony Point into the Hudson, its giant boulders strewn about like a giant's marbles, left there by the continental advance of the inexorable ice, millions of years before. If George had ever succeeded in making his trip to Europe, he would have seen boulders like these on the shore of Lake Geneva, where the alpine glaciers had pushed them.

King's Ferry had been the scene of innumerable passages,

but the spectacle Washington witnessed those bright August days in 1781 must have surpassed them all. Hour after hour the boats crossed and recrossed, making a continuous vivid line from Fort Lafayette on the east side to the beach below the guns of Stony Point, high above on the west. The late summer sun glinted off the water, throwing sharp spears of light against the arms and uniforms of the two nations. The French made a brave splash of color against mountains and water; the Americans were drab by comparison but they had won the respect of the French nobility, the officers who rode beside them and whose names were a social register of old French families.

By the twenty-fifth, the crossing was completed. In the afternoon, Washington left the Ferry and joined the advance right column at Ramapo, where it was encamped for the night. He proposed to stay in front of the troops, removing any obstacles that might obstruct their advance, which he desired to be as fast as possible.[2]

To hide his intentions from the British, for a time at least, Washington contrived the first stage of the march to have the appearance of a feint toward New York. Thus his men were to advance in three columns, two American and one French, by separate routes to a reunion at Trenton. The prospect before them was a hundred and thirty miles of gradual descent from the peaks of the Hudson Highlands to the New Jersey plains and the major pivot point of the march, Philadelphia.

For Washington the road led first to Benson's Tavern, on a plateau overlooking the river within sight of Teller's Point, then by familiar roads past former headquarters—Suffern's, the Hopper house, through wild, beautiful country and along roads shaded by oaks, elms, chestnuts, hemlocks, larches and a dozen other varieties. Here was the Pompton Plains, and the lush countryside around it, in which the French officers delighted, making friendly overtures to the prosperous Dutch settlers along the way.

As they inspected the country around Totawa Falls, these officers made quick comparisons with their own land. The

American soil needed manuring and was not as good as the best French soil, they thought. But they were enchanted with the rich farms, the great herds of cattle, the endless fruit. They sampled the buckwheat and maize of the region and found it good. One officer was astonished by the non-existence of gardens and walls; he seldom saw a fence.

The inhabitants welcomed the French. Drawn by understandable impulses, the women of the Jersey countryside brought provisions to the French encampments in their own wagons, dressing themselves to the nines for the occasion.

To the officers, the progress through New Jersey was as fresh and exciting as it was an old story to Washington. They wrote of the heavy stand of timber between Somerset and Princeton, and they were charmed with the little college town whose sixty houses numbered only ten more than the students in its college. Trenton, they found, had a hundred houses. Here the armies crossed the Delaware; ferryboats carried the troops, while the wagons forded the river, which reminded the visitors of the Loire at home. From the other side, the road was broad and comparatively straight to Philadelphia, along the flatlands of the riverbank. The French thought Burlington a handsome town, and Bristol a pretty little place of forty or fifty houses. Nearly all of them remarked on the famous Red Lion Tavern, sixteen miles from Philadelphia.

The passage of the troops through that city excited everyone in the placid town except, one supposes, the Quakers. A newspaper reported the event as follows:

"On Thursday, the 30th of August, at one o'clock in the afternoon, His Excellency the Commander-in-Chief of the American armies, accompanied by the Generals Rochambeau and Chastellux, with their respective suites, arrived in this city. The General was received by the militia light horse in the suburbs, and escorted into the town; he stopped at the City Tavern and received the visit of several gentlemen: from thence he proceeded to the house of the Superintendent of Finance (Robert Morris), where he now has his headquarters.

About three o'clock he went up to the State House and paid his respects to Congress. He then returned to the Superintendent's, where His Excellency the President of Congress (Thomas M'Kean) with the Generals before mentioned, General Knox, General Sullivan, and several other gentlemen, had the pleasure of dining with him. After dinner some vessels belonging to this port, and those lying in the stream fired salutes to the different toasts which were drank. In the evening the city was illuminated, and His Excellency walked through some of the principal streets, attended by a numerous concourse of people, eagerly pressing to see their beloved General." [3]

Speaking of the dinner in his house on South Front Street, Robert Morris notes that the toasts were numerous, ". . . The United States, His Most Christian Majesty, His Catholic Majesty, The United Provinces, The Allied Armies, Count de Grasse's speedy arrival, &c. &c."

On September 3, the French passed in review as the city watched. A sharp-eyed reporter for the *Pennsylvania Packet* did not fail to note that Washington and Rochambeau stood uncovered, while the President of Congress, upholding that body's republican dignity, would not take off his hat. On the following night, the French minister, Monsieur de la Luzerne, entertained the generals and members of Congress at a dinner in his house on the north side of Chestnut Street, between Sixth and Seventh streets.

It must have seemed at times to Washington that the war was over, so ready was everyone to entertain him, as though no major military operation portended which demanded speed and concentration. While the entertainments were still going on, he left Philadelphia on September 5 and set off for Head of Elk, that curiously named important transportation point, near present-day Elkton, Maryland. Head of Elk was the "head" of navigation on Elk River, an estuary of Chesapeake Bay stretching northeast to within forty miles of Philadelphia.

He had seldom made a more anxious journey. Over him there hung a question unanswered: Had the French fleet really landed, or was it made of phantom ships, as it so often seemed, which were always promised or on the way, yet never furled their sails in an American harbor? Washington remembered, too, the last time he had marched troops down this road to Head of Elk. Then he had been on his way to meet Clinton's forces, and the effort had ended in the defeat at the Brandywine. Now here he was again, cursed as always with insufficient equipment and inadequate transport, and if the French fleet did not arrive, with its troops and guns and blockading power, a far worse disaster could result.

He rode fast, in a mood more somber as the miles clattered off. Three miles past Chester he sighted a horseman flying down the road toward him, and he saw that it was an express. Here was the news, good or bad.

It was news that gave Washington what was perhaps his happiest moment of the Revolution. Admiral de Grasse had arrived in the Chesapeake with twenty-eight ships and three thousand troops. He had, it appeared, received Washington's letter to him, with the details of allied movements, present and projected, as the fleet lay off Cape Henry, and had immediately dispatched a reply by Captain de la Laune, of the cutter *Serpent*, who took the pouch up the bay to Baltimore. De la Laune arrived in that city at 1 P.M. on September 4. By six o'clock, General Mordecai Gist had redispatched the message, with a covering letter of his own, by an express who was told to ride day and night. He reached Washington sometime during the early afternoon of the fifth.

With the virtual certainty that the plan to trap Cornwallis was on the verge of being executed, and all the means were at last to hand, the General was transformed as few had ever seen him. He turned around and rode back to Chester, where Rochambeau, who had been coming down the Delaware on a boat, inspecting the river defenses, was expected to land shortly. He could not wait to tell his fellow commander the glorious news. "I have never seen a man moved by a greater or more sincere joy than was General Washington," the Duc de Lauzun wrote afterward in his memoirs. The Count de Deux Ponts recalled that the General, "cold by nature," was so transported that "his features, his countenance, his manner immediately changed. He threw off his character as arbiter of North America, and was for a moment content with that of a citizen, happy in the good fortune of his country. A child, whose wishes had been satisfied, could not have experienced a more lively sensation of pleasure, and I think I am honoring the feelings of this rare man in seeking to describe them in all their vivacity."

Rochambeau must certainly have been astonished by the transformation, if indeed it was that marked. As his vessel approached the wharf, he saw Washington waiting for him, his hat off in one hand, his handkerchief clutched in the other, waving his arms like a man possessed. So far was he from his customary dignity that, when the French leader stepped ashore, Washington performed a Gallic gesture by embracing him.

After a brief but ecstatic celebration, the march was resumed. Now Washington was so eager to reach Mount Vernon, which he had not seen for six years and four months, that he rapidly outstripped his French companions, who chose not to try to maintain the pace. Apparently the General wanted to have a day to himself on the plantation before the French officers arrived to be his guests.

He left Head of Elk on September 8. Mount Vernon was one hundred and twenty miles away. At Baltimore the exasperating delays of ceremony awaited him. Captain Nicholas Moore's Light Dragoon militia were waiting to escort him into town, and the artillery companies had their cannon ready for salutes. There was no escaping. He stayed the night at the Fountain Inn, and although he had ridden sixty miles that day and had an equal distance to go the following day, he had to receive the citizens who called to wish him well. As usual, the city was illuminated in his honor.

Although it was Sunday morning, Washington did not bother to attend church next day. He was in the saddle early and, with a single aide to accompany him, set out for Mount

Vernon. As he rode the highways he knew so well, he viewed them with a cold military eye and saw that they would have to be repaired if he were to get his forces over them without an undue number of breakdowns. Sand and mud would be the enemies that must be defeated before he got to Cornwallis. To-day, fortunately, the sun cast a warm September glow on the land, and before it set at six-twenty, he dismounted at last before the portico of Mount Vernon.

He had little space to enjoy its pleasures. By dinnertime on the tenth, Rochambeau and his staff and Washington's own family had arrived, filling Mount Vernon with a large company of guests who would appreciate the sumptuous table that the plantation was able to set even in wartime. De Chastellux arrived on the eleventh. Jonathan Trumbull, Jr., the young New Englander in Washington's suite who had never seen a Southern plantation before, summed it up: "A numerous family now present. All accommodated. An elegant seat and situation, great appearance of opulence and real exhibitions of hospitality and princely entertainment."

Undoubtedly everyone would have liked to stay on to enjoy these delights, but Cornwallis would not wait if he scented what was in store for him. On the morning of the twelfth, Washington's servants left Mount Vernon at 5 A.M., instructed to go ahead and provide forage for the horses along the route, and to engage quarters in Fredericksburg for the party. Washington was not far behind his servants.

Like a stroke of lightning, an express brought news to him on the road, between Colchester and Dumfries, that turned the world over again. It was incredible, but there was the message. De Grasse, it said, had discovered that the British fleet was lying off the Virginia Capes, had sought them out, engaged them, and the contesting vessels had disappeared from the sight of land lookouts. The outcome of the battle was in doubt until they reappeared. Gloom enveloped Washington, as it had on the way to Chester. He dared not let himself think what would happen if the British fleet reappeared over the horizon, master of the sea.

The cavalcade rested on the night of the twelfth in Fredericksburg, and probably at Hanover Court House the following night. Now they rode by farms belonging to the Custises, all familiar, loved territory to Washington, and approaching Williamsburg, he knew that he would again see Lafayette and other old comrades. But the shadow of uncertainty hung blackly over him as they neared the encampment of the armies.

Only Rochambeau and a few staff officers had been able to keep Washington's hard pace; the others in the party, most of them much younger men, were constantly astonished to find the "old man" outstripping them in the saddle. But twelve, including the two generals, remained as they rode through the encampment of the Virginia militia. At the French camp, he was received and embraced by Lafayette, who headed a welcoming party. There was a rolling of drums and the booming of a twenty-one-gun salute. As he rode into the ranks of the troops waiting for him, the troops of his own army, it was impossible to think entirely of De Grasse and his fate. These were faces well known to him—Lafayette's light infantry, the Pennsylvania Brigade, and the others who had endured. As Freeman remarks, he rode on, "doubtless with infinitely more emotion than he permitted himself to show."

Dinner that night was joyful in spite of everything. The food was good, the company most congenial, and the band of General Saint-Simon, commander of the French forces De Grasse had landed, played the dinner music. One of the selections was a quartet from Grétry's *Lucille*, which in the opera praises family unity. There was a spirit at the table of utmost cordiality and good cheer between the French and the Americans.

Sometime during the night, or perhaps the next morning, Washington's last doubt was dispelled. De Grasse sent a dispatch, reporting that he had returned with a triumph that was reassuring if not complete. He had captured two frigates, and the British had broken off the engagement.

For his headquarters in Williamsburg, Washington chose the Wythe house, that gem of colonial elegance which shines so brightly in the Restoration today. From this house, Washington set out on Monday, September 17, to visit Admiral de Grasse—to meet at last the man on whom his hopes had rested for so long, and who had begun to seem more legendary than real. The General describes the trip in his journal:

"In company with the Count de Rochambeau, the Chevalier Chastellux, Generals Knox and Duportail, I set out for the interview with the Admiral, and arrived on board the *Ville de Paris* (off Cape Henry) the next day by noon, and having settled most points with him to my satisfaction except not obtaining an assurance of sending ships above York—and one that he could not continue his fleet on this station longer than the first of November, I embarked on board the *Queen Charlotte* (the vessel I went down in), but by hard blowing and contrary winds, did not reach Williamsburg again till the twenty-second."

So ended Washington's sea voyage, the second one of his life—except for two fishing trips in the presidential years, the only other such excursion he made after the youthful voyage to Barbados.

His troubles with De Grasse were not yet over. There was another anxious period when it seemed that the elusive Admiral was about to cruise off again to engage the British fleet, but his own officers decided against it in a council of war. Toward the end of September the plan of operation against Cornwallis was at last settled in detail, the ships and troops were in position, and on September 28 the order for the general advance was given.

Camping that night only a mile from the enemy, the armies and the generals alike slept under the trees, but there is little reason to believe in the hardy Washington legend which asserts, as Irving perpetuated it, that the General "slept under a mulberry-tree, the root serving for a pillow." Freeman does not dignify this tradition by denying it, but he locates headquarters with as much exactness as possible "on the present line between York and Warwick Counties, about 1060 yards northwest of the junction of Jones's and Great Run." The site was level ground on the west side of Jones's Run, with a spring nearby and an old field lying before it. Rochambeau pitched his tents about five hundred yards away, and there is no reason to believe that Washington's own marquee was not raised for his comfort, in spite of Irving's assertion that "Washington and his staff bivouacked on the ground in the open air. . . ." Freeman states it correctly: "The General, his staff and doubtless most of the senior officers bivouacked under the trees," but with the clear implication that they were, as usual, in tents.

In any event, it was from his position on Jones's Run, possibly in a farmhouse nearby, that Washington directed the concentration of forces which slowly, inexorably, squeezed Cornwallis' army into submission in the early weeks of October, until on the seventeenth the besieged lord sat down and wrote the historic document for which Washington had waited so long. With one simple sentence the ordeal, for all practical purposes was over: "Sir, I propose a cessation of hostilities for twenty-four hours, and that two officers may be appointed by each side, to meet at Mr. Moore's house, to settle terms for the surrender of the posts at York and Gloucester."

Now came the final act of the military drama, that surrender scene which has been preserved in a painting nearly as erroneous as the depiction of the Delaware crossing, though not so famous.[4] But then, the reality of that October 19 called for a photographer, not a painter. It is a matter for regret that some of Henry Luce's better men were not on hand to record what must have been one of the most moving scenes in American history.

Down the shameful surrender road, lined on one side by French troops and on the other by the Continental Army and the militia, the defeated British troops were to march. The people had come to see them, people from miles around, peering over the heads of the soldiers.

About one o'clock in the afternoon the French, trim in the gaiters they had produced from their knapsacks, marched to the west side of the York–Hampton Road and took up positions.

They stepped to the music of their own band, and since the
French have always possessed the finest military bands in the
world,* there was good reason for the populace to be delighted
with its sound, which they applauded loudly. After them came
the Americans, with a band playing only "moderately well,"
according to one observer.

And at last General George Washington, riding between
the lines. As he passed down that half mile of serrated military
power, he must have seen, as Freeman notes, not troops but
symbols of the six years he had lived with these men—symbols
of the Jersey retreat, the icy Delaware, the autumn heat of
White Plains and the terrifying storm and cold of Morristown,
the starvation of Valley Forge, the incredible rout of Germantown. Blood and thirst and hunger and misery, and with it
unbelievable patience and courage and endurance: that was
what the Continental Army represented. It had known more
than its share of deserters and "sunshine patriots," and traitors,
and soldiers in spite of themselves, but it had survived—and it
had conquered.

To these men, and their French allies who had clinched
the victory, the British came to surrender. One who watched
their progress describes it: "They marched through both armies
in a slow pace, and to the sound of music, not military marches,
but of certain airs, which had in them so peculiar a strain of
melancholy, and which together with the appearance before
me, excited sentiments far different from those I expected to
enjoy." [5]

The "certain airs" the British bands and pipers played were
almost certainly a march which could not have been more
aptly named, "The World Turn'd Upside Down"; by another
ironic coincidence, the ballad to which the melody had often
been attached in one of its numerous adaptations was the old
English popular song, "When the King Enjoys His Own
Again."

* The author knows this is a sweeping statement, but he is prepared to put
up an argument against anyone who wishes to challenge it.

As they came down the York road to these wistful strains, the British troops marched with a slow, measured tread which prolonged their unhappy progress. Those who watched them waited to see one man: Cornwallis. But when a smartly gotten-up British general officer appeared, his staff behind him, it was not Cornwallis, though probably few if any of the principals present knew it at the moment. This officer rode directly to Rochambeau and began to address him. Count Dumas, in his memoirs, asserts that the British general sought to surrender his sword to the French commander, but that he, the Count, prevented this error by interposing his horse, while Rochambeau simultaneously pointed toward Washington. But it must be doubted that any sword was involved in the ceremony, portraiture to the contrary, since the terms of surrender explicitly permitted the British commander to be spared this traditional gesture of humiliation. Dumas is the only noteworthy contemporary reporter of the scene who mentions a sword; no American witness confirms the statement.

In any event, the British officer, whom Washington and Rochambeau were now close enough to see was obviously not Cornwallis, did make a mistake in his generals, after which he bowed in apology and turned his horse to Washington. This handsome, courteous Irishman then introduced himself as Brigadier Charles O'Hara, of the Guards. Cornwallis, he said, was indisposed, which was at least understandable, though disappointing. Some would have thought it an outright breach of good manners, unless Cornwallis was wounded or stricken with a serious disease. Washington displayed no emotion, however, but gravely indicated to O'Hara that, as a deputy second in command to Cornwallis, he must deal by protocol with the American leader's second in command, General Benjamin Lincoln. Again O'Hara bowed and went to confer with Lincoln. The two men then settled, briefly, the details of capitulation.

If omitting the ceremony of the sword had spared the feelings of the British generals, there was nothing about the actual surrender which could be anything but galling to the British regulars who were compelled to perform it. They had to enter a circle in an open field, ringed by French hussars, and there, regiment by regiment, they must lay down their arms and march back between the French and American lines.

When this heartbreaking business began, the Hessian troops came on in perfect order, but the British lines were spotted with drunken soldiers and their customary rhythmic precision was absent in places, although the larger part of them dressed and marched well. They carried their colors cased, and their bands played the music Washington had ordered in the surrender terms—only English and German marches. This was in retaliation for the arrogant British demand at Charleston that the drums of the surrendering Americans not be allowed to beat a British march. At Charleston, connoisseurs of surrender music have noted, the band of His Majesty's Grenadiers burst out with "God Save the King" as it entered the gate of the Charleston fort, while the American drums and bugles, hampered alike by the surrender terms and the deficiencies of native musical literature, were compelled to resort to the "Turks' March."

At the circle of capitulation outside Yorktown, the British troops presented arms before they laid them down, along with their cartridge boxes. As they did so, many failed to manage the act without emotion—weeping, swearing or, in a last gesture of defiance, trying to break their musket locks by dashing the weapons to the ground.

Both French and American officers gathered around to watch this scene of ignominy, peering over the shoulders of the hussars, but Washington was not present. Gloating was not in his character, nor, as Freeman points out, was it "his habit to spend time over a finished task."

Military etiquette demanded that the victors entertain the vanquished at dinner that night, and there was doubtless a good deal of preliminary embarrassment over the prospect. But General O'Hara and his staff surprised and delighted everyone, particularly the French, those masters of sang-froid. The British gentlemen appeared to be at ease, and O'Hara was particularly charming, so much so that some of those present may have wondered who were the guests.

After it was over, Washington sat down to compose a historic document of his own, a dispatch announcing the victory to Congress, which Tench Tilghman was to have the honor of delivering. Its beginning was a classic example of the General's restraint: "Sir, I have the Honor to inform Congress that a Reduction of the British Army under the Command of Lord Cornwallis, is most happily effected. . . ."

The campaigns were over.

# Chapter 6

## York State

If Washington himself had been writing these recollections of his travels, he might reasonably have shuddered at the memory of the places he occupied in New York State, at least those on the east side of the Hudson. Newburgh and West Point, on the opposite shore, stood in a somewhat different light, but those in Westchester and Dutchess counties bore the atmosphere of retreat, of treachery, and of painful indecision.

[1776]   The General's military introduction to this region was gloomy enough. After the Battle of Harlem Heights on September 16, 1776—"Monday's battle," as it was known to the Americans; "this scrape," as Sir Henry Clinton termed it —there was a momentary pause in operations, during which it became obvious that the British meant to try something else before winter set in. What they had in mind became more apparent by October 13, when Clinton executed a maneuver comparable to General MacArthur's Inchon exploit in Korea by landing the main body of his troops nine miles farther up the Sound, at the American rear. Washington's position on Harlem Heights thus became untenable, and at a council of war it was decided to fall back from there into Westchester, leaving only enough forces to defend the newly completed Fort Washington, on the heights overlooking the Hudson.

The British gibed at their departure. One Tory wrote: "The cowardly rebels, besides being very successful in the use of their legs, are the noisiest rascals in the world. Not sobered down by being driven from every post they have formed, they are now wasting their powder in celebrating the capture of a few cattle from Long Island. Yesterday morning, before daybreak, a party of them stole over from Eastchester, and carried off four old working oxen, a mangy dog and two kittens, and they are so rejoiced at this success of their arms, and the prospect of a good dinner, that Mr. Washington has ordered a *feu de joie,* and the usual complement of bad cider-rum."[1]

Washington established his new headquarters at the Miller house, in White Plains. The retreat, or "strategic withdrawal," to put the best face on it, had been through a countryside parched and burned by a summer of intense heat that had persisted into the late fall. The fields were brown, and the problem of water had become acute. Most houses were supplied by wells of the "moss-covered bucket" type, which had been adequate until the American troops swept by them, followed by the advancing British and Hessians. The double invasion left the wells almost dry. In addition, many of the inhabitants were terrified by the enemy even before they arrived. In New Rochelle, which the British occupied temporarily, some of the people fled to shelter in the nearby woods and left their houses to the mercy of the troops.

The house Washington occupied at White Plains was not of a kind to provide him with cheer in the midst of drought and terror. It stood at the foot of a hill, in a dense stand of timber, a clapboard house with the usual center-hall arrangement on the first floor, a kitchen annex, and an attic so small that it was uninhabitable.[2]

The Commander-in-Chief did not see much of it. On the twenty-third of October, his first day there, he spent most of the time reconnoitering on horseback, forming posts, choosing the places for breastworks and redoubts. Five days later the battle was fought on Chatterton's Hill, a mile from the town and west of the Bronx River. The Miller house was north of White Plains, east of the river.

It was a victory, and yet it was not a victory. The British had not taken White Plains, or routed the Americans, yet Washington thought it prudent three days later to remove his army to stronger positions on the heights of North Castle, two miles farther back and five from White Plains. An indecisive few days elapsed, then the British unexpectedly began to retreat. They might be going back to New York or toward the Jerseys: an American council of war decided it was the Jerseys. Consequently Washington split his army, sending one body of troops to New Jersey and the remainder of his forces to Peekskill, where they would be in a position to command both river and countryside. He would follow to Jersey, and General Heath would take the command at Peekskill.

Washington left the Miller house on the morning of November 10, probably with little regret. He never revisited it, though the allied armies of America and France occupied the neighborhood under quite different circumstances in the spring and summer of 1781, and Washington himself returned to the village, at an unestablished headquarters, in 1778.

Arriving at Peekskill about sunset of the tenth, the General established himself in the Birdsall house, which stood on the southwest corner of Main and Division streets. The house had been erected by one of the village founders, shortly after the first settlement in 1764, and it endured until the latter part of the nineteenth century before it was torn down. Washington was not long in this house ( he was off to New Jersey on November 12) but it earned a few more paragraphs in history because it was here, in this same month of November 1776, that General Charles Lee stopped after his failure to trap the famous Captain Rogers, and immediately embroiled himself in a quarrel with Heath, who told his side of it in his memoirs.

Shortly after he left Westchester, as related in Part 2, Chapter 3, Washington saw his last stronghold at the rim of New York, Fort Washington, fall to the British, and its able commanders, Greene and Putnam, driven across the river, where they were all compelled to flee on the ignoble road to the Delaware.

The British press missed no opportunity to twit the Americans, particularly homespun Yankees like Putnam, and his departure from Westchester occasioned this advertisement:

"LOST, an old black dog, of the American breed; answers to the name of Putnam;—had on a yellow collar with the following inscription, 'Ubi libertas ibi patria, 1776. Long Island:' is an old domestic animal,—barks very much at the name of N(ort)h, and has a remarkable howl at that of Howe. Was seen in Long Island some time ago, but is supposed to have been alarmed at some British troops who were exercising there, and ran off towards Hellgate. As he was a great favorite of the Washington family, they are fearful some accident has happened to him."[3]

[1777]    As the Continental Army struggled back up from the Delaware in the early months of 1777, the British journalists took due note of its difficulties. One remarked: "A deserter from the rebel army at Westchester [that would have been Heath's forces] who came into New York this morning, says that the Congress troops are suffering extremely for food and rum; that there is not a whole pair of breeches in the army, and that the last news from Mr. Washington's camp was, that he had to tie his up with strings, having parted with the buttons to buy the necessaries of life."[4]

Later, and on a somewhat higher plane, the *Pennsylvania Evening Post* reported with mock solemnity on May 15: "A late letter from England says—'Mr. Rigby has proposed in the cabinet a scheme for adjusting all disputes with America. His plan is to decide the quarrel after the Roman fashion, by single combat. Mr. Rigby offers himself as the champion of England; he will box Washington, Lee, or Putnam. This is at least as good a mode of reconciliation as that projected by the Howes."[5]

With all his buttons apparently intact, and having signed no contracts for a bout with Mr. Rigby, either indoors or outdoors, Washington came out of Jersey and back into York State briefly in July. On the fifteenth, he was at the entrance to that lofty, tangled piece of Hudson River highland known as the Clove, in Orange County, New York. Here he paused at Suffern's Tavern for five days before he entered the Clove itself, which was succinctly described by the ubiquitous De Chastellux.

"The Clove is extremely wild," says the Count, "and was scarcely known before the war: It is a sort of valley, or gorge, situated to the westward of the high mountains between New Windsor and King's Ferry, and at the foot of which are West Point and Stony Point, and the principal forts which defend the river."[6]

On Sunday, July 20, Washington moved eleven miles into the Clove, as far as Galloway's, an old log house. There, says Colonel Pickering in his journal, with quiet satisfaction, "The General lodged in a bed, and his family on the floor about him. We had plenty of sepawn* and milk, and all were contented."

[1778]     Exactly a year later, with the New Jersey victories behind him, Washington returned on July 20 to White Plains, where he remained until the sixteenth of September with the army encamped about him. He could not help remarking on the turn of fortune since he had last been there, unhappily, at the Miller house. "It is not a little pleasing, nor less wonderful to contemplate," he wrote General Nelson, "that after two years' maneuvering and undergoing the strangest vicissitudes that perhaps ever attended any one contest since the creation, both armies are brought back to the very point they set out from, and that which was the offending party in the beginning is now reduced to the use of the spade and pickaxe for defense."

But the maneuvering was far from over. Less than a month later Washington was writing to General Sullivan, informing him that the army was to be pulled back again from White Plains. And again it was because of his doubt as to which di-

---

* Pickering used a variation of supawn, meaning hasty pudding or, more commonly, mush. The word has its origin in the language of the Algonquins.

rection the British would go next, and the constant failure of his intelligence to inform him accurately. Now he thought the enemy might be contemplating an adventure toward Boston, or, on the other hand, the fighting might be centered at the posts around New York. By placing the troops farther north at Fredericksburg (then in Dutchess, now in Putnam, County), almost directly across the river in a line from Newburgh, he would be able to move quickly in any direction.

For his headquarters Washington chose the village of Patterson, near the Connecticut line. He was there about the sixteenth or seventeenth of September 1778. The British countermove was to send a reinforcement of troops to its army in New Jersey and make some threatening gestures toward West Point, which caused Washington to send General Putnam across the river to the threatened territory, since it would have been a calamity indeed to lose the Point, while he himself went up to Fishkill, where he would be nearer that important post and better able to view events in New Jersey.

In the village of Fishkill, which was fifteen miles west of Fredericksburg, Washington lodged intermittently for a good part of the war. Probably he was most often at the house of John Brinckerhoff, a solid structure built in 1738 and intact more than a century and a half later. At other times he stayed in the house of John's nephew, Colonel Derrick Brinckerhoff.

Fishkill did not appear to be a place of high sociability, as the Jerseys had been. Later in the war, when Baron Steuben had his quarters near the village, he termed it a "center of dullness . . . the last place in the world for mirth." He had, he says, "two disciples at chess, Mrs. Washington and my colleague, but unhappily one is thinking too much of her home, and the other is making verses during the game. Their progress, therefore, is so little that both are tired of it, and so I have been obliged to learn backgammon, of which I am equally tired."

Washington, one supposes, was always too busy to be bored. It might be added, in passing, that his diaries and letters, forty-five volumes of them including indexes in the standard editions, never once mention a state of boredom worthy of notice (not counting such items as dull days when rain kept him inside on a journey) except in the single instance of his last days at Newburgh, when he was impatiently awaiting the official end of the war and sought to pass the time by his tour of the Northern posts.

During this first visit to Fishkill, he spent one day, October 8, in the performance of a commander's duty not often mentioned elsewhere. He went a few miles down the river to the Robinson house, the country place of his Virginia friend of the early days, Beverly Robinson, who had sheltered him in New York on his way to Boston and introduced him to his beautiful sister-in-law Mary Philipse. Now, little more than twenty years later, Beverly Robinson was a Loyalist, Mary was married to one, and the summerhouse had been commandeered as a hospital for the Continental Army.

Dr. Thacher helped to show the Commander-in-Chief through the wards, and in his *Military Journal* left a snapshot of this "perfect gentleman and accomplished warrior" on the occasion of his visit. "He is remarkably tall, six feet,* erect and well proportioned," wrote the doctor. "The strength and proportion of his joints and muscles appear to be commensurate with the pre-eminent powers of his mind. The serenity of his countenance, and majestic gracefulness of his deportment, impart a strong impression of that dignity and grandeur which are his peculiar characteristics, and no one can stand in his presence without feeling the ascendancy of his mind, and associating with his countenance the idea of wisdom, philanthropy, magnanimity and patriotism. There is a fine symmetry in the features of his face indicative of a benign and dignified

---

* As a physician, Thacher's height guess was nearer the mark than most, but it was still surprisingly far from accurate. In his obvious awe of Washington's commanding presence, Thacher also overlooked the physical characteristics more worldly observers noted—the long arms and large hands, and the almost classic proportions of his thighs and legs, so valuable an asset to a man in those trouserless days.

spirit. His nose is straight, and his eyes inclined to blue. He wears his hair in a becoming queue, and from his forehead it is turned back and powdered in a manner which adds to the military air of his appearance of ostentation. His uniform dress is a blue coat, with two brilliant epaulettes, buff-colored under clothes, and a three-cornered hat with a black cockade. He is constantly equipped with an elegant small sword, boots and spurs, in readiness to mount his noble charger."

After October 9, Washington returned to his headquarters near Fredericksburg and stayed there until November 28, except for a second trip to Fishkill for the purpose of discussing confidentially with John Jay the advisability of a plan Congress was then considering to invade Canada, in combination with the French troops. The two wisely decided to oppose this plan. On the twenty-eighth of November, Washington left once more for Jersey, this time to the social delights of the winter at Middlebrook.

[1779]     In the spring of 1779, he returned by the same route as two years before, through the Clove, where he stayed near the tavern, in a position to watch the enemy's movements. Colonel Wadsworth did not take the happy view of the Clove his friend Pickering had recorded in 1777. "This is a most villainous country," Wadsworth wrote to Samuel Webb on June 17, "rough, rocky and a bad climate. Rattlesnakes and robbers are plenty. It was an infringement on the right of wild beasts for man ever to enter this Clove. . . ."

From the Clove, Washington removed to a new Westchester headquarters at New Windsor, which may have been more civilized in its surroundings but to the General became "my dreary quarters" during the time he stayed there, in the William Ellison house, on a hill just south of the village. It must have been the state of his mind that made the quarters seem dreary, because the house itself was pleasant, a Dutch stone house a story and a half high, with three dormer windows in front, much like Steuben's headquarters at the Verplanck house near Fishkill. From its high bluff, the house looked out across the Hudson to the Beacon hills.[7]

On the twenty-first of July, he moved to West Point, where he remained until November 28, supervising the construction of the strong works in and around the fortress. While he was busily occupied through the summer and fall, he lived in John Moore's house, a mile north of the Point in a locality that afterward came to be known as Washington's Valley. Although Moore was a successful New York merchant who could afford it, his house was so large and elegant that it was popularly known as "Moore's Folly," and is even designated that way on some contemporary maps. The 1800 acres of property around it included the site of West Point itself; the American government bought the whole tract from Moore's son Stephen in 1790. (Stephen's son, Richard Channing Moore, it may be added, secured the family's name in history by becoming the noted Bishop of Virginia.)

Of his life at Moore's Folly, Washington himself has left the best description, in a letter to Dr. John Cochran. "Since our arrival at this happy spot," he wrote. "we have had a ham (sometimes a shoulder) of bacon to grace the head of the table; a piece of roast beef adorns the foot; a dish of beans, or greens (almost imperceptible) decorates the center. When the cook has a mind to cut a figure (which, I presume, will be the case tomorrow) we have two beefsteak pies, or dishes of crabs, in addition, one on each side of the center dish dividing the space and reducing the distance between dish and dish to about six feet, which without them would be near 12 feet apart. Of late he has had the surprising sagacity to discover that apples will make pies, and it's a question if, in the violence of his efforts, we do not get one of apples instead of having both of beefsteaks. If the ladies [he meant Mrs. Cochran and her friend Mrs. Livingston, who were coming to dine next day] can put up with such entertainment, and will submit to partake of it in plates once tin but now iron (not become so by the labor of scouring) I shall be happy to see them." [8]


[1780]    From this plentiful table and fine house, in the majestic highlands, Washington went directly in December to the misery of the winter at Morristown, with its violent storms and excruciating cold. He remained in New Jersey through the spring and early summer of 1780 until it seemed in July that Clinton meant to attack Rhode Island. In moving to ward off this blow, or meet it, Washington returned to Westchester on July 31, and quartered overnight at the Robinson house, no longer a military hospital but reconverted to a residence.

About this time there appeared in the London *Chronicle*, for the benefit of the enemy, a view of the General written by a correspondent in New Jersey more than six months before. The British, picking up the *Chronicle* to discover the progress of the colonial revolt, could read that the legendary commander directing it was "a tall, well-made man, rather large boned, and has a tolerably genteel address, his features are manly and bold, his eyes of a bluish cast, and very lively; his hair a deep brown, his face rather long, and marked with the smallpox; his complexion sunburnt, and without much color, and his countenance sensible, composed and thoughtful. There is a remarkable air of dignity about him, with a striking degree of gracefulness. . . ." [9]

The tall, well-made man at that moment was planning frustration for the invaders. He paused at the Robinson house only momentarily on his way to Kingsbridge, from where he hoped to confront the enemy with such a menacing front that they would have to give up the Rhode Island campaign, if that was what they intended, or else be compelled to take on the American army at the spot, if the time was ripe.

From the Robinson house, the General went on to Peekskill, and there he learned that British intelligence had presumably reported his movements, and the maneuver had achieved the effect he hoped. The British fleet sailing toward Rhode Island had put back, alarmed for the safety of New York City itself. To encourage them in this worry, Washington brought his troops back across the river to the vicinity of Tappan, New York, more often called Orangetown in those days; it was then in Orange County, but is now in Rockland, about two miles from the western landing of Dobbs Ferry and very near the New Jersey line. "A most excellent country, inhabited chiefly with Low Dutch," a captain of the Pennsylvania line wrote of it.[10]

Headquarters at Tappan was in the De Wint house, a one-story brick and stone dwelling. It was a fascinating old Dutch residence, built in 1700 of materials brought in part from Holland. Johannes de Wint, a West India planter, owned it at the time Washington stayed there, and it was in his parlor, which George used for an office, that Major André's death warrant was signed a few weeks later. This parlor was graced by a fireplace decorated with eighty-nine Dutch tiles, each representing a scene from the Scriptures or the Apocrypha. They were purple on a white ground, and the effect was sometimes startling, combined with the literal Teutonic character of the art itself, as for instance one tile showing the whale holding Jonah by his waistband.* Massive white oak beams held up the ceiling of the room, and it had capacious closets.

Several traditions cling to the Tappan house, a few worth repeating. It is said that when Washington's aide rode up to the place for the first time in 1780, to secure its accommodations for the General, he found only a Mrs. Blauvelt, a married daughter of De Wint, at home. As it happened, she was a Loy-

---

* This tiled fireplace was a particularly fine example of a type of ornamentation found often in better-class homes of the period. Admiral de Ternay's beautifully restored headquarters at Newport, for example, in one of a row of waterfront houses which belonged to the city's merchant princes, has several Dutch-tiled fireplaces depicting biblical scenes. In one of these, Jonah is represented, seized by the whale in a pose that is a variation on the De Wint tile. Not all such tiles were biblical. Many depicted flowers, or pastoral scenes, or beasts of a form not classified in this world.

alist, but she was also either sensible or resigned, or perhaps impressed by the honor, no matter what her politics. In any event, she made no objection at all to receiving the American commander, and entertained him well during his stay.

Another tradition says that Washington liked to walk out in the morning, very early, to a nearby spring, where he took a long draught of the cool water to start his day.

Still another, connected with a later visit than the one in 1780, relates the story of a benevolent Tappan lady who visited the American camp every day on errands of mercy. One day she talked to a soldier sentenced to death for desertion, and seeing his opportunity, he persuaded her to plead for him with the General. Early the next morning she was at headquarters. The officer of the day told her Washington was at worship with his family, but that when she saw the front door open and Washington pacing the hall inside, she could enter.

As the story goes, Washington heard her plea and said: "Madam, I would willingly do anything in my power to please you, but your request is a hard one. I am afraid he is a bad man. For your sake, however, I will see what can be done."

Apparently—a point that casts serious doubt on the whole story—Washington was able to reverse the decision of the court-martial, because the lady found the deserter saved the next morning, and he overwhelmed her with his gratitude.

This kindly little tale has a realistic ending, however, unlike most traditional stories about Washington. The reprieved man deserted again, was recaptured, and this time he was shot, vindicating Washington's judgment but dealing a hard blow to humanitarianism.[11]

The hardest blow of all to Washington's own belief in his fellow man was then in the making as he stayed at Tappan. There was a brief interlude in northern New Jersey in the early autumn of 1780 before he set off from the Hopper house for the interview with Rochambeau in Hartford, but the mood of relief and hopefulness in which he rode back from that meeting was shattered abruptly when he reached the Robinson house on the morning of Monday, September 25, and learned of Arnold's treachery.

The Robinson house was a singularly apt setting for the climactic scene of the brilliant, eventful tragedy that was Benedict Arnold's life, a tragedy that has left so many doubts and questions still unanswered.* Robinson had chosen the house for its seclusion and for the magnificent scenery of the Hudson Valley, between Peekskill and Garrison, that opened before him. Sugar Loaf Mountain rose from the back lawn, and from its summit one could see the "majestic, solemn, wild and melancholy" view of the river where it widens into the splendid curve of Newburgh Bay, with Storm King Mountain thrusting up its bold prominence in the distance, and West Point beyond. The house itself was a rambling old mansion, with low ceilings, heavy, uncovered joists, fireplaces with no mantel shelves, and stairways with unusually short flights and broad landings.[12]

After the grim episodes of Arnold's treachery and André's execution that autumn, Washington was at Preakness, New Jersey, in the Dey house, but on December 6 he was back in his old "dreary quarters" at the Ellison house in New Windsor, where he proposed to spend the winter. He stayed until June 25, 1781.

It could not have been as dreary that winter as he had thought it before. Martha was with him, and she did her best to make the house the customary center of polite society. Of course it was small for entertaining. De Chastellux considered it "much

* Most of the doubts and questions remaining, however, have been answered with the publication in October 1953 of James Thomas Flexner's book, *The Traitor and the Spy*, a superb summary of all that is known about Arnold and André and their fateful conspiracy. When this volume is taken in conjunction with Carl Van Doren's *Secret History of the American Revolution*, the interested reader has in his possession the best and most complete (as well as the most readable) scholarship available on the unforgettable drama whose center stage was the Robinson house.

less" than the place the General had enjoyed at Preakness, and a sergeant in the Guard called it "not large, but comfortable in cold weather."

De Chastellux visited the Washingtons in December, meeting them in their carriage when he was still two miles from New Windsor. They were going to call on Mrs. Knox, about a mile farther on, but would have turned back if De Chastellux had not politely refused to interrupt their visit. Washington sent his aide, Colonel Humphreys, back to the Ellison house with the Count, and promised to return in half an hour.

That day, says the Count, he dined with the family and several officers as guests, at an excellent dinner. Later in the afternoon they drank tea together and sat in conversation until it was time for supper. Washington took an active part in the talk. Once he asked De Chastellux what books he read with most pleasure as a professional soldier. The Count cited the *King of Prussia's Instructions to his Generals*, and the *Tactics of M. de Guilbert*.

The winter that year was delightfully mild compared with the onslaughts at Morristown and Valley Forge; not until after New Year's did the river freeze at Newburgh. Martha came just before Christmas, so dinner on that day was her first entertainment. Sergeant Uzal Knapp was sent out to see if he could get a turkey for the occasion, but he had a difficult time of it. The soldiers, newly settled in the neighborhood, had depleted the supply of turkeys for miles around, both legally and illegally, and the sergeant was in distress until he came to the house of General James Clinton, who was off fighting in the North. Molly, his wife, came to the door and, when she heard the sergeant's errand, gave him "three for the General" from the private stock she had locked up for her own family.

Christmas dinner, with the help of Clinton's turkeys, proved to be a gala affair. Two young French officers had come over from Rochambeau's headquarters at Newport, and there was Governor George Clinton and his lady (it may have been his daughter), some of the neighborhood gentry, the staff officers, and Molly Clinton, who was eligible for the guest list not alone because of her generosity but because she was a general's wife. All told, twenty persons sat down to eat turkey, chickens, beef and mutton; there were plenty of pies, puddings, apples, nuts and cider, and spiced wine for after dinner. Sergeant Knapp, in charge of the Guard Band, had them playing seasonal dinner music throughout the meal. The band was stationed in the passageway leading to the largest room in the house, where the table was laid, and Sergeant Knapp relates that he saw all the distinguished people go by him and assemble around their chairs at the table, when "the General, standing, asked a blessing with solemn tones and closed eyes."

[1781]     There were visitors from the French army throughout the winter. One of them, Count Dumas, recalls in his memoirs how Washington, Lafayette, Dumas and other French officers visited West Point one day soon after the fine Christmas dinner, on January 22, 1781. They viewed the works, took the garrison's salute, and then in the late afternoon prepared to mount their horses for the return to New Windsor. Washington noted that Lafayette, who had never fully recovered from his Brandywine wound, appeared so tired he could scarcely mount his horse.

Count Dumas recalls that Washington said quickly, when he noticed Lafayette's fatigue, "It will be better to return by water. The tide will assist us in ascending against the stream." Of the subsequent perilous voyage the Count relates:

"A boat was soon manned with good rowers, and we embarked. The cold became excessive; we had to make our way between the large flakes of ice which the river brought down. A heavy snow and the obscurity of the night soon rendered the danger more imminent and the management of the boat, which filled with water, became increasingly difficult. We coasted the rocks which lined the right bank of the Hudson, between West Point and New Windsor, at the foot of which

The Revolution: Journeys and Headquarters

it was impossible to land. General Washington, perceiving that the master of the boat was very much alarmed, took the helm, saying, 'Courage, my friends; I am going to conduct you, since it is my duty to hold the helm.' After having with much difficulty made our way against the stream and the ice, we landed, and had to walk a league before we reached the head-quarters."

A month after this excursion came the first real break in the ranks of the official family. With the notable exception of Charles Lee, it was the first time anyone close to Washington had suggested that there were imperfections in the image of the Commander-in-Chief. It was a clash between two proud men, but the prouder was Alexander Hamilton.

Washington stood waiting for Hamilton in the upper hall of the New Windsor headquarters one February day. Of infinite patience in large matters, the General was inclined to be impatient in small ones. He had sent word he wanted to see Hamilton, and the Colonel had sent back word he would be there shortly. Ten minutes elapsed, and when Hamilton appeared, the conversation is said to have flared at once into an impulsive quarrel.

"You have kept me waiting at the head of these stairs these ten minutes," Washington said sternly. "I must tell you, sir, you treat me with disrespect."

"I am not conscious of it, sir," Hamilton replied, matching him in offended dignity, "but since you have thought it necessary to tell me so, we part."

"Very well, sir, if it be your choice," Washington said curtly.

As soon as the flare-up was over, Washington regretted it, but Hamilton did not. The General may have recalled that when he was Hamilton's age he was as sensitive and proud and full of quick tempers, but he had fought hard and successfully to overcome these faults. He sent a kind, conciliatory note to his Colonel, suggesting that their differences could be amended in a few moments of candid conversation. Hamilton coolly

209

declined the honor. He made it plain that nothing would persuade him to stay.

In a letter to his father-in-law, Hamilton confessed that he had never liked the General (though it could hardly have been true), and he asserted that Washington did not have the proper consideration for others, a most intemperate statement. In an even more savage vein, he wrote to McHenry that "the Great Man" ought to "for once repent his ill humor."

The winter was more profitably interrupted in March by the visit to Hartford and Newport, and in May there was the conference at Wethersfield with the French commanders.

On June 25, 1781, Washington left his New Windsor winter quarters, sending Martha down to Virginia while he joined the main body of the troops in their camp at Peekskill. There, briefly, he made his headquarters in the Van Cortlandt house, erected by this rich and influential family only eight years before.

Claude Blanchard, the Commissary of the French army, who had met and admired him at Newport, encountered the General there on June 29. Blanchard was riding to look at some winter barracks with a view to establishing a hospital in them when he met Washington on the road. The General recognized him and invited him to dine at three o'clock. Blanchard wrote of the dinner:

"I repaired thither; there were twenty-five covers used by some officers of the army and a lady to whom the house belonged in which the General lodged. We dined under the tent. I was placed alongside of the General. One of his aides-de-camp did the honors. The table was served in the American style and pretty abundantly: vegetables, roast beef, lamb, chickens, salad dressed with nothing but vinegar, green peas, puddings and some pie, a kind of tart, greatly in use in England and among the Americans, all this being put upon the table at the same time. They gave us on the same plate beef, green peas, lamb, &c."[13]

This method of service, which appears to have shocked Monsieur Blanchard, has survived in the American army to the present day, as any G.I. can testify without benefit of scholarship.

On July 2, Washington marched the troops to Valentine's Hill, by way of the new bridge over the Croton River about nine miles south of Peekskill, making a stop at this bridge and at the church near Tarrytown. It was sunrise when they reached the Hill, four miles from Kingsbridge. By the maneuver, Washington hoped to surprise the British outposts at the northern end of New York Island. The French army, meanwhile, had marched down from Newport, by way of Providence, Plainfield, Windham, Bolton, Hartford, Farmington, Newtown and Ridgebury, Connecticut. On the day of Washington's march, they had reached Bedford, New York, and Lauzun's legion made a forced march the next day to East Chester.

The result of this marching and reconnoitering was very small, from a military standpoint, except that the French at last made a junction with the Americans at Phillipsburg, twelve miles from Kingsbridge. Washington established headquarters at Joseph Appleby's house, on the road from Dobbs Ferry to White Plains, on an elevation still known as Washington's Hill, while Rochambeau quartered at the Odell house, about a mile and a half away.

From this point the French and Americans conducted a joint reconnaissance in force of the British positions at Kingsbridge on July 22. Washington and Rochambeau dined together the following night at the Van Cortlandt house, a mile north of Kingsbridge. There was further reconnaissance and planning for an attack upon New York, but these plans were interrupted by the news from Newport that a French fleet and an army aboard it was headed from the West Indies for Chesapeake Bay, under Count de Grasse. The French naval officers were disinclined to force New York Harbor, and in any event, the Count had promised his services for only a short time. With these and other factors taken into consideration, Washington decided at Phillipsburg to give up the projected assault on New York from the north, and to concentrate his forces for an attack on Cornwallis in Virginia, in conjunction with the French fleet—in brief, the plan evolved at Wethersfield, Hartford and Newport. Thus, on Sunday, August 19, 1781, the entire French army and six regiments of Americans, with Colonel Scammel's light troops, began the long march toward King's Ferry, across the river, and down through New Jersey, Pennsylvania and Delaware.

The junction of the armies at Phillipsburg had given other Frenchmen an opportunity to see the Washington they had heard so much about, and they were eloquent in his praise. The Abbé Robin, a chaplain in one of the regiments, was especially impressed with Washington's effect on the population. He wrote: ". . . They consider him in the light of a beneficent God, dispensing peace and happiness around him. Old men, women and children, press about him when he accidentally passes along, and think themselves happy, once in their lives, to have seen him—they follow him through the towns with torches, and celebrate his arrival by public illuminations. The Americans, that cool and sedate people, who in the midst of their most trying difficulties have attended only to the directions and impulses of plain method and common sense, are roused, animated and inflamed at the very mention of his name; and the first songs that sentiment or gratitude has dictated, have been to celebrate General Washington."

On this high note of impending triumph, Washington departed Westchester and rode off to Yorktown and the final victory. But he was not through with York State. After the surrender of Cornwallis, he spent the winter in Philadelphia. Then, in March, he came back up to rejoin the main army at Newburgh, New York, eight miles above West Point.

[1782]    Of the hundred or more headquarters Washington established during the Revolution, this one was distinguished in several ways. For one, the fifteen months and eighteen days he spent in it was the longest consecutive period he lived in any of the houses he had occupied in seven states, from Massachusetts to Virginia. It was, too, the last major headquarters of the Revolution, though not the last in time. Finally, it is doubtful if any other Washington shrine except Mount Vernon (or possibly Valley Forge) has been seen in our own time by so many Americans as the Hasbrouck house at Newburgh. The restoration is excellent; nowhere else, in following Washington's war footsteps, is the atmosphere of the times evoked so strongly.

The house itself, of course, has some novelties of its own to offer, particularly the odd construction of Washington's living and dining room, with its seven doors and one window. Burger Mynders built the oldest part of the house, in the early years of the eighteenth century. Jonathan Hasbrouck acquired it at the time of his marriage and added a north addition; again, in 1770, he enlarged it to accommodate his family. Not long after, he died and his widow temporarily left the place to Washington and his family when he arrived there on Sunday, March 31, 1782.*

The cares of the war substantially behind him, Washington began to relax at Newburgh, and with the aid of Martha, enjoyed an active social life, as well as the first moments of leisurely camp life he had known for weary months.

One of the first events he attended was the celebration of the birth of the French Dauphin at West Point on May 31, at which he gave a dinner for more than five hundred people in a bower 214 by 70 feet, erected by the soldiers with materials dragged in from the woods. At this dinner, reported General Heath, "Thirteen toasts were drank, announced by the discharge of cannon. At evening there was a grand feu-de-joy, opened by the discharge of 13 cannon, three times repeated.

* Title to the house became vested in New York State in 1849, and in 1850 the Assembly placed it in the hands of the Board of Trustees of Newburgh, so that the proper measures could be taken for its preservation.

The feu-de-joy, being fired in the dusk, had a pleasing appearance to the eye, as well as the ear; and was so ordered for that purpose."

Another observer was the indefatigable Dr. Thacher, who wrote of the celebration in his journal: "At half-past eleven o'clock, the celebration was concluded by the exhibition of fireworks very ingeniously constructed of various figures. . . . Washington was unusually cheerful. He attended the ball in the evening, and with a dignified and graceful air, having Mrs. Knox for his partner, carried down a dance of twenty couple in the arbor on the green grass."

With this kind of example, the anxiety of other hosts, when Washington was to come for dinner, may well be imagined. Here is Colonel Webb, writing from his quarters at the Robinson house, in haste on June 6, to a colleague nearby:

"General Washington dines with me tomorrow. He is exceedingly fond of salt fish. I have some coming up, and though it will be here in a few days, it will not be here in time. If you could conveniently lend me as much fish as would serve a pretty large company for dinner tomorrow (at least for one dish) it will oblige me, and shall in a very few days be returned in as good done fish as ever you see.

"Excuse this freedom, and it will add to the favor—Could you not prevail upon somebody to catch some trout for me early tomorrow morning?"

Early in the autumn the French and American troops came together once more, for the first time since Phillipsburg. By agreement with Rochambeau, they were to be concentrated on the Hudson in case Sir Guy Carleton should attempt to prolong hostilities from his position in New York, though Sir Guy, judging by his public statements, was bored with the war and anxious to end it officially.

The meeting of the victorious allies was like a vast pageant. On August 31 the Americans moved first to the rendezvous site at Verplanck's Point. A good part of the Connecticut and Massachusetts troops came down the river from Newburgh in boats, "which being in motion and in regular order on the water, made a most beautiful appearance," Dr. Thacher noted. Next day, a Sunday, the rest of the army except for the West Point garrison followed. By September 18 the French troops, which had begun moving from Virginia as early as June 23, had joined them, camping on the American left about ten miles away.

A visiting nobleman, come to watch Washington's review of the French army on September 20, found the American encampment inspiring. "It consisted of about six thousand men," he says, "who for the first time since the beginning of the war were decently uniformed, well armed, properly equipped, and camped in tents of a regular model. I passed through all the camp with pleasure, astonishment and admiration. All the soldiers seemed to me well looking, robust and well chosen. The sentinels were well equipped, very attentive, sufficiently well disciplined in the use of their arms, and so strong was the contrast with the incorrect notions I had formed concerning these troops, that I was obliged frequently to say to myself that I beheld in this army the same which formerly had no other uniform than a cap, on which was written Liberty. I noticed on a little hill which looked over the camp an assemblage of tents, which I recognized easily as the quarters of General Washington." [14]

These men whom the French nobleman so admired were the survivors, the tough men who had endured everything, including at times the scorn of their own countrymen, and now that the war was virtually over, they knew themselves as a proud, fighting army for the first time, where before they had been only grim, desperate and determined men bound together by something stronger than the drill discipline of regular troops. Remembering their dark history, they must have known a deep, quiet pride when they heard the profuse compliments of the French military men, to whom war was a science and an art, a game to be played well. One of these officers had said, watching the Americans march in maneuvers, that they possessed "that exactness, order and silence which distinguish veteran armies. . . ." Rochambeau himself was astonished at the difference since the last time he had reviewed them. According to Dr. Thacher, he turned to Washington and exclaimed, "You must have formed an alliance with the King of Prussia. These troops are Prussians." And Thacher added, "Several of the principal officers of the French army who have seen troops of different European nations, have bestowed the highest encomiums and applause on our army, and declared that they had seen none superior to the Americans."

But Rochambeau well understood at what cost the Americans had arrived at this state. In his memoirs, he writes of walking between a double line of Washington's troops on September 14, drawn up for his inspection, and he records from his command knowledge that they were "equipped, armed and clothed for the first time in the Revolution, partly from material and arms brought from France, and partly from the British storehouses taken from Cornwallis, which the French generously gave up to the American army. General Washington made his drums beat the French march during the whole time of this review, and the two armies met again with evident marks of reciprocal satisfaction."

Rochambeau did not think it necessary to underline the irony of the fact that the American army, in its moment of triumph, owed its fine outward appearance to the generosity of the French and the spoils from enemy storehouses—after eight years of war. But this was only surface. The "order and silence" his officer had spoken of—that was the result of suffering and survival. It was the difference, to cite a modern instance, between the hastily assembled National Guard troops who marched off to the Pacific in 1941, and the hard, quiet men who strode down the streets in the victory parades of 1945.

In any event, the grand review of September 21, the day after the French army had paraded for Washington, was the high point of the Continental Army. The French officer who so admired their discipline describes their appearance:

"The army was drawn up at the head of their camp. Twenty-four battalions of the states of New Jersey, Massachusetts, Rhode Island, Connecticut and New York formed a line of two miles extent. The most exact uniformity, the neat dress of the men, the glittering of their arms, their martial look, and a kind of military luxury gave a most magnificent appearance to this assemblage of citizens armed in defense of their country....

"The day was terminated with an entertainment of more than ninety covers, served with true military magnificence in the praetorium of the consul (for I rather express myself thus than by saying in the tent of the general). In fact, everything in this army bears a particular character, and things uncommon ought not to be described by common expressions. A band of American music, which played during the dinner, added to the gaiety of the company."[15]

The paradings and reviews of both forces went on well into October. The French army at last set out for Boston on the twenty-second, from where they would sail for the West Indies, on the way home; and on the twenty-sixth, virtually certain now that there would be no more hostile operations, the American army recrossed the Hudson in boats to West Point, and then moved up to New Windsor, two miles below Newburgh, where they prepared to establish their last cantonment of the war. Washington returned with them to the Hasbrouck house.

This cantonment, about three miles southwest of the present Newburgh, was described by General Heath as "regular and beautiful," and it is so today, a place of calm, rolling pastures and gentle ravines, not greatly changed from the time of the Revolution, except for cultivation and the disappearance of timber stands.

Having toured the armies, Washington toured the nearby countryside in November. He called it in his account book "a tour to Poughkeepsy—thence to Esopus [Kingston] & along the Western Frontier of the state of New York," by which he meant the frontier bordering the Hudson. The trip cost him a little more than forty-three pounds. Its progress could be embodied in the reception at Kingston, which he reached on the sixteenth of November. He had spent the previous night with Colonel Cornelius Wynkoop at his home in Stone Ridge, the present Marbletown.

In Kingston, says a local history, he was "greeted with great rejoicing on the part of the citizens. He put up at the public house of Evert Bogardus, but accompanied by his staff, he dined with Judge Dirck Wynkoop in Green Street. In the evening there was a gathering of ladies in the Bogardus ballroom, which was honored for a short time by the attendance of the General, when the ladies were severally introduced to him. The next morning at an early hour he left the village and continued his journey." [16]

Back at Newburgh, he welcomed visitors as usual, although now it was often a matter of bidding old friends farewell. De Chastellux came on December 6 to pay his final respects. As always, he gave the General's quarters a sharp critical appraisal and reported:

"The headquarters of Newburgh consists of a single house, neither vast nor commodious, which is built in the Dutch fashion. The largest room in it (which was the proprietor's parlor for his family, and which General Washington has converted into his dining room) is in truth tolerably spacious, but it has seven doors and only one window. The chimney, or rather the chimney back, is against the wall, so that there is in fact but one vent for the smoke, and the fire is in the room itself. I found the company assembled in a small room which served by way of parlor. At nine supper was served, and when the hour of bedtime came, I found that the chamber to which the general conducted me was the very parlor I speak of, wherein he had made them place a camp-bed. . . . The day I remained at headquarters was spent either at table or in conversation." [17]


[1783]    As the winter wore away, Washington became conscious of a growing discontent in his victorious but idle army. Now that there were no campaigns to worry about, and they were clothed and fed, the men had time to talk, to wonder when they were going home. Scuttlebutt flew about the cantonment. It was said that when peace was declared, Congress intended to dismiss the army without doing anything about the considerable amount of back pay owed to officers and men. Those who had suffered most at the hands of the reluctant Congressmen during the war predicted that the troops would be sent home without so much as a thank you. In this state of mind, it was easy for an army now sure of itself and united in another common grievance to talk about insisting on satisfaction, by force, if necessary.

Washington was aware of the rumors and the discontent and the threats. "I must stick close to my flock this winter," he had written at the start of it. By March the agitation was approaching a dangerous climax, because now it was spearheaded by a group of rebellious officers whose memories were short enough to make them believe the whispers that Washington was not really the army's friend and protector, that in the crisis he would side with Congress.

Hearing that the agitators had called a secret meeting to decide on a course of action, the General determined to step in and forestall it. The method he chose seemed almost naïve. He planned simply to call a meeting of his own before the others could assemble, and read a statement to the officers, outlining his position and appealing to their honor and humanity to prevent any "precipitate and dangerous" action.

He had not been in a happy frame of mind himself. He chafed at the delay in ending the war, and he was tired of the "rugged and dreary mountains" around him, longing for the tidelands of Virginia, and his eyes bothered him from the excessive use he had given them. Lately he had been "trying" spectacles.

On the fifteenth of March, 1783, Washington pocketed the statement he had been writing and walked over to the big wooden building his soldiers had completed a few weeks before. They called it the Temple, but it was used with complete catholicity as both chapel and dancing academy.

Outwardly he was calm, but his agitation over this untimely, and to him unseemly, rebellion was evident in his omission of the customary formalities, which were habitual with him. The men were already assembled, and he walked to the lectern without so much as a bow or an acknowledgment of their presence, and began reading.

As he went along in his manuscript, which had been written, probably, with a hurried and troubled hand, the lines close together and no paragraphing, he stumbled and stopped. Reaching in his pocket, he took out his new glasses, and as he fumbled with them, putting them on, he remarked to his intent audience, "Gentlemen, you must pardon me. I have grown gray in your service and now find myself growing blind."

The noble sentiments in his written statement may have convinced the minds of the rebels, but the simple, unaffected comment, made in passing, won their hearts. Whether the distant possibility is admitted that it was a calculated gesture (see Part 5, Chapter 2 of this volume), it seemed to his listeners a human, touching thing. The rebellion was over, at least in the dangerous phase it had assumed. Colonel Humphreys wrote that night, "Matters have turned complete to our wishes," and the General himself, surrounded with new expressions of devotion, declared with satisfaction that "the occasion, though attended for opposite purposes, has turned out to be one of the happiest circumstances of the war."

With his house in better order, the General prepared with a relatively clear mind for the May conferences with Sir Guy Carleton which were to settle the details of the British evacuation of New York and the other posts the enemy possessed. Sir Guy came up the river in a frigate to Dobbs Ferry, the place of meeting, while Washington, accompanied by Governor Clinton and their suites, with four companies of light infantry as guards, came down from Newburgh.

The conferences, on May 6 and 7, were held in the Van Brugh Livingston house, on a hill overlooking the river at the eastern end of Dobbs Ferry; Washington made his headquarters on the other side at Tappan. The two commanders got along amiably. On May 8, Carleton entertained the Americans aboard his frigate. When they arrived, a salute of cannon greeted them, and when they departed, Sir Guy ordered a seventeen-gun salute in honor of Washington's rank—probably the first salute fired by the British to honor thus an American officer. It may even have been the first salute to the new nation.

With the meeting satisfactorily concluded, Washington returned to Newburgh. In these last days of his military command, he lived with increasing simplicity, as the letter of a young Scot testifies. George Bennet arrived at Newburgh in April, a few weeks before the conference with Carleton. He had come to New York from Jamaica, but found he could not travel to Philadelphia at that disordered moment without proper credentials, which he had come to seek from Washington. After the General had explained that Congress had passed resolutions seeking to forbid the admission of British subjects to America, and therefore he could not properly provide a pass, he went on to remark that Bennet should have no difficulty anyway, advised him about roads, and told him to seek out Robert Morris when he got to Philadelphia. Then he invited the visitor to dinner, an "honor which I could never have expected and would by no means decline," Bennet wrote.

At the table, he continued, Washington "placed me on the left hand of Mrs. Washington. He was on her right and he drank his first glass of wine with me. The company besides consisted of about fifteen officers. The dinner was good, but everything was quite plain. We all sat on camp stools and there was nothing to be seen about his house but what every officer in the army might likewise have in his. Mrs. Washington was as plain, easy and affable as he was, and one would have thought from the familiarity which prevailed there that he saw a respectable private gentleman dining at the head of his own family.

"General Washington is now just fifty years old. He is a tall, genteel figure of a man, rather exceeding six feet in height. His countenance is grave, composed, mild and penetrating. His nose is long and of the Roman shape, his eyes a little hollow under the eyebrows but active and lively. His whole countenance is expressive of sagacity, of prudence, and of moderation, and his figure altogether has something of the solemn and majestic, which impresses respect in every beholder. . . .

"In his dress he was perfectly plain, an old blue coat faced with buff waistcoat and britches of the latter, seemingly of the same age and without any lace upon them, composed his dress. His shirt had no ruffles at the wrists, but of very fine linen. He always wears boots, and never uses a carriage but when Mrs. W. is with him, and that is only in winter. His hair is a little gray and combed smoothly back from the forehead and in a small queue—no curls and but very little powder to it."

If Washington seemed a simple man to the young Scot, it must be said that his mind was occupied with simple matters in these spring and early summer days at Newburgh. He wanted to visit a dentist, and he was anxious to buy books. He was ordering trunks to carry his papers back to Mount Vernon; he corresponded with Barbé-Marbois about Martha's health: "bilious fevers and colics attack her very often, and reduce her low." Yet the traveler wanted to go home, to a life far different from the relative simplicities of his military headquarters. As Dr. Freeman remarks, "He was dreaming of a time when he could look peacefully out on the silent Potomac and ride over his broad acres and plan new shade trees, and dress his dinner table with a French plated silver service and offer his guests old claret and Madeira, with meals prepared by a good German cook."

There was only a little more time to spin out before he could go. He spun some of it that summer with the tour to the Mohawk Valley and the Northern posts, and he passed a few more weeks in the fall at Rocky Hill. As winter came on, he must have been doubly impatient. At the last moment, as he was preparing to leave West Point, he was caught in a great snowstorm at Tappan for three days, in his old quarters at the De Wint house, where Johannes' wife, Elizabeth, helped him and the other stranded officers pass the time with cards—the first time he had played, or so said Colonel Humphreys, since the Revolution began.

At last, late in the month, Sir Guy Carleton sent him the exact dates on which he planned to evacuate New York and Washington could take possession. On November 18, he turned his back on the Hasbrouck house for the last time, left the Hudson highlands behind him, and began a leisurely progress down through Westchester, pausing at Edward Couenhoven's hostelry in Tarrytown at the corner of Main Street and Broadway, as the intersection would be known there and in thousands of other American towns, and stopping in Yonkers to dine with General Lewis Morris and to lodge at the Van Cortlandt house. Then on Friday morning, November 21, 1783, he came finally to the outer limits of New York City. He had left it more than seven years before at the head of a retreating, half-beaten army. He returned to it a conqueror.

# PART 3

## WASHINGTON IN NEW YORK CITY

### Chapter 1

### As Commander-in-Chief

When Washington returned to New York City in April 1776, after the triumph at Boston, he must have been reminded of the spring days he had spent there only three years before, when he had brought Martha's son Jack up from Mount Vernon to register him at King's College. The chief social event of his five days in the city, between May 26 and May 31, had been the strenuous farewell given to his old acquaintance, Lieutenant General Thomas Gage, Commander-in-Chief of the British military forces in America.

[1773]    Gage had spent the better part of twenty-two years in America, since the King had sent him to fight the French in 1755, and Washington had played a role, minor though it was, in the victory which brought him distinction and promotion. The General had been somewhat more popular in America than most British commanders, at least among the conservative merchants and upper-class citizens, and New York society was intent on giving him a farewell befitting his distinguished station and long residence. They proffered the customary "elegant entertainment" on May 27, and Washington attended as a guest. Then, the day before he was to

225

start home, he had dinner with General Gage. Presumably they discussed old campaigns, especially Braddock's fatal march, which they had shared, and no doubt found pleasure in each other's company.

Scarcely more than two years later they were the opposing generals in the struggle for Boston. It had been Gage who, as Governor of Massachusetts in 1774, tried to suppress the growing rebellion by seizing Sam Adams and Hancock, and ended by directing the first battles of the war at Lexington and Concord, after which he found himself besieged by his old friend Washington. At that juncture the world must have made very little sense to Thomas Gage. Replaced by Howe, he had resigned his commission and gone home in October 1775.

[1776]     Now, six months after his departure, Washington was returning to the scene of their last conversation, a general in his own right, fresh from a victory over Gage's countrymen and confident he could win others. If the British leader had been the vindictive kind, he might have derived ample satisfaction from the record of what happened to General Washington during that hot, tense summer in New York.

The change from the Boston he had left nine days before must have been startling. There, as Mercy Warren had reported, "a dead silence reigns through the long, extended lines. The total stagnation of business within, and the still calm without the walls of Boston resemble that serenity which often succeeds the most violent concussion in the world of nature."

New York, on the other hand, was nervous and excitable, stirring with a restless activity. One of Washington's most observant colonels, Loammi Baldwin, described it: "The city is grand, the buildings lofty and elegant. The streets are not so fine, I think, as those in Boston, but the buildings exceed. ... The manners of the people differ something from the natural inhabitants of Boston, having Jewish, Dutch and Irish customs." It was a city divided, as before, but the Sons of Liberty

226

nominally held the upper hand and the rebels were more numerous, though the Loyalists had the security of knowing that the British warships in the harbor could destroy the town any time they wished.

Washington arrived there on April 13. Martha came four days later, having been delayed on the road by the illness of Jack. Until her arrival, her husband had been living at the house of William Smith, who became one of the most articulate Loyalists in the city and left a diary, still unpublished, which is a superb account of life in the city from the Tory viewpoint. His home was directly opposite Governor Tryon's former quarters on Broadway. (The Governor had taken refuge on one of the British warships in the harbor.)

When Martha arrived, Washington established new headquarters in a more comfortable place, far out in the country at the mansion of Abraham Mortier, who had been for years Paymaster General of the British forces. The Mortier house stood at the southeast corner of Varick and Charlton streets, now in the southwestern reaches of Greenwich Village, considered remote in those days because it was two and a half miles from the fort on the Battery. The region it lay in was called Lispenard's Meadow, part of the estate where Washington had landed the year before, en route to Boston; later it became known as Richmond Hill.

Abigail Adams was disdainful of the Mortier mansion. "The house is convenient for one family, but too small for more," she told her husband. For the Washingtons it would be home for an indefinite time, and they proceeded to furnish it, with feather bed, bolster, pillows, bed curtains, crockery and glassware. Anticipating the time, approaching sooner than he thought, when he would not have the comforts of home, General Washington also purchased camp equipment, at the more favorable New York prices: sleeping and dining tents, eighteen walnut camp stools and three camp tables of the same wood.

There was scant amusement in New York. Martha could not re-establish the comfortable social life of Cambridge in this

227

tense city, and her husband was busy day and night.* Washington was not at all content to have her stay there. Like everyone else, he was apprehensive of the imminent prospect of enemy bombardment, and for Martha there was also the danger of smallpox. It was this latter peril that impelled him to take her along when he was summoned to Philadelphia on May 21, to advise and consult with Congress. There, although she agonized in advance about the process, she submitted to inoculation, and remained for a time to recover from the experience after her husband returned to New York on June 5.

Where the Washingtons stayed in Philadelphia during this time is not clear. Where they did *not* stay, however, makes a wry sort of social footnote. John Hancock, then the President of Congress, had extended a cordial invitation to the General and his lady when he wrote on May 16, presenting Congress' desire for consultation. "I request the favor," he added, "that you will please to honor me with you and your lady's company at my house, where I have a bed at your service, and where every endeavor on my part and Mrs. Hancock's will be exerted to make your abode agreeable. I reside in an airy, open part of the city, in Arch Street, corner of Fourth St." When the travelers arrived in the city, however, they were greeted with a regretful note from the President, asserting that he could not meet them because of a severe attack of the gout.

Thus the gout came between the Hancocks and the Washingtons socially for the first time. As noted in Part 2, Chapter

* In Appendix IV-L, pp. 635–37, Freeman discusses the interesting question of where, if anywhere, Washington maintained a downtown office to transact his military business between the time he left Smith's house and his departure for Philadelphia on May 21. (After his return it is fairly certain he maintained his office in the Mortier house.) Tradition has placed this business headquarters variously in the general vicinity of Chatham Square, on Pearl Street across from Hanover Square, and at number 180 Pearl Street, opposite Cedar Street. Analyzing the evidence, none of which is to be found in orderly books or other contemporary records, Freeman concludes that the office, if it existed, was on an elevation near what was called the "Oyster Battery," at Morris and Greenwich streets.

2, it caused a certain coolness thirteen years later, when Washington the President came to Boston on the grand tour, only to find Governor Hancock in bed with the same affliction.

Back in New York again, Washington found a brief relaxation from the mounting tension all about him in an entertainment given by the Provincial Congress at Fraunces' Tavern (which the official invitation misspelled Frances's) on June 18. This dinner was gaily described in a letter from Captain Caleb Gibbs, of Washington's Guard, to his "Dear Penelope":

"This afternoon, the Provincial Congress of New York gave an elegant entertainment to General Washington and his suite; the general and staff officers, and the commanding officer of the different regiments in and near the city. Many patriotic toasts were offered and drank with the greatest pleasure and decency. After the toasts, Little Phil, of the Guard, was brought in to sing H——'s new campaign song, and was joined by all the under officers, who seemed much animated by the accompanying of Clute's drumsticks and Aaron's fife. Our good General Putnam got sick and went to his quarters before dinner was over, and we missed him a marvel, as there is not a chap in the camp who can lead him in the Maggie Lauder song."

The song Little Phil sang with such success was probably the one that began:

> *When virtuous ardor, from motions sincere*
> *Nerves the arm of a soldier, what foe can he fear?*
> *Undaunted he fights, and his glorious name*
> *Immortal shall flourish through every campaign.*

It ended, a mouthful for any singer:

> *Let spirit and union dispel party strife,*
> *While struggling for freedom and empire and life;*
> *Ungenerous sentiments nobly disdain*
> *Fir'd with the idea of such a campaign.*

*Then wreaths shall be twined of unfading renown,*
*Our brows to encircle and actions to crown;*
*And the clarion immortal, of sonorous fame,*
*Shall transmit to all ages, this glorious campaign.*[1]

Washington ate often, then and later, at the tavern of his friend, "Black Sam" Fraunces, later his steward during the New York term of his presidency. The tavern's longroom, which was restored by the Sons of the American Revolution in 1907 and is the only part of the place remaining largely unaltered, was a favorite spot for New York gay dogs and the city's numerous clubs and societies to hold their parties. The room has two fireplaces and five windows on the street—originally over a piazza, which has since been removed.

Black Sam's family was immortalized by tradition shortly after the congressional dinner party, in a way that demonstrated the city's hysterical state of mind. On June 22, Mayor David Matthews was arrested on Washington's orders and the existence of a widespread liaison between the British, operating from their ships in the harbor, and both civilians and soldiers in the city, including some of Washington's own Guard, was disclosed. It was more liaison than plot, because the plotters themselves, under questioning, were vague about their plans, although they were ambitious enough to have contemplated seizing the city.

Rumor swirled through the taverns and over dinner tables: Washington and some of his staff were to be assassinated. When the expected British fleet arrived to reinforce the ships already there, it was to be the signal for a bloody uprising. The troops were to be slaughtered by their own cannon. The torch was to be applied to New York City at nine different places. A force of two hundred Tories was lurking in the woods and swamps on remote parts of the island.

Whether Sam's family and establishment became the heroes of the piece then or later is not clear, but the rumor that has survived until the present moment, and was accepted by at

230

least one nineteenth-century historian, is that someone at Fraunces' Tavern exposed the core of the plot, which was to poison Washington. Sometimes it is a waiter, William Collier, who is the particular hero; in other versions it is Sam's wife, or her housekeeper. The most popular form of the story is that the heroine was Sam's good-looking daughter Peggy, who pretended to be a part of the conspiracy in order to expose it.

In its most widely circulated form, the story relates that Peggy listened to the evil urgings of Thomas Hickey, identified as a member of Washington's Guard, and consented to serve the General with a plate of poisoned green peas. For what happened next, one could refer, out of numerous instances, to an *Elementary History of the United States*, by G. P. Quackenbos, published in 1886 and adopted as a text by the public schools of Brooklyn.

"Fixing his [Washington's] eyes upon the guilty man," this text relates, "he put a spoonful of peas on his plate, and asked him, 'Shall I eat of these?' 'I don't know,' stammered the man, turning deadly pale. Washington took some on his knife, and again asked, 'Shall I eat of these?' The man could not say a word, but raised his hand as if to prevent it."

Somehow this statement got out of the quiet of the classroom and into the newspapers, where it created widespread indignation—not because it was a story without a word of truth in it, but because of that one phrase, "Washington took some on his knife . . ." Did Washington eat peas with his knife? Some quite eminent newspapers thundered that the school children of America were being taught that Washington had no table manners and wasn't a gentleman. A writer in the Cleveland *Leader* was one of the few to defend poor Quackenbos. He did so on the ground that the "whole literary United States at the time of Washington . . . seemed to be a mutual admiration society," and unfavorable gossip was not likely to be repeated.[2]

Thus the truth of the whole affair, which was more sordid than romantic, was obscured for generations of Americans by such fruitless arguments over non-existent occurrences.

At the time, the plot's importance to Washington was not so much the disclosure of treachery, which was to be expected, but the possible extent to which disaffection had touched his army. Most of the dozen or more conspirators sent off to prison in Connecticut with Mayor Matthews were civilians, but Thomas Hickey, a counterfeiter and deserter of low character, had implicated eight other members of the Guard in the plot, and had boasted that at least seven hundred soldiers had declared themselves for the King and stood ready to turn their coats when the time came. Hickey's companion, Michael Lynch, and other soldiers involved boasted further of the inroads treachery had made in the army.

Discounting the utterances of men with no reputation for truth, it was still plain that there was serious disloyalty in the army. Since Hickey seemed to be the worst of the lot that had been caught up in the net, Washington determined to make an example of him. He was court-martialed, convicted of "mutiny, sedition and treachery," and sentenced to be hanged on June 28.

Hickey died badly in the presence of nearly twenty thousand people, shortly before noon. He refused the consolation of religion, calling the chaplains cutthroats, broke down in sobbing, then wiped his tears and cried out angrily against "Greene," although it is not certain whether he meant the General or a fellow conspirator. As he swung to his death, the effect on the emotional throng was electric. One newspaper reported somewhat mysteriously that "during the execution, Kip, the moon-curser, suddenly sank down and expired immediately."

Washington summed up the whole episode succinctly in his General Orders for the day, pointing out the moral lesson he hoped to impress on his army:

"The unhappy fate of Thomas Hickey, executed this day for mutiny, sedition and treachery, the General hopes will be a warning to every soldier in the army to avoid those crimes, and all others, so disgraceful to the character of a soldier, and pernicious to his country, whose pay he receives and bread he eats—and in order to avoid those crimes the most certain method is to keep out of the temptation of them, and particularly to avoid lewd women, who, by the dying confession of this poor criminal, first led him into practices which ended in an untimely and ignominious death."

Two days after this event, Martha left the city for Virginia. She had returned to New York from Philadelphia, successfully recovered from her inoculation, during the week of June 16, but Washington could not permit her to stay in a city which hourly faced British attack of one kind or another. Her son Jack and his wife had gone soon after May 13, and she would have company at Mount Vernon. Most of the other officers' wives were departing the threatened city as June ended—except for the lovely, unpredictable young wife of Nathanael Greene. Catherine was returning as the others were leaving, causing no end of gossip among the ladies.

Early in July the expected British warships, carrying the troops evacuated from Boston, appeared off Sandy Hook. There seemed, in fact, to be a concentration of British troops and an attack was considered imminent, but whether upon Long Island or the city itself no one could be certain. Washington's headquarters in the Mortier house was frantic with activity. The aides, those "beardless boys," as one observer wrote disparagingly, were hurrying about on missions, interviewing prisoners, copying letters, carrying orders, helping non-combatants to get out of the city, and hearing applications of every kind. Obviously Washington needed help, and at this opportune moment Tench Tilghman appeared on the scene.[3] The florid-faced young man with gray eyes and reddish-brown hair quickly became one of the General's best-loved and most trusted aides, relieving the commander of a great part of his detail work. Tilghman was a Marylander whose father and friends there and in Philadelphia were staunch Tories, but he had been converted to the rebel cause by George III's speech to Parliament after Bunker Hill. "I was convinced no terms were to be expected but blind submission, and from that moment I was determined never to submit to them," he wrote. He joined up as a volunteer, and soon after he had come to the Continental Army in New York by way of the Pennsylvania militia, he entered Washington's family.

Tilghman had come just in time to be present at a historic moment. At six o'clock on July 9, the soldiers not on active duty were assembled by brigades, and the brigade commanders standing before their men began to read, in their own time and in the loudest voices they could muster, from copies of a document—a document which began, "When, in the course of human events . . ." Washington did not, according to tradition, sit on his horse with the men about him in a hollow square to hear the reading. Probably he was in his office, well aware of the document's significance and appreciative of its language, but too busy for meditation, or to make himself available for a tableau.

At the end of the reading, some of the brigades gave the regulation three cheers, others exploded in a patriotic shout. But for the moment they had no further opportunity to celebrate; the orders were to keep them in quarters and on duty because the attack might come at any moment.

The citizenry were in a mood to celebrate, however, and in the evening they were free to do so. There was a good deal of cheering and spontaneous huzzaing in the streets as the crowds, particularly the young men, strolled about looking for mischief. An undercurrent of unspoken communication drew many of them together at Bowling Green, where they stood looking up at the equestrian statue of George III in the robes of a Roman emperor, a third larger than life. It was by all odds the finest piece of statuary in New York. Of gilded lead, it stood on a fifteen-foot-high white marble pedestal. The King gazed out over the lowly multitude of his erstwhile colonial subjects with what the Sons of Liberty thought an unbearably disdainful air. To most of them even his leaden presence profaned the atmosphere of liberty, particularly at the moment of declared independence. A few determined Sons hoisted themselves over the ten-foot fence, crossed the grass of the oval and climbed up the base, where they applied ropes and bars to the statue and soon brought horse and rider crashing to the ground while a triumphant cry swelled from the crowd packed in the streets.

Appropriately, and thriftily, the broken pieces were gathered up and sent to Litchfield, Connecticut, where the lead was melted into bullets to be hurled back at George's loyal subjects. Only a piece of the horse's tail survived; it may be seen today in the museum of the New York Historical Society.

This act relieved the feelings of the Sons of Liberty, but it did little for the nerves of the other citizens as July dragged on and the storm failed to break. August came in with the hottest weather that the oldest inhabitant could remember. Soldiers and civilians sweltered and speculated about the British. A spirit of panic was abroad in the city, and nearly every day some new rumor set off terror-stricken milling in the streets. It was estimated that the British fleet lying between Sandy Hook and Staten Island harbored forty thousand regulars, preparing for an assault on Manhattan. Confronting such a force with an inadequate army, Washington had called for volunteers. Fear and patriotism alike had produced a rush of recruits whose costumes evidenced their haste to enlist in the cause.

Never had an army boasted such a variety of uniforms. There were homemade working clothes, green hunting outfits, red coats left over from the French and Indian War, Delaware volunteers in dark blue coats with red facings, and riflemen from New Jersey with short red coats and striped trousers. No two soldiers in the Pennsylvania regiments seemed to match: some had brown coats faced with buff, others blue coats faced with red, or brown coats faced with white and held together with pewter buttons. Most wore buckskin breeches and black cocked hats with white bindings. Doing their commander proud, the Virginians were the most resplendent in white smock-frocks, ruffled at the neck, elbows and wrists. They wore black stockings, their hair was in queues, and their round-topped black hats were broad-brimmed. They were nearly a match for the Guards, the elite corps, whose blue coats, faced with buff, were worn over red waistcoats and buckskin breeches. White tape bound their black felt hats, and their bayonet and body belts were of white.⁴

These motley troops were committed at last, just as the August heat and the waiting had become nearly unendurable. The General Orders of August 23 told the story in solemn, portentous words: "The enemy have now landed on Long Island, and the hour is fast approaching on which the honor and success of this army, and the safety of our bleeding country will depend. Remember, officers and soldiers, that you are free-men, fighting for the blessings of liberty, that slavery will be your portion, and that of your posterity, if you do not acquit yourselves like men."

They did acquit themselves like men in that much-debated Battle of Long Island, which began on August 27, whatever the rights or wrongs of the strategy may be. To Washington it was a terrible slaughter of brave men, as he watched from behind a redoubt the rout of Stirling's division, and saw the Maryland battalions methodically cut down.*

At the end of the second day of confused struggle, it was obvious that the whole American army would be chopped up piecemeal if a retreat were not ordered. The decision was taken in the old Dutch stone church in Brooklyn, where Fulton and Flatbush avenues now intersect, at a hasty council called at five in the afternoon. Even then the disaster might have been total if a fog had not mercifully cloaked the retreat across the East River on the following night. Washington stayed at the point of crossing the whole night, mounted on his gray horse, anxiously calculating the race against time. He and his aides were in the last boats to leave the Brooklyn shore at six o'clock

---

* The hill from which Washington watched the battle would be today the block bounded by Court, Clinton, Atlantic and Pacific avenues, in Brooklyn.

on the morning of August 30, and the British were breathing hard on their heels.

For once Washington was too exhausted to send his report to Congress that Friday. It had been three days of shock and flight, demanding every ounce of his resources. Yet he began his dispatch almost apologetically when he was able to write it on Saturday:

"Inclination as well as duty would have induced me to give Congress the earliest information of my removal, and that of the troops, from Long Island and its dependencies to this city the night before last; but the extreme fatigue which myself and family have undergone, as much from the weather since as the engagement on the twenty-seventh, rendered me and them entirely unfit to take pen in hand. Since Monday scarce any of us have been out of the lines till our passage across the East River was effected yesterday morning, and for forty-eight hours preceding that, I had hardly been off my horse, and never closed my eyes, so that I was quite unfit to write or dictate till this morning."

In later dispatches, Washington sought to put the best official face on the matter, but the fact was that the American army had been soundly whipped. The reasons for it were hotly argued in New York and elsewhere, and are still debated by scholars today.

A nearly equivalent amount of confusion and tradition surrounds Washington's movements in the September days following the retreat. They were confusing days, as he prepared to abandon the city to the British. The army began moving northward to Fort Washington and Kingsbridge on September 13, and it seems probable that he changed headquarters, beginning that day, from the Mortier house to the Roger Morris house on Harlem Heights, which he occupied on September 17. His stopping places in between are not verifiable, but they can be arrived at with more prospect of accuracy than the traditional accounts of his actions as the Americans retreated from New York Island.

On the night of the fourteenth, he may have been at Robert Murray's house, near the present Thirty-sixth Street and Fourth Avenue, although Freeman states that he was already established in the Morris house, prepared to ride to any point at which the British might be landing on the island. That point proved to be Kip's Bay, at about eleven o'clock next morning. Hurrying there with his aides, at about the foot of what is now Thirty-fourth Street, Washington gazed upon the sight so utterly dismaying to a commander, one he would see more than once—his troops fleeing in wild panic before the advancing British and Hessians. He did his best to rally them, but they were beyond recall. He did not, as tradition says, throw down his hat and cry, "Are these the men with which I am to defend America?" nor did he shout, "Good God, have I got such troops as these?" nor did he and his generals whip the Connecticut militiamen with canes to make them fight. Such language or behavior would not have been Washington's way. He was angry enough, and he exerted himself as much as it was humanly possible to stem the retreat. More than that he did not and could not do, and it was not enough. The British losses were absurdly small; the Americans lost their pride, twenty officers and three hundred men captured, large supplies of baggage and stores and heavy cannon, and they lost New York Island in the bargain, through one small, disgraceful encounter. The British threw a line across the island and prepared to advance northward.

Whether Washington stopped at the home of Charles Ward Apthorpe, at the present corner of Ninety-first Street and Ninth Avenue, is not determined, but the story is probably untrue that in this splendid house, one of the best on the island, he lingered nearly too long with his host, who was a Loyalist but a peaceable one, and departed only an hour before the British officers rode up.

The disgrace of Kip's Bay, on Sunday, September 15, was followed on Monday by another determined effort to rout the Continentals. The Battle of Harlem Heights, as Freeman notes, has had an entirely disproportionate number of words written about it, considering the small number of men involved in the action. The site itself, as he says, has had a respectable body of literature built around it, a great deal of it conflicting and contradictory.[5]

To the casual tourist who surveys the battleground today, the action can best be visualized from the grounds of the Jumel Mansion, as the house of Washington's former comrade-in-arms, Roger Morris, came to be called in the later and more gaudy years of its history. The house is open to the public today, in an excellent state of preservation; its history would make a book by itself.

From this mansion, situated in present terms between 161st and 162nd streets and Edgecombe Avenue and Jumel Terrace, Washington rode out shortly after seven o'clock on the morning of the sixteenth, as the British and American advance guards clashed. His command post was the so-called Point of Rocks, where Ninth Avenue and 126th Street intersect. Now, however, he rode to his army's advance position on the north side of West 125th Street, between Manhattan Avenue and the Hudson.

It was somewhere in this neighborhood, as Washington hesitated, trying to decide whether to order an attack, that the British appeared far below him, blowing a derisive call on their bugles—not any of the military signals, but one familiar to an old Virginia fox hunter: the call given when the fox has been killed and the huntsmen are ending the chase.* "I never felt such a sensation before; it seemed to crown our disgrace," Joseph Reed wrote later.

At any rate, the musical taunt decided Washington on an advance, though a limited one, and the battle properly began.

---

* The apotheosis of scholarship may have been reached by Dr. Freeman in his footnote on this bugle call (IV, 198), disclosing his well-known capacity for infinite detail, which is likely to astound the non-scholarly reader. The call, he notes, "may have been the 'whoo-whoop.' The length of the blasts on a horn of one key is given in Joseph B. Thomas, *Hounds and Hunting Through the Ages*, 130."

Then it was that the American troops redeemed themselves from the panicky flight of the day before and, in their turn, pursued the fleeing British. General Clinton attributed his defeat to the "ungovernable impetuosity of the light troops." Whatever the reason, it gave the Continental Army and its commander a buoyant lift that helped them forget Long Island and Kip's Bay. With his customary understatement, Washington wrote to Congress: "The affair I am in hopes will be attended with many salutary consequences, as it seems to have greatly inspirited the whole of our troops."

A month later, Washington and the army were on the move northward once more, as detailed elsewhere, leaving New York Island until the end of the war.

[1783]    When once more he returned to the city, he came as the conquering general in November 1783, taking possession as his last official act before he resigned his post as Commander-in-Chief and hastened on to Mount Vernon. With Governor Clinton and an assortment of other dignitaries, he had ridden down through Westchester, past the place of defeat at Fort Washington, past the place of victory, mere skirmish though it might be, at Harlem Heights. The Continentals now were encamped somewhat below this battleground, waiting to enter and occupy the city, while the British rear guard rested sullenly nearby, waiting for the order of evacuation.

At the Widow Day's tavern in the village of Harlem, at the present corner of 125th Street and Eighth Avenue, Washington paused from November 21 to 24 while the details of the official entry were being settled. On the twenty-fourth, he was told that Carleton intended to leave at noon the next day.

The column assembled early on the morning of the twenty-fifth, a clear, sparkling, late autumn day with a sharp wind out of the northwest. As the procession moved down into town, Washington noted how war had changed the city. Along the Boston Road, on which they rode, there was not a tree or a

fence rail remaining; the British troops had used every scrap
of wood to keep themselves warm. The occupied city appeared
shabby, like a recluse coming out of retirement into the sun.

Now they passed the fields near Kip's Bay, with its memories
of panic and shame, and rode on, perhaps stopping at the Beekman house to refresh themselves. General Knox and the troops
had preceded Washington and Clinton downtown, according
to plan, which provided that the army should first occupy the
city and secure order, and then Governor Clinton would officially take over its administration. For his own part, though
he was the man the entire population waited joyously to see,
Washington had cast himself in the role of spectator, merely
the Governor's guest.

There was no doubt of who played the hero's role in the
eyes of the populace when they caught sight of Washington
astride his splendid gray mount, as the cavalcade arrived at the
Bull's Head Tavern, on the Bowery between Bayard and Pump
streets. The people had waited there by order, on the line
which that morning had divided British and American troops,
and now they set up a great cry of welcome that shattered the
November air. General Knox rode up with the citizens' welcoming committee, which had assembled earlier at the Bowling
Green, and there was a good deal of handshaking and re-form-
ing of columns. Clinton, riding a bay gelding, fell in beside the
General, the Westchester Light Dragoons took up escort
positions, and the civilians followed behind.

Slowly the column flowed down Chatham Street, between
lanes of people who knew not whether to cheer or weep, and
tried to do both, until it reached Tea Water Pump, near Pearl
Street. There another contingent of civilians joined the procession, and Knox and the former officers with him split off to
proceed by a shorter route, for sentimental reasons: the veterans
of the Revolution wanted to take part in the grand welcome
that would greet their chief at Cape's Tavern, the immediate
goal.

As Washington turned into Broadway, he was met by the

eight hundred soldiers who had faced the British that morning, along with other units, and these joined in the procession. The tearful, joyously shouting crowds who lined the broad thoroughfare had seen the British troops leave, and they had watched the hated enemy marching up and down their streets for interminable years. Like the citizens of Paris in World War II, they greeted the liberating force with an emotion nearly too deep for words, but unlike the Parisians, they saw in these liberators their countrymen, whose appearance was a reminder of the terrible odds which had prevailed against victory. One woman who watched wrote, years afterward:

"We had been accustomed for a long time to military display in all the finish and finery of garrison life; the troops just leaving us were as if equipped for show, and with their scarlet uniforms and burnished arms, made a brilliant display; the troops that marched in, on the contrary, were ill-clad and weatherbeaten, and made a forlorn appearance; but then they were *our* troops, and as I looked at them and thought upon all they had done and suffered for us, my heart and my eyes were full, and I admired and gloried in them the more, because they were weatherbeaten and forlorn."

The procession came at last to a halt at Cape's Tavern, on the west side of Broadway at the corner of Thames Street, a site where the famous City Hotel was erected in the nineteenth century. There occurred the official presentation of addresses, after which Washington went inside and the ceremony of entrance was over.

While all this was happening, a seriocomic affair had taken place down at the Battery. There another part of the ceremony, and a symbolically important one in the eyes of victor and vanquished, was to be enacted with the raising of the American flag over Fort George and the firing of a thirteen-gun salute. This would be something of an insult thrown in the teeth of the departing British, whose troop-laden boats were still plying out to the warships. The men and commanders on these ships were already in a state of indignation because for days the

French and American merchantmen who shared the harbor with them had been flying their own and each other's flags.

But when the company of light infantry arrived at the flag-pole with the Stars and Stripes, they discovered that the beaten foe, not quite daring to cut down the pole, had tried to avoid a parting indignity by cutting the halyards, taking off the cleats and greasing the pole.

There was an excited council of war at the base, while the British stopped rowing in the harbor and those already aboard hung on the rails to see how the Americans would resolve their dilemma. Like the site of the Battle of Harlem Heights, this thin slice of history has enjoyed a quantity of analysis far beyond its importance. Freeman suggests, and a contemporary account in the Clinton Papers supports him, that someone simply got a ladder. At any rate, the colors were raised, the cannons fired, and New York City passed into American hands.

As might be expected, the next few days were virtually given up to "elegant entertainments." The citizens of the city who had returned from exile gave one on the twenty-eighth at Cape's Tavern for some three hundred gentlemen, including, of course, General Washington and Governor Clinton. On December 1, the Governor was the host at Cape's. The French Ambassador, Washington, "the principal officers of this state and of the army" and a hundred others "passed the day and evening with great conviviality."

Washington must have sat through these occasions with impatience. He did not intend to stay in the city a day longer than was necessary before he made his long-deferred journey home. There was one more ceremony, however, which he had no wish to avoid, although he did not anticipate it, and that was the farewell to his officers. He set the time for it at noon in Fraunces' Tavern, on December 4.

With his usual promptness, he stepped into the longroom almost as soon as the clock had finished striking. Looking about at the faces of those waiting for him, not all of them familiar, he could reflect sadly on how few of those who started the conflict with him had survived to the end. Congress had commissioned twenty-nine major generals, but of these only three —Knox, Steuben and McDougall—were there in the longroom: six were dead, one a traitor and seven had resigned. The others had not been able to attend. Of the forty-four men made brigadiers during the war, only one was present. And of the others of lesser rank who stood up as Washington entered, Freeman has this to say of them: ". . . they were typical of the hundreds who had remained at their posts in poverty and shabbiness while their families at home had pinched and patched though speculating neighbors had grown fat. The poorest officers, many of them, had been among the finest. . . ."

It was one of the few supremely emotional moments in the life of this most controlled of men, and Washington temporarily lost his superb composure as he looked about him. Much has been written of his aloofness, of the marble idol who had none of Lincoln's humanity, yet he was moved to public tears on the really great occasions of his life: when he was given command of the Continental Army, when he resigned his command, when he was inaugurated as President, and as he prepared for this last farewell.

If they had not been so moved themselves, one supposes that the assembled officers might have felt some embarrassment at seeing their calm, confident, serene commander hardly able to speak. They watched him turn away abruptly and try to keep the affair moving by going through the motions of eating some of the collation which Black Sam had laid out for his distinguished guest. But the General could not get the food past the emotion that clutched at his throat, and he gave up, filling a wineglass instead. Gratefully the others followed his example. The familiar motion gave them, too, the opportunity to gain control of themselves.

When all the glasses were full, Washington spoke. The room was suddenly very quiet. In the silence they could hear the General's voice, queer and choked, saying to them, "With a heart full of love and gratitude, I now take leave of you. I most devoutly wish that your later days may be as prosperous and happy as your former ones have been glorious and honorable."

They tried to answer him, each in his own way, but the result was only a confused murmuring of sound, before they raised their glasses and drank the wine. Again there was silence as the glasses were sipped and memories crowded about. They could not look at each other. Washington spoke once more, his voice shaking as the tears blinded him: "I cannot come to each of you, but I shall feel obliged if each of you will come and take me by the hand."

The first to come was Henry Knox, and he was entitled to be first because he had given eight years of the most faithful service to his General. Not one of the senior officers had been so unswervingly loyal as Knox. When he came forward and held out his hand, Washington's reserve broke completely. Frankly weeping, he embraced his Chief of Artillery and kissed him on the cheek. With precedent thus established, he would have to perform the same act for them all, even those whom he did not know, but since they were all as much affected, it became simply an unashamed outpouring of sentiment from men who had seldom, if ever, indulged themselves in the luxury. No one tried to say anything to the General; each one came to him, received the embrace and passed on. Describing the scene years later, Benjamin Tallmadge recalled vividly what they felt: "The simple thought that we were then about to part from the man who had conducted us through a long and bloody war, and under whose conduct the glory and independence of our country had been achieved, and that we should see his face no more in this world seemed to me utterly insupportable."

To Washington, also, the scene had become insupportable. He could endure no longer this violent wrenching of his emotions, to which he was so unaccustomed. As the last man stepped away, he went to the door, raised an arm in a farewell salute and left them. Walking down the stairs, his iron control reasserted itself; he could not face the crowds outside in such a state. Only the taut muscles in his cheeks and the thin, drawn line of his lips showed the tight rein he was holding as he walked out of Fraunces', through a guard of honor, and down the street to the slip at Whitehall. Every inch of space along the way and in the area around the wharf was packed with men, women and children, pushing and crowding to get even a glimpse of him. He did not wave and smile to the cheering throng, as other departing heroes would have done. He could not. He was tense, still controlling himself with a mighty effort, unable to say a word, his face a mask.

He walked onto his barge, ready to take him across the harbor to Jersey City (or Powles Hook), where he would begin the long ride homeward. The craft shoved off immediately at his signal. As the water widened between boat and shore, he turned and gave to the white flutter of hands raised in farewell the same embracing gesture he had given his officers as he left them. Then he turned his back on New York, on the British ships in the harbor preparing to make sail, on the Revolution itself, and stood alone with his cloak wrapped tight against the bite of the December wind, a lonely figure against the bright sky arching over a liberated city and a free nation.

# Chapter 2

## As President

No President of the United States has ever approached the office with so much private misgiving and public acclamation as George Washington, when he became the first Chief Executive in 1789. There have been Vice-Presidents called upon to assume the duties of suddenly deceased Presidents who were appalled by the magnitude of a responsibility they had never thought to confront, but these were lesser men and they were not in Washington's peculiar situation. The enthusiasm which greeted the accession of other national heroes has been the end result of campaigning and the product of that great American pastime, politics. But for Washington there was no campaign, the country was only beginning to formulate the rules of its national game, and his immense popularity was due solely to his primary role in winning the war that made the presidency possible, a role that could never be duplicated by his successors.

When the office came to the man, it found him at Mount Vernon, still in the process of reorganizing and forwarding his private affairs, which had fallen into serious neglect after his eight years' absence with the armies. He had slipped back easily into the quiet, peaceful life of the plantation, absorbed with the one subject that interested him more than any other—agriculture—and content to enjoy the gracious hospitality of tidewater Virginia.

In these circumstances it is understandable, and believable, that he should declare to his former Chief of Artillery, Henry Knox, "In confidence I tell you (with the world it would obtain little credit) that my movements to the chair of government will be accompanied by feelings not unlike those of a culprit who is going to the place of his execution, so unwilling am I, in the evening of a life nearly consumed in public cares, to quit a peaceful abode for an ocean of difficulties, without that competency of political skill, abilities and inclination which are necessary to manage the helm . . . ." [1]

In the same vein, he recorded privately in his diary on April 16, as he left home for New York: "About ten o'clock I bade adieu to Mount Vernon, to private life, and to domestic felicity, and with a mind oppressed with more anxious and painful sensations than I have words to express, set out for New York in company with Mr. Thomson and Colonel Humphreys, with the best disposition to render service to my country in obedience to its calls, but with less hope of answering its expectations."

[1789]     Of all the journeys George Washington made in his lifetime, this ride to New York was perhaps most remarkable. From beginning to end it was a triumphal procession that would have honored a Roman conqueror. At this moment he reached the peak of his prestige. The people had honored him as Commander-in-Chief and trampled on each other for the privilege of seeing him, but there were other generals. As President-elect of the United States, however, he stood alone. Entrusted with the direction of an experiment about which men still disagreed violently, and which even the boldest approached with some misgivings, Washington embodied in his person and his office all the hopes and fears of the nation. He was war hero, father of the country and First Citizen, all in one.

He was no farther away from home than Alexandria, a town that had known him well most of his life, when he was given the first intimation of what awaited him. A large body of his friends and neighbors met him at some distance from town, and according to one contemporary account, their "attachment to him was such that, not satisfied with attending him to the verge of their own state, they crossed over in numerous crowds to Georgetown, where they surrendered him over to the arms

of an affectionate sister state . . . ." [2] By this time it must have
been clear to Washington that the progress to Boston in 1775,
tumultuous as it had been, would be far surpassed.

At Georgetown the ferry transported him with his escort
into the arms of another welcoming committee. The Alexan-
drians were hosts at an early dinner in Wise's Tavern, and
afterward the Georgetown people went with him out of town
as far as Spurrier's Tavern, where the Baltimore committee
waited. Thus he was passed along the entire route from hand
to hand, committee to committee, tavern to tavern, street after
street lined with cheering citizens come to honor the man who,
as one paper remarked, had "bid adieu to the peaceful retreat
of Mount Vernon in order to save his country once more from
confusion and anarchy." [3]

At Baltimore he rested Friday night, April 17, at Grant's
Fountain Inn. Fortunately for the sake of that rest, he arrived
too late for a public dinner, but the committee insisted on entertaining him at supper. It was after ten o'clock before he
could retire. Yet he was on his way again at half past five on
Saturday morning. The escort was there promptly to ride with
his carriage, but after they had traveled seven miles, he alighted
and bade them good-by, insisting that they trouble themselves
no further. "We shall only add on this occasion," wrote an
admiring correspondent, "that those who had often seen him
before, and those who never had, were equally anxious to see
him . . . ."

He was in Wilmington, Delaware, on Sunday and reached
Philadelphia about one o'clock the next day, escorted into town
by the President of the state, the Governor, the Speaker of the
Assembly, the Chief Justice, the Attorney-General, other officials, two city troops of horse, the county troop, a detachment
of artillery, a body of light infantry, and "a numerous concourse of citizens on horseback and foot."

When he crossed Gray's Ferry bridge into the city, the most
startling incident of his journey occurred. The bridge had
been decorated with laurel and other evergreens by Gray him-

self, Charles Willson Peale and other eminent Philadelphians, but the really elaborate part of its ornamentation were the arches of laurel at each end, intentionally reminiscent of the Roman arches used to welcome returning heroes. As he passed beneath one of these arches, an admiring newspaper reported, "a lad, beautifully ornamented with sprigs of laurel, assisted by certain machinery, let drop above the Hero's head, unperceived by him, a civic crown of laurel."[4]

What Washington thought of this blessing which appeared to drop literally from heaven, he did not record, but he must have been shaken. He had never been so thoroughly welcomed.

At the head of the procession, he rode on horseback so that everyone might see him. People were jammed against each other on the streets, in the doors and windows, and they hung from trees like so many monkeys. Philadelphia had never seen such a turnout. The parade halted at the City Tavern, where at three o'clock the President sat down with two hundred and fifty others to a public dinner. As he ate, a band played appropriate airs from opera, and the tunes of the Revolution. When the wine was passed, the usual toasts were supplemented by "The State of Virginia." Ships in the harbor broke out the colors of various nations, including Great Britain.

Washington spent that night at Robert Morris's house on Market Street, and in the morning received the endless addresses from state, city and societies before he departed.* As he came into Trenton, surrounded by the customary escort, he encountered at the bridge south of the city a scene to which, as a correspondent truly noted, "no description can do justice."

---

\* A tradition related by Jephtha Simms, in his *Frontiersmen of New York*, says that between Philadelphia and Trenton, Washington came upon something which touched him. Stephen Ogden, a soldier who had fought at the Battle of Monmouth and suffered a terrible wound in the hips, was standing beside the road with his three sons, Charles, Ephraim and Jacob. Washington did not recognize the old soldier, though it was said he had consoled Ogden personally as he lay wounded on the battlefield, but he could not help smiling as he saw the three youngsters lined up, powdered and ruffled, dressed in their best. They had taken off their hats and held them over their left breasts. Washington saluted the boys gravely and remarked, "Good morning, sirs."

### Washington in New York City

It must be supposed that the President approached this place with thoughts of himself as General. Here he had captured the Hessians and turned back the British at Assunpink Creek the day before the Battle of Princeton. The ladies of Trenton had evolved a plan and a program to commemorate the historic event when the President should pass by, and the result was formidable.

A triumphal arch twenty feet wide had been raised at the bridge. It was supported by thirteen columns, each twined with evergreen wreaths and covered with laurel. Large gilt letters on the front of the arch proclaimed: "The Defender of the Mothers Will Also Protect the Daughters!" Above this inscription, at the center of the arch, was a dome constructed of artificial flowers and evergreens, circling the dates of Washington's victories there, written in large gilt letters. An effulgent sunflower surmounted the dome, intended to be symbolic of the motto, "To you alone," since it was always pointed toward the sun.

The ladies who had conceived this pageantry and all the matrons of consequence in town, leading their daughters, were drawn up in imposing lines. Standing before them were thirteen young girls, dressed in white flowing robes and ornamented fore and aft with wreaths and chaplets of flowers. While Washington sat in front of this choir on his horse, they scattered flowers at his feet from the baskets they carried, meanwhile singing him a "sonata," as the contemporary accounts put it, music written for the occasion to words composed by no less a personage than Major Richard Howell, who five years later would be Governor of New Jersey. The Major's apostrophe to civic virtue ran:

> Welcome, mighty Chief! once more,
> Welcome to this grateful shore:
> Now no mercenary foe
> Aims again the fatal blow—
> Aims at thee the fatal blow.

*Virgins fair, and matrons grave,*
*Those thy conquering arms did save,*
*Build for thee triumphal bowers.*
*Strew, ye fair, his way with flowers—*
*Strew your Hero's way with flowers.*

The mighty Chief bowed low to the virgins fair and matrons grave, and requested them to accept his most grateful thanks. Before he left town he wrote a letter thanking them again for the "novel and grateful" manner with which they had received him, and for "the exquisite sensation he experienced in that affecting moment." It had reminded him, he said, of the "astonishing contrast between his former and actual situation at the same spot," which had now, he was happy to see, been adorned with elegant taste, including the "innocent appearance of the white-robed choir." All this, he concluded, had "made such impressions on his remembrance, as, he assures them, will never be effaced."

The impression made on the welcomers by their own welcome was quite as affecting. "The scene was truly grand," one observer wrote. "Universal silence prevailed—nothing was to be heard but the sweet notes of the songsters—and the mingled sentiments which crowded into the mind in the moments of solemn stillness during the song, bathed many cheeks with tears. . . ."[5]

Having heard the "sonata" and expressed his thanks, Washington rode on to Samuel Henry's City Tavern, at the southwest corner of Second and Warren streets, where he dined and afterward held a reception in the inn's parlors. It was late in the afternoon, according to one authority, before he climbed into his carriage and journeyed on to Princeton, where he is said to have spent the night at the home of the college's president, the Rev. Dr. John Witherspoon.[6] A contemporary account, however, asserts that he slept at Joseph Vandegrift's tavern, on North Warren Street, and set out again at sunrise next morning, accompanied by an escort eight miles out of town.[7]

There is no doubt whatever that he was in New Brunswick the next day. Artillery salutes and the ringing of bells roused the whole countryside as he approached, and a band of music joined the military units which came to escort him. He passed into the city between lines of troops, raised his hand to salute the "great number of the fair daughters of Columbia" who waved at him from the windows and doorways, and proceeded to the house of Major Thomas Egbert, where he received addresses. Presumably he ate there, too, though no record of it seems to exist. At five o'clock he crossed the river and resumed his journey, pausing for the night at nearby Woodbridge. Thursday morning he passed through Rahway and entered Elizabethtown between eight and nine o'clock, in a tumult to which by now he was nearly accustomed.

Alighting at Samuel Smith's tavern, he met the committee from New York and sat down with them to eat breakfast. Where he ate and what happened afterward runs into a tangle of conflicting testimony from contemporary sources. But there is some evidence to show, and logic supports it, that in Elizabeth he was conducted to the home of Elias Boudinot, a wealthy lawyer of considerable culture, who as President of Congress had signed the treaty of peace with England.[8]

Boudinot lived in a large, square house that seemed old-fashioned even in its own time. It had a gabled roof and tall chimneys, an imposing façade broken by a huge door with a brass knocker, and it was surrounded by expansive lawns and gardens, enormous trees, shrubbery and vines. A private drive wound through this rural beauty from the old Elizabethport road. Washington and the other distinguished guests stepped from their carriages (or perhaps alighted from their horses) into an entrance hall spacious enough for a cotillion.

What meal they ate there is difficult to say. It was too early for dinner, though nearly correct for luncheon in our own time. Since Washington still had to review troops at Elizabethtown Point and be rowed across the bay to New York, it is quite possible that Boudinot thought the President's dinner might be considerably delayed and had therefore prepared a collation to tide him over.

The guests seated themselves in a spacious, paneled dining room, and ate with the family silver from a china table service. Both china and silver were used a hundred years later at a luncheon for President Harrison at the Lawyers' Club in New York. The china was especially notable, having the Boudinot arms on every piece. The silver had been collected from the best silversmiths of Paris and London, with a smattering of New York work.

The committee from Congress included Henry Knox, the new Secretary of War; John Langdon, the New Hampshireman who was then President of the Senate; John Jay and a dozen others. After the meal, these gentlemen went with Washington to the review of troops, and then he got on board the barge that was to take him across the bay to New York.

The barge was an extraordinary affair, built for the occasion and rowed by thirteen masters of vessels, dressed in white uniforms. Commodore James Nicholson commanded this distinguished crew. As the barge glided away from the Jersey shore, an escort of other boats slipped into line behind it and the procession moved through the strait between New Jersey and Staten Island. There, in the full expanse of New York Harbor, it was joined suddenly by dozens of other craft decked out with flags, pennons and bunting.

If Washington thought he had seen everything in the way of procession ceremonials, he was disabused when his barge passed Bedloe's Island. A sloop under full sail bore down upon him, and as it cruised gracefully alongside, a choir of twenty-five ladies and gentlemen began to sing an ode composed for the occasion, although someone had tactlessly set it to the music of "God Save the King."

No sooner had the President recovered from this surprise

than a smaller craft pulled up on the other side and a twelve-man glee club on it began to sing an ode of their own.

The harbor was alive with ships, those with guns sounding salutes. Some carried bands playing at full tilt, the Spanish man-of-war *Galveston* displayed every flag and signal that could be crowded on her lines, and a continuous swelling roar of sound from human throats afloat and ashore mingled with the bells of churches and the concussion of shore batteries, while a brilliant sun poured down from an absolutely clear April sky.

Washington stepped off the barge about two o'clock at Murray's Wharf, at the foot of Wall Street, into a city where all other activity had stopped except his welcoming, and whose inhabitants nearly to a man were packed into every inch of space along his route. The President's old friend, Governor Clinton, was there to receive him at the ferry stairs, which had been carpeted and its rails hung with red cloth. As President and Governor shook hands, and Washington stood again on the soil of the island he had liberated and departed from in tears six years before, a new burst of sound rose from the crowd, in the wildest, most unrestrained ovation the city had ever heard.

Most of the city's policemen were on hand to force a passage for the procession, which was led by military officers, regiments of soldiers and militia officers, then the congressional committee, Washington and Clinton walking together, government department heads, the Mayor and aldermen, clergy, foreign ministers, and the citizenry pouring in behind.

Along the way every door and window, every roof, was filled with craning heads, and the houses and stores were decorated from street to attic, with Washington's name woven into innumerable designs and into arches across the street. Future celebrities riding up Broadway would pass through a storm of confetti and ticker tape, but Washington was deluged with a steady rain of flowers. Bells and cannon added to the uproar until it seemed that there was nothing in the world but sound.

Some versions of the tour say that Washington stopped at the City Coffee House and met Clinton and the Mayor there, but it is more likely that the procession went directly from the ferry slip to the new presidential home. This was number 3 Cherry Street, in a section later known as Franklin Square, destined in the next fifty years to degenerate from its fashionable post-Revolutionary state into one of the worst slums on the continent. Walter Franklin, a merchant of substance, had built the house and given his name to it, but at the time of Washington's residence it was owned by Samuel Osgood, one of the Treasury commissioners, later Postmaster General, who had married Franklin's widow. Osgood had removed himself and his family temporarily at the government's request.*

There had been some objections to appropriating the Franklin house for the President. A good many people thought it was too far out in the country, though it was only a dozen squares or so from the new Federal Hall. But everyone agreed it would be a charming place for Washington to spend his first summer in New York. Its windows looked out toward the bay and Long Island, and only the foliage of its sloping gardens partially hid the East River. West and northwest the President could survey a pastoral landscape of sun-sleepy meadows, gentle hills and sparsely populated valleys between them.

Inside the house there was an atmosphere of quiet good taste. One who lived in it later, remembering his childhood there, described it as "a handsome old house, with thick walls, richly carved staircase, deep window seats, wainscoted partitions, and open fireplaces quaintly tiled with blue Indian china. The wallpaper in the second hall was of never failing interest to us children, with its gay pictures of men and women of full size, walking in beautiful gardens, sitting by fountains with parasols, or sailing on lakes with guitars or flutes in their hands."

* The publishing house of Harper & Brothers stood near this site toward the end of the nineteenth century.

By the time he reached this new home, Washington must have been ready to eat supper and retire, but he understood that the obligations of his office, as well as his own natural courtesy, would not allow it. He stationed himself in the drawing room and received every dignitary who came to pay his respects. Elias Boudinot, who had come along from Elizabeth, describes the end of the ceremonies: "And then we dined with His Excellency Governor Clinton, who had provided an elegant dinner for us. Thus ended our commission."

And thus Washington came to rest in New York City as President of the United States. He would shortly discover that the Franklin house was much too small for his ménage, which included besides Martha and her two grandchildren (Jack's children, who had come to live with them after their father's death immediately following the Yorktown battle), four secretaries and a retinue of servants. But until another house could be found, Franklin's undersized mansion would have to do.

The city into which Washington stepped next day was one that had been living in a state of continuous excitement for a month or more. As one antiquarian remarks, "Fresh paint and rents advanced with unusual celerity." Modern New Yorkers may find a gloomy comfort in knowing that the city was considered even then the most expensive place in the country to live. A visiting Parisian complained that it cost more than France, and he mentioned the outrageous board-and-room rentals of four to six dollars a week.

Aside from the joy of those who expected to turn an honest dollar, the establishment of New York as the national capital was regarded with mixed feelings in and out of Congress. The location was not a settled matter, but beyond that fact, people were uncertain whether the new government they had created was itself there to stay. It had been one thing to argue the question of union and quite another to see it actually functioning, complete with Constitution and President, a new Congress and all the other appurtenances of federal control. Some thought it monarchy in another form; others considered the whole scheme unworkable, or at least improbable, and these included not a few members of the new Congress itself.

This body had been called to assemble on March 4, but it was April 1 before enough members had appeared to make a quorum. That was owing not to lack of interest but to the difficulties of March travel, the stains of which were upon the members who had made long journeys as they straggled into the city one by one, on horseback, in stages, a few in their own chariots.

One of those who watched the Congress assemble was Fisher Ames, newly elected Congressman from Massachusetts, a New England conservative who would soon become one of the leading voices of Federalism. Arriving about the middle of March, he found little to cheer him. In a letter to a friend in Boston, he complained:

"We have twenty-six representatives; and as thirty are necessary to make a quorum, we are still in a state of inaction. . . . I am inclined to believe that the languor of the old Confederation is transfused into the members of the new Congress. This city has not caught the spirit, or rather the want of spirit, I am vexing myself to express to you. Their hall will cost £20,000 York money. They are preparing fireworks, and a splendid barge for the President, which last will cost £200 to £300. We lose £1,000 a day revenue. We lose credit, spirit, everything. The public will forget the government before it is born. The resurrection of the infant will come before its birth. Happily the federal interest is strong in Congress. The old Congress still continues to meet, and it seems to be doubtful whether the old government is dead, or the new one alive. God deliver us speedily from this puzzling state, or prepare my will, if it subsists much longer, for I am in a fever to think of it." [9]

By April 4, when the House had assembled, Ames was disposed to think better of Federalism's chances. He wrote again: "The House is composed of sober, solid, old-charter folks, as we often say. At least, I am sure that there are many such. They have been in government before, and they are not disposed to embarrass business, nor are they, for the most part, men of intrigues. . . . It will be quite a republican assembly. It looks like one. Many who expected a Roman senate, when the doors shall be opened, will be disappointed. Admiration will lose its feast. . . . The Senate will be a very respectable body."

Thus the republicans, even in that lower-case era, were concerned about whether government was "disposed to embarrass business."

As Washington moved about in the six days between his arrival and his inauguration, he contrived to call upon as many members of the new Congress as he could. One of those he met had no compunction about embarrassing business, or contradicting Fisher Ames to his face, or even, in the end, defying the President himself. This man was William Maclay, a salty Pennsylvania farmer who became leader of the Administration's opposition in Congress, providing the General with something he had hitherto never experienced. Maclay's diary remains one of the most continuously fascinating records of the time, and a refreshing change in viewpoint from the idolatry of Washington. Among men in public life, only John Adams' diary and letters equal Maclay's journal in bitter criticism of the hero.*

Senator Maclay reported his first meeting with the President on April 28, two days before the inauguration, as follows: "This

---

* The Senator from Pennsylvania deserves further mention. Born in 1734, in Chester County, of North Ireland stock, his trail crossed Washington's as early as 1750, when he fought the French and went with General Forbes as a lieutenant in the expedition against Fort DuQuesne. Later, in 1763–64, he took part in Colonel Henry Bouquet's famous foray against the Indians. Like Washington, he was a surveyor for a time.

After his marriage in 1769 to Mary McClure, whose father, John Harris, was the founder of Harrisburg, he settled down on 300 acres of land at Mifflintown and practiced law. In 1772 he laid out the town of Sunbury and lived there until 1786, when he moved to Harrisburg. During the Revolution he was an ardent patriot, serving in the militia, acting as commissary officer at Sunbury, and helping to organize frontier defenses against the Indians.

day I ought to note with some extraordinary mark. I had dressed and was about to set out, when Gen. Washington, the greatest man in the world, paid me a visit. I met him at the foot of the stairs. Mr. Henry Wynkoop just came in. We asked him to take a seat. He excused himself on account of the number of his visits. We accompanied him to the door. He made us complaisant bows—one before he mounted and the other as he went away on horseback."

The casual irony of Maclay's pen was in that "greatest man in the world" phrase, and it will be noted that to him Washington was still "General." In fact, one of the more popular occupations in the weeks and days before the inauguration was to argue about what Washington should be called. A friend of General Gates, John Armstrong, had written to him early in April: "All the world here are busy in collecting flowers and sweets of every kind to amuse and delight the President in his approach and on his arrival. Even Roger Sherman has set his head at work to devise some style of address more novel and dignified than 'Excellency.' Yet in the midst of this admiration there are skeptics who doubt its propriety, and wits who amuse themselves at this extravagance."

The newspapers debated the question editorially, families tossed it about over the dinner table and the new government's officials found themselves unable to agree. Chief Justice McKean asserted that the President should have a title, and one not hitherto appropriated by any other ruler. James Madison

---

Maclay began his political career in the state legislature, as representative for Northumberland County from 1781–85. Later he held a variety of other posts—member of the Supreme Executive Council, Judge of the Court of Common Pleas, Deputy Surveyor. As a United States Senator in the first Congress organized under the Constitution, 1789–91, he represented rural Pennsylvania, and by lot was the short-term Senator, Robert Morris being his colleague.

The basis of his opposition to Washington was his unalterable hatred of Federalism. He fought the entire Hamiltonian program, and he may have been the first Jeffersonian Democrat.

He was ousted from Congress by his Federalist opponents after his first term, but he served another term in the Pennsylvania state legislature before he died in 1804.

declared that in his opinion "President" was enough. Congress appointed a joint committee to resolve the question, but its members could not agree. They decided to leave it up to Washington.

By any title, the new President would shortly take office and the city had worked itself into a frenzy of anticipation. Everyone who could get to New York for the occasion had elbowed his way into town. The fortunate ones visited their friends and relatives; the less fortunate, and there were thousands of them, had no other shelter than tents in vacant spaces downtown, or nothing at all on curbstones and in the fields.

A Miss Bertha Ingersoll, one of the visitors, wrote to her friend Miss McKean, of Philadelphia: "We shall remain here if we have to sleep in tents, as many have to do. Mr. Williamson had promised to engage us rooms at Fraunces' Tavern, but that was jammed long ago, as was every other decent public house; and now while we are waiting at Mrs. Vandervoort's in Maiden Lane, until after dinner, two of our best beaux are running about town, determined to obtain the best places for us to stay at which can be obtained for love, money, or the most persuasive speeches."

A Boston girl had worse difficulties, both en route and in finding lodgings, but she concluded her letter home, "I have seen him! and though I had been entirely ignorant that he was arrived in the city, I should have known at a glance that it was General Washington; I never saw a human being that looked so grand and noble as he does. I could fall down on my knees before him and bless him for all the good he has done for this country."

That was the general feeling, particularly among the ladies, although it was not a matter of either sex or age. There were aged people who announced they wanted only to look upon Washington before they died, and the young fry gave him the kind of adulation they would reserve for crooners in another era.

Thursday, April 30, was Inauguration Day. At nine o'clock

in the morning every church bell in town began a clangorous salute to the occasion, but after an agreed interval, they changed their pealing to the slow tolling that called the churchgoers on Sundays. There followed an impressive mass demonstration of faith as people of every belief crowded their churches until they had to stand on the walks outside, while inside the pastors prayed for the safety of the President.

Washington was up early, as usual, and by the time the official procession reached his door at noon he was ready to enter his coach, which was cream-colored and of an elaborate, almost monarchical design that must have shocked Maclay's democratic soul. The Washington coat-of-arms was emblazoned on its sides, decorated about with a scroll depicting the Four Seasons; Fritz, Washington's German coachman, drove the four bay horses, and he along with the two footmen and postillions were dressed in scarlet and white livery. All except Fritz had come from the Mount Vernon staff.

The coach was not the only bright spot in the inaugural parade. Captain Harsin's Grenadiers made a vivid splash of color, with their blue coats faced with red and embroidered with gold lace, cocked hats surmounted by a white feather, white waistcoats and breeches, and black spatterdashes buttoned tightly from shoe to knee. Surveying them, Maclay must have been reminded once more of monarchy: these men, chosen as the tallest and finest in the city, were dressed and drilled in obvious imitation of Frederick the Great's guard.

Shortly after noon the procession wound away from the President's house, led by a troop of horse, followed by foot soldiers, the sheriff on horseback, the committees from House and Senate, the President with his suite and assistants, dignitaries who would be admitted to the Senate chamber, other gentlemen in coaches, and less distinguished citizens on foot. Between lines of cheering watchers, the parade passed through Queen (later Pearl), Great Dock and Broad streets to the new Federal State House in Wall Street. The troops formed double lines through which Washington walked into the building.

For a month or more this edifice had been the center of promenades, fashionable and proletarian. The sidewalks before it were thronged every pleasant afternoon with curious citizens and visitors, who were entranced by the way this old City Hall, which had served New York for nearly a century, had been cleverly transformed into the first national building the country had ever possessed. This had been done on the outside largely by arranging the cornice to admit thirteen stars, while the pediment above the four Doric columns contained the American eagle and other national insignia. Each window, too, was surmounted by a tablet on whose surface was engraved thirteen arrows entwined with olive branches.

Those fortunate enough to get inside, other than members of Congress, were greeted with what Washington saw as he entered it on Inauguration Day, presumably for the first time. He came into a vestibule with a marble floor, glistening under the light from a dome rich with ornamentation. The chamber of the House was octagonal, with an arched ceiling forty-six feet high, and large windows beneath which were fireplaces. There was no other means of heat. Two galleries looked down on the chamber. The chairs of the Represetnatives were covered with light blue damask, to match the window curtains. The Senate chamber was not so large, but it was more elaborately decorated. A sun and thirteen stars shone resplendently in its light blue arched ceiling, the curtains and chair coverings were of light crimson damask, and the handsome fireplaces were of American marble. The President's chair, covered by a crimson canopy, was raised three feet above the floor.

Washington came into this chamber with his escort, and after meeting the members of Congress there, stepped out with them directly onto a balcony twelve feet deep, opening to views of Broad and Wall streets, and for that day covered by a white-striped red canopy and curtains to match.*

* That part of the iron railing on the front of the balcony between its two pillars, a section containing a centerpiece of thirteen arrows, is in the museum of the New York Historical Society.

As he came out on the balcony, a tremendous shout of acclamation rose from the citizens jammed elbow to elbow in the
streets as far as anyone could see. Washington acknowledged
the ovation by coming to the front of the balcony, laying his
hand on his heart, and bowing. One would think that, after the
welcomes he had heard all the way from Alexandria to New
York, another would not ruffle him, but at this great moment of
his life, as on other such peaks, he was momentarily overcome.
He turned and groped for a chair in which he sat rather heavily.

Then came the moment for which the whole nation had
waited. Washington rose and moved forward, with Robert R.
Livingston, Chancellor of the State of New York, who was to
administer the oath. A quiet, deep and profound, fell on the
multitude below as the President-elect, tall and distinguished in
his dark brown, American-made suit, worn with a steel-hilted
dress sword, white silk stockings and silver shoe buckles, laid
his large hand on the Bible, which reposed on a cushion of
crimson velvet resting in turn on a table covered with a crimson velvet cloth. They repeated the now familiar oath, after
which Livingston turned to the railing and proclaimed in a
ringing voice, "Long live George Washington, President of
the United States."

A new tumult of sound welled up from below, mingled with
the roar of a thirteen-gun salute. Washington stood bowing for
a minute or two, then he turned and went back into the Senate
chamber with the members of Congress. There they took their
seats and the President ascended the chair of his office. In a
moment he began to read his inaugural speech.

Of the several contemporary accounts of it, the most interesting are those of William Maclay and Fisher Ames, whose person-
alities and political outlooks produced sharply contrasting views.

"This great man was agitated and embarrassed," says Maclay,
"more than ever he was by the leveled cannon or pointed musket. He trembled, and several times could scarce make out to
read, though it must be supposed he had often read it before.

*264*

He put part of the fingers of his left hand into the side of what I think the tailors call the fall of the breeches, changing the paper into his left [right] hand. After some time he then did the same with some of the fingers of his right hand. When he came to the words, 'all the world,' he made a flourish with his right hand, which left rather an ungainly impression. I sincerely, for my part, wished all set ceremony in the hands of the dancing masters, and that this first of men had read off his address in the plainest manner, without ever taking his eyes from the paper, for I felt hurt that he was not first in everything."

For all its candid observation, this was one of the most charitable things Maclay ever wrote about the President. By contrast, here is part of Ames's sympathetic observation of the same scene. He termed it "very touching" and "quite of the solemn kind. His aspect grave, almost to sadness; his modesty, actually shaking; his voice deep, a little tremulous, and so low as to call for close attention; added to the series of objects presented to the mind, and overwhelming it, produced emotion of the most affecting kind upon the members."

After it was over, Washington, accompanied by the Vice-President, the Speaker of the House, and both houses of Congress, proceeded in solemn procession to St. Paul's Chapel, at Broadway and Vesey Street, where they attended a service performed by the Right Rev. Dr. Samuel Provost, Bishop of the Episcopal Church in New York, and also chaplain of Congress.

That concluded the ceremonies. After church everyone went home, including Washington, to prepare for the evening. The official festivities that night were confined to fireworks and transparent paintings; the inauguration ball would not be held until May 7.

As soon as it was dark, everyone crowded into the lower end of the island around the Battery to see the fireworks and the transparencies. Washington went down in his carriage with Colonel Humphreys and Tobias Lear, first to Chancellor Livingston's house, then to Knox's, where they could get the best view of the fireworks. On the way, one supposes, they were driven by a route which provided an opportunity to see the illuminations.

All the public buildings and most of the private dwellings, except those too poor to afford the candles, were alight in every window. On John Street, the theatre glowed with transparencies, including one in which Fame was depicted descending angellike from heaven to place the symbol of immortality on Washington's brow. As the carriage passed Bowling Green, Washington could see himself portrayed in a huge transparency, with a figure labeled Fortitude bending over him, and Justice and Wisdom, representing the two branches of government, one on each side.

Near the Green, on Broadway, the French and Spanish ministers had tried to outdo each other, with spectacular results. The French minister had called upon his sister, who was an artist, to draw pictures illustrating American history, past, present and future. These were arrayed before the mansion, illuminated by lamps which bordered the doors and windows. The Spanish minister was more in the classic vein, with intimations of Thomas A. Edison. His principal transparency before the house showed the Graces, surrounded by emblems symbolizing practically everything, and in the windows he had placed panoramas arranged so that they seemed to be moving. The ships in the harbor were illuminated too. One, the *Carolina*, resembled a pyramid of stars set against the black curtain of the night.

But the climax of the evening was a two-hour display of fireworks on the Battery, under Colonel Bauman's direction, which was said to be the most beautiful ever devised in the country. A story which has no proof except that Elias Boudinot's daughter Catherine told it all her life relates that, as the Boudinot family watched the fireworks, Washington stood near them, somewhere outside Chancellor Livingston's house.

Little Catherine, then about eight, had been allowed to come out of the house to watch a fire balloon go up, and her father was sending her back in when Washington exclaimed, "No, you pretty little yellow bird, you shall see as well as anybody," and thereupon hoisted her to his shoulder.[10]

When the last rocket had flared, the crowd was still not willing that the day should end. The taverns were already full with those who meant it to go on for some time. The new President was more than ready to go to bed, but he had a difficult time getting there. "We returned home on foot," Tobias Lear wrote in his diary that night, "the throng of people being so great as not to permit a carriage to pass through it." [11]

In the week following, Washington spent a good deal of time arranging his social schedule, settling matters of protocol, and establishing rules to govern his office. He realized that regulations for seeing visitors and entertaining were essential, if he were to have any time for the business of being President. He decided at once to return no visits. Dinner invitations would be extended only to high officials and "strangers of distinction." Courtesy calls were to be paid Tuesday afternoons (Tobias Lear wrote of the first one that "we had a numerous and splendid circle"), but foreign ministers and strangers would be received on other days. Mrs. Washington would hold her levees, when she arrived, on Friday evenings. State dinners would be held on Thursday nights. In between would come such visitations as that on May 6, when Washington attended the Columbia College commencement in St. Paul's Chapel.

With no more than a week's breathing space to prepare for it, the night of the Inauguration Ball arrived. Among the three hundred persons present, according to the *New York Packet*, were a "numerous and brilliant collection of ladies," which pleased Washington. The ladies were more than pleased when they entered with their escorts: each one was given a beautiful fan, made especially in Paris, which disclosed a striking medallion portrait of Washington in profile when it was opened.

Everyone exclaimed over these gifts and the magnificence of the decorations in the Assembly Room, on the east side of Broadway a little above Wall Street. (There appears to be no foundation for the tradition that it was held in the Delancey mansion on the Bowery Road.) The guests probably admired each other, too, and the ladies did not get all the attention. Consider, for example, what a gentleman of high fashion wore to an affair of this kind in 1789, as described by one of them, recalling a party at about the same time:

"I was dressed in a light French blue coat, with a high collar, broad lapels, and large gilt buttons, a double-breasted Marseilles vest, nankeen-colored cassimere breeches, with white silk stockings, shining pumps. and full ruffles on my breast and at my wrists, together with a ponderous white cravat, with a pudding in it, as we then called it; and I was considered the best dressed gentleman in the room."

Among the women, the favorite ball costume of the New York belles at the moment was a celestial blue satin gown, worn with a white satin petticoat. Around her neck she might wear an Italian gauze handkerchief with satin border stripes. Her hair would be done up in detached curls, with a pouf of gauze, adorned with wreaths of flowers, for headdress. Her gown would billow out over a court hoop, all but concealing the feet, dainty or otherwise, encased in matching celestial blue shoes, dotted with rose-colored rosettes. Besides this shade of blue, ladies that season were partial to dark gray, yellow and bright green.

Surveying the assemblage of beauty, President Washington naturally exercised his prerogative, as he always did, and chose the prettiest. He danced with three of the most beautiful women present: Mrs. Peter Van Brugh Livingston, Lord Stirling's sister; Elizabeth Schuyler Hamilton, Alexander's wife; and a minuet with a favorite partner of the Morristown days, then the lovely Miss Van Zandt and now Mrs. James Homer Maxwell. In such pleasant company, he hardly noticed that the ball went on until two in the morning, very late indeed for him.

Of course the inauguration festivities did not end with the official party. There was a holiday air in the city, and among the high officials there was much entertaining. On May 11, Washington sent Senator Maclay a ticket and an invitation to share his box at the John Street Theatre that night, his first appearance there since the inaugural. Arriving, Maclay found himself in excellent company: besides the President and Governor Clinton, there were the foreign ministers, the Senators from New Hampshire, Connecticut and South Carolina, and his Pennsylvania colleague, Robert Morris, along with an assortment of ladies. But Maclay found no enchantment in either the company or the drama.

"I am old, and notices or attentions are lost to me," he wrote. "I could have wished some of my dear children in my place; they are young and would have enjoyed it. Long might they live to boast of having been seated in the same box with the first Character in the world.

"The play was the 'School for Scandal.' I never liked it; indeed, I think it an indecent representation before ladies of character and virtue. Farce, the 'Old Soldier.' The house greatly crowded, and I thought the players acted well; but I wish we had seen the 'Conscious Lovers,' or some one that inculcated more prudential manners."[12]

A week after the Inauguration Ball, the minister of France, Count de Moustier, gave another elegant affair, plainly trying to outdo the Americans, of whom he secretly had a rather low opinion, as Gouverneur Morris discovered later.* Madame de

* What Gouverneur Morris discovered was not flattering to American society. As minister to France, Morris spent an evening a few years later with Count de Moustier, who had meanwhile returned to Paris, and afterward reported: "I find that, notwithstanding public professions as to the public proceedings of America, both De Moustier and Madame de Bréhan have a thorough dislike to the country and its inhabitants. The society of New York is not sociable, the provisions of America are not good, the climate is very damp, the wines are abominable, the people are excessively indolent."

Bréhan, his sister, was hostess for the affair, and she declared frankly that she had "exhausted every resource to produce an entertainment worthy of France." What she produced would be worthy today of the Radio City Music Hall. There were two sets of cotillion dancers, the men in complete military uniform, one set in the colors of France and the other in those of America, representing the grand alliance. Blue ribbons and American flowers adorned the heads of four ladies, while the other four sported the red ribbons and flowers of France.

For the refreshment of the guests, the Count and his sister had set aside a large room, one of whose walls was lined with shelves like a department store. On them were fruits, ices and wine in bewildering array. Servants standing behind a table in the center of the room brought from the shelves whatever the hungry or thirsty guest might choose.

On the Tuesday afternoon following this affair, Washington held his regular reception, and among those coming to pay their respects was Senator Maclay, who attended by agreement with a party of Pennsylvanians. As they entered the drawing room, the honest Senator recorded in his diary, "I went foremost, and left them to follow and do as well as they could. Indeed, they had no great thing of a pattern, for I am but a poor courtier." Glancing about, Maclay noted with his customary disdain the presence of the foreign ministers, especially the newly arrived Dutch minister, Van Berkel, "gaudy as a peacock." Then he found himself next to the President and engaged in conversation, which he reported verbatim as follows:

"How will this weather suit your farming?" Washington inquired.

"Poorly—sir; the season is the most backward I have ever known," Maclay replied. "It is remarkably so here, but by letters from Pennsylvania vegetation is slow in proportion there."

"The fruit, it is to be expected, will be safe; backward seasons are in favor of it, but in Virginia it was lost before I left that place."

"Much depends on the exposure of the orchard. Those with a northern aspect have been found by us [in Pennsylvania] to be the most certain in producing fruit."

"Yes, that is a good observation and should be attended to."

With this final thrust of repartee the conversation ended, and the Senator says he "made [his] bow and retired."

There were already stirring in Congress republican objections to these levees and state dinners and the other entertaining—dark suspicions that the monarchy so lately shed had returned under another name.

These suspicions were not shared by the ladies of New York, who were delighted to be the social center of the new nation. As soon as Martha arrived, on May 27, they were swept into the brilliance of her Friday evening levees, which she conducted with that talent which seemed to be part of the natural equipment of Virginia ladies. Washington appeared at these functions as a private gentleman, meaning that he did not wear hat or sword, in contrast with his Tuesday afternoon dress, when he usually wore a much more ornate costume.

A constellation of prominent ladies gathered about Martha's Friday evenings, some of them old friends, some new: Mrs. Jay, Mrs. Adams, Mrs. Hamilton, Mrs. Robert Morris, Mrs. Ralph Izard, Mrs. Knox, Lady Mary Watts, Lady Kitty Duer, Mrs. Beekman, Mrs. Prevost, Mrs. Livingston, Mrs. Elbridge Gerry and Mrs. Rufus King. These ladies, and others whose husbands held official positions or were prominent socially or in some other way, required no special invitation, as was the custom in eighteenth-century English and French drawing rooms. A few others were invited particularly; and some of these swooned for joy at having "arrived," when the postman brought their invitations. Everyone, no matter what her station, was required to wear formal dress.

The evening before Martha's first levee, Washington gave what was probably the first of his Thursday state dinners. The guests included John Adams, Clinton, the French and Spanish ministers, the Governor of the Western Territory (Arthur St. Clair), John Jay, and a half dozen members of Congress. Senator Paine Wingate, of New Hampshire, has left a description of the event:

"It was the least showy dinner that I ever saw at the President's. As there was no clergyman present, Washington himself said grace on taking his seat. He dined on a boiled leg of mutton, as it was his custom to eat of only one dish. After the dessert a single glass of wine was offered to each of his guests, when the President rose, the guests following his example, and repaired to the drawing room, each departing at his option, without ceremony."

The new Administration's social season was thus off to a brilliant start, but it came to a halt abruptly in June, when the President, who had not been feeling well for some time, took to his bed with a dangerous illness. It was not easy to get Washington into bed when he was ill. In his recollections, George Washington Parke Custis, Martha's grandchild, who was brought up with his sister as part of the Washington family, remembers that the President's "aversion to the use of medicine was extreme; and even when in great suffering, it was only by the entreaties of his lady, and the respectful yet beseeching look of his oldest friend and companion in arms (Dr. James Craik) that he could be prevailed upon to take the slightest preparation of medicine." He refused, wisely as it turns out now, to take any of the eighteenth-century potions devised for colds. "Let it go as it came," he always said. He was extremely solicitous of other people's colds and illnesses, however. One visitor to Mount Vernon who retired with a bad cough, after declining to take the remedies Washington offered, heard the door of his room gently open, "and on drawing my bed curtains, to my utter astonishment, I beheld Washington himself, standing at my bedside, with a bowl of hot tea in his hand."

The illness that seized Washington in New York was so serious that there was no question of his going to bed. He had a high fever and endured intense pain. What he suffered is not certain. Washington called it "a very large and painful tumor on the protuberance of my thigh." Tobias Lear termed it a "violent tumor" and another source describes it as "a malignant carbuncle." The doctor's diagnosis was anthrax. At that moment, Washington's mother was dying of cancer in Virginia, and later in life, he had a somewhat similar growth removed from his cheek, which he called cancer but paradoxically appears to have been non-malignant.

By June 19 an anxious hush had settled upon the city, and it was whispered that the President might not live. The sidewalks before his house were laid with straw and a chain was stretched across the street to prevent the passage of carriages.

He had the attention of several physicians, including Dr. Samuel Bard, a "society doctor" who was considered the best in New York. His reputation was understandable. He had entered King's College at fourteen to take his premedical work, and then had gone for further study to London and Edinburgh, where the famous Scottish medical school was then at the peak of its renown.* He had returned to New York an M.D. in 1765 and immediately built a practice, at first with his father, which was the envy of every other doctor in town. Later he helped to found New York Hospital, the school which became Columbia's College of Physicians and Surgeons, the New York Public Library, the New York Dispensary, and in his retirement, the Protestant Episcopal Church at Hyde Park, New York, the village where he died of pleurisy at seventy-nine. By an odd chance, this man who became Washington's personal physician in New York had been a Loyalist during the Revolution.

Bard's presence in the Washington case was due more to

---

* The Seven Years' War was raging when Bard went to London in 1760, and on the way over his ship was captured by a French privateer and taken to Bayonne. There he spent five dreary months in prison before his father learned his whereabouts and prevailed upon his friend Benjamin Franklin to use his influence at the French court to obtain young Samuel's release.

his formidable reputation than to his usefulness in this particular instance. His specialty was obstetrics, and his practice otherwise was entirely internal medicine. He did no surgery. Yet it must be admitted that he directed the operation which saved the President's life, whether or not he actually made the remark attributed to him, when he is said to have told the surgeon, "Cut away—deeper. Don't be afraid. See how well the President bears it." Bard may not have been a surgeon, but he understood how vitally important it was to go deep enough to get all of the affected area.

Before the operation, according to another tradition, Washington took advantage of a moment alone with Dr. Bard to fix him with the most commanding gaze he could summon and ask for the physician's candid opinion of his chances.

"Do not flatter me with vain hopes," he is supposed to have insisted. "I am not afraid to die, and therefore can bear the worst."

Dr. Bard told him the outlook was hopeful, but he admitted that he was not without apprehensions. Washington sighed.

"Whether tonight or twenty years hence makes no difference," he remarked, "I know that I am in the hands of a good Providence." *

By July 3, so great was his recuperative power, Washington was able to write to his friend James McHenry: "I have now the pleasure to inform you that my health is restored, but a feebleness still hangs upon me, and I am much incommoded by the incision which was made . . . . This prevents me from walking or sitting . . . . I am able to take exercise in my coach, by having it so contrived as to extend myself the full length of it."

Three weeks later, he was even able to joke a little about his convalescence in a letter to Bushrod Washington, which was, he said, "among the first acts of my recommencing business,

* Providence," or sometimes "Heaven," was Washington's usual way of referring to the Deity. Not a particularly religious man, in spite of the efforts of his admiring biographers to make him so, he did not use the word "God" often until his late life, and then mostly in official utterances.

after lying six weeks on my right side . . . . Not being fairly on my seat yet, or in other words, not being able to sit up without some uneasiness, it must be short."

He had missed the celebration of July 4, but part of it had come to him. A committee from the New York State chapter of the Society of the Cincinnati had visited him that day, and its chairman, Baron Steuben, had presented him with an address from the Society. Later the Society marched in procession to St. Paul's Chapel, the veterans stepping to the music of a band and escorted by Colonel Bauman's artillery. At the chapel, Alexander Hamilton gave an oration in honor of their comrade, Nathanael Greene, who had died three years before. The misanthropic Maclay, who had no love for the Cincinnati, regarding them as a Federalist institution, gave his own account of the service:

"The church was crowded. The Cincinnati had seats allotted for themselves; wore their eagles at their buttonholes, and were preceded by a flag. The oration was well delivered; the composition appeared good, but I thought he should have given us some account of his virtues as a citizen as well as a warrior, for I supposed he possessed them, and he lived some time after the war, and, I believe, commenced farming."

Maclay hardly did justice to the memory of a man whose "virtues as a citizen'" were so excellent that he impoverished himself after the Revolution by making good on the defection of a dishonest contractor, one of those to whom Greene had given personal notes in his determination to get supplies for the Continental Army during his service as Quartermaster General. He "commenced farming" only because the grateful people of Georgia gave a plantation to this man who, as commander of the Southern Department, had saved the South from the British.

For the moment, Washington was spared the attentions of the Senator from Pennsylvania, though it was to be a short-lived truce. Convalescing slowly from his operation, the President was able for a time to take only the carriage trips he mentioned; it was September before he could walk from Franklin Square to the Battery with his characteristic light, firm step. By good fortune the summer that year was cool, and since he was necessarily relieved in part of the burdens of entertaining and attending other functions, he was able to look about as he toured the town in his carriage, and to see a little more of the city that was temporarily his home.

For all its bustle and pretensions, New York was still a small town; the great era of expansion would not begin for nearly fifty years. Where the New York *Times* would one day be born, near the present City Hall on Printing House Square, stood the Brick Church, and there the city proper ended. Where the gloomy pile of the Tombs later rose on Centre Street, Washington saw the Fresh Water Pond, a small lake sixty feet deep. Along Canal Street toward the Hudson River, muddy paths and rudimentary roads cut through marshy fields. Not even real estate men expected the city would ever push that far into the country.

Water carts, supplied from the Tea Water Pump, near the head of Pearl Street, rolled through the streets every day, while the driver shouted "Good, fresh drinking water." It could be bought by the cask or gallon. The streets, in fact, were as alive with hawking cries as ever were the byways of Dickens' London. Early in the morning the clamoring began with the milkman's "Milk, ho!" as he strode along with a yoke over his shoulders, tin cans suspended from it on both sides. After him came the chimneysweeps, usually Negro boys, and the wood dealers, and the vendors of good things to eat, from clams to hot corn.

The city had an appearance unlike any other in America or abroad. Already it was a bewildering mixture of cultures and architecture and neighborhoods. Its churches, with their mossy roofs and trim churchyards, had an Old World look, much like the village churches of England and the Netherlands, but they were tucked in at random among houses which were put together in all the varying English styles, with a generous mixture of Dutch and French designs. The little hotels and the numerous small stores were more English than anything else, but they avoided a consistent pattern. Many of the streets retained lovely rows of shade trees, and there were gardens and flowers everywhere, giving the city in places the odd illusion of a country village. It was democratic in many respects, sheltering even then most of the elements that made it the "melting pot" of the nineteenth century, but it was also feudal in other respects: slaveholding was as common as it was in the South, and no family of any social standing was without them.[13]

As Washington rode, and later walked, about the town he was the object of a constant if respectful watchfulness on the part of the population. As the first chief magistrate, the symbol of a republic not yet out of swaddling clothes, he was the novelty and wonder of the age. By some mysterious communication, it was known when he left the house, and what direction he took, so that everywhere people watched his progress. They were not so unmindful of his high office as to follow him, or obstruct his way, but they gaped with mingled curiosity, admiration and affection.

Washington Irving often told the story (in which as much faith may be placed as in the numerous traditions related as fact in his life of the President) that his old Scotch nurse once stopped Washington at the corner of Broadway and Wall Street when he was out for a stroll and asked George to bless her wee bairn, who was then six years old. The President patted Irving's head and went on.*

As a man interested in property values, the President inspected real estate with a speculator's eye while he rode about town during his convalescence. He had heard something on this score from his Cabinet and members of Congress who complained about the high rents in New York. The rental market was tight, and government salaries were low—in brief,

---

* Irving, when he was an old man, told this story to another small boy, George Haven Putnam, and added, "But you can't see now the spot on my head that the President touched." The small Putnam went home and puzzled over the remark until his father enlightened him: "Irving wears a wig."[14]

Washington, D.C., in our own time. James Madison had been house hunting for his friend Edmund Randolph, the new Attorney General, but he reported himself unable to find a place fit to live in that suited the salary of the office, $1500 a year. The lowest-priced dwelling he could find cost $250 annually; Randolph had allowed himself only £50 Virginia currency, which was $166.66. In the end, he had to pay half again as much. He wrote to his wife, breaking the news as gently as possible:

"I have a house at a mile and a half or thereabouts from Federal Hall, that is, from the most public part of the city. It is, in fact, in the country, is airy, has seven rooms, is well finished and gentlemanlike. The rent, £75 our money. Good water is difficult to be found in this place, and the inhabitants are obliged to receive water for tea, and other purposes which do not admit brackish water, from hogsheads brought every day in drays. At our house there is an excellent pump of fresh water, I am told. . . . I am resolved against any company of form, and to live merely a private life."

Randolph got off easy, comparatively, in the matter of rents. The house to which Washington moved the following February cost $2500 a year.

Meanwhile, the President had other matters, both large and small, to give him concern. About this time he made that discovery which has delighted so many sufferers—a good dentist. The man was John Greenwood, as remarkable a figure in his way as Dr. Bard, and one who had a war record more to Washington's liking. He had been a scout with Arnold on the march to Quebec and had fought in the Trenton campaign, but it must be added that when his enlistment ran out he refused to stay with the army. He shipped as a privateer, with a mercenary motive: to get enough money to study dental mechanics. He came by this desire honestly; his father, Isaac, a Boston ivory turner and maker of mathematical instruments, also performed some dentistry on the side, and may have been that city's first dentist.

John had been apprenticed before the war as a cabinetmaker, but his privateering enabled him to become a dentist about 1784. Like his father, he was inventive and is credited with originating the foot-power drill, spiral springs to hold artificial teeth in place, and with pioneering the use of porcelain to make false teeth.

When Washington came to Greenwood in New York, he had already been the victim of several practitioners of the art who only succeeded in adding to the oral misery he had endured all his life. His teeth had always been bad: he experienced his first extraction when he was scarcely more than twenty-one, and his diary shows that this painful operation became a more or less regular occurrence thereafter. He was using false teeth by the time he found Greenwood, but they were ill-fitting dentures and are said to be the reason why Stuart's famous portrait gives Washington a queer look about the mouth. He may have laughed even less than his serious nature allowed for the same reason, because laughter was sometimes painful and was never really comfortable.

Greenwood was an expert at making false teeth, and he also specialized in replacing decayed teeth with "live" ones which he bought from people poor enough to sacrifice good teeth for money. While he took beeswax casts of Washington's jaws, he probably recounted how he had enlisted as a fifer boy in the Revolution, but deserted when he heard of the fight at Concord and walked to Cambridge, hoping to reach his parents in Boston, observing the Battle of Bunker Hill on the way. After the casts were made, he carved upper and lower plates from a hippopotamus tusk, working human teeth into the lower plate, where they were fixed permanently with gold pivots.

Before he was through, Greenwood made several more sets for Washington, who would go to no one else the rest of his life. Two of the sets still exist and are regarded as superb examples of early dental artistry. After the President left New York, he sent to Greenwood from Virginia the last one of his natural teeth, apparently extracted some time before, to be used as a pattern in the making of a new set. Greenwood kept the tooth and it was passed down from generation to generation in the family, to the present century.

Along with his physical troubles that summer in New York, Washington began to suffer for the first time from the barbs of political life. It was a new experience. He had never been a politician before, and did not intend to be one now, but he was increasingly aware of an unorganized opposition to his Administration, still largely underground but the emanations of which came to him second and third hand from his friends.

Ironically, it was one of the President's critics, John Adams, who bore the first of the whisperings, and for some of the same reasons for which he later criticized Washington. Dr. David Stuart, who had married Jack Custis's widow, wrote to the President on July 14: " I have been much concerned at the clamor and abuse against him [Adams] . . . . It has given me much pleasure to hear every part of your conduct spoke of with high approbation, and particularly your dispensing with ceremony occasionally and walking the streets, while Adams is never seen but in his carriage and six. As trivial as this may appear, it appears to be more captivating to the generality than matters of more importance . . . an error of judgment is more easily pardoned than one of the heart."

Washington, replying, noted that "one of the gentlemen whose name is mentioned in your letter, though high-toned, has never, I believe, appeared with more than *two* horses in his carriage, but it is to be lamented that *he* and *some others* have stirred a question which has given rise to so much animadversion, and which I confess has given me much uneasiness. . . ."

He may have been referring here to the criticism and argument that continued to surround his refusal to return visits and the appointing of official days to receive them. Before he had adopted these rules, Washington recalled in his reply to Dr. Stuart, "I should have been unable to attend to *any* sort of business unless I applied the hours allotted to rest and refreshment to this purpose, for by the time I had done breakfast, and thence till dinner, and afterwards till bedtime, I could not get relieved from the ceremony of one visit before I had to attend to another."

Washington was aware that he was also being criticized for entertaining only "official characters." But he reminded Stuart that the Presidents of Congress had previously involved themselves in "insuperable difficulties" on this account, so that their "table was considered as a public one, and every person who could get introduced conceived that he had a *right* to be invited to it. This although the table was always crowded (and with mixed company, and the President considered in no better light than as a Maître d'Hôtel) was in its nature impracticable and as many offenses given as if no table had been kept."

He went on: "So strongly had the citizens of this place imbibed an idea of the impropriety of my accepting invitations to dinner that I have not received one from any family (though they are remarkable for hospitality, and though I have received every civility and attention possible from them) since I came to the city, except dining with the Governor on the day of my arrival, so that if this should be adduced as an article of impeachment there can be at least *one* good reason adduced for my not dining out—to wit, never having been asked to do so."

By August, when he was able once more to attend the business of Congress, Washington was more sensitive to this opposition than he had been before, and on its part, the opposition was prepared to defy him. They met head-on in an argument over whether the matter of negotiations for treaties with the Southern Indians should be dealt with at once and passed by the Senate in the form which Washington and his Cabinet had already agreed upon, or whether it should be referred to committee for study and debate. Meeting with the Senate on Saturday, August 22, Washington asserted that the problem had already been discussed thoroughly and the Senate had only to ratify what had been proposed. The opposition took this as an attempt to dictate to Congress (shades of modern times!) and, led by Maclay, succeeded in getting the bill referred to com-

George Washington's America

mittee, while Washington sat in his chair, his face dark and severe, hardly able to believe that he, the President, the revered Father of the Country, had been set aside by a Pennsylvania farmer and his friends. There was an emotional, unspoken impasse, of which Maclay wrote:

"We waited for him to withdraw. He did so with a discontented air. Had it been any other man than the man whom I wish to regard as the first character in the world, I would have said, with sullen dignity."

Over Sunday, however, he regained the control that he always sought in such a crisis, and Maclay had a different report on Monday: "The Senate met. The President of the United States soon took his seat, and the business began. The President wore a different aspect from what he did Saturday. He was placid and serene, and manifested a spirit of accommodation; declared his consent that his questions should be amended."

On Thursday of that week, Maclay attended the regular state dinner, and it seemed there were strong overtones of the growing dissension in his acid report of the occasion. The guests included John Adams, Clinton, Jay, John Langdon, Tristram Dalton and three or four other members of Congress, with their wives, if they had them, as well as Tobias Lear and Robert Lewis, Washington's sister's son, who had come recently to be a secretary. The President and his wife sat opposite each other in the middle of the table, with the secretaries at the ends. "It was a great dinner," the irascible Senator records, meaning the elegance of the assemblage, "and the best of the kind I ever was at," but he could not help adding his compulsive sour note, "The room, however, was disagreeably warm." Then he gives us this detailed and fascinating description:

"First was the soup; fish roasted and boiled; meats, gammon, fowls, etc. This was the dinner. The middle of the table was garnished in the usual tasty way, with small images, flowers (artificial) etc. The dessert was, first apple pies, pudding, etc., then iced creams, jellies, etc.; then watermelons, muskmelons, apples, peaches, nuts.

"It was the most solemn dinner ever I sat at. Not a health drank, scarce a word said until the cloth was taken away. Then the President, filling a glass of wine, with great formality drank to the health of every individual by name round the table. Everybody imitated him, charged glasses, and such buzz of 'health, sir,' and 'health, madam,' and 'thank you, sir,' and 'thank you, madam,' never had I heard before. Indeed, I had liked to have been thrown out in the hurry, but I got a little wine in my glass, and passed the ceremony. The ladies sat a good while, and the bottles passed about; but there was a dead silence almost. Mrs. Washington at last withdrew with the ladies.

"I expected the men would now begin, but the same stillness remained. The President told of a New England clergyman who had lost a hat and wig in passing a river called the Brunks [Bronx]. He smiled, and everybody else laughed. He now and then said a sentence or two on some common subject, and what he said was not amiss. Mr. Jay tried to make a laugh by mentioning the circumstances of the Duchess of Devonshire leaving no stone unturned to carry Fox's election. There was a Mr. Smith, who mentioned how Homer described Aeneas leaving his wife and carrying his father out of flaming Troy. He had heard somebody (I suppose) witty on the occasion, but if he had ever read it he would have said Virgil. The President kept a fork in his hand when the cloth was taken away, I thought for the purpose of picking nuts. He ate no nuts, however, but played with the fork, striking on the edge of the table with it. We did not sit long after the ladies retired. The President rose, went upstairs to drink coffee; the company followed. I took my hat and came home."

Aside from the political and personal overtones of this account, it will be seen that the Washingtons were eating well. That was due to the superior marketing and managerial abilities of Sam Fraunces, who was the steward of the President's household. Every morning he went to the Fly Market and bargained shrewdly for Washington's table, though not shrewdly enough, if one may believe an anecdote which crops up now and then. This story says that Sam one morning saw a fine shad at the Fly Market, the first of the season, and bore it home triumphantly, serving it for the General's breakfast.

"What is that, Sam?" the President is said to have inquired, observing it.

"Why, sir, it is a shad," Sam told him.

"It is very early in the season for shad," Washington remarked suspiciously. "How much did you pay for it?"

"Two dollars," the steward admitted reluctantly.

Washington was indignant. "Two dollars!" he cried. "I can never encourage such extravagance at my table. Take it away. I will not touch it."

Sam took away his shad penitently, and after breakfast, served it to himself without scruple at his own table.[15]

It was at another dinner table, five days after the Senator's uncomfortable occasion, that Washington, in the midst of some rare and honest merriment with Baron Steuben, who was "remarkably cheerful and facetious," was handed the letter which told him that his mother had died in Fredericksburg exactly a week before, at the age of eighty-two.

He was not surprised to hear the news—it had been expected —and since he had never been close to his mother, he was not seriously affected, although he wrote a dutiful letter to his sister Betty on September 13, in which he remarked sententiously that "awful and affecting as the death of a parent is, there is consolation in knowing that Heaven has spared ours to an age beyond which few attain, and favored her with the full enjoyment of her mental faculties, and as much bodily strength as usually falls to the lot of fourscore. Under these considerations and a hope that she is translated to a happier place, it is the duty of her relatives to yield due submission to the decrees of the Creator. When I was last at Fredericksburg, I took a final leave of my mother, never expecting to see her more."

284

Mary Washington's bequests to her son were an odd mixture of practicality and sentiment. There was, of course, the expected real estate he knew he would get, consisting of lands on Accokeek Run, in Stafford County. But there was also her Negro boy, George, her best bed and bedspread of Virginia cloth, curtains, a quilted blue and white quilt, her best dressing glass and her next best dressing glass, another bed, bedstead bolsters, a pillow, a pair of sheets, a blanket and a counterpane. Doubtless Martha was most appreciative of all these bequests.

By September, Washington's own physical condition was nearly back to normal. He wrote to Dr. James Craik: "My disorder was of long and painful continuance, and though now freed from the latter, the wound given by the incision is not yet closed. Persuaded as I am that the case has been treated with skill, and with as much tenderness at the nature of the complaint would admit, yet I confess I often wished for your inspection of it. During the paroxysm, the distance rendered this impracticable, and after the paroxysm had passed, I had no conception of being confined to a lying posture on one side six weeks, and that I should feel the remains of it more than twelve. The part affected is now reduced to the size of a barley corn, and by Saturday next (which will complete the thirteenth week) I expect it will be skinned over. Upon the whole, I have more reason to be thankful that it is no worse than to repine at the confinement."

In this letter, he complains of the want of exercise and the cares of his office, which he has no doubt will "hasten my departure for that country from whence no traveler returns," but Dr. Craik surely discounted this gloomy prediction from his old friend and patient. It was the kind of thing Washington often wrote; from his early years onward, he frequently considered himself not long for this world, but he survived diseases and disorders which had killed thousands upon thousands of his countrymen, and died at last of a bad cold that turned into pneumonia.

*285*

As for exercise, his own diary at the time belies his complaint. On October 5, for example, he records that he "exercised on horse-back between the hours of 9 and 11 in the forenoon, and between 5 and 6 in the afternoon, on foot." Next day he "exercised in a carriage with Mrs. Washington in the forenoon," and the day after exercised on horseback again, besides walking an hour in the afternoon.

He had more time for exercise and relaxation now, since Congress had adjourned on September 26, and instead of limiting his jaunts on horseback or in the carriage to an hour, he could take his time and pause to make leisurely inspections. One day, for example, he visited two lovely gardens, Mr. Perry's, on the west side of the Bloomingdale Road, just west of the present Union Square, and Mr. Williamson's, a flower and nursery garden which was actually the horticultural annex of a tavern, on the east side of Greenwich Street, extending three blocks up from Harrison Street.

In the bright autumn weather, he sometimes spent the whole day in the open, as he did on October 10, when he recorded in his diary: "Pursuant to an engagement formed on Thursday last, I set off about 9 o'clock in my barge to visit Mr. Prince's fruit gardens and shrubberies at Flushing, on Long Island. The Vice-President, Governor of the State, Mr. Izard, Col. Smith and Major Jackson accompanied me. These gardens, except in the number of young fruit trees, did not answer my expectations. The shrubs were trifling, and the flowers not numerous. The inhabitants of this place showed us what respect they could, by making the best use of one cannon to salute. On our return we stopped at the seats of General and Mr. Gouverneur Morris [Morrisania] and viewed a barn of which I have heard the latter speak much belonging to his farm—but it was not of a construction to strike my fancy—nor did the conveniences of it at all answer their cost. From hence we proceeded to Harlem, where we were met by Mrs. Washington, Mrs. Adams and Mrs. Smith. Dined at the tavern kept by

*286*

a Captain Mariner [Marriner] and came home in the evening."*

On these excursions the master of Mount Vernon could forget that he was President and indulge himself in the subject he enjoyed most. The critical tone of these diary entries shows how much he was enjoying himself; it was the kind of note-taking he would have done, though verbally, on an inspection of Mount Vernon.

The remainder of the autumn was occupied with his tour of the Eastern states, described elsewhere. The President may have enjoyed this tour of duty, but its political effect was summarized bluntly by John Trumbull, Governor Jonathan Trumbull's painter son, who wrote to Oliver Wolcott in December: "I see the President has returned all fragrant with the odor of incense. It must have given him satisfaction to find that the hearts of the people are united in his favor, but the blunt and acknowledged adulation of our addresses must often have wounded his feelings. We have gone through all the popish grades of worship, at least up to the *Hyperdoulia*. This tour has answered a good political purpose, and in a great measure stilled those who were clamoring about the wages of Congress and the salaries of officers."

[1790]    Washington came back from New England to a New York winter that, for once, was extremely mild until February. He was able to "exercise" nearly every day by horse or carriage, often with Martha and the two grandchildren. These carriage excursions followed a regular route, which was called "the 14 miles round." That meant driving out of town on the Kingsbridge Road, over Murray Hill along the line of

---

* Captain William Marriner, who owned taverns both in Harlem and on Ward's Island for years after the war, had fought in a little-known phase of the Revolution. He and Captain Adam Hyler were leaders in a kind of whale-boat privateering off New York Island, designed to hamper the movement of British supplies as much as possible.

the present Lexington Avenue, and up the island to Mc-Gowan's Pass, at 108th Street, then across the top, paralleling the Harlem River, to the Bloomingdale Road, and down the west side home.

Congress returned and succeeded in getting a quorum of both houses by January 6, 1790. They had much to discuss: Indian troubles on the Ohio and in the South, relations with Great Britain and France, Hamilton's scheme to refund the public debt, and the exceedingly delicate question of where to locate the government permanently.

Meanwhile, social life resumed and Senator Maclay submitted himself to its duties with worse grace than before. "Dined this day with the President," he wrote on January 14. "It was a great dinner—all in the taste of high life. I considered it as a part of my duty as a Senator to submit to it, and am glad it is over. The President is a cold, formal man, but I must declare that he treated me with great attention. I was the first person with whom he drank a glass of wine. I was often spoken to by him. Yet he knows how rigid a republican I am."

The mildness of the weather, with the exception of a bad Christmas storm, enabled the President to pursue his agricultural inspections. A week or so after the Senator's unhappy dinner he was off to the Baron de Poellnitz' farm, near Murray Hill, to see a new threshing machine in operation. The Baron, who was an assiduous inventor of agricultural tools and machines, including a threshing machine and a horse-hoe, kept his farm largely for experiments, which was exactly Washington's cup of tea. The President contrived to visit the place whenever he could, and the Baron astutely took advantage of his interest to propose that the government establish an experimental farm of its own, but there is no record that Washington ever proposed this measure to Congress, where Maclay would certainly have risen in his wrath to defeat it.

Soon after the first of the year, Washington was given relief from the crowded house on Franklin Square. Count de Moustier returned to Paris, leaving vacant his fine six-story mansion on lower Broadway, and the government quickly secured it for the President. Undoubtedly Maclay and the other republican critics disapproved the move, because it was one of the most aristocratic houses in the city, but Washington was delighted.* He took charge of the moving process himself, and as soon as the Count had moved out, walked through the place, assigning rooms, disposing the furniture, and directing that new stables be built. Nearly every day in early February he walked to his new lodgings, measuring, conferring with his carpenters, and laying out his stable according to his own exact dimensions.

On his fifty-eighth birthday, while New York and most of the nation's cities were celebrating the event, Washington chose to move. So much furniture was carried over during the day that two of the President's official family slept there that night. After dinner the following day, he and Martha and the children arrived with their personal belongings.

Martha must have had little to do. Washington records in his diary that he spent the twenty-fourth "employed in arranging matters about the house and fixing matters," and on the twenty-fifth he was "engaged as yesterday," though he had to stop in the afternoon and receive a congressional committee which had brought for his consideration a bill to take a census of the nation's inhabitants.

By March 4 he was entertaining in full style again, and there was old William Maclay at his table, grumbling as usual: "Dined with the President of the United States. . . . He seemed to bear in his countenance a settled aspect of melancholy. No cheering ray of convivial sunshine broke through the cloudy gloom of settled seriousness."

If Washington was really gloomy, it may have been because he needed a trip to get him away from official duties for a time.

* The house was the Macomb house, on the west side of Broadway below Trinity Church, about where number 39 Broadway is today. Subsequently it became a hotel known as Bunker's Mansion House, and enjoyed another incarnation as a boardinghouse, after which it disappeared entirely.

He undertook one in April, a tour into the wilds of Long Island, where his diary carefully notes the condition of the houses he stayed in. The route ran from Brooklyn to Flatbush, then to New Utrecht and over to Jamaica, where he spent his first night, April 20. They had dined that day in New Utrecht, at the house of a Mr. Barre, where, Washington said, "the man was obliging but little else to recommend it."

The morning of the twenty-first was clear and pleasant. The party rode out along the road to South Hempstead, where they stopped to feed the horses, then turned southward until "we came in view of the sea," presumably somewhere in the vicinity of the present Freeport. He stopped that night at "Squire Thompson's," dined the next day at Hart's Tavern, in Brookhaven Township, then struck across the island to the north side, "passing the east end of the Brushey Plains." He stayed that night in Setauket, in the house of a Captain Roe, "tolerably decent with obliging people in it." Passing through Smithtown on the following day, he dined at Huntington and lodged for the night in Oyster Bay. The host was a Mr. Young. Leaving him before six o'clock next morning, Washington journeyed past Glen Cove (then called Mosquito Cove), and breakfasted at Henry Onderdonk's house, "at the head of a little bay, where we were kindly received and well entertained." Onderdonk operated a grist mill and two paper mills. The party dined that day at Flushing, and by late afternoon they were in Brooklyn again, crossing the ferry to New York Island before sundown.

The journey must have put Washington in better spirits, because Maclay dined again with the President less than two weeks later and reported him "in more good humor than I ever saw him, though he was so deaf that I believe he heard little of the conversation."

The President was, indeed, a little deaf and his eyesight compelled him to wear glasses when he was working, but he was not in the sorry condition that the Senator implied, as far as his hearing was concerned. He had, however, acquired a cold, and three days after the dinner with Maclay, he was in bed. A day later, May 10, he was seriously ill with pneumonia. A doctor was summoned from Philadelphia, on the advice of Dr. Bard, and there were frequent consultations with New York specialists. By the fifteenth of May, it was whispered about once more, as it had been the year before, that the President would not live. Maclay, calling to see how Washington did, reported this awful prospect in a tone of what may have been grim satisfaction: "Every eye full of tears. His life despaired of. Dr. MacKnight told me he would trifle neither with his own character nor the public expectation; his danger was imminent, and every reason to expect that the event of his disorder would be unfortunate."

As he had so many times, Washington astonished everyone with his rapid recovery from what would have been a fatal illness to most people. He was so much better by May 24 that he was able to ride out in his carriage, but nonetheless his convalescence was slow. He suffered a "general debility" through most of the summer of 1790.

While he was recuperating he must have been pleased to read a letter that had arrived while he lay ill, from the executor of Benjamin Franklin's estate, Henry Hill, with an accompanying bequest from the "great and invaluable" doctor, as Washington called him in returning his thanks. Franklin had bequeathed to Washington "my fine crabtree walking stick with a gold head curiously wrought in the form of the cap of Liberty." This he gave to "my friend and the friend of Mankind, General Washington. If it were a sceptre, he has merited it, and would become it." *

Curiously this suggestion of the sceptre came at a moment when criticism of Washington's "royalist" habits had been renewed, just before his illness. The faithful Dr. Stuart reported these new rumors to the President, who in his reply appeared particularly incensed by the complaint of Colonel

* This cane is in the National Museum at Washington, D.C.

Bland, reported to have remarked that Washington's bow was stiff and haughty.

"That I have not been able to make bows to the taste of poor Colonel Bland (who, by the by, I believe never saw one of them) is to be regretted, especially too as (upon the occasions) they were indiscriminately bestowed, and the best I was master of. Would it not have been better to throw the veil of charity over them, ascribing their stiffness to the effects of age, or to the unskillfulness of my teacher, than to pride and dignity of office, which God knows has no charms for me? For I can truly say I had rather be at Mount Vernon with a friend or two about me than to be attended at the seat of government by the officers of state and the representatives of every power in Europe. . . ."

In this letter to Dr. Stuart, Washington appended a melancholy addendum about the state of his health. "I have already had within less than a year two *severe* attacks, the last worse than the first," he wrote. "A third more than probable will put me to sleep with my fathers; at what distance this may be I know not. Within the last twelve months I have undergone more and severer sickness than thirty preceding years afflicted me with, put it all together. I have abundant reason however to be thankful that I am so well recovered, though I still feel the remains of the violent affection of my lungs, the cough, pain in my breast, and shortness in breathing not having entirely left me. . . ." [16]

A week before Washington penned this gloomy estimate, Thomas Jefferson had written to a friend: "The President is perfectly reestablished, and looks better than before his illness." Jefferson, in fact, was at that moment preparing to embark with Washington on a three-day fishing excursion off Sandy Hook. In perfect June weather, the craft cruised along the fishing banks, and the President himself hauled in "a great number" of sea bass and blackfish.

Independence Day fell on Sunday that summer of 1790, so it was celebrated on Monday with parading and saluting all day, music and the steady beating of drums adding to the uproar. Congress adjourned and went to Washington's house, where they "got some wine, punch and cakes." The ceremonies of the day, and the oration by Brockholst Livingston, took place in St. Paul's, where everyone repaired from the President's house. Washington thought Livingston's speech a "sensible oration," but Maclay, who sat in a pew next to the President's, remarked, "I could not hear him well. Some said it was fine. I could not contradict them."

Through the hot weeks of summer, Congress debated that year the question of where to establish itself. A good many members were willing to settle for New York City, but it was considered essential that the federal government have a federal site. The city had gone so far as to place under construction a new and imposing presidential home near the Battery, overlooking Bowling Green, where the old fort had once stood. But neither city nor state would consent to cede the ten square miles of territory, with accompanying federal jurisdiction, which Congress demanded. Various tracts were suggested—Harlem Heights, the lower portion of Westchester, Brooklyn Heights—but it was impossible to reach an agreement. Washington himself preferred Harlem Heights, if the final choice should be New York City.

There were other claimants for the honor. Pennsylvania wanted the national capital on the banks of the Delaware. Maryland, Virginia and Delaware wanted it on the Potomac. South Carolina made no claims for herself, but opposed Philadelphia because the Quakers, she said, "were eternally dogging Southern members with their schemes of emancipation." As for the Philadelphians, they were only concerned lest New York should get the honor. "Do as you please," wrote the fiery Dr. Benjamin Rush to a friend in the Senate, "but tear Congress away from New York in any way. Do not rise until you have effected this business."

The question was settled by a political deal, made over a dinner table and engineered jointly by Jefferson and Hamil-

293

ton. The latter had before Congress his Assumption Bill, whereby the federal government would assume state debts through the mechanism of his funding system. Jefferson and his supporters naturally opposed this as a dangerous exercise of federal power. The two men are supposed to have argued the matter for a half hour one morning as they walked up and down before Washington's house, having both arrived at the same time to see him.

At the dinner conference, which included two or three key Senators, a deal was made. Jefferson, who had been won over by Hamilton, agreed to provide the Virginia votes necessary to get the Assumption Bill passed, and in return Hamilton and Robert Morris would muster enough Northern votes to insure that the seat of government would finally be established on the Potomac. Soon after, the funding system squeaked through both houses by a small majority, as a result of the deal, and Congress decided to erect the federal city on the site it now occupies.

Meanwhile, before it adjourned on August 12, Congress voted to reconvene for its next sessions in Philadelphia, thus soothing everyone's feelings.

Washington took advantage of the early adjournment to add the postscript to his New England tour by visiting Rhode Island, a journey previously described, and returned to the city only long enough to pack his belongings and prepare for a welcome holiday at Mount Vernon before he would have to return to Philadelphia in November.

On a Monday morning, August 30, he left New York for the last time. It was a sad procession for everyone but Washington, who was going home to Mount Vernon and could not have been unhappy if he tried. New Yorkers, one supposes, felt that their brief glory was coming to an untimely end. Nevertheless, they sent off the President in a final burst of ceremony—a parade of officials and military down to the barge, which lay at McComb's Wharf, in the North River. Martha and her husband climbed into the boat, and as the traditional thirteen-gun salute sounded, the thirteen oarsmen in white jackets and black caps bent to their oars, and the barge skimmed over the bay in "serene and beautiful" August weather. This time there were no tears. Mount Vernon and a new life in Philadelphia were waiting over the horizon.

PART 4

WASHINGTON IN PHILADELPHIA

Chapter 1

As Soldier and Civilian

Long before he came to live there as President,
Washington knew and loved the old city by the Schuylkill. He
was respected and admired in Philadelphia at a time when he
was virtually unknown in New York. By reason of social connections, military associations dating from the war with the
French, and a kind of natural affinity, Washington always
found himself welcomed more cordially in Philadelphia, and
by the best families, than anywhere else in the colonies outside his native Virginia.

[1757]    The solid foundation for this pleasant relationship
was laid in the days of the struggle with France, when he visited the city in the course of his military tribulations as a Colonel of Virginia militia. He went there for the first time in
1756, on his way to Boston and the interview with Governor
Shirley. The following year he returned, with unexpected leisure, to see more of the city. Disappointed at the outcome
of his visit to Shirley, he had asked Dinwiddie's permission to
attend the conference of provincial governors in Philadelphia
called by Lord Loudon, the new British commander, in the
hope that he could impress the irascible Scot sufficiently so
that Loudon would remove him from the ranks of underpriv-

ileged militia and get him a royal commission in the regular military establishment.

Dinwiddie's permission had been grudging, to say the least: "I cannot conceive what service you can be of in going there, as the plan concerted will of course be communicated to you and the other officers, however, as you seem so earnest to go, I now give you leave. . . ." George did not argue the point; he knew why he was going and what he hoped to gain there. But when he reached the city on February 21, 1757, he found that Loudon had not yet arrived. Other distinguished personages were present, including Dinwiddie, Governor Horatio Sharpe, of Maryland, Governor Arthur Dobbs, of North Carolina; and William Denny, Pennsylvania's Governor, who was in residence at the Shippen house.

Since these gentlemen were all known to him, especially Dinwiddie and Sharpe, he was invited to spend some time in their company, while everyone waited for the British commander. He saw more of Governor Sharpe than of the others, perhaps because Sharpe was now his immediate superior and they had much in common to discuss. The young Colonel's accounts show that he ate and drank with Sharpe, played cards with him and the others, and attended the dancing assembly. These regular assembly affairs included cards as well as dancing, with rum punch to enliven an evening that customarily lasted for six hours.

The preliminaries to the conference proved to be more enjoyable for George than the event itself. Loudon arrived on March 14 with a ringing of bells and a salute from the Association Battery, and sat down immediately with the governors. They learned little enough of his plans, but he heard a good deal from them about the problems of the colonies. Whenever he had the opportunity, George improved his time with Loudon, and it seemed to him that the commander was favorably impressed. However, he failed to get even the promise of what he had come for, and early in April he rode back to Alexandria in as dark a mood as he had left it.

[1773]    By the time he came again to Philadelphia for a visit, having made two brief trips in between, it was May 1773 and he was a person of substance and considerable distinction. He had in tow Martha's son, Jack Custis, whom he was about to enter in King's College, New York, with the hope that it would improve his lagging mental industry and save him from a precipitate marriage with Nellie Calvert. (It did neither.)

Jack must have been impressed with the way his stepfather was received. Twice he was invited to dinner by the Governor, and much of his time was occupied with entertaining and being entertained by some of the city's foremost citizens.

[September–October 1774]    All told, then, Washington had visited Philadelphia five times before he arrived in September 1774 as a delegate to the first Continental Congress, and he must have felt himself much at home as he rode into town with two of the Virginia delegates, Patrick Henry and Edmund Pendleton.

There was a different atmosphere in the city this time. Although it was Sunday, the accustomed Sabbath quiet of the Quaker stronghold was sorely disturbed by the comings and goings of the delegates pouring in from every colony except Georgia. They were greeting each other, getting themselves established in headquarters, making social engagements and discussing the business before them. They buzzed with indignation and resolve. As John Adams wrote to Abigail, "Every gentleman seems to consider the bombardment of Boston as the bombardment of the capital of his own province."

Washington found quarters with a friend, Dr. William Shippen, a noted physician and anatomist, and breakfasted with him next morning before he walked down to the meeting place of the delegates, the City Tavern. There he found himself among strangers, except for a few of the Maryland and Pennsylvania men. These representatives were among the ablest men in their provinces. Accustomed to writing and making speeches, many of them were brilliant at it, and most were burning to do it in this crisis. Washington had neither of these talents, and so he found himself sitting almost on the sidelines. No one appointed him to a committee; he failed to make John Adams's list of convention celebrities; and he was overshadowed in his own delegation by Patrick Henry and Richard Henry Lee.

It was not so much a question of what Washington did for the Congress as of what the Congress did for him. There it could be said he had improved himself. By confining his activities of necessity to work behind the scenes, which consisted largely of wining and dining with his colleagues, he contrived to meet a high percentage of important people. (He was entertained in no less than thirty-one private homes.) Men like Benjamin Harrison, Joseph Reed and Thomas Mifflin were influential leaders whose careers would shortly be entangled with his own. Mixing with them and others smoothed off whatever remained of the provincial in him. He came away from the session in October feeling that he had won valuable friendships and been respected if not particularly admired.

Among the non-delegates who admired him to the point of ecstasy was Dr. Solomon Drowne, a Philadelphia physician, who wrote to his sister in Providence, on October 5, a letter containing this impassioned piece of free verse:

> *A Day or two after*
> *By curiosity led forth (all conquering*
> *Power) my willing Feet transferred me where*
> *I might survey America's great Patriots*
> *Retire from weighty Council.—A Prospect*
> *Glorious!—At the pleasing View, how glow'd*
> *My Bosom!—As many as the Weeks*
> *The Year contains, so many constitute*
> *Th' illustrious Band.—With manly gait,*
> *His faithful Steel suspended by his Side,*
> *Pass'd W-shi-gt-n along, Virginia's Hero.*

> *\*\*\* much is wanting \*\*\**

Lost in admiration of his own muse, Dr. Drowne concluded his fit: "I am in great Haste, and can go no further in this heroic and truly sublime Strain. I have not even time to give the lines their proper measure. This Col. W-sh-gt-n is a man noted as well for his good sense as his Bravery. I heard he said he wished to God the Liberties of America were to be determined by a single Combat between himself and G——e."

Which may be the most unlikely of all the remarks Washington is said to have made.


[May 1775]    When he returned to Philadelphia seven months later, in May 1775, the fateful events of Concord and Lexington had occurred and the business of war was at the top of the agenda. The Colonel came in martial array and mood. At Baltimore he stopped on the sixth to review the volunteer companies, and stayed to have dinner with the admiring citizens. He may have been already attired in the uniform which drew attention to him a few days later in Philadelphia, the red and blue outfit of his French and Indian War days. Charles Willson Peale painted him in it, a portrait well known today.

As Colonel Washington and his Virginia friends came within six miles of Philadelphia on May 9, after they had left Baltimore, George encountered the first of the welcoming delegations he was to see so many times during his life that the day would come when he pleaded for omission of the honor. These welcomers were said to number about five hundred, including officers of the military companies and leading citizens.*
Four miles farther on, the procession encountered a band and

---

* The number seems excessive, considering the nature of the occasion, even though Freeman prints it without question and at least one contemporary source so reckons it. It is more credible, however, if one considers that the Philadelphia Light Horse, Washington's frequent escort as Commander-in-Chief and as President, numbered about two hundred and fifty at full strength, and adds to that the turnout which patriotic fervor was able to produce in the city as each of the state delegations appeared and was similarly escorted.

a body of foot soldiers and riflemen. Thus the Virginians were escorted into town in style.

They found the spirit of both city and Congress considerably different than it had been when they left it last. Sectional jealousies and individual struggles were lost in the overwhelming events which had swept up the delegates and nearly everyone else. Only the Loyalists and those who would correspond to our present-day isolationists resisted the tide.

This time, too, Washington was a far more conspicuous figure in Congress than he had been before. John Adams noted: "Colonel Washington appears at Congress in his uniform, and by his great experience and abilities in military matters is of much service to us."

The story of how the Colonel became a General as Congress chose the man who would lead the new Continental Army is too long and complicated to rehearse here, involving as it does the intricate maneuverings between the Northern and Southern factions, and the state of mind that prevailed in the two Houses. It is enough to say that the reasons for choosing Washington were complex and surprising in some aspects, and that the decision, when it came, did not please everyone, including several in the Virginia delegation itself, and particularly disappointed John Hancock, who thought until the last moment that the honor would fall upon him. It was an honor he badly wanted, but he swallowed his chagrin manfully when he saw the choice was inevitable. Those who had championed other leaders during the discussions of the Committee of the Whole also accepted what they could not defeat, and to give the appearance of unity, which everyone recognized was essential, no other name was proposed after Thomas Johnson, of Maryland, put Washington's before the assemblage. He was elected unanimously.

Washington, of course, did not attend the momentous session. He knew that he was being considered, but he did not believe he would be chosen, and whenever he allowed himself to think of it as a possibility, dismay and reluctance gripped him, and he could not bear to listen to the deliberations.

About dinnertime, however, he understood that the hand pointed at him and there was no escape. The delegates, filing out of the hall, seized his hand and showered him with congratulations, and he heard for the first time the music of a word that was admittedly sweet to his ears—"General."

He dined that day at Burns's Tavern, "in the fields," which was located according to which Philadelphia authority you choose: on Tenth Street (Hiltzheimer); Ninth Street above Arch (Scharf); or on the Commons, at Tenth and Vine streets (Eberlein and Hubbard). After dinner he performed his first official military duty, sitting down with a congressional committee to work out the rules and regulations that would govern the army.

Washington approached his command with the same genuine reluctance with which he later came to the presidency, obsessed by a strange if honest fear that he was not equal to the task. His strong emotional feeling about it was evident in the tears that filled his eyes, if the story is true, as he discussed the matter with Patrick Henry, protesting that he lacked the training for such an important command—a protest that was technically true. He assured his fellow Virginian solemnly:

"Remember, Mr. Henry, what I now tell you: from the day I enter upon the command of the American armies, I date my fall, and the ruin of my reputation."*

In any event, the commitment had been made, and if Washington was alone at first in fully understanding the awful responsibility thrust upon him, the men who had honored him realized it when, at a dinner soon afterward, the first toast proposed was "To the Commander-in-Chief of the American

* The story of Washington's tears and what he said is Benjamin Rush's later remembrance of what Patrick Henry told him, and therefore secondhand, but as Freeman says, "It has the ring of sound money on the historical counter."

Armies." Dr. Benjamin Rush described the scene that followed:

"General Washington rose from his seat, and with some confusion thanked the company for the honor they did him. The whole company instantly rose and drank the toast standing. This scene, so unexpected, was a solemn one. A silence followed it, as if every heart was penetrated with the awful but great events which were to follow the use of the sword of liberty which had been put into General Washington's hands by the unanimous voice of his country."

When the toasts and the acclamation and the committee meetings were over, Washington went back to his lodgings, and it must be supposed he lay in his bed and tried to face the task that lay before him. He was forty-three years old, with excellent experience in border warfare and a good general knowledge of military affairs. But he had never commanded large bodies of men, and he had never fought a major engagement. He was expected to confront and defeat British regulars in unknown but undoubtedly formidable quantity, and of a quality he had good reason to respect, with an army still to be drawn, for the most part, from a manpower pool which would not exceed 175,000 men at the maximum. He could not foresee that he would be compelled to get along with a pitiful fraction of the strength that might reasonably be expected from such resources.

To supply this army, he would have four cities to draw upon: Philadelphia, 34,000; New York, 22,000; Boston, 15,000; Charleston, 12,000.[1] Out of these 83,000 inhabitants would have to come enough skilled artisans, enough producers of essential supplies, enough workers of every kind to maintain the armies in the field. Only a man of Washington's extraordinary character could have contemplated such a prospect without feeling himself hopelessly defeated before he had even started to fight against the immense resources of the British Empire.

On the night of June 22, he was ready to embark on the

task, with whatever courage and resolution he could muster. A farewell supper was given him at the City Tavern, that historic spot where so much of his life had been determined, then and at other times. In the morning he and his generals, Lee and Schuyler, set out for Boston, a journey that has been described elsewhere in these pages. They left the city to the blare of bands and in the pomp of military pageantry, which somehow outraged John Adams. He rode back to town and, perhaps out of the jealousy of Washington that nagged him, he wrote: "Such is the pride and pomp of war. I, poor creature, worn out with scribbling for my bread and my liberty . . . must leave others to wear the laurels I have sown."

[1776]   It may be that Adams was less anxious to share the laurels when he saw Washington on the General's occasional war visits to Philadelphia, and observed the crushing weight he carried. They met next in May 1776, when the Commander-in-Chief came down to Philadelphia briefly from New York for consultations with Congress, bringing Martha with him to be inoculated for smallpox. That, it will be remembered, was the time John Hancock's gout prevented him from entertaining, though it is likely Washington would have declined in any event, not wanting a host to share Martha's risk. Adams could assess the kind of constant tension under which Washington now labored by the fact that his concern for the safety of New York had led him to station horses at the various stopping places between the two cities, so he could return "with the utmost expedition" if the British attacked.

Philadelphia had frequent glimpses of him throughout the war, for varying periods of time, and the more acute observers in Congress must have seen beyond the grave mask and understood why it was that Washington so seldom smiled in those years.

[1777]    Of these glimpses—quick snapshots of a man constantly in motion—the city would remember longest, perhaps, the August Sunday in 1777 when the army marched through the city on its way to the Brandywine. Washington meant them to remember it, and in fact that was the purpose of making a display of this march—to intimidate the Loyalists, if possible, and to reassure the fainthearted patriots who had been frightened by the proximity of Howe's army and the stories of its overwhelming strength. Having decided to put on a show for the population, Washington was faced with the necessity of minimizing as far as possible his army's deficiencies in equipment, and of emphasizing its spirit, which was high at the moment. To make as brave an appearance as possible, he directed that the nondescript clothes the men wore (in place of the uniforms they did not have) should be washed, and what arms they had should be burnished. Each man was also to wear in his hat a "green sprig, emblem of hope."

As the troops marched up to the city, they were halted a mile away and inspected to see that no ragged edges were showing. Then the drums beat again and the army, which more nearly resembled a body of armed civilians, began the march, Washington and his aides riding at its head. They paraded down Front Street, up Chestnut to the Common. Their order was that of a force marching into alien country: first the cavalry, light horse and mounted regiments; then the pioneers, the road-builders with their axes; then Nathanael Greene, heading the first brigade of infantry, commanded by that valiant preacher, Peter Muhlenberg, who preached a last sermon to his Virginia congregation, so it was said, and then took off his clerical robes to disclose his uniform. "I leave you now to join General Washington," he is supposed to have said. "Let those brave men who will, follow me." After the infantry came the artillery, and more regiments, and the massed drum-and-fife corps. Washington had given the musicians exact instructions. They were to play "a tune for a quick step, with such moderation that the men may step to it with ease, and without dancing along, or totally disregarding the music."

Washington had given other specific directions for this march, recognizing the realities of the situation and mindful of the effect he intended to create on the watchers. He recognized, for instance, that it was more than probable some of the reluctant soldiers, passing through the crowded city streets, would take advantage of the opportunity to slip away into the throng and desert, which would not be difficult, since they wore no uniforms, for the most part. To discourage such ideas, the General had made it plain that any deserter in this manner who was caught would be given thirty-nine lashes. He also had ordered that no women be permitted in the line of march; they would have to be gotten around Philadelphia in some other manner.*

After the army had finished its two-hour progress through the city, crossed the Schuylkill on the floating bridge, and marched off toward Brandywine, the people and the members of Congress and the other dignitaries went home to think about what they had seen. Whatever good impression may have been made on the people was doubtless obliterated in the next few weeks by the successive disasters of Brandywine and Germantown, and the British occupation of the city. As for Congress and the officials, some had been cheered, some had been

* Washington's General Orders in this matter, issued August 4, 1777, demanded a reduction of the "multitude of women, particularly those pregnant or having children with them." For readers unacquainted with this problem, it may be explained that each brigade was allotted a quota of "washerwomen," the number varying with time and circumstance. Some of these were legitimate, and sweated over their tubs under the trees to keep the army's linen in order, but inevitably every brigade acquired an additional quota of washerwomen who never saw a tub. These included not only prostitutes, professional and otherwise, but wives who refused to let their husbands leave them, and similarly devoted sweethearts. Washington's army had apparently accumulated an unreasonable number of female camp followers, and he was anxious not to give the respectable and otherwise ignorant citizens of Philadelphia a bad impression.

In passing, it may be noted that some historians have questioned Molly Pitcher's status in the army, not only the details of her traditional feat but whether she was in fact the wife of an artilleryman, as tradition asserts.

dispirited, and some had tried to be judicious about it, among these John Adams.

"The army . . . I find to be extremely well armed," he wrote, displaying either a profound lack of military knowledge or careless observation, "pretty well clothed, and tolerably disciplined. . . . Much remains yet to be done. Our soldiers have not yet quite the air of soldiers. They don't step exactly in time. They don't hold up their heads quite erect, nor turn out their toes exactly as they ought. They don't all of them cock their hats; and such as do, don't all wear them the same way."

This was a most charitable estimate of the army's condition.

[1778–1779]   When the city next saw Washington, it was not so much the army that was in question as its leadership. The loyalty and integrity of three of his generals had been questioned, and Henry Laurens had been compelled in honor to resign as President of Congress after his brother John had shot General Lee in a duel. But somehow little of this unpleasantness had tarnished Washington's name. When he came down from his Middlebrook headquarters in December 1778 to discuss with Congress the campaigns for the following year, he was received with deference and a round of elaborate entertaining, in which he was joined by Martha, who was already in the city.

The entertainments were so numerous, in fact, that Nathanael Greene, who was with the Commander-in-Chief, complained: ". . . I spent a month in the most agreeable and disagreeable manner I ever did a month in my life. We had the most splendid entertainment imaginable; large assemblies, evening balls, etc. It was hard service to go through the duties of the day. I was obliged to rise early and to go to bed late to complete them. In the morning a round of visiting came on. Then you had to prepare for dinner, after which the evening balls would engage your time until one or two in the morning.

Our great Fabius Maximus was the glory and admiration of the city. Every exertion was made to show him respect and make his time agreeable, but the exhibition was such a scene of luxury and profusion they gave him more pain than pleasure." And Joseph Reed could second him: "The night being frequently devoted to pleasure, Nature will make her demands in the day, and many a report have I known delayed because the committee had been dancing all night."

To Washington, all this was in shocking contrast to the horrors and anxieties in the field from which he had so recently come; it lent support to his gloomy conviction that the war could not be won unless his countrymen showed a far more resolute determination to win it.

On the day appointed by Congress and his own General Orders as a day of Thanksgiving, the thirtieth of December 1778, he poured out his misgivings in a letter to Benjamin Harrison. "If I was to be called upon to draw a picture of the times and of men from what I have seen and heard, and in part know," he wrote, "I should in one word say that idleness, dissipation and extravagance seems to have laid fast hold of most of them. That speculation, peculation, and an insatiable thirst for riches seems to have got the better of every other consideration and almost of every order of men. That party disputes and personal quarrels are the great business of the day, whilst the momentous concerns of an empire, a great and accumulated debt, ruined finances, depreciated money and want of credit (which in their consequences is the want of everything) are but secondary considerations and postponed from day to day, from week to week, as if our affairs wear the most promising aspect. After drawing this picture, which from my soul I believe to be a true one, I need not repeat to you that I am alarmed and wish to see my countrymen roused."

Yet, alarmed and dismayed as he might be, courtesy demanded that Washington do his share of entertaining, nor could he refuse to attend parties and dinners. He himself gave an elaborate dinner for Congress at the City Tavern on January 1779, and the next night found him dancing at the house of Samuel Powel, on the west side of Third Street, between Walnut and Spruce streets. But there was special significance in that party. One of his partners, Mrs. Bache, disclosed it in a letter to her father, Benjamin Franklin. While they were dancing, she said, Washington remarked that it was his twentieth wedding anniversary. It was also, by coincidence, the good doctor's birthday.

The day before he left Philadelphia to return to Middlebrook, February 1, Washington sat for his portrait to Pierre Eugène du Simitière. In his notebook the artist recorded that it was "a drawing in black lead of a likeness in profile of His Excellency, General Washington, form of a medal, for my collection. . . . The General, at the request of the Hon. Mr. Jay, President of Congress, came with him to my house this morning and condescended with great good nature to sit about three quarters of an hour for the above likeness, having but little time to spare, being the last day of his stay in town." *[2]

Next day the General said good-by to his host, Henry Laurens, left the disturbing "idleness and dissipation" of Philadelphia behind him, and returned to the realities of his Middlebrook headquarters.

[1781–1782]   By the time he was next a visitor for any respectable period, the anxieties were largely in the past and the decisive victory of Yorktown was behind him. He was coming up to Philadelphia from Mount Vernon, with Martha, and everyone was eager to do some honor to the conqueror. In Annapolis, according to a contemporary account, he was accompanied to the home of Governor Thomas Lee "by the honest acclamations of the Whigs" and in the bargain "a few Tories, to expiate their crimes and shuffle off this opprobrium

---

* The original of Du Simitière's drawing has been lost, but engravings have made the portrait itself well known. It was first printed at Madrid in 1781.

of their characters, feebly joined in applauding the man whose late successes had annihilated their hopes, and whose conduct is a satire on their principles." [3] That evening he spent "at the Governor's elegant and hospitable board, with festive joy enlivened by good humor, wit and beauty," and the following evening he attended an assembly "prepared for the ladies, to afford them an opportunity of beholding their friend, and thanking their protector with their smiles."

Delayed by such pleasant adulation, Washington came to Philadelphia on November 26, 1781, and settled down for the winter at the new home of Benjamin Chew, 110 South Third Street, between Walnut and Spruce. Here the unfortunate Spanish agent, Don Juan de Mirailles, had lived before he died on his visit to the Morristown camp. The house was immediately north of Samuel Powel's place, where Washington had been a guest during the winter of 1778–79.

In this winter of victory, Washington was entertained with the same overwhelming hospitality that had so dismayed him in the dark years of the war. Except for a comparatively quiet Christmas dinner with Robert Morris and his family, the calendar was filled with large and elegant affairs.

The minister of France entertained George and Martha, Catherine Greene, "and a very polite circle of the gentlemen and ladies," with an "oratorio composed and set to music by a gentleman whose taste in the polite arts is well known . . . ." [4]

On New Year's Day, the Society of the Friendly Sons of St. Patrick gave him a dinner at the City Tavern. The next day came an occasion more to Washington's liking, when Alexander Quesnay de Glouvay, a French teacher, gave a theatrical program at the Southwark Theatre, on the corner of South and Apollo (later Charles) streets, between Fourth and Fifth. The chief attraction was Beaumarchais's comedy, *Eugénie*, given in French and much admired by the audience, most of whom did not speak the language. This was followed by a farce, *The Lying Valet*, and after it came "several curious dances, followed by a brilliant illumination, consisting of thir-

311

teen pyramidal pillars, representing the thirteen states. On the middle column was seen a Cupid, supporting a laurel crown over the motto—Washington, the pride of his country and the terror of Britain. On the summit was the word Virginia, on the right Connecticut, with the names Greene and Lafayette, on the left the word Pennsylvania, with the names Wayne and Steuben; and so on according to the birthplace and state proper to each general. The spectacle ended with an artificial illumination of the thirteen columns."

What the pride of his country and the terror of Britain thought of this bill, he did not record. He could not have understood *Eugénie*, and he had, even at this early date, seen enough tableaux and illuminations to last him a lifetime. At one point he was uncomfortable and embarrassed, when a prologue to the play was given, addressed directly to him. Being a confirmed theatregoer whenever he could find the opportunity, it may be he enjoyed simply being in the theatre, with the long ordeal nearly over and the more lasting pleasures of Mount Vernon at last in sight.

[1787]     It was nearly five years later that he left those pleasures to take his role in the great drama of the Constitutional Convention. His journey got off to an inauspicious start when he found himself on the first night out, at Major Snowden's, "feeling very severely" with "a violent headache and sick stomach. . . ." But he went on the next day, feeling well recovered, through rainy, squally weather which delayed his crossing at Havre de Grace and compelled him to stop overnight at the ferry crossing. On Sunday, May 13, 1787, he was in Philadelphia once more, escorted into town by his old friends, the Light Horse,* who had met him at Gray's Ferry. He had in-

---

* The Philadelphia Light Horse, or the "City Light Horse," as Washington usually called them, was known later as the First Troop Philadelphia City Cavalry. Organized on November 17, 1774, they came to occupy much the

tended to lodge at the boarding establishment of Mrs. Mary House, Fifth and Market streets, but the Morrises pressed him to stay with them, and he removed his baggage to their home on the south side of Market Street, below Sixth. "On my arrival," he notes, "the bells were chimed."

Washington was among the first, if not the first, arrival at the Convention. While the other delegates were gathering, he performed the usual social amenities, including some that were not so usual. One night he accompanied Mrs. Morris and other ladies "to hear a Mrs. O'Connell read (a charity affair) the lady being reduced in circumstances had had recourse to this expedient to obtain a little money. Her performance was tolerable . . . ." This took place at the College Hall, Fourth below Arch Street.

On another evening he went to a dinner party at Dr. Franklin's, where the guests were treated to a cask of porter just brought over from London. The wine, wrote the knowledgeable Franklin, "met with a most cordial reception and universal approbation." At eighty-one, the elder statesman was then near the end of his remarkable career (he died three years later), but although he stooped a bit when he walked and was inclined to squint through his spectacles, there was nothing in the least wrong with his intellect or his wit. Washington, in his prime at fifty-five and towering over his friend, was a vigorous contrast physically, but he was no match for Franklin's charm and eloquence.

The delegates were slow in arriving and the entertaining continued. On a warm Sunday afternoon, May 20, he dined with the Morrises and other company at their eighty-acre farm

---

same position in the city's society as the equally famous Seventh Regiment in New York City. One of Washington's biographers says of the Light Horse: "That troop proved time and time again, as Lee's and Washington's Legion subsequently proved in the Carolinas, that there *is* room in society for the order of gentlemen, and that in time of stress it is well for the State to have a class to call on who will die as gayly as they dance, and will pour out their blood, as they were wont to do their fortunes, for faith and honor, for sentiment and ideals."[5]

called The Hills on the east bank of the Schuylkill, north of Fairmount Hill. The house itself stood on Lemon Hill, in a district which is now part of Fairmount Park.

On the day after this jaunt, the General dined and drank tea at the splendid home of William Bingham, then a member of Congress from Pennsylvania and later a Senator, on Third Street above Spruce. In this house, one of the finest private homes of its day, the mistress was the former Anna Willing, who had married Bingham seven years before, and had then made his mansion one of the city's social centers. Her dinners and salons, over which she presided with exceptional charm (she was one of the town's reigning beauties), were considered the pinnacle of elegance.

Every day brought Washington into some new entertainment devised for him or for the pleasure of the delegates. One morning he rode out to Thomas Mifflin's country place on the Ridge Road, at Schuylkill Falls, in what later was the 28th Ward, and had breakfast, after which he journeyed about the hills and valleys visiting other gentlemen in their rural establishments. That day he dined with his old friend Benjamin Chew, where the household was celebrating the marriage of Chew's daughter Peggy to Colonel John Eager Howard, of Baltimore. After dining, he drank tea "in a very large circle of ladies."

One of the country homes he visited more than once was Belmont, now also part of Fairmount Park, where lived one of Washington's best Philadelphia friends, Richard Peters, who was later judge of the United States District Court for Pennsylvania, from 1792 until he died in 1818.

On Sundays, with the true instinct of a man in public life, Washington divided his churchgoing so that no faith would be offended. He attended "the Romish church," as he put it, on the twenty-seventh, and heard high mass celebrated there. This church was St. Mary's, on Fourth Street above Spruce.

That same week he went to a large party—more than a hundred guests—at the estate of William Hamilton, Bush Hill, where Andrew Hamilton, the defender of John Peter Zenger, had once lived. Situated on the north side of what was later Buttonwood Street, between Seventeenth and Eighteenth streets, this handsome place was also the home of John Adams during part of his vice-presidential term, before it was destroyed in a fire, about 1808.

As the summer came on, Washington found relief from the work of the Convention and the heat of the city in further excursions out of town, or at least to nearby points of particular interest to him. The master of Mount Vernon found his way as soon as possible to William Bartram's celebrated Botanical Garden, the first in the United States. John Bartram, a noted botanist, had founded the gardens in 1728 on the west side of the Schuylkill, a short distance below Gray's Ferry. Before he died in 1777, John had heard Linnaeus refer to him as the greatest natural botanist in the world. His son William had continued his work with only slightly less distinction. Washington toured the seven acres of the gardens and returned an indifferent verdict. They were "stored with many curious plants, shrubs and trees, many of which are exotics," he admitted, but it "was not laid off with much taste, nor was it large. . . ."

The road to the gardens led also to one of the city's most popular resorts, where Washington and the other delegates spent a good many of their relaxing hours. This was Gray's Ferry, three miles southwest of town; here George and Robert Gray, the proprietors, had laid out pleasant walks, planted ornamental shrubbery, and inaugurated concerts, fireworks and other diversions to please the citizenry. It was a favorite rendezvous for outdoor parties and public fetes.

On July 22, Washington visited another agricultural experiment at Spring Mills, near Conshohocken, known to him in the Revolution as Matson's Ford. He left the city at five o'clock that morning, breakfasted at General Mifflin's, spent the day with him and others at the Mills, and returned to the General's for dinner. He made the trip not to see the grist mill there, which was probably the first to be built in Pennsylvania, but to inspect a vineyard and bee colony belonging to Peter Legaux, a Frenchman who had arrived in America two years before. In his diary Legaux recorded that his visitors "asked a number of questions, and testified their highest approbation with my manner of managing bees, which gave me a great deal of pleasure."

When the Convention adjourned in July for ten days, so that a committee could draft its work into a form for adoption, Washington took advantage of the break to go fishing. On July 30, he hitched his horses to Gouverneur Morris's phaeton, and with Morris set off for the neighborhood of Valley Forge "to get trout." Headquarters was to be Jane Moore's 275-acre farm in Upper Merion Township, Montgomery County, about a mile west of the Schuylkill on Trout Creek.

Fish were not the only thing on Washington's mind, judging by the fact that he allowed Morris to go fishing by himself the first day while he rode over to the place of the winter encampment at Valley Forge. But whatever thoughts rose in his mind as he surveyed the spot which had nearly been the graveyard of all his hopes, he wrote in his diary no more than what a tourist might have recorded—"visited all the works which were in ruins, and the encampments in woods where the ground had not been cultivated."

Yet one supposes he rode about the place, apparently alone, with the memories tumbling in his brain. On one side he could see the broken ridges of the earthworks, covered over with grass now. The log huts where the soldiers had shivered and starved were empty and falling apart. On the hill stood the stone house that had been his headquarters. He must have remembered, with a keen and bitter recollection, those dreary weeks, but he was not a man to sentimentalize about the past. As he rode back to the fishing camp, he stopped to chat with some farmers he saw working in the fields, discussing the uncertainties of raising buckwheat and the problems of cattle raising.

A few days after the fishing trip he rode up to Trenton and

examined the newly rebuilt steel furnace belonging to Nan-
carrow and Matlack. It was, boasted the *Pennsylvania Packet*,
"much the largest and best constructed furnace in America,
being charged with fourteen tons of iron at that time, convert-
ing into steel."

Although he made no comment about his thoughts at Valley
Forge, he was not quite so reticent on August 19, when he
traveled over to Whitemarsh, where he had camped with the
army just before going into those quarters. He wrote that he
"traversed my old encampment and contemplated on the
dangers which threatened the American army at that place."

This was the range of Washington's side traveling. For the
rest he attended closely to the business of the Convention and
the steady round of formal and informal entertaining in the
city. By September 17 the work was done. Eleven states had
approved the Constitution; Vermont and Rhode Island still
held back. Governor Randolph and George Mason, among
the Virginia delegation, and Elbridge Gerry, of Massachusetts,
were the only three delegates present who refused to sign, except for the New York delegation, which had bolted the Convention to show its wholehearted distaste for what the disgruntled members called "a concoction." Only Alexander
Hamilton among their number approved the document: it represented historic victory for his principles.

After the adjournment, in more harmony than might have
been expected at the beginning, the members dined together
at the City Tavern and made their farewells. Washington returned to his lodgings and "retired to meditate on the momentous work which had been executed . . . ."

During his long stay in the city, Philadelphians and the members of the Convention alike had enjoyed an unusual opportunity of seeing their "first character in the world" at work and
at play. In the minds of many he undoubtedly appeared as the
logical leader of the new order the Convention had been de-
vising. Certainly he commanded the profound admiration of
most common citizens. Jacob Hiltzheimer, a Philadelphian

317

who had been a stablemaster in the Continental Army, wrote in his diary that he and his wife had gone to see "that great and good man Gen. Washington" as he walked in the evening on Market Street. "We had a full view of him and Major Jackson, who walked with him," Jacob noted, "but the number of people who followed him on all sides was astonishing. . . ."

Such open adulation was nearly as prevalent in the highest circles as it was among the populace. One of those who saw Washington frequently during the convention was Charles Biddle, Vice-President of Pennsylvania from 1785 to 1787, who "dined several times in company with him, and had the honor of his company to dine with me." Then and later, when their acquaintance was an everyday matter, Biddle saw Washington as "a most elegant figure of a man, with so much dignity of manner that no person whatever could take any improper liberties with him. I have heard Mr. Robert Morris, who was as intimate with him as any man in America, say that he was the only man in whose presence he felt any awe. You would seldom see a frown or a smile on his countenance, his air was serious and reflecting, yet I have seen him in the theatre laugh heartily." [6]

He was, in brief, the kind of man no one would think of calling by his first name, or by an affectionate nickname—a personality type found in nearly everyone's acquaintance. At the same time, he enjoyed the love and trust of widely dissimilar parts of the population. With these two essential attributes, he appeared to be the one man most qualified to give the office of President of the United States, when it was filled, the dignity it required to command respect, and the public support it must have to endure.

Washington rode away from Philadelphia toward Mount Vernon on September 18. Of those who said farewell and watched him depart, there must surely have been many who experienced an inner awareness that he would ride back again as President.

Chapter 2

As Leader of the Nation

Like any other householder, the President of the United States was beset with moving problems when Congress transferred the seat of government from New York to Philadelphia in 1790. The actual process of transferring furniture and arranging the new household he entrusted to his faithful secretary, Tobias Lear, while he and Martha spent a few autumn weeks at Mount Vernon, but he showered poor Lear with the most minute instructions as to how it must be done.

[1790–1791]   Anticipating Washington's arrival, the city of Philadelphia had appropriated the house of the President's old friend, Robert Morris, for his official residence. It stood on the south side of Market Street, sixty feet east of Sixth Street. Morris obligingly moved to the nearest house westward. The President had often been a guest in the house, of course, and knew something of its history. Built sometime before 1772, it had been occupied originally by Mary Masters, a widow, then by her daughter, also Mary, who married Richard Penn. It had been General Howe's headquarters when the British occupied the city, and Benedict Arnold had lived there after the evacuation. John Holker, the Consul General of France, had it for his residence after Arnold departed, and while he inhabited it, fire partly destroyed the building on January 2, 1780. It was then that Robert Morris bought the land and what remained of the mansion, ordered it "rebuilt and repaired," and in 1785 obtained a deed for it.

Benjamin Rush's son Richard, who grew up to become a noted American statesman and diplomat during the early nineteenth century, describes in his *Reminiscences* how the place

319

looked to him as a boy of ten, when Washington lived there: "It was a large double house. To the east a brick wall six or seven feet high ran well on toward Fifth Street, until it met other houses; the wall enclosed a garden, which was shaded by lofty old trees, and ran back to what is now Minor Street, where the stables stood. To the west no building adjoined it, the nearest house in that direction being at the corner of Sixth and Market, where lived Robert Morris." *

Washington's own description of it, in a letter to Lear as he passed through Philadelphia on the way to Mount Vernon, was less flattering. It was, he said, "the best they could get. It is, I believe, the best *single house* in the city; yet without additions it is inadequate to the *commodious* accommodation of my family. These, I believe, will be made." **

In this letter he indicated specifically how the rooms were to be divided, and he noted their limitations. "The first floor contains only two public rooms," he informed Lear. ". . . The second floor will have two public [drawing] rooms, and with the aid of one room with the partition in it in the back building, will be sufficient for the accommodation of Mrs. Washington and the children, and their maids, besides affording me a small place for a private study and dressing room. The third story will furnish you and Mrs. Lear with a good lodging room, a

* The melancholy fate that has overtaken so many historical sites befell the beautiful Robert Morris house. It was demolished in 1833 and three stores took its place, to be followed by successively modern business fronts. The Pennsylvania Society of the Sons of the Revolution has marked the site.

** ". . . Inadequate to the commodious accommodation of my family"— that was the constant complaint of the master of Mount Vernon during the years of his presidency. It will be recalled that New York was building him a house large enough, but it was not finished before the government was moved. This structure became successively the residence of Governors Clinton and Jay, then it was used as the Custom House, and ultimately destroyed. The Port Authority Building stands approximately on the site today. In Philadelphia, it is said, the mansion the city built for the President was *too* large when it was finished, and Washington would not live in it. Later it became the first home of the University of Pennsylvania, and after that the site of the Philadelphia Post Office.

public office (for there is no place below for one) and two rooms for the gentlemen of the family. The garret has four good rooms which must serve Mr. and Mrs. Hyde (unless they should prefer the room over the washhouse; William, and such servants as it may not be better to place in the addition (as proposed) to the back building. There is a room over the stable (without a fireplace, but by means of a stove) may serve the coachman and postillions, and there is a smokehouse, which possibly may be more useful to me for the accommodation of servants than for smoking of meat. The intention of the addition to the back building is to provide a servants' hall, and one or two (as it will afford) lodging rooms for the servants, especially those who are coupled. There is a very good washhouse adjoining to the kitchen (under one of the rooms already mentioned). There are good stables, but for twelve horses only, and a coach house which will hold all my carriages." [1]

In subsequent letters Washington urged his secretary not to let the construction work—bow windows on the south front, and the addition in back—delay "the main point (that is, the removal)" before bad weather set in. The rooms would be painted as soon as Morris moved out, and the furniture Lear was not able to place at once could be stored temporarily.

The sure hand for details of a man accustomed to running large establishments is everywhere evident in George's correspondence about the new house. He was even mindful of the impression servants might make on visitors who came to see the President. Thus he left it to Lear as to whether or not to bring their New York washerwoman, but he advised against keeping two of the kitchen flunkeys, a Mrs. Lewis and her daughter, "especially as it is in contemplation to transplant Hercules or Nathan from the kitchen at Mount Vernon to that in Philadelphia and because the dirty figures of Mrs. Lewis and her daughter will not be a pleasant sight in view (as the kitchen always will be) of the principal entertaining rooms in our new habitation." [2]

He also advised Lear that the Morrises had insisted upon

"leaving the two large looking glasses which are in their best rooms because they have no place (they say) proper to remove them to, and because they are unwilling to hazard the taking of them down. You will therefore let them have, in place of them, the choice of mine. The large ones which I purchased from the French minister they do not incline to take, but will be glad of some of the others. They also will leave a large glass lamp in the entry or hall, and will take one or more of my glass lamps in lieu of it. . . ."

Early in November the moving process had been completed, the alterations made, and the details of servants and looking glasses carried out. Congress was preparing to meet, and Washington departed Mount Vernon once more for Philadelphia on November 19. He had a slow, irritating journey over roads made nearly impassable by incessant rains. At Spurrier's Tavern, ten miles south of Baltimore, where he had been compelled to stay the night and was still waiting for his dinner, Washington came as near to intemperate language as he ever did in a letter to Lear. "The roads are infamous," he declared.

After five more days of hard traveling, he arrived in Philadelphia on Saturday, November 27, 1790, and settled down in his new home. He found the house in good order, thanks to the efficient Lear, and the state entertaining began almost at once. Following previous custom, Washington received as President of the United States between three and four o'clock on Tuesday afternoons, in the first-floor dining room at the rear of the house. Lear or someone known to Washington had to introduce the callers; it was not proper for a man to introduce himself. State visitors, of course, were properly presented by a Cabinet member. At the first levee on December 7, Thomas Jefferson introduced the day's distinguished foreign guest, Ignatius Palyrat, the new Consul General from Portugal.

A visitor arriving at the levee would be conducted by a servant to the dining room, from which chairs and tables were removed for the occasion. Probably the first person he noted in the room would be Washington himself. The tall, commanding figure of the President dominated the room as he stood before the fireplace, facing the door. He was usually dressed in rich black velvet coat and breeches, his powdered hair dressed and gathered at the back in a silk bag. He wore yellow gloves, a white or pearl-colored satin vest, and in one hand carried a cocked and cockaded hat. There were buckles at his knees and on his shoes. His long sword, with its finely wrought, polished steel hilt, was worn at the left hip beneath his coat, so that only the hilt and the end of the sword showed. The sword was encased in a scabbard of white polished leather.

He insisted that those who performed the introductions pronounce the visitor's name distinctly. That was not alone because of his bad hearing, but because he had that valuable political asset, embodied most notably today in the person of James A. Farley, of associating a man's name and appearance and never forgetting them. A levee visitor, no matter how obscure or how brief his appearance before Washington, was always highly flattered to hear himself called by name if the President saw him again. There were no handshakes at the levees; Washington simply bowed, holding his hands so that the visitor could see plainly that no clasp was to be given. Not even his best friends were given his customary firm grip on these occasions. He did not want it to be said of him that he made distinctions.

The visitors at the levee, as they entered, made a circle about the room. They were expected to be reasonably prompt, and to encourage that idea, the door was closed at three-fifteen. As soon as this was done and he knew the circle for the day was complete, Washington began making the rounds of it, beginning on the right and stopping to talk a little with each man. When he had completed the circle, he was standing again in front of the fireplace. That was the signal for each visitor to approach him in turn, make his bow and retire. The ceremony was over by four o'clock.[3]

On Christmas Eve, 1790, Martha held her first levee.* Here are the enthusiastic observations of two society ladies, old and young, who were enchanted with the affair. Abigail Adams, John's wife, writing to Mrs. William S. Smith, recorded: " . . . I went with Charles [her third child] to the drawing room, being the first of my appearance in public. The room became full before I left it, and the circle very brilliant. How could it be otherwise, when the dazzling Mrs. Bingham and her beautiful sisters (the Misses Willing) were there; the Misses Allen, and Misses Chew; in short, a constellation of beauties?"

Miss Sally McKean, daughter of Thomas McKean, Chief Justice of Pennsylvania, wrote loftily to a friend in New York: "You never could have had such a drawing room; it was brilliant beyond anything you could imagine, and though there was a good deal of extravagance, there was so much of Philadelphia taste in everything that it must be confessed the most delightful occasion of the kind ever known in this country."

The levees and entertainments during the holiday season were, of course, the dressiest and most unrepublican of the year. Senator Maclay went so far as to adorn himself in a new suit for the one on the twenty-eighth, and congratulated himself that he had not omitted "this piece of duty," as he called the presidential levee, since he had arrived in Philadelphia. He concluded glumly that "if there is little harm in it there can not be much good."

On New Year's Day, 1791, a Saturday, having performed his duty on Tuesday, he had no intention of joining the members of Congress and other citizens in paying the compliments

* Christmas Eve was not celebrated in America at that time as it was later, nor was Christmas Day the holiday it is now. It took successive waves of German and Middle European immigration to establish firmly the custom of "the night before Christmas." In colonial America, and for several decades after, there was considerable variance in the Christmas celebration. Schools were open and churches closed in some parts of the country, although the religious character of the day was observed in most places. New Year's Day was the major national holiday, and remained so for years. In the better social circles, New Year's week was a whirl of partygoing, the high point of the society year.

of the season, but fate overtook him in a most embarrassing way and caught him without his new suit.

"Just as I passed the President's house," he reported, "Griffin called to me and asked whether I would not pay my respects to the President. I was in boots and had on my worst clothes. I could not prevail on myself to go with him. I had, however, passed him but a little way when Osgood, Postmaster General, attacked me warmly to go with him. I was pushed forward by him; bolted into his presence; made the President the compliments of the season; had a hearty shake by the hand.* I was asked to partake of the punch and cake, but declined. I sat down, and we had some chat. But the diplomatic gentry and foreigners coming in, I embraced the first vacancy to make my bow and wish him good morning."

Having been defeated for re-election by his Federalist opponent, Maclay was about to be removed as a thorn in Washington's congressional side. (Washington was sometimes angered by Maclay's blunt opposition in the Senate, but he would have been nearly unbelieving if he could have seen what the Senator confided to his diary.) On January 20, just before he left Philadelphia, Maclay dined with the President, and realizing that "I have now seen him for the last time, perhaps," he proposed to "take a review of him as he really is. In stature about six feet [Maclay even minimized the Royalist's height], with an unexceptionable make, but lax appearance. His frame would seem to want filling up. His motions rather slow than lively, though he showed no signs of having suffered by gout or rheumatism. His complexion pale, nay, almost cadaverous. His voice hollow and indistinct, owing as I believe to artificial teeth before his upper jaw, which occasioned a flatness of . . ."

Here, unfortunately, the dismal catalogue of George's de-

---

* A puzzling reference. Either Maclay was mistaken in his recollection of the incident, or the evidence offered by several of his contemporaries must be disregarded when they assert that Washington never shook hands with anyone at these functions. It is possible, of course, that the President decided to make an exception of the Senator in this particular instance, but it seems unlikely.

fects ends abruptly. When the journal was resurrected and first published in 1890 (in the late twenties it was re-edited by Charles A. Beard), the editor, Edgar Maclay, discovered that the remainder of the page on which this description was written had been torn off and lost.

For a man in the pitiful condition Maclay described, Washington seemed in remarkably good spirits that first winter in Philadelphia. Recovered from his New York ailments, and refreshed by the autumnal weeks at Mount Vernon, he appeared to enjoy the heavy social obligations he was required to perform, and often found time for such other amusements as his favorite, the theatre. He was frequently at the Southwark, on the corner of South and Apollo (now Charles) streets, between Fourth and Fifth. His favorite plays were the *School for Scandal*, which had so outraged poor Maclay, and a two-act comedy, *The Poor Soldier*. These were often given command performances for his pleasure.

At the theatre, he and his party customarily filled the entire first tier of boxes, arriving promptly in time for a six-fifteen curtain. The manager could always be certain of a full house when Washington came. The President brought his own large party and his attendance was the signal for a turnout of society and as many lesser citizens as could crowd themselves into the little theatre.[4]

Washington's good mood in these months was noted by that careful observer, Abigail Adams, who wrote to Mrs. William S. Smith on February 21: "On Thursday last I dined with the President, in company with the ministers and ladies of the court. He was more than usually social. . . . He asked very affectionately after you and the children, and at table picked the sugar-plums from a cake, and requested me to take them for Master John."

In April he felt well able to make the Southern tour (described in Part 5, Chapter 1) which was the necessary complement to his presidential tour of New England. Returning North in June, he paused at Mount Vernon for a few welcome days before he rode up to Georgetown on June 27 to meet the commissioners named under the Residence Act, and begin with them the discussions preparatory to laying out Washington, D.C., then designated as the Federal City. After three days of conference, he set off for Philadelphia at an unusually early hour, even for him—four in the morning.

This time, perhaps inspired by the new country he had seen in the South, he determined to look at unfamiliar portions of the landscape nearer at hand, and proceeded along a road he had not traveled before—from Fredericktown, Maryland, by way of York and Lancaster to the capital. Because he came unannounced to the cities along the way, they had no opportunity to prepare any lavish welcomes, which suited Washington perfectly. He was able to pass through with a minimum of ceremony, and consequently had the time and opportunity in some of the towns to walk through the streets and see how the citizens he governed were living these days.

The local politicians, unprepared as they were, did their best on short notice. In Fredericktown, for example, the bell-ringers hurried over to the Lutheran and Calvinist churches and pulled their ropes enthusiastically while the artillery on Cannon Hill fired fifteen rounds, and a hastily assembled band serenaded the President that evening. Before he could get away the next morning he was obliged to receive an address, "drawn in great haste."

As he traveled, he wrote occasionally in his diary the kind of brief descriptive comment he had made on his stopping places during the New England tour. Some of them were hardly flattering. At Taneytown, Maryland (he called it Tawny town), where he lodged on the night of July 1, he summed up the village as "but a small place with only the street through which the road passes, built on—the buildings are principally of wood."

Passing over the state line dividing Maryland and Pennsylvania, he looked in vain for the clearing in the timber which was supposed to mark the boundary, but the trees were too thick. Nine miles from Taneytown, he passed through Little-town, observing, ". . . they are of similar appearance, but the latter is more insignificant than the former." Seven miles farther, however, he came to Hanover, "commonly called Mc-Alister's town," which he described as "a very pretty village with a number of good brick houses and mechanics in it."

That night he lodged in the more considerable settlement of Yorktown, Pennsylvania, and after dinner walked through the principal streets of the place. Here the surprised citizens succeeded in getting the courthouse illuminated at nightfall, and the Independent Light Infantry gave him a fifteen-round volley before his lodgings.

What his appearance meant to serious, thoughful men, not given to the adulation of public figures, was expressed by a Moravian pastor, who wrote in his diary that when Washington came to Yorktown at two o'clock in the afternoon "all the bells of the town rang in honor of the event as if the voices of the Archangels sounding in harmony commanded attention. I could not repress my tears at the thought of all this, indeed I cried aloud, not from a sense of sadness, from a feeling of very joyfulness. . . ." [5]

Having arrived on a Saturday, Washington was of course expected to go to church on Sunday morning, and since there was no minister of his own Episcopal faith in the town, he was compelled to attend the services of the church which dominated Yorktown, the Dutch Reformed, notwithstanding that they were conducted in the Dutch language, "not a word of which I understood." And he added with his characteristic humor of gentle irony, "I was in no danger of becoming a proselite to its religion by the eloquence of the preacher."

He went on to Lancaster that day, arriving there at six in the evening of July 3. He well understood that he would be insulting the inhabitants if he rode on next morning. "This being the anniversary of American independence, and being kindly requested to do it, I agreed to halt here this day and partake of the entertainment which was preparing for the celebration of it," he wrote. It appears to have been an exceedingly mild celebration. The President walked about Lancaster in the morning, received an address from the Corporation and the compliments of the clergy in the afternoon, dined between three and four o'clock, and afterward drank tea with Mrs. Hand. No more is recorded in his diary.

Next day he was in Philadephia, which he had not seen for three months, feeling that the Southern tour had improved his health, although he complained of a "slight indisposition" a few weeks after his return, which he said was "occasioned by a tumor, not much unlike the one I had at New York in 1789. . . ."

He was not long in the city. Philadelphia lay in its August steam bath, Congress had adjourned until October, and there was nothing to keep him from Mount Vernon. On his last night in the city, September 14, he entertained a distinguished traveler to America, François René, Viscount de Chateaubriand. The Viscount, a sophisticated and worldly man, described his encounter with the President in seemingly contradictory terms when he published the account of his travels more than a quarter century later.*

He informed Washington that he intended to find the Northwest Passage by an exploration of the polar sea. The President looked dumfounded by this intelligence and expressed polite astonishment, and the Viscount replied gallantly, "But it is less difficult to discover the Northwest Passage than to create a nation, as you have done."

The dinner-table conversation centered on the French Revolution, and Washington proudly showed his visitor the key

* Chateaubriand, who has been called by some authorities the father of French romanticism, was acknowledged as the master prose stylist of his day in France. Unfortunately his travel writings were in the tradition of Father Hennepin—that is, full of rich, beautiful prose and imaginative flights, and lamentably short on facts. The Viscount, like the good father, supplied facts if none existed, and somehow he always appears as the hero of his own adventures.

As an example of Chateaubriand's fancy at work, he told Washington and a good many other people that he was off to penetrate the polar seas. The farthest north and westward point he reached was Niagara Falls.

to the Bastille that Lafayette had given him, obviously believing it to be authentic.

". . . Those keys of the Bastille were but silly playthings which were about that time distributed over the two worlds," Chateaubriand commented dryly in his book.[6] "Had Washington seen like me the conquerors of the Bastille in the kennels of Paris, he would have had less faith in the relic. The gravity and the energy of the revolution were not in the sanguinary orgies. At the time of the revocation of the edict of Nantes, in 1685, the same populace of the Faubourg Saint-Antoine demolished the Protestant church at Charenton with as much zeal as it despoiled the church of St. Denis in 1793."

But having disposed of Washington's naïveté, he added: "I left my host at ten in the evening, and never saw him again; he set out for the country the following day, and I continued my journey. Such was my interview with that man who gave liberty to a whole world. Washington sunk [sic] into the tomb before any little celebrity had attached to my name. I passed before him as the most unknown of beings; he was in all his glory, I in the depth of my obscurity, my name probably dwelt not a whole day in his memory. Happy, however, that his looks were cast upon me! I have felt myself warmed for it all the rest of my life. There is a virtue in the looks of a great man."

As he set off for Mount Vernon next morning, the great man had prepared himself in little things far in advance of his homecoming. A series of letters to Anthony Whiting, then his superintendent at the plantation, described the preparations that were to be made. The instructions were specific in the smallest details. "I request that you would pay particular attention to the meats, that I may have such as are fat and proper for the table while I am at home, which will be till the middle of October," he wrote to Whiting late in August. ". . . By fat meats, I mean mutton, lamb, veal (if there are any calves young enough); perhaps a small beef also."

After a few weeks at Mount Vernon, he was ready to take up his office again—except that somehow he had made "a strange mistake." The President of the United States had thought Congress was to reconvene on the last Monday of October, instead of the fourth, and suddenly he found himself compelled to make a hurried departure from Mount Vernon, lest his mistake be discovered publicly. He admitted it in a letter to James McHenry, marked "private," and confessed further that he would never have caught himself unless by accident, if Lear had not written a letter reminding him of the date.

In spite of this near embarrassment, he arrived in Philadelphia on October 21, in plenty of time to make his opening address to Congress on the twenty-fifth, in the Senate chamber of the legislative hall at the corner of Chestnut and Sixth streets.

The remainder of the year, with one exception, was placid enough. The exception came on December 8, if one may believe a secondhand account, when dispatches arrived informing the President that General St. Clair, who was in the Miami country subduing the Indians, had himself been surprised and subdued by the Miamis, with a loss enumerated in these first reports as six hundred men killed and wounded. According to Lear, who was present, it was one of the few times Washington ever completely lost his temper, stamping about and raging at St. Clair for repeating what was essentially the Braddock disaster. With his knowledge of frontier fighting against Indians, Washington had warned St. Clair specifically against the danger of surprise, but the General had nevertheless been surprised. After what was described as a "paroxysm of passion," Washington recovered his ordinary calm.[7]

The other events of the fall were much more peaceful. As he had been so often in bringing up Martha's children and grandchildren, the President found himself cast in the ungrateful role of fatherly adviser to a child not his own. The "child" this time was his dead brother Samuel's daughter, Harriet Washington, a frivolous and extravagant young lady for whose guidance he now found himself more or less responsible.

*331*

Most of his letters to Harriet were admonitory. "Your Affectionate Uncle" attempted, in a delicate way, to apprise her of what every young girl should know. Jack Custis would have chuckled if he could have read these missives; in tone and substance they were like many "Your Affectionate Uncle" had written to him in college, and like the ones he wrote later to Jack's son George.*

Before his first complete year of residence in Philadelphia had quite ended, Washington was presented on December 30 with a gift he considered particularly appropriate, and one he treasured. It was a silver-mounted box made out of an oak that allegedly had sheltered Sir William Wallace, the Washington of Scotland, after he had been defeated by Edward I at the Battle of Falkirk in the fourteenth century. This gift had been brought to the President from the Earl of Buchan by Archibald Robertson, a Scotch artist, along with a request from the Earl that Washington allow Robertson to paint his portrait.

Robertson was received hospitably and the request for sittings granted. When he had presented the box, Washington invited him to stay for dinner, an occasion Robertson described as follows:

"The dinner, served at three o'clock in the afternoon, was plain but suitable for a family in genteel and comfortable circumstances. There was nothing specially remarkable at the table but that the General and Mrs. Washington sat side by side, he on the right of his lady, the gentlemen on his right hand and the ladies on her left. It being on Saturday, the first course was mostly of eastern cod and fresh fish. A few glasses of wine were drunk during dinner, with other beverage; the whole closed with a few glasses of sparkling champagne, in about three quarters of an hour, when the General and Colonel Lear retired, leaving the ladies in high glee about Lord Buchan and the 'Wallace box.'"

* Harriet cost her affectionate uncle a respectable sum of money and an undetermined amount of worry before she happily ended his responsibility for her on the Fourth of July, 1796, by marrying Andrew Parks, of Baltimore.

[1792]   So ended the first year of the presidential residence in Philadelphia. It had been an eventful and, on the whole, a good one. The second year, 1792, which began with the customary New Year's entertaining, closed Washington's first term, and closed it for the most part quietly, aside from the political struggles in Congress. His birthday was celebrated on Tuesday evening, the twenty-first, with a ball given by the City Dancing Assembly, which had been giving balls since 1748 and continued for more than a century afterward. "One of the most brilliant displays of beauty ever exhibited in this city" attended the affair, according to Dunlap's *American Daily Advertiser*. On the next night, the New City Dancing Assembly, a rival organization, entertained the President. More conservatively, the *Advertiser* reported that it was "remarkable, we hear, for a brilliant display of beauty, taste and elegance."

One of the most candid, if unflattering, portraits of Washington at this point in his career has been provided by a critic who could hardly be considered unbiased, yet whose political outlook and background made him a far shrewder judge than Senator Maclay, who was constricted by his provincial, partisan character. The critic was Edward Thornton, secretary to George Hammond, the British minister. In two letters written home to his friend, Sir James Bland Burges, Thornton views Washington with a natural British bias, but perhaps sees him more clearly than most Americans, blinded by his prestige and his military accomplishments.

"His person is tall and sufficiently graceful," Thornton says in his letter of April 2, 1792, "his face well formed, his complexion rather pale, with a mild philosophic gravity in the expression of it. In his air and manner he displays much natural dignity; in his address he is cold, reserved, and even phlegmatic, though without the least appearance of haughtiness or ill-nature; it is the effect, I imagine, of constitutional diffidence. That caution and circumspection which form so striking and well known a feature in his military, and in his political character, is very strongly marked in his countenance, for his eyes

retire inward (do you understand me?) and have nothing of
fire or animation or openness in their expression. If this circumspection is accompanied by discernment and penetration, as
I am informed it is, and as I should be inclined to believe from
the judicious choice he has generally made of persons to fill
public stations, he possesses the two great requisites of a statesman, the faculty of concealing his own sentiments and of dis-
covering those of other men. A certain degree of indecision,
however, a want of vigor and energy, may be observed in
some of his actions, and are indeed the obvious result of too
refined caution.

"He is a man of great but secret ambition, and has sometimes, I think, condescended to use little arts, and those, too,
very shallow ones, to secure the object of that ambition. He
is, I am told, indefatigable in business, and extremely clear and
systematic in the arrangement of it; his time is regularly divided into certain portions, and the business allotted to any
one portion rigidly attended to. Of his private character I can
say little positive. I have never heard of any truly noble, generous, or disinterested action of his; he has very few who are
on terms of intimate and unreserved friendship; and what is
worse, he is less beloved in his own state (Virginia) than in
any part of the United States. After all, he is a great man, circumstances have made him so; but I cannot help thinking that
the misconduct of our commanders has given him a principal
part of that greatness."

Before he wrote again, Thornton had been invited to dine at
the President's house, an event he found "dull and unenter-
taining," because, so he thought, "the President's reserve, the
effect partly I think of pride, partly of constitutional diffidence, throws a restraint on the whole party. The conversation
was in consequence uncommonly phlegmatic and trivial,
though as the party contracted into a smaller circle, the Secretary of State's strictures on monarchs began to throw a certain portion of animation into it.

"This gentleman [Thomas Jefferson] is, or affects to be, a
334

most rigid republican; a warm admirer of Thomas Paine, and a vigorous stickler for revolutions and for the downfall of all aristocracy. The death of the King of Sweden [Gustavus III] made it extremely probable, he said, that there would be a revolution in that country during the minority of his successor.

"The most dignified character in this country [Washington] has a good deal of (I cannot call it republicanism, for he affects state, he loves to be treated with great respect, and . . . is not a little flattered, I conceive, by the particular attention of Mr. Hammond not to visit him but in full dress) a certain dislike to monarchy. If Kings were Presidents, or if the President were a King, I believe that aversion would cease. At present he cannot but conceive himself much inferior in dignity and importance to any of them. When he travels, it is in a very kingly style; for on his last journey he foundered five horses, and I am informed that his secretaries are not admitted into his carriage, but stand with their horses' bridles in their hands till he is seated, and then mount and ride before his carriage." [8]

Thornton's estimate had enough of truth in it to leaven the adulatory views of Washington held by most of those who observed him, but in many respects he was far wide of the mark, as a reader who knows no more of the man than what he has seen in these pages could easily determine. If Washington traveled about in state, when the occasion called for it, it was no better than several other well-to-do Americans might command, and not as splendid as plain John Adams could turn out when he chose. Washington was accustomed most of his life to the luxuries of the time, because of his economic and social status, but he had no ambition to live like a king. If he had been free to live as he chose, it would unquestionably have been as a gentleman farmer.

He was ambitious, as Thornton said, during the earlier part of his life, and there was a coldness, an aloof dignity about him, and his natural demeanor was grave. But he could be moved to tears, and he had his intervals of humor; his letters glint here and there with a glancing, ironic wit. He was not unaware of his faults, and some of them he strove to correct.

If he could have read the British secretary's letters, however, the part that possibly would have wounded him more than anything else was the oblique implication that he had no regard for his horses. As a Virginia gentleman who had virtually grown up in the saddle, Washington loved horses, and if Thornton had gone around behind the Morris house in Philadelphia, he would have seen how well the President took care of his mounts and the teams that drew his carriage.

The stables were on Minor Street, a short thoroughfare running between Fifth and Sixth streets back of the house. Its sixteen stalls housed what may have been the finest horseflesh in America. Washington came in every morning without fail to inspect the stables, and he insisted on as high standards in the care of them as he did in his own home. Kingly or not, he must have known the satisfaction of a horseman when six of these handsome animals pulled around from Minor Street with his white carriage, liveried coachman and two postillions riding atop.

He drove into the country to visit his friends whenever he could, and he rode as often as possible for exercise, but he had to be in constant attendance on Congress, and there was the interminable state entertaining to be done, as well as a thousand other demands on his time.

One of the most persistent of these demands was the request to sit for a portrait. He was good-natured about it for years, but in July 1792, importuned by an unknown painter named Williams, he wrote in irritation to Henry Lee, who had recommended the man to his attention: ". . . To be frank, I am so heartily tired of the attendance which from one cause or another has been given to these people, that it is now more than two years since I have resolved to sit no more for any of them, and have adhered to it, except in instances where it has been requested by public bodies, or for a particular purpose (not of the painters), and could not without offense be refused."

Such a case had been the Earl of Buchan's friend Robertson, the Scottish painter to whom he had sat just a few months before. However, Lee must have shown this letter to Williams, who shrewdly got himself a sponsor, and one he was sure would prevail upon his unwilling subject—Washington Lodge No. 22 of the Masons, in Alexandria. When they applied in Williams' behalf, since the finished portrait had been promised to them, Washington could not very well turn down his fraternal brothers, especially those from Alexandria. He consented. The portrait was an extremely bad one—it showed Washington as a Mason, wearing the Past Master's collar and jewel—but the Alexandria lodge proudly hung it.

Another view of Washington in these Philadelphia years of his presidency was that of Dr. Ashbel Green, the chaplain of Congress from November 5, 1792, until the government was transferred to Washington. Here was a man who could not be suspected of bias either political or secular, and yet there were overtones of both Maclay's and Thornton's feelings about Washington in the sympathetic observations Dr. Green made of the President in his reminiscences. "There was more of the indefinable quality called *presence* in President Washington than any person I have ever known," he wrote. "In his general manners he was eminently courteous and kind; and yet to the last, I could never speak to him without feeling a degree of embarrassment such as I have never felt in the presence of any other individual, man or woman, with whom I was well acquainted."

Dr. Green was present to hear all the speeches Washington made at the opening of congressional sessions. (Jefferson was the first to send his messages instead of reading them in person.) The chaplain's description of Washington's appearance on these occasions is excellent reporting:

"Twelve o'clock at noon was the usual hour agreed on for his opening speech, and in no instance did he fail in a punctual attendance at that hour; indeed, he commonly crossed the threshold of the door where the Congress sat exactly when the clock was striking the hour of twelve. The two houses always assembled to receive him in the Senate chamber.* When he entered, all the members of both houses rose from their seats and stood up until he had taken his seat, which he did immediately after bowing to his audience. When he was seated, he looked around on the audience for a minute or two, and then took out his spectacles from a common red morocco case, and laid them on his knee, and then took from his side pocket his written speech. After putting on his spectacles he rose and began his address, which he read closely. He read distinctly and audibly, but in no other respect was his reading excellent. Dr. Witherspoon had heard George the Third deliver one of his speeches to the British Parliament, which he said was in the very best style of elocution. This could not be said of the speeches of Washington; his elocution had no glaring fault, and no high excellence."

[1793]    As he began his second term, the President had much more to worry him than his elocution. His first four years in office had been a relatively calm prelude to the cares, both personal and political, which beset him soon after a joint committee of Congress informed him on February 15 of his re-election.

The year 1793 had begun with an event which agitated the city from Congress to the humblest dwelling, caused a deluge of sermons from the pulpits, and precipitated enough arguments to take the minds of a good many heated citizens off politics for a few weeks. This strange and wonderful occurrence was the ascent in a balloon of Blanchard, "the bold aeronaut," from the prison yard at Sixth and Walnut streets.

Beginning at daybreak on the morning of January 9, can-

* Dr. Green was in error on this point. Washington read three of his speeches in the House.

non salutes marked the hours until the moment, shortly after ten o'clock, when the balloon was to rise. Meanwhile, every citizen who could shove his way into the neighborhood waited in the confident expectation that Monsieur Blanchard would shortly be dashed at their feet.

Washington was present, and at ten o'clock promptly handed Blanchard a document, signed by him, requesting the aid of the inhabitants in whatever part of the country the bold aeronaut came down. The President shook the balloonist's hand, spoke a few words of encouragement to him and stepped back. At five minutes past ten Blanchard leaped into the spangled blue gondola, suspended beneath the yellowish bag covered with a net. For the occasion, *Dunlap's American Daily Advertiser* noted, Monsieur Blanchard was tastefully gotten up in "a plain blue suit, a cock'd hat and white feathers. . . ."

He sailed off to the unbelieving cheers of the crowd. At about half past six that evening he was encountered once more on the streets of Philadelphia, alive and well, and on his way to report to the President. His flight was anything but spectacular by modern standards, but it was viewed with awe at the time. He had floated forty-six minutes and come down fifteen miles away, east of Woodbury, New Jersey. There he took a carriage and returned to Philadelphia.

Before the year was over, Washington may well have wished that he could leap into a balloon and escape the vexations of his office. The basis of his troubles was the old one on which Maclay had put his blunt finger: the spirit of "republicanism" opposed to the "federal" ideas of Hamilton and of Washington himself. In present-day terms, it was essentially the question, never decided in our history, of the proper balance between the federal government on the one hand and the states on the other.

To reduce this immensely complex question and situation to its simplest terms, the problem in Washington's day centered on how much authority and power the federal government should be permitted by the sovereign people, who took

the idea of democracy seriously. Washington and his supporters in the Administration believed that the principles of the
new Constitution, and indeed the nation it had created, could
not survive in a hostile world unless the trust and confidence
of the people were placed in a central authority. The republicans were not so much against the Constitution and the idea of
union, though both were attacked still in some quarters, as
they were against the spirit of a "ruling power" which they
thought they saw in Washington's Administration. A brilliant
figure like Jefferson could oppose this spirit in practical political terms by attacking the measures which he considered
strengthened federal control. But the lesser republicans, especially the Maclay-like rural representatives in Congress,
who possessed more zeal for the common man than brains, assailed even the tangible evidences of presidential rule.

It was in such an outburst of misguided democratic sentiment that one Representative rose to move that the mace of
the House be destroyed, and the silver in it given to the public
mint. The criticism of Washington's levees, his state coach and
the other appurtenances of his office were now outspoken,
where before they had been only whispers and innuendo.

This could have been put down to the growing pains of a
new republic if the whole question had not been painfully
complicated by events in France, which created for the first
time a division between Washington and the American people
—a division that was unacknowledged by Washington but
seized upon happily by his opponents.

As he took his second oath of office on March 4, 1793, the
French Revolution was at its height. The Republic had been
proclaimed the previous September. A month before, Lafayette had tried to persuade the army to help restore the
deposed Louis XVI, but they had refused and Washington's
old friend and comrade-in-arms had been made a prisoner of
war by the Republic. The execution of Louis on January 21,
1793, had been followed immediately by declarations of war
on England and Holland—the Republic was already at war

with Austria—and four days after Washington's inauguration Spain was added to the list of French enemies.

To the average American, and in fact to the average Congressman, the French people were only doing what Americans had just done. They had overthrown monarchical tyranny, and further, were now warring against the other tyrannical monarchs of Europe. A great wave of sympathy for the French welled up in America. It led some ardent republicans to call each other "citizen," and in politics it created a tremendous popular pressure for the Administration to do something to help its recent gallant ally, France. "The French helped us to achieve a free republic, it is only fair to help them now," was the popular thought.

Since the close of the American Revolution, the clash of political opinion had found a new outlet in the press. During the war there had been a patriot press and a Tory press, then briefly a nearly unanimous patriot press, but now there had risen a bitter, violent, partisan press in which newspapers were little more than political propaganda organs. Washington had paid no attention to the slurs and insults of the Tory publishers, but at this time he found himself assailed quite openly in free American newspapers, and nowhere more caustically than in the republican papers of Philadelphia, which had become screaming partisans of the French Republic.

This was the atmosphere in which Washington took the oath of office in the Senate chamber. Thornton was an observer of the scene, and as a loyal subject of his King, who was at war with France, not an impartial one. Describing the ceremony to his friend Sir James, the British secretary noted that the portraits of the King and Queen of France, presented to Congress during the war and thereafter hung in the Senate, had been covered over with a curtain. "Alas! poor Louis!" Thornton commented with justifiable irony, and he quoted:

> *Deserted at his utmost need*
> *By those his former bounty fed!*

Thornton went on to inform Burges that in the house of a certain "great man" the key to the Bastille (so disdained by Chateaubriand) which had been presented by Lafayette was hung in a glass frame, opposite an engraving of the unfortunate Louis. As for the political decorations in Jefferson's drawing room, said Thornton, they consisted of three busts—Franklin, Paul Jones and Lafayette, "three gentlemen, the first of whom had talents without virtue, the second deserved hanging, and the last, not improbably, may meet with that fate."

Washington was torn in both directions. He was naturally sympathetic in principle with popular revolts against tyranny, but this particular revolt was against gentlemen and friends like Lafayette, and against His Most Christian Majesty, who had been so resoundingly toasted for years in America as one of the nation's saviors. More than most Americans, Washington was aware of how much the help of France under Louis had meant to the American cause; without it, there would have been no victory. He was also aware, in the present crisis, that the new American Republic, still struggling to establish itself firmly, still not enjoying the consent of the whole population, was in no position to inject itself into a struggle between great powers. These and other considerations led him to his declaration of American neutrality on April 23, an act which provoked howls of rage from the superpatriots who were willing to fight England all over again for the sake of the French. It took no prescience to see that Washington faced a rough passage in his second term.

Along with these public troubles, he was having difficulties at Mount Vernon. In March he had to make a quick journey there when his nephew, Major George Augustine Washington, son of his brother Charles (and one of Lafayette's aides), died of tuberculosis. It meant not only the loss of a much-loved relative but the creation of a domestic problem, since the Major had been in charge of the estate as manager since 1789.

Before he could readjust the affairs of the plantation, the

news came of the French declarations against England and Holland, and he had to hurry back to Philadelphia to undertake the "restraining, as far as a proclamation would do it, our citizens from taking part in the contest."

Washington undoubtedly expected some public protest against his proclamation of neutrality, but he was obviously astonished and indignant at the manner in which his opposition now boldly assaulted him. To have his conduct questioned and his character, hitherto almost sacred in the eyes of the public, blackened in the public prints was to him insupportable. In Philip Freneau's *National Gazette* and Benjamin Franklin Bache's *Aurora*, he read that he had issued "a royal edict," that his use of executive powers was "unwarrantable and daring," that he had shown he was partial to England and against France, and that he had flouted Congress and the people. The Constitution, said the pro-French press, did not give the President the right to make policy, either foreign or domestic.

(If all this has a familiar sound to the modern reader who has read the newspapers faithfully during the regimes of Presidents Roosevelt and Truman, he need not be alarmed: that noise he hears is only history repeating itself.)

To these charges in the opposition newspapers, Washington replied that the publications were "outrages on common decency." In August of that year, when the agitation over the Citizen Genêt affair was at its height, and the Cabinet had met to determine what action, if any, the government should take on the activities of the French agent, the President lost his temper completely in a Cabinet meeting at which Knox read a satiric newspaper account of the funeral of the monarchist Washington after his death on the guillotine. Then, according to Jefferson's famous report of the incident, "The President was much inflamed; got into one of those passions when he cannot command himself; ran on much on the personal abuse which had been bestowed on him; defied any man on earth to produce one single act of his since he had been in the government which was not done on the purest motives; that he had never repented but once the having slipped the moment of resigning his office, and that was every moment since; that *by God* he had rather be in his grave than in his present situation; that he had rather be on his farm than to be made *Emperor of the world;* and yet that they were charging him with wanting to be a King. That that *rascal Freneau* sent him three of his papers every day, as if he thought he would become the distributor of his papers; that he could see in this nothing but an impudent design to insult him: he ended in this high tone. There was a pause. Some difficulty in resuming our question. . . ."

Meanwhile, there was trouble enough on his farm. Anthony Whiting had succeeded Major Washington as manager of Mount Vernon, but the President knew that things were not going well there. Whiting did not reply to his employer's letters in the prompt, methodical manner demanded of his superintendents, answering each point the President raised in the regular weekly letter of instruction. In fact, Whiting often failed to answer at all; though Washington did not know it, he was dying.

In May, Whiting wrote that his health was bad. This was the first knowledge Washington had of the situation, and he was quick to offer medical advice. "From my own experience (and the measure was recommended to me by eminent physicians)," he wrote, "wearing flannel next the skin is the best cure for and preventative of the rheumatism I ever tried. And for your other complaint, which you suppose to be in your lungs, a vegetable and milk diet I should suppose would be proper, avoiding as much as possible animal food. Of this, however, the doctors must be a better judge, and if you choose to have any in these parts consulted, and will state or get your case stated, I will lay it before the person highest in reputation here as a physician, and send you the result."

This generous offer was too late. Whiting died in the early part of June, probably of the same disease that had carried off his predecessor. Washington made a hurried trip to Mount

Vernon for the second time that year, returning on July 11 to find himself in a raging hornet's nest of politics and the beginnings of a serious yellow fever epidemic. His state of mind as he tried to catch up on his correspondence and work is reflected in the letter he wrote to Governor Henry Lee, of Virginia, on July 21:

"I should have thanked you at an earlier period for your obliging letter . . . had it not come to my hands a day or two only before I set out for Mount Vernon, and at a time when I was much hurried and indeed very much perplexed with the disputes, memorials and what not with which the government were pestered by one or other of the petulant representatives of the powers at war, and because since my return to this city (nine days ago) I have been more than ever overwhelmed with their complaints. In a word, the trouble they give is hardly to be described.

"My journey to and from Mount Vernon was sudden and rapid, and as short as I could make it. It was occasioned by the unexpected death of Mr. Whiting (my manager) at a critical season for the business with which he was entrusted. Where to supply his place I know not; of course my concerns at Mount Vernon are left as a body without a head, but this by the bye. . . ."

The yellow fever brought him a short respite from his political troubles. Beginning in a lodging house early in July, the epidemic flashed through the city until those who were still alive had joined by August 25 in a panicky exodus to the country. Before the disease died out in early November, it took four thousand lives.

Washington stayed longer than seemed prudent, but in September he went with Martha to Mount Vernon, leaving the hot, stricken city behind. "It was my wish to have continued there longer," he wrote Tobias Lear on September 25, "but as Mrs. Washington was unwilling to leave me surrounded by the malignant fever which prevailed, I could not think of hazarding her and the children any longer by my continuance in the city, the house in which we lived being, in a manner, blockaded by the disorder, and was becoming every day more and more fatal. . . ."

Congress, disorganized by the epidemic, did not know when or where it would be able to reconvene, but in November, Washington thought it best to come up from Virginia before the weather made traveling too difficult, so that he would be available to the legislators. He decided to take a house in nearby Germantown, and found one on the west of the main street, now Germantown Avenue, about six miles northwest of Independence Hall. It was a substantial stone building owned by a colonel who had fought with Washington in the Revolution, Isaac Franks.

Congress met in Philadelphia on December 2 (the inhabitants having slowly returned to the city during the latter part of November) and the President delivered his address to them on the following day.

It had been a hard year, and his face showed the strain of the preceding months. There had been his troubles with the plantation, which were far from over, and the violence of the dispute over foreign policy—also far from being concluded. Added to that were the perils of yellow fever and the insults of the partisan press. It had been a year full of sad events. In July, Tobias Lear's beloved twenty-three-year-old wife, who had been his childhood sweetheart, died suddenly; the President attended her funeral. This occurrence further disrupted his household, since Lear was Washington's most trusted secretary and he was some time recovering from his grief before he married Fanny Bassett Washington, widow of the lately deceased Major Washington. (By sad coincidence, she too died in the last year of Washington's presidency.)

Small wonder that his correspondence at the end of 1793 shows a sharp temper out of keeping with his usual courteous tone. Much of his irritation was taken out on the Mount Vernon overseers. He had engaged a new manager, William Pearce, who had taken over in October, but Pearce was slow in getting affairs in hand, and meanwhile the crops were endangered by the overseers' lack of enterprise.

One of them, a man named Hyland Crow, had the temerity to ask for a raise in wages. Fortunately for him, he had produced the best crop on the plantation the previous season, so Washington agreed to raise him to forty pounds, but any further attempt to get more, he warned, would be fruitless. He gave his reason in one of those long, complicated sentences into which emotion often led him, but which must nevertheless have been quite clear to Mr. Crow:

"Forty pounds per annum, clear of all expenses, whether the winds blow high or blow low, whether the ground is deluged with rain, or laid waste by a parching drought, by either of which, and by many other casualties, crops may be destroyed, though the expenses incurred in the making do not lessen, nor the mouths which are to be fed, nor the backs which are to be clothed do not decrease, is equal to the chance of double that sum in a proportion of the crop which, was it not for the labor spent in making meadows and other jobs, some on and others off the farm, I had much rather give, but have been restrained from doing it to avoid grumbling; and because I may apply the hands at such places and in such a manner as to me, or my manager, should seem most conducive to my interest, when no other was to be affected by it. . . ."

He had been disillusioned to discover, as he wrote Pearce, that Whiting "drank freely, kept bad company at my house and in Alexandria, and was a very debauched person." That, he concluded, was why his former manager had not looked more scrupulously into the overseers' conduct, "and more minutely into the smaller matters belonging to the farms, which, though individually may be trifling, are not found so in the aggregate; for there is no adage more true than an old Scotch one, that 'many mickles make a muckle.' " This was one of Washington's favorite saws, and he quoted it often.

By the end of the year, he was laying about right and left amid the overseers. He threatened to have Pearce put Hyland

Crow off the plantation for his "insufferable neglect" of his fall plowing and other duties. "And look ye, Mr. Crow," George wrote, " I have too good reasons to believe that your running about and entertaining company at home, contrary to your agreement . . . is the cause of this . . . irremediable evil in the progress of my business. . . . I sent a horse to you for the plow, because I never intended (as he has got stiff and unfit for the road) that he should ever go out of a walk; instead of which I learn you were figuring away at the races with him, and have converted him into the very thing I parted with because of his unfitness for. I am very willing and desirous to be your friend, but if your conduct does not merit it, you must abide the consequences from Yrs, etc."

This and similar letters were written just before Christmas, but the master of Mount Vernon did not even add, "Greetings of the season."

[1794]   The year that succeeded, while not quite so stormy, was distinguished as the year of the Whiskey Rebellion. This bloodless revolt was in itself a manifestation of republicanism, because it questioned the right of the government to tax, the sufferers in this case being the farmers of western Pennsylvania, whose distillery profits they had no intention of sharing with the government.

This matter did not come to a head until October. Meantime there was the accustomed routine to be followed in the Morris house, including the entertaining of visitors. One of these, Henry Wansey, a British traveler, was lucky enough to be invited to breakfast on June 6, 1794, and thus saw Washington informally. His description of the meal is a small, intimate snapshot of the family at home:

"The President, in his person, is tall and thin, but erect; rather of an engaging than a dignified presence. He appears very thoughtful, is slow in delivering himself, which occasions some to conclude him reserved, but it is rather, I apprehend, the effect of much thinking and reflection, for there is great appearance to me of affability and accommodation. He was at this time in his 63rd year . . . but he has very little the appearance of age, having been all his lifetime so **exceeding** temperate. There is a certain anxiety visible in his countenance. . . .

"Mrs. Washington herself made tea and coffee for us. On the table were two small plates of sliced tongue, dry toast, bread and butter, &c., but no broiled fish, as is the general custom. Miss Custis, her granddaughter, a very pleasing young lady of about sixteen, sat next to her, and her brother, George Washington Custis, about two years older than herself.* There was but little appearance of form: one servant only attended, who had no livery; a silver urn for hot water was the only article of expense on the table. She appears something older than the President, though I understand they were both born in the same year [Martha was born June 21, 1731]; short in stature, rather robust; very plain in her dress, wearing a very plain cap, with her gray hair closely turned up under it. She has routs or levees . . . but the anti-Federalists object even to these, as tending to give a super-eminency, and introductory to the paraphernalia of courts." [9]

About a week or so after this breakfast, Washington took advantage of a lull in business to spend a short time at Mount Vernon. There he had a narrow escape from serious injury or death while he was out riding on a Sunday morning. Trying "to save myself and horse from falling among the rocks at the Lower Falls of the Potomac, whither I went . . . to see the canal and locks," he wrenched his back badly, and it bothered him for some time.

Returning to Philadelphia on July 7, after a miserable all-day ride in the rain two days before, he stayed in the city only a month, when the summer heat drove him out as far as Georgetown, where he and Martha took a house.

Before his departure, he concluded as many state duties as

---

* Wansey had his dates mixed. George was two years *younger* than Nelly.

possible, including a reception for a delegation of Chickasaw Indians, headed by Chief Piomingo, who had recently helped the government put down the obstreperous Creeks. This ceremony was witnessed by young John Quincy Adams—it happened to be his twenty-eighth birthday—who had just been given his commission as minister to Holland. In his diary, Adams wrote down an amusing description of how the Great White Father entertained his children, the Chickasaws:

"Five chiefs, seven warriors, four boys and an interpreter constituted the company. As soon as the whole were seated, the ceremony of smoking began. A large East Indian pipe was placed in the middle of the hall. The tube, which appeared to be of leather, was twelve or fifteen feet in length. The President began, and after two or three whiffs, passed the tube to Piomingo, he to the next chief, and so all around. Whether this ceremony be really of Indian origin, as is generally supposed, I confess I have some doubt. At least these Indians appeared to be quite unused to it, and from their manner of going through it, looked as if they were submitting to a process in compliance with *our* custom. Some of them, I thought, smiled with such an expression of countenance as denoted a sense of *novelty* and of *frivolity* too, as if the ceremony struck them not only as new, but also as ridiculous. When it was finished, the President addressed them in a speech which he read, stopping at the close of every sentence for the interpreter to translate it. Observed that the interpreter, at the close of every sentence, concluded by repeating the same word twice over. The sound was something like this, Tshkyer! Tshkyer! . . ." *

* If the Indians were smiling, it was probably because of the East Indian pipe, with its lengthy tube. The Indian pipe was, of course, a straight clay stem, varying in length but not often more than two feet. The ceremony was anything but strange to them, and it was unquestionably Indian in origin (at least in America), antedating the coming of the white man. The exclamation at the ends of sentences which Adams noted was common usage, often translated as, "I have spoken," although it had many variations. Ordinarily it followed the end of every complete statement, and the exclamation and pause would be used to lay down a belt of wampum.

From the house in Germantown (the same one he had lived in the year before) Washington issued on August 7 his proclamation to the insurgent farmers of Pennsylvania, warning them they must not oppose the duties levied upon spirits and stills, because it was the law of the United States. He sensed that he had to take a firm stand in this matter. If the spirit of rebellion against the federal establishment were permitted to thrive in one place, it would certainly crop up in another. By making a show of force against the rebels, he guessed shrewdly, he would not only achieve victory without bloodshed but at the same time would enhance the prestige of the government.

On Tuesday, September 30, he was ready to leave Philadelphia for Carlisle, where the troops were to rendezvous, and there he intended to pause while awaiting further information from the insurgent counties. On the eve of his going, Martha wrote to Fanny Bassett Washington, the Major's widow: "The insurgents in the back country have carried matters so high that the President has been obliged to send a large body of men to settle the matter, and is to go himself tomorrow to Carlisle to meet the troops. God knows when he will return again. I shall be left quite alone with the children."

In spite of Martha's tragic view of it, Washington's leave-taking was no dramatic departure for the wars. He rode quietly out of town with Secretary of the Treasury Hamilton and his own private secretary, Bartholomew Dandridge. They stopped that night at a place called the Trap, twenty-five miles from Philadelphia.

He was in Reading on October 1, and in Lebanon the following night, pausing to view the canal running from Myerstown toward Lebanon. The locks between the two towns were, he thought, "admirably constructed." At Harrisburg, on the night of October 3, he found the 1st New Jersey Regiment, about 560 men, on its way to the rendezvous (he had passed other troops along the way) and reviewed them as he went to his quarters. "After dinner," he noted in his diary, "walked through and round the town, which is considerable for its age (of about 8 or 9 years). The Susequehanna at this place abounds in rock fish of 12 or 15 inches in length, and a fish which they call salmon."

Fording the Susquehanna, at a point nearly a mile wide, on the morning of October 4, he found his faithful escorts, the Philadelphia Light Horse, waiting to accompany him to Carlisle, seventeen miles away.

Two miles from the rendezvous point, he was met by the state's Governor, Thomas Mifflin, and Governor Richard Howell, of New Jersey, with the entire body of cavalry which had thus far arrived, and the Pennsylvania Infantry. Reviewing these and other troops at Carlisle before he went to his quarters, Washington was pleased by their number, about three thousand men, and their smart military appearance. Some of the officers of the Revolution who were present declared there had been no body of cavalry as strong as this one in the war.

After dark that night, Washington was further encouraged by a display of federal sentiment that must have seemed cheerful after the snipings of his republican enemies in Philadelphia. The citizens illuminated their courthouse and displayed a transparency whose front portion proclaimed in large letters, "Washington Is Ever Triumphant." One side advertised "The Reign of the Laws," while the other warned, "Woe to Anarchists."

Next day was Sunday, but politics were not entirely suspended. Washington went to the Presbyterian church, where the minister preached a sermon recommending order and good government, particularly the government of the United States.

Early on Monday, Washington was busy organizing his army—or rather, as he put it, "urging and assisting General Mifflin to do it, as I no otherwise took the command of the troops than to press them forward, and to provide them with necessaries for their march, as well and as far as our means would admit. . . ."

Dandridge concerned himself with the supply problem, notably the supplies of his employer. Blankets, tents and such equipment were ordered in case the campaign compelled them to cross the mountains. In a private letter to the Secretary of State on October 9, Dandridge added this succinct note: ". . . As the President will be going, if he proceeds, into the country of whiskey, he proposes to make use of that liquor for his drink. . . ."

Next day the troops began marching toward the next rendezvous point, at Bedford. Washington set out with his staff on Sunday morning, October 12, about seven o'clock, dined at Shippensburg and lodged that night at Chambersburg, going on the following day to Williamsport. He spent the night of the fourteenth at a place long familiar to him, Berkeley Springs, West Virginia, which he called the Warm Springs, or Bath.

As they left Bath and began to traverse the rough roads and rocky hills to the west, the going became difficult for the carriage horses, but Washington noted that "they performed it however well."

At Cumberland, which was reached on the sixteenth, he was met by a party of horse commanded by his nephew, Major George Lewis, and General Samuel Smith, of the Maryland line, who escorted him to town and accompanied him while he reviewed the troops drawn up to greet him. That night he slept in the house of Major Lynn, another Marylander and an old Continental officer, "where I was well lodged and civilly entertained."

Preparations for the final stage of the march to Bedford and the subsequent campaign were made at Cumberland. It was not an easy task to move 3200 men over the mountains, as General Washington well knew, but he had expert assistance from officers who had seen much service in the Revolution. The whole force began to move on the nineteenth. Washington reached Bedford that night, stopping at the house of David Espy, a Bedford County official.

By this time the insurgent counties had taken a soberer view

353

of the rebellion, as Washington learned from his intelligence reports. They were, he informed the Secretary of State from Fort Cumberland, "much alarmed at the serious appearance of things." The distilling farmers were not prepared to take on the formidable army the government had mustered against them, and confident that the purpose of the demonstration was about to succeed, Washington proposed to go with the army no farther than Bedford. There a plan could be laid to meet all the possible contingencies, and he would then return to Philadelphia, where Bache's *Aurora* was asserting that the President could not constitutionally command the army while Congress was in session.

When Washington left Bedford on October 20 to meet Congress and "attend to the civil duties of my office," after giving the troops final orders, he left a small company of relatives behind him. According to Robert Welford, the army's Surgeon General, he had been escorted five miles out of Fort Cumberland toward Bedford on the nineteenth by a cavalry detachment under Major George Lewis; taking the Major aside when the escort turned back, Washington had told him: "George, you are the eldest of five nephews that I have in this army. Let your conduct be an example to them, and do not turn your back until you are ordered." Besides George Lewis, there was Major Lawrence Lewis, General Morgan's aide; Howell Lewis, of Captain Mercer's troops; and Samuel and Lawrence Washington, both in Major Lewis' cavalry.

After Washington left the troops at Bedford, they marched onward in two divisions into the insurgent counties, but found no armed resistance. Several of the leaders were arrested. The other rebels stood about and glowered, and noting their "sour and malignant temper," a detachment under Major General Morgan was ordered to camp in the territory for the winter, taking the position, one supposes, of occupying troops and revenue agents simultaneously. That was the end of the insurrection.

As for the President, he traveled home in the miserable weather which so often accompanied his journeys. Writing to Hamilton on Sunday, October 26, from Wright's Ferry on the Susquehanna, he reported:

"Thus far I have proceeded without accident to men, horse or carriage, although the latter has had wherewith to try its goodness, especially in ascending the North Mountain from Skinner's by a wrong road—that is, by the old road which never was good and is rendered next to impassable by neglect. . . . I rode yesterday afternoon through the rain from Yorktown to this place, and got twice in the height of it hung (and delayed by that means) on the rocks in the middle of the Susquehanna, but I did not feel half as much for my own situation as I did on account of the troops on the mountains, and of the effect the rain might have on the roads through the glades."

It rained that Sunday, too, and on Monday, but by Tuesday, the twenty-eighth of October, Washington was back in Philadelphia before noon, "without encountering any accident on the road, or anything more unpleasant than the badness of the ways after the rains had softened the earth and made them susceptible of a deep impression of the wheels."

After he opened Congress on November 19, he relaxed a little for the remainder of the year. As always, he found welcome relief at the theatre. On the night of December 4, he went to see the Old American Company on Cedar Street. The bill was altogether remarkable. It began with a comedy, *The Young Quaker, or The Fair Philadelphian*, written by one O'Keefe, and "performed in London with the most unbounded applause" (*Aurora*). After it came a pantomime ballet titled *The Two Philosophers*, and to this was added a new musical piece called *The Children in the Wood*. A Mr. Martin brought the curtain down with "Dr. Goldsmith's celebrated epilogue in the character of Harlequin," and the evening concluded spectacularly "with a LEAP through a Barrel of FIRE."

355

[1795]     With the coming of the new year, 1795, Washington had much to be thankful for on the day he proclaimed as Thanksgiving, Thursday, February 19. He attended services in Christ Church, on Second Street above Market, and heard the Rev. William White preach on "the connection between religion and civil happiness." This was the church Washington regularly attended in Philadelphia, both during the Revolution and in the years of his presidential residence, except for the winter of 1781–82, when he went to St. Peter's at Third and Pine because it was nearer Benjamin Chew's house, where he was staying. As President, he sat in a pew ten yards in front of the reading desk, along with Martha and his secretaries. According to the Rev. Mr. White, his behavior was always "serious and attentive," but the pastor admitted years later, in answer to an inquiring letter from another minister, that he never saw Washington kneel.

There was reason to kneel that February in 1795. He had come safely through the French crisis without precipitating the country into dangerous conflict, and he had demonstrated the basic unity of the nation in the episode of the Whiskey Rebellion. If one may take seriously a letter he wrote six days after Thanksgiving, he had narrowly escaped death again a few months before, a circumstance hitherto undisclosed. In a letter of introduction to Thomas Pinckney, on behalf of a Dr. Tate, he recommended the physician as one "possessed of the valuable secret of curing cancerous complaints." He went on to disclose that he had himself "experienced the fruits of his skill in this art, being cured by him of an irritable spot on my right cheek which had for years been increasing in pricking and disagreeable sensations, and in June last assumed the decided character of a cancer, of which I was perfectly relieved by Dr. Tate in about two months by an easy course, under the operation of which I felt no confinement, or other inconvenience at the time, nor any injury to my constitution since. . . ."

From the vantage point of modern medicine, it can be safely assumed that Washington did not have a skin cancer, and that

356

Dr. Tate certainly had no "cure" for the disease, but on the other hand, whatever Washington did have, Dr. Tate apparently cured it, and the President was spared another serious illness.

With these unhappy events behind him, he celebrated Thanksgiving with a truly thankful heart, and the following Monday joined the rest of Philadelphia in celebrating his birthday, which had this year fallen on Sunday. At the end of a long day of federal salutes, parading, addresses, and the City Dancing Assembly's ball, the President rose after supper and proposed a toast: "The Dancing Assembly of Philadelphia—may the members thereof, and the fair who honor it with their presence, long continue in the enjoyment of an amusement so innocent and agreeable."

One who saw him that night, Justice James Iredell, of the Supreme Court, wrote to his wife that he had never seen Washington "in better health and spirits. The crowds of gentlemen that waited on him in the day were innumerable, and in the Assembly at night it was scarcely possible to move. I came off a little after eight, having business of great importance to attend to, and indeed the room was much too crowded to be comfortable."

Justice Iredell did not, naturally, appreciate the party nearly so much as one of "the fair" who attended it. Mrs. Iredell would probably have preferred the description set down by the lovely Charlotte Chambers, daughter of General James Chambers, of the Pennsylvania line, granddaughter of Benjamin Chambers, the founder of Chambersburg. It was the year before her marriage to Israel Ludlow, and Charlotte was spending a gay winter in Philadelphia. In a letter home to her mother, she described the birthday ball from a strictly feminine standpoint:

"Dr. Rodman, master of ceremonies, met us at the door and conducted us to Mrs. Washington. She half arose as we made our passing compliments. She was dressed in a rich silk, but entirely without ornament, except the animation her amiable heart gives to her countenance. Next her were seated the wives of the foreign ambassadors, glittering from the floor to the summit of their headdress. One of the ladies wore three large ostrich feathers. Her brow was encircled by a sparkling fillet of diamonds; her neck and arms were almost covered with jewels, and two watches were suspended from her girdle, and all reflecting the light from a hundred directions. Such super-abundance of ornament struck me as injudicious; we look too much at the gold and pearls to do justice to the lady. However, it may not be in conformity to their individual taste thus decorating themselves, but to honor the country they represent.

"The seats were arranged like those of an amphitheatre, and cords were stretched on each side of the room, about three feet from the floor, to preserve sufficient space for the dancers. We were not long seated when General Washington entered, and bowed to the ladies as he passed round the room. 'He comes, he comes, the hero comes!' I involuntarily but softly exclaimed. When he bowed to me, I could scarcely resist the impulse of my heart, that almost burst through by bosom, to meet him. The dancing soon after commenced."

It was an exciting week for Charlotte. The ball was on Monday, and on Friday night she went to Martha's levee, wearing a gown of white brocade silk, trimmed with silver and white silk, "high-heeled shoes, embroidered with silver, and a light blue sash, with silver cord and tassel tied at the left side. My watch was suspended at the right, and my hair was in its natural curls. Surmounting all was a small white hat and white ostrich feather, confined by brilliant band and buckle."

To her mother she described the levee: "The hall, stairs and drawing room of the President's house were lighted by lamps and chandeliers. Mrs. Washington, with Mrs. Knox, sat near the fireplace. Other ladies were seated on sofas, and gentlemen stood in the center of the room conversing. On our approach, Mrs. Washington arose and made a curtsey—the gentlemen bowed most profoundly—and I calculated my declension to her own with critical exactness. The President, soon after, with that benignity peculiarly his own, advanced and I rose to receive and return his compliments with the respect and love my heart dictated. He seated himself beside me, and inquired for my father, a severe cold having detained him at home. . . ." [10] *

In contrast with such amiable society, the President found himself embroiled once more with the republicans in Congress, the republican press and a large body of public opinion. The issue this time was the peace treaty with Great Britain which Jay had negotiated. One of the republican newspapers had procured, by means which have not entirely fallen into disuse by the press, the text of the treaty and printed it before Washington had time to study it. There was an outburst of public indignation such as Washington had never experienced. Americans thought Jay had signed away a good many of the rights they had fought for, although actually it was a most skillfully negotiated document. There was a hue and cry in the press and in Congress. Mobs swirled in the streets of Philadelphia and hanged Jay in effigy; Hamilton, whose influence on the making of the treaty had been strong, was publicly stoned while he was making a speech in defense of it.

After the Senate had ratified the treaty in June, at the end of a violent special session, Washington retreated to the peace of Mount Vernon on July 15. But the issue of the treaty would not let him rest. There was so much public agitation, even after ratification, that he felt compelled to return to the city. He left on August 6 and arrived in the capital on the eleventh.

During his absence, a mass meeting of Philadelphia citizens had burned a copy of the treaty, hung at the end of a long pole, before the residence of the British minister. There was a spirit of riot abroad in the hot, dry August weather. Washington met immediately with the Cabinet on the treaty question, and after

---

* Charlotte tells her mother in another letter, dated March 11, of a visit from Martha, when the First Lady noted a picture of her husband hanging over the fireplace, and remarked that she had never seen a correct likeness of the General. Charlotte quoted her as adding that "the only merit the numerous portraits of him possessed was their resemblance to each other."

lengthy debate, his views prevailed. The ratification process went forward.

Most of the opposition now appeared to be centered in the seaport towns, which were aghast at what they considered the treaty's severe hampering of American trade. But by late August, Washington was convinced that "the current is turning," and by September 8, he felt justified in returning to Mount Vernon. There he helped to celebrate, somewhat after the event, the early August wedding of Tobias Lear and Fanny Washington, George Augustine's widow.

Returning to Philadelphia on October 20, Washington had several weeks to wait before Congress reconvened in December. He improved the time with his "civil duties," as he called them, and prepared as best he could to face the tense situation that would confront him in the new Congress, where the treaty situation was yet unsettled.

On Tuesday, December 8, he came before Congress and faced the legislators, many of them his bitter accusers. The Pennsylvania legislature had adjourned at noon and was there to hear this most important of opening addresses. The best report of the scene is, unfortunately, a biased one, though it was written by one of the most talented journalists of the day, the Englishman, William Cobbett, who called himself Peter Porcupine. In *Porcupine's Gazette,* his newspaper, he was as vituperative as Bache and Freneau—but on the other side. Washington had no better defender in the press, because Cobbett had a sharp eye, imagination, absolute fearlessness and a biting pen, specially skilled in needling his enemies, who were numerous. Writing of Washington, however, whom he intensely admired, he was inclined to put the best possible face on things. Of the scene in Congress Hall, he wrote:

"When the President arrived at the House this day, he found it in that state of composed gravity, of respectful silence, for which the Congress is so remarkable, and which, whatever witlings may say, is the surest mark of sound understanding.—

The gallery was crowded with anxious spectators, whose orderly behavior was not the least pleasing part of the scene.

"The President is a timid speaker: he is a proof, among thousands, that superior genius, wisdom, and courage are ever accompanied with excessive modesty. His situation was at this time almost entirely new. Never, till a few months preceding this session, had the tongue of the most factious slander dared to make a public attack on his character. This was the first time he had ever entered the walls of Congress without a full assurance of meeting a welcome from every heart. He now saw, even among those to whom he addressed himself, numbers who, to repay all his labors, all his anxious cares for their welfare, were ready to thwart his measures and present him the cup of humiliation, filled to the brim. When he came to that part of his speech where he mentions the treaty with His Britannic Majesty, he cast his eyes towards the gallery.—It was not the look of indignation and reproach, but of injured virtue, which is ever ready to forgive. I was pleased to observe that not a single murmur of disapprobation was heard from the spectators that surrounded me; and if there were some amongst them who had assisted at the turbulent town meetings, I am persuaded they were sincerely penitent. When he departed, every look seemed to say: God prolong his precious life." [11]

In spite of the exaggerations, Cobbett's report was true in the sense that Washington had once more succeeded in frustrating his more extreme enemies simply by the tremendous weight of his prestige and character. As the year ended, he probably felt more certain that the "current is turning." At least we know he had a pleasant dinner on Christmas Eve, because there is the testimony of Theophilus Bradbury, Representative from Essex County, Massachusetts, who was one of about twenty members of Congress, and the Vice-President, who sat down with the President that night. Bradbury describes the occasion in a letter to his daughter Harriet, the wife of Major Thomas Hooper:

"In the middle of the table was placed a piece of table furniture about six feet long and two feet wide, rounded at the ends. It was either of wood gilded, or polished metal, raised only an inch, with a silver rim round it like that round a tea board; in the center was a pedestal of plaster of Paris with images upon it, and on each end figures, male and female, of the same. It was very elegant and used for ornament only. The dishes were placed all around, and there was an elegant variety of roast beef, veal, turkeys, ducks, fowls, hams, &c.; puddings, jellies, oranges, apples, nuts, almonds, figs, raisins, and a variety of wines and punch. We took our leave at six, more than an hour after the candles were introduced. No lady but Mrs. Washington dined with us. We were waited on by four or five men servants dressed in livery."

[1796]    Whatever might be the prospect for the year 1796, Washington was certain of one thing: It would be his last in office. In a few more months, the quarrels in Congress, the barbs of the republican gazettes, the cares and responsibilities of the presidency would be forever behind him, and he could retire to the deep peace of Mount Vernon at last. The knowledge gave him strength to face whatever lay ahead in the last year of his term.

It proved to be, on the whole, not a bad one. The worst of the crises was past, and although there remained a highly vocal opposition to the Administration, Washington appeared to have regained a large part of whatever public prestige he had lost during the past two years. His birthday was celebrated with the greatest good will and gaiety the city had ever shown, possibly because the citizens sensed it would be the last he would spend with them. As a visiting traveler[12] put it, "On General Washington's birthday . . . this city was unusually gay; every person of consequence in it, Quakers alone excepted, made it a point to visit the General on this day. As early as eleven o'clock in the morning he was prepared to receive them, and the audience lasted till three in the afternoon. . . ."

At noon Speaker Robert Hare, of the Senate, and Speaker George Latimer, of the House, led the members of Congress, friends and enemies alike, to call on the President and congratulate him. He bowed to all of them in the back parlor of the Morris house, and gave them wine and cake.

For more than four hours he stood there, receiving the Society of the Cincinnati, the clergy, militia officers, citizens of distinction, foreign ministers and other dignitaries. Besides the usual parlor, another had been opened to accommodate the crowd, and since this one fronted on the street, the windows were black with spectators peering in from outside. Upstairs, Martha received the ladies of the city in her own suite, and after the gentlemen had paid their respects to the President, most of them went up to greet her as well. At night there was a grand public ball and supper.

More than one of those who came to pay their respects thought they had never seen Washington looking so cheerful, and it seems certain that his good humor stemmed from his anticipation of early retirement. It was much on his mind these days, although it was months before he could announce it officially. John Adams, writing to Abigail, tells of a dinner party on March 24, at which the President drew him into close conversation after the other gentlemen and their ladies had withdrawn to the parlor, and talked politics in an almost intimate way, unusual for him. "He detained me there till nine o'clock, and was never more frank and open upon politics," Adams reported. "I find his opinions and sentiments are more exactly like mine than I ever knew before, respecting England, France, and our American parties. He gave me intimations enough that his reign would be very short. He repeated it three times at least, that this and that was of no consequence to him personally, as he had but a very little while to stay in his present situation."

Another visitor to the Morris house that spring got the same impression of serenity, and in telling of it, added a gracious footnote to the surrender at Yorktown. This visitor was an Englishman, Thomas Twining, a British government official from the East Indies, who came to America on a brief visit in 1796. On his way to Philadelphia he called on Tobias Lear, then living near Georgetown, and in that period of his life not working for Washington. Lear, who apparently knew Twining or knew of him through his English business connections, gave the visitor a letter of introduction to the President, and along with it a miniature of Washington to be delivered to him.

On Friday, May 13, Twining arrived in Philadelphia with his letter and picture, and at one in the afternoon he called at the Morris house, which he was surprised to discover had no imposing façade, and indeed was next door to a hairdresser's establishment. Twining relates what happened to him:

"Having stated my object to a servant who came to the door, I was conducted up a neat but rather narrow staircase, carpeted in the middle, and was shown into a middling-sized well-furnished drawing room on the left of the passage. Nearly opposite the door was the fireplace, with a wood fire in it. The floor was carpeted. On the left of the fireplace was a sofa, which sloped across the room. There were no pictures on the walls, no ornaments on the chimney-piece. Two windows on the right of the entrance looked into the street. There was nobody in the room, but in a minute Mrs. Washington came in, when I repeated the object of my calling, and put into her hands the letter for General Washington, and his miniature.

"She said she would deliver them to the President, and inviting me to sit down, retired for that purpose. She soon returned, and said the President would come presently. Mrs. Washington was a middle-sized lady, rather stout; her manner extremely kind and unaffected. She sat down on the sofa, and invited me to sit by her. I spoke of the pleasant days I had passed at Washington [meaning the new city], and of the attentions I had received from her granddaughter, Mrs. Law.

"While engaged in this conversation, but with my thoughts turned to the expected arrival of the General, the door opened and Mrs. Washington and myself rising, she said, 'The President,' and introduced me to him. Never did I feel more interest than at this moment, when I saw the tall, venerable upright figure of this great man advancing towards me to take me by the hand. . . . The General, having thanked me for the picture, requested me to sit down next the fire, Mrs. Washington being on the sofa on the other side, and himself taking a chair in the middle. . . .

"In the course of the conversation, I mentioned the particular regard and respect with which Lord Cornwallis always spoke of him. He received this communication in the most courteous manner, inquired about his lordship, and expressed for him much esteem. . . . After sitting about three-quarters of an hour, I rose to take leave, when the General invited me to drink tea with him that evening. I regret to say I declined this honor on account of some other engagement—a wrong and injudicious decision, for which I have since reproached myself. . . .

"The General's age was rather more than sixty-four. In person he was tall, well-proportioned, and upright. His hair was powdered and tied behind. Although his deportment was that of a general, the expression of his features had rather the calm dignity of a legislator than the severity of a soldier."[13]

On June 1, Congress ended its session and the President, impatient to be at Mount Vernon, hurried to finish his own duties. The legislators must have been in even greater haste. Writing to Tobias Lear on June 3, Washington told him that his mother and son had passed through Philadelphia on the way to visit him. "It was with great difficulty a carriage could be procured to take her on," he wrote, "for it so happened that Congress closed their session yesterday, that members were struggling for, and bidding on each other for conveyances, and your mother's anxious desire to get to you would not permit her to wait. At length, after some unavailing attempts, Mr. Craik succeeded in getting a carriage and pair of horses, which I hope will take her safe down."

Washington expected a heavy summer social season at Mount Vernon—"crowded with company all the while we shall be at it," as he said. The ministers of France, Great Britain and Portugal were expected, along with "other strangers."

Anticipating these visitations, he forwarded specific instructions to his manager, William Pearce, on June 5: "In a few days after we get there, we shall be visited, I expect, by characters of distinction; I could wish, therefore, that the gardens, lawns and everything else in and about the houses may be got in clean and nice order. If the gardener needs aid to accomplish as much of this as lies within his line, let him have it, and let others rake and scrape up all the trash of every sort and kind about the houses, and in holes and corners, and throw it (all, I mean, that will make dung) into the stercorary [a covered repository for fertilizer] and the rest into the gullied parts of the road coming up to the house. And as the front gate of the lawn (by the ivies) is cracked and scarcely to be opened, I wish you would order a new one (like the old one) to be immediately made, and that with the new ones you have just got made, and all the boarding of every kind that was white before, to be painted white again. If Neal and my own people cannot make the front gate above mentioned, get someone from Alexandria to do it, provided he will set about and finish it immediately. This must be the way up to the house.

"Let the rooms in the servants' hall, above and below, be well cleaned, and have the beds and bedsteads therein put in order, after which have a good lock put on the door of the west room above, and order Caroline, or whoever has the charge of these rooms, to suffer no person to sleep or even to go into it without express orders from her mistress or myself. Let exactly the same things be done with the rooms over the kitchen, as there will be a white cook with us that will require one of them, and the other may also be wanted for some other servants or use, it being likely there will be a call for all these places and things. And I hope, especially as there is no ice to keep fresh meats, that you will have an abundant supply for the demands that will probably be made thereon during our stay at home. And besides, will ascertain from the butcher in Alexandria the stated days on which beef and veal are killed, that we may know what dependence to place on him. Tell the gardener I shall expect everything that a garden ought to produce, in the most ample manner.

"Take care to keep a sufficiency of oats, and the best of your old hay on hand. I shall have eight or ten horses of my own with me and there will be many others with visitors."

Having laid the groundwork for an active summer, Washington left Philadelphia on June 13. The season was all that he expected, and more, since a delegation of visiting Indians who had failed to see him in Philadelphia turned up at Mount Vernon and had to be entertained. "I hope and expect that the proposed visit from the Cherokee chiefs will be so managed as not to take place before the month of November," the master of Mount Vernon wrote to James McHenry. "I have already been incommoded at this place by a visit of several days from a party of a dozen Catawbas, and should wish while I am in this retreat to avoid a repetition of such guests."

The Catawbas were not the only disruption of Mount Vernon's social summer, though they must have been by far the most sensational. Washington apparently took time from his duties as host to brood about his enemies. In a letter to Jefferson, he remarked that until the last year or so he had never thought probable, hardly even possible, that while he was doing his best to establish the nation and keep it out of war, "I should be accused of being the enemy of one nation, and subject to the influence of another, and to prove it, that every act of my administration would be tortured, and the grossest and most insidious misrepresentations of them be made by giving one side only of a subject, and that too in such exaggerated and indecent terms as could scarcely be applied to a Nero, a notorious defaulter, or even to a common pickpocket."

He did not spend the whole summer in Mount Vernon. Conscious of the major public act which immediately confronted him, he was back in Philadelphia by Sunday, August 21, prepared to write and publish his Farewell Address to the American people, which would retire him at last from public office.

Having written the address, the publication of it was a problem. As a President with more enemies than friends in the newspaper business (or so it often seemed to him), he had to find a gazette that possessed the requisite dignity and circulation, and at the same time was friendly to him. The paper he chose was *Claypoole's American Daily Advertiser*, formerly Dunlap's. On September 15 he sent a message to the publisher, David C. Claypoole, requesting him to make a private visit, an invitation which must have stirred Claypoole's best reporting instincts, since he surely understood that he was about to be given an exclusive story.

Claypoole's own account of the interview, written later, relates that Washington received him kindly in the drawing room, where he sat alone, and asked the publisher to draw up a chair. Then the President told him that for some time he had contemplated retiring from public life, and intended to do so at the end of his present term. There were several "thoughts and reflections," he said, which he wanted to communicate to the people in the form of an address, and he had selected the *Daily Advertiser* to print it. He paused. Claypoole took it that he should make some kind of reply, and so he thanked the President for having selected his paper, "especially as I viewed this choice as an evidence of his approbation of the principles and manner in which the work was conducted." To this, says Claypoole, Washington "silently assented." Then he wanted to know when the publication could be made. They agreed on Monday, September 19, and Washington promised to deliver the copy next morning, Friday. That ended the interview.

"After the proof sheet had been carefully compared with

the copy and corrected by myself," Claypoole relates, "I carried two different revises to be examined by the President, who made but few alterations from the original, except in punctuation, in which he was very minute. . . . I waited on the President with the original, and in presenting it to him, expressed my regret at parting with it, and how much I should be gratified by being permitted to retain it, upon which in the most obliging manner, he handed it back to me, saying that if I wished for it, I might keep it, and I then took my leave." *

After the publication of the address, there was a noticeable letdown in the political tensions surrounding Washington, and all but the most virulent of the opposition newspapers stopped taking shots at him on every possible occasion. Now, it seemed, everyone wanted to do him honor. As the year closed, the noted Indian chiefs, most of whom venerated the Great Chief Conotocarious, made lengthy journeys to pay their final respects to "the White Father Who Sits in Philadelphia," as he was often called in their interminable speeches. John Watts, the King of the Cherokees, came with several chiefs of the tribe and their wives, including the widow and children of Hanging Maw, a friend of the government who had been treacherously murdered by a white man. From the Mohawk Valley came the famous and traveled Mohawk chief, Colonel Joseph Brant, who had been in England, where he was received by the King. With him came one of Washington's best Indian friends, the Seneca chief Cornplanter, whose eloquence is still remembered and quoted today. John Adams noted on December 3 that Washington had "dined four sets of Indians on four several days the last week."

[1797]    The farewell of the people themselves appeared, by unspoken consent, to have been reserved for the last celebration of his birthday in Philadelphia. Justice Iredell gave his

---

* This original is in the New York Public Library.

wife, in a letter written on February 24, perhaps the best summary of that day:

"The President's birthday was celebrated here with every
possible mark of attachment, affection and respect, rendered
affecting beyond all expression by its being in some degree a
parting scene. Mrs. Washington was moved even to tears, with
the mingled emotions of gratitude for such strong proofs of
public regard, and the new prospect of the uninterrupted enjoyment of domestic life; she expressed herself something to
this effect. I never saw the President look better, nor in finer
spirits, but his emotions were too powerful to be concealed.
He could sometimes scarcely speak. Three rooms of his house
were almost entirely full from 12 to 3, and such a crowd at
the door it was difficult to get in. At the [Ricketts] Amphitheatre at night it is supposed there was at least 1200 persons.
The show was a very brilliant one, but such scrambling to go
to supper that there was some danger of being squeezed to
death. The Vice-President handed in Mrs. Washington, and
the President immediately followed. The applause with which
they were received is indescribable. The same was shown on
their return from supper. The music added greatly to the interest of the scene. The President stayed till between 12 and 1."

When the clergy called in a body that day, according to
custom, the President appeared "unusually cheerful," Dr. Ashbel Green recalls, in his reminiscences. He even did what he
had never done before, and made a little joke.

"Gentlemen, I feel the weight of years. I take a pair of sixes
on my shoulders this day," he remarked.

The Rev. Dr. Green is at humorless pains to explain that
Washington could not make little jokes. "This great man was
not in his proper element when he attempted a pleasant con-
ceit," Green writes. "I never witnessed his making the attempt but on this occasion. And if his allusion, as I suppose
must have been the case, was to the fifty-sixes used in weighing heavy articles, it was surely far-fetched and not very obvious. He entered his sixty-sixth year at this time."

After his birthday celebration, Washington went to the theatre as usual, the New Theatre this time, and saw a double bill presented by his "particular desire." The principal attraction was a new comedy, *The Way to Get Married*. Following it came a comic ballet, *Dermot & Kathleen, or Animal Magnetism*.

The only really emotional scene of his prolonged leave-taking came on Friday, March 3, 1797, the day before he was to leave the presidential chair. A large company came to dine with him, including the foreign ministers and their ladies, his successor John Adams (Abigail was home in Quincy), Thomas Jefferson and "other conspicuous persons of both sexes." Bishop White, who was present, says that "during the dinner much hilarity prevailed, but on the removal of the cloth, it was put an end to by the President, certainly without design. Having filled his glass, he addressed the company with a smile on his countenance, as nearly as can be recollected in the following terms: 'Ladies and gentlemen, this is the last time I shall drink your health as a public man. I do it with sincerity, and wishing you all possible happiness!' There was an end of all pleasantry. He who gives this relation accidentally directed his eye to the lady of the British minister (Mrs. Liston) and tears were running down her cheeks."[14]

Next day was Inauguration Day. No one knew better than the new President that Washington could not be anything but cheerful about it. Those who witnessed President Eisenhower's serious, almost glum countenance and President Truman's cheerful grin on Inauguration Day, 1953, will note the parallel moods, and for somewhat the same reasons, in the report of that March 4, 1797, which John Adams gave his wife.

"A solemn scene it was indeed," he wrote, "and it was made affecting to me by the presence of the General, whose countenance was as serene and unclouded as the day. He seemed to me to enjoy a triumph over me. Methought I heard him say, 'Ay! I am fairly out and you fairly in! See which of us will be happiest!' When the ceremony was over, he came and made

me a visit, and cordially congratulated me, and wished my administration might be happy, successful, and honorable. . . .
In the chamber of the House of Representatives was a multitude as great as the space could contain, and I believe scarcely
a dry eye but Washington's."

That night the merchants of Philadelphia gave a public dinner to Washington in Ricketts Amphitheatre, at the southwest
corner of Sixth and Chestnut streets. The guests met at Oeller's
Hotel, near the Amphitheatre, and paraded to the hall. As they
entered, a march which had been written for the President
resounded from a large military band, and a huge transparency
was unveiled, showing Washington, full length, being
crowned with a wreath of laurel by Fame, and delivering to
her his Farewell Address, meanwhile taking leave of the Genius
of America, represented by a female figure holding the Cap
of Liberty in her hand, with an altar before her inscribed
"Public Gratitude." Emblematic devices representing some of
Washington's honors in public service were worked into the
painting, along with "a distant view of Mount Vernon." The
creator of this masterpiece was no less a personage than the celebrated Charles Willson Peale.

Samuel Richard, master of the City Tavern and Merchants'
Coffee House, had outdone himself as steward of the affair.
He gave the 240 guests a dinner which included—presumably
to the accompaniment of widespread indigestion—four hundred dishes, "of the most choice viands which money could
purchase or art prepare. . . ."

If there was a sour note in the inauguration air, it came
from the *Aurora's* editorial columns, where Bache delivered a
few parting republican shots at Washington. There are strong
echoes here of the journalistic extremists of today, and several
newspapers would doubtless give profitable employment to the
writer of these words about Washington. The words themselves have a strangely reminiscent sound:

"When a retrospect is taken of the Washingtonian admin-

372

istration for eight years, it is the subject of the greatest astonishment that a single individual should have cankered the principles of republicanism in an enlightened people, just emerged from the gulf of despotism, and should have carried his designs against the public liberty so far as to put in jeopardy its very existence. Such, however, are the facts, and with them staring us in the face, this day ought to be a jubilee in the United States."

And again: "If ever a nation has been debauched by a man, the American nation has been debauched by Washington. If ever a nation has been deceived by a man, the American nation has been deceived by Washington. Let his conduct, then, be an example to future ages. Let it serve to be a warning that no man may be an idol. Let the history of the federal government instruct mankind that the mask of patriotism may be worn to conceal the foulest designs against the liberties of the people."

Washington remained bitter about his newspaper opposition to the last; he could never view it with Jefferson's equanimity, a composure which was tested as severely as Washington's when he, in turn as President, became the subject of scurrilous abuse. Washington wrote his old friend Henry Knox on March 2: "To the wearied traveler who sees a resting place and is bending his body to lean thereon, I now compare myself, but to be suffered to do this in peace is, I perceive, too much to be endured by some. To misrepresent my motives, to reprobate my politics, and to weaken the confidence which has been reposed in my administration are objects which cannot be relinquished by those who will be satisfied with nothing short of a change in our political system. . . ."

But he found consolation in the days lying ahead of him. He added in his letter to Knox: "The remainder of my life (which in the course of nature cannot be long) will be occupied in rural amusements, and though I shall seclude myself as much as possible from the noisy and bustling crowd, none more than myself would be regaled by the company of those I esteem at Mount Vernon, more than twenty miles from which, after I arrive there, it is not likely I shall ever be."

There was a final bustle of moving preparations, and on March 9, General Washington, no longer President, left Philadelphia with his family. Along the way to Mount Vernon he sent back letters of instructions to Tobias Lear—what to do with furniture, things to buy, things to sell, a long list of small details, and evidently with Martha and the children peering over his shoulder, because he adds a plaintive P.S. to a note written from Chester: "On one side I am called upon to remember the parrot, on the other to remember the dog. For my own part I should not pine much if both were forgot."


[1798]     He visited Philadelphia only once more in the three years remaining to him. About a year and a half after he left the city, the man who had promised he would travel no farther than twenty miles from home came into Philadelphia on November 10, 1798. All the way along the route he had been given the highest military honors, much in the old manner; by this time Adams had made him Commander-in-Chief of the armies.

Arriving on November 10, he stayed until December 14, lodging at the boardinghouse of the Widow Rosannah White, at 9 North Eighth Street.

During this reprise, he was treated with the overflowing hospitality Philadelphia had always given him. He dined at a different place nearly every night. One evening he spent with Robert Morris and his family, and heard the details of his friend's hard luck. The meeting took place in jail. Morris had been imprisoned for debt the previous February, and it was August 1801 before he was released. They dined in the debtors' apartment of the Walnut Street Prison, at Sixth and Walnut streets. On Saturday, December 8, Washington sat as an honored guest in Federal Hall and heard President Adams open the third session of the Fifth Congress, and would not have changed places with him for a fortune.

On a Friday morning, December 14, his carriage rolled out of Philadelphia for the last time. He never saw it again.

# PART 5

# WASHINGTON AND THE SOUTH

Chapter 1

The Presidential Tour

As a Southerner who loved his own state so much he called it "the country," as though it had a national identity, Washington oddly did not discover the South below Virginia until politics impelled him to it in 1791. What he discovered on that presidential journey of 1887 miles through the Carolinas and Georgia was both pleasing and displeasing to him.

[1791]    The South possessed the worst inns and the most beautiful women he had ever seen. Its welcome to him, on the whole, was colder than the tour of acclamation through New England had been, because here the stubborn opposition to the Constitution had been translated into animosity toward the Administration. But on the other hand, his reception in such cities as Charleston, Savannah and Augusta was all any human being, let alone the President, could ask for.

No journey he ever undertook had been planned so thoroughly. He laid out an itinerary (so that important mail might reach him properly) which was an exact day-by-day scheduling from town to town, listing the mileage, providing for halts and for nearly every imaginable contingency. He deviated from this itinerary only slightly. The tour did not come out precisely on schedule simply because the eight days he allowed for casualties were not needed.

377

As he wrote later, "Having obtained before I left Philadelphia the most accurate account I could get there of the places and roads through and by which I was to perform my tour, and the distances between the former, I formed my line of march accordingly, fixed each day's journey and the day to halt, from neither of which have I departed in a single instance except staying, from a particular circumstance, two days in Columbia and none at Charlotte, instead of one at each, and crossing James River at Carter's Ferry in place of Taylor's, as was the original intention."[1]

There was nothing about the beginning of the tour to suggest its later smoothness. It was off to a wild start, soon after Washington left Philadelphia on Monday, March 21, 1791, accompanied by his aide, Major Jackson. They rode in the President's own chariot, drawn by four horses, followed by a light baggage wagon with two horses, five saddle horses, including his own mount, and five servants: his valet, two footmen, the coachman and a postillion.

The rough going began three days out, at the southern end of the Chesapeake Bay crossing, when the vessel on which Washington was embarked attempted to navigate late in the evening the mouth of the Severn River, leading up to Annapolis, and promptly ran aground on Greenbury Point. Washington irritably laid this to the "ignorance of the people on board, with respect to the navigation of it. . . ."[2]

After "much exertion and difficulty," the vessel was floated again, but their situation was not appreciably better. No one aboard had any knowledge of the channel; the darkness was nowhere penetrated by a light; and heavy squalls began to blow the boat around, to the accompaniment of "constant lightning and tremendous thunder." In no time they were aground once more, this time on Horne's Point. The craft refused to budge, and as Washington put it, "not knowing where we were, we remained, not knowing what might happen, till morning."

The President of the United States was hardly accustomed

to the primitive accommodations he had to put up with that night. He lay in his greatcoat and boots, "on a berth not long enough for me by the head, and much cramped." When daylight came, the ship was still aground, but the return of visibility showed that they were only a mile from Annapolis, whose comforts they could have enjoyed had they only known it. A sailboat put out from Annapolis, when the inhabitants saw the ferry's plight and realized the President was aboard, and in it Washington and most of his baggage were conveyed to shore. As soon as he had settled himself at Mann's Tavern, Governor John Eager Howard came to call and asked him to dine with the prominent citizens that day, and at his own house the next.

After his dinner with the Governor, Washington took a busman's holiday and went to an evening session of the Maryland Assembly, where he listened to the debates until half past ten. At nine the next morning, the twenty-seventh, he left Annapolis with the usual escort, while the guns boomed.

Stopping at Bladensburg that night, he was up early and in Georgetown at eight o'clock, where he was to meet the commissioners planning the new Federal City: Chief Justice Thomas Johnson, of Maryland, David Stuart and Daniel Carroll. He met both the commissioners and a welcoming committee, who dined him royally at a public dinner in Sutter's Tavern, where he lodged.

Washington found the commissioners snarled in a disagreement with the landholders of Georgetown and Carrollsburg, and concluding that "their fears and jealousies of each other" might turn out to be against the public interest, he asked the contending elements to meet him at his lodgings. He does not record what he told them, but in his diary next day he remarks blandly that "the parties to whom I addressed myself yesterday evening, having taken the matter into consideration, saw the propriety of my observations, and that whilst they were contending for the shadow they might lose the substance. . . ." The upshot was that they agreed to surrender the land neces-

379

sary to establish the Federal City. Having untied this knot, the President was ready to resume his journey—a short run down to Mount Vernon on the twenty-ninth.

After a nine-day stopover at his plantation, he set off southward again on April 7, "with horses apparently much refreshed and in good spirits," and their master in an equally happy state. There were certain family obligations to be met on this stage of the tour, and they could not be hurried. At Dumfries, Virginia, he stopped to drink tea with his niece Mildred, John Augustine's daughter, who had married Thomas Lee, eldest son of Richard Henry Lee, a little less than three years before. On the next night, he dined and lodged with his sister Betty Lewis, in Fredericksburg—"my Sister Lewis," as Washington always called her.

Fredericksburg insisted on dining and entertaining him the following day, so that it was Sunday morning, April 10, before he could leave his friends and well-wishers, and get on with his journey. He traveled thirty-five miles before nightfall, stopping at Kenner's Tavern, a distance that enabled him to reach Richmond easily, early the next afternoon. Along with the entertaining that Governor Henry Lee and the city's prominent citizens provided during the three days he stayed there, he had an opportunity to view a project close to his heart and pocketbook: the canal, sluices, locks and other navigational works between Richmond and Westham, all the property of the James River Navigation Company.

At Petersburg, which he reached on April 14, he attended his first assembly of the tour, and there began counting the Southern belles, as he did at each such occasion. There were between sixty and seventy of them at Petersburg.

Beyond Petersburg, Washington and Major Jackson found themselves in the back country, where the roads and the quality of the lodgings were alike uncertain. On the night of the fifteenth, they stopped at the house of one Oliver, "which is a good one for horses, and where there are tolerable clean beds," but the next morning, after a journey before breakfast over roads which had raised choking clouds of dust, it began to rain and the party decided to stop at the only inn short of Halifax, North Carolina. However, this place, Washington discovered, had "no stables in which the horses could be comfortable and no rooms or beds which appeared tolerable," and everything else had "a dirty appearance." They had to go on to Halifax, making the day's journey forty-eight miles. At six o'clock they arrived in this city on the south bank of the Roanoke River, having started a little after five that morning.

The district's Representative in Congress, Colonel John B. Ashe, was at home in Halifax, and it was a matter of planned courtesy to stay over a day and attend the customary public dinner. Tarborough was the stop on the next night, and after dining "at a trifling place called Greenville" on the following day, the party lodged on the evening of the nineteenth at Allan's ordinary, "a very indifferent house without stabling, which for the first time since I commenced my journey, [the horses] were obliged to stand without a cover."

On the way to Newbern, North Carolina, Washington paused for breakfast at what he took to be a public house, the home of a Colonel Allan, and was "kindly and well entertained without knowing it was at his expense, until it was too late to rectify the mistake." Pausing at Newbern for a public dinner and a dancing assembly (seventy ladies) in a structure called the Palace, "a good brick building . . . now hastening to ruins," Washington made a report to Tobias Lear: "We have, all things considered, come on tolerably well, yet some of the horses, especially the last two bought, are not a little worsted by their journey, and the whole, if brought back, will not cut capers as they did at starting out. . . ."

Resuming the journey on April 22, he dined at Trenton, and after an overnight stop at an indifferent ordinary ten miles farther, pressed onward forty-four miles the following day. "The whole road from Newbern to Wilmington (except in a few places of small extent)," Washington wrote in his diary, "passes through the most barren country I ever beheld, especially in the parts nearest the latter, which is no other than a bed of white sand. In places, however, before we came to these, if the ideas of poverty could be separated from the sand, the appearances of it are agreeable, resembling a lawn well covered with evergreens, and a good verdure below from a brook or coarse grass which, having sprung since the burning of the woods, had a neat and handsome look, especially as there were parts entirely open, and others with ponds of water, which contributed not a little to the beauty of the scene."

Of Wilmington he formed a better impression, describing it as having "some good houses pretty compactly built." Its population was said to be 1000, but the President noted that it was "agreed on all hands that the census in this state has been very inaccurately and shamefully taken by the marshal's deputies, who, instead of going to people's houses and there, on the spot, ascertaining the numbers, have advertised a meeting of them at certain places, by which means those who did not attend (and it seems many purposely avoided doing it, some from an apprehension of its being introductory of a tax, and others from religious scruples) have gone with their families unnumbered. . . ."

In Wilmington, too, he found "very good lodgings," which were more than welcome after the series of third-rate country inns in which he had eaten and slept. Wilmington gave him a public dinner and ball (sixty-two ladies), along with illuminations and bonfires, and it was Tuesday before he could leave the city's hospitality, having arrived on Sunday.

On the morning of Saturday, April 30, he had reached Georgetown, South Carolina, descending the river three miles to get to it. The Georgetown citizens turned out their infantry company, handsomely uniformed, saluted him with cannon, gave him a public dinner, and in the afternoon he was "introduced to upwards of 50 ladies who had assembled (at a tea party) on the occasion."

Leaving Georgetown the following morning, a Sunday, he crossed Santee Creek and the Santee River, at Lynch's Island,

and after a day's journey of thirty-four miles, stayed that night at the Manigault plantation, one of the great Southern estates, where he must have felt more suitably entertained.

After breakfast on Monday morning at the country seat of Governor Charles Pinckney, of South Carolina, eighteen miles from Manigault's, Washington came after six more miles to Haddrel's Point, where a barge waited to take him over to Charleston. Here was a scene reminiscent of his triumphal entry into New York. The barge was rowed by a dozen American captains of ships, "most elegantly dressed," and on the way over, other boats filled with ladies and gentlemen attended him, including two waterborne bands. At the wharf he was met by the Governor and other officials, including the state's two Senators, Pierce Butler and Ralph Izard, and there was a cheering parade up the street to his lodgings. Governor Pinckney entertained him at what he called a private dinner, Washington noted wryly, although there were fifteen or eighteen gentlemen present.

He stayed a week in Charleston, more than ordinarily encouraged to do so, perhaps, by the experience he had on his first full day there, when about two o'clock he was visited "by a great number of the most respectable ladies of Charleston-- the first honor of the kind I had ever experienced, and it was as flattering as it was singular." Many of these must have been among the "256 elegantly dressed and handsome ladies" who came to the assembly the following night, at the Exchange.

On the morning of the assembly, President Washington became a general again as he rode out to satisfy a matter of military interest remaining from the Revolution. There must always have been a doubt in his mind about the tactical defense of Charleston, questions unanswered as to why General Lincoln had to surrender it to Clinton in 1780 after Moultrie had twice defended it successfully. He had been compelled to form his opinion from dispatches, letters and the personal explanations of the commanders involved. Now he examined for himself the lines of attack and defense, and was "satisfied that

*383*

the defense was noble and honorable, although the measure was undertaken upon wrong principles and impolitic." He also inspected the ruins of Fort Johnson and Fort Moultrie.

Again and again in his diary the President remarked upon Charleston hospitality and the charm of its women, as well as their abundance. Attending a concert at the Exchange, he noted that there were "at least 400 ladies, the number and appearance of which exceeding anything of the kind I had ever seen," and the ball at the Governor's house produced "a select company of ladies."

Besides dining with Pierce Butler, General Moultrie, the Governor and others anxious to entertain him, and paying numerous other calls, Washington found time to see most of the gracious city by riding through its streets on horseback. One morning before breakfast he visited an orphanage, and presented himself amiably to the awestruck boys and girls, who were probably astounded to see so distinguished a figure at such an hour in the morning.

He described the city, in his diary, as containing about 1600 dwelling houses and nearly 16,000 people, evenly divided between Negroes and whites. The inhabitants, at least those of his own kind, seemed to him "wealthy, gay and hospitable," and he was delighted to see that they appeared "happy and satisfied with the general government."

As he left Charleston on May 9, about six o'clock, a corps of the Cincinnati and most of the principal gentlemen of the city followed him hospitably as far as the bridge over the Ashley River, and a "select party of particular friends" went even farther. They dined on May 11 at Pocotaligo, where the parishioners of Prince William County had prepared a reception for him.

A committee from Savannah met him at Purisburg, twenty-five miles up the river from that city, and provided him with a handsome eight-oared barge, rowed by eight American captains of vessels, to carry him down the waterway. The procession stopped at a river-front place called Mulberry Grove, and Washington went ashore to pay his respects to Nathanael Greene's widow, who still lived on the plantation the state had given her husband. One regrets that Washington was not a more voluminous diarist, that he might have told us how the pretty, vivacious, intelligent Catherine appeared now, more than a decade after they had danced half the night at her husband's "pretty little frisk" in New Jersey. Had Greene's ill-fortune in the postwar years, and her removal from the gay society she had always known, sobered this beauty who was the subject of scandalous whispers, who flaunted bravely into embattled New York when every other wife was leaving? Washington had been captivated by her, along with half the officers in his camp. Unfortunately the laconic President provides no enlightenment. "I called upon Mrs. Greene . . . and asked her how she did," he informs us succinctly.

In any event, the pause at Mulberry Grove lengthened to seven hours a river journey that should have taken only four. He found the city illuminated, and the Mayor and wardens ready to conduct him to "very good lodging" and to a public dinner at the Coffee Room.

Savannah had its pleasures arrayed for him: dinner with the Cincinnati; the dancing assembly, with "100 well-dressed and handsome ladies"; an inspection of the 1779 battlefields, accompanied by General Anthony Wayne and others; and dinner with two hundred citizens "in an elegant bower erected for the occasion on the bank of the river below the town," followed by "a tolerable good display of fireworks."

The President observed in his diary that Savannah stood upon "what may be called high ground for this country." He noted, too, that it was "extremely sandy, which makes the walking very disagreeable and the houses uncomfortable in warm and windy weather, as they are filled with dust whenever these happen. The town on three sides is surrounded with cultivated rice fields which have a rich and luxuriant appearance. On the fourth or backside it is a fine sand. The harbor is said to be very good, and often filled with square-rigged vessels. . . ."

As in Charleston, he was visited by delegations of ladies, both Saturday and Sunday. After he had received them on Sunday, May 15, he set out for Augusta, Georgia, stopping again at Mulberry Grove to dine with Mrs. Greene. He reached Augusta on the morning of the eighteenth, and enjoyed the customary reception, complete with artillery, Governor Edward Telfair, and "many well dressed ladies." He spent two more days in the city, attending the assembly (sixty to seventy ladies), viewing the remains of the British fortifications, the falls above the town, and the streets of the city.

Having crossed the Congaree River in a flat-bottomed boat at a rope ferry, he found himself in Columbia, the new capital of South Carolina, on Sunday, May 22. He had planned to spend only a day there, Monday, but a foundered horse obliged him to remain over Tuesday as well. To make up for it, he started at four o'clock Wednesday morning for Camden, South Carolina, leading the sick horse slowly along behind, and reached his destination at two o'clock that afternoon. He viewed the British works there next day and went on toward Charlotte, stopping en route to see the ground where General Greene had fought Lord Rawdon's troops at the Battle of Hobkirk's Hill, in April 1781. Six miles beyond this place he saw the bloody fields where Cornwallis had dealt General Gates a stinging blow in August 1780. The Commander-in-Chief was seeing terrain which had been only names and maps to him until now.

By Saturday the twenty-eighth he was in Charlotte, North Carolina, well on the way home. There he dined with General Thomas Polk, stayed overnight, and set off again next day toward Salisbury, where he arrived in time for breakfast on the thirtieth. The citizens of Salisbury gave him the prescribed public dinner, and in the afternoon he drank tea "with about 20 ladies, who had been assembled for the occasion."

Thirty-five miles from Salisbury he came to Salem, "a small

but neat village, and like all the rest of the Moravian settlements, is governed by an excellent police, having within itself all kinds of artisans. The number of souls does not exceed 200." As in the Pennsylvania settlements, Washington appeared to take a special interest in the Moravian way of living. He spent a day with them, visiting the shops of the tradesmen in the morning and inspecting the "houses of accommodation for the single men and sisters of the fraternity, and their place of worship." He invited six of the principal citizens to dine with him that afternoon, and in the evening he went to hear them perform the music of their church "on a variety of instruments."

Governor Alexander Martin had come down to Salem to meet him, and in his company Washington set out at four o'clock on June 2 (one wonders what the Governor thought of the President's traveling habits) for Guilford, North Carolina, "where there was a considerable gathering of people who had received notice of my intention to be there today and came to satisfy their curiosity." This was an oblique reference to Washington's feeling that a good many of the people who came to look at him on his travels (everywhere, not just in the South) were inspired more by curiosity than by respect and devotion, an idea that offended him.

By this time, too, he was weary of ceremony and attention; he scented the green fields of Mount Vernon near at hand, and consequently was in no mood to dally any longer than necessary. He prevailed on the Governor to dismiss the party of light horse which met them outside Guilford, and to countermand his orders for similar attentions on his progress through the state. He even persuaded Martin not to ride with him from Guilford to the state line.

Shortly after six o'clock on the morning of June 4, a Saturday, he crossed the boundary and came once more into "the country," his beloved Virginia. Next day, about noon, at the Staunton River, he met Colonel Isaac Coles, a former member of Congress from the district, and accepted his pressing invitation to stop with him, to refresh himself and his horses.

Washington adds that he left his servants and the horses "at one of the usually indifferent taverns at the ferry, that they might give no trouble or be inconvenient to a private family."

He stayed with the Colonel all of the following day, June 6, departing at daybreak of the seventh. He was detained again at Charlotte Court House, fifteen miles farther on, where he had stopped for breakfast, by the necessity of reshoeing some horses.

The remainder of the journey through Virginia was without particular incident, except that he had difficulty crossing the James River at Carter's Ferry, finding the regular ferryboat laid up for repairs. He had to cross piecemeal in a small river boat. Beyond the ferry he found the roads "very bad" and the weather "very sultry," and in the bargain lost his way, but about three o'clock on the tenth he reached his Sister Lewis' in Fredericksburg. On June 12 his carriage pulled up at the portico of Mount Vernon in time for dinner, so far ahead of his schedule that he had fourteen days to remain at home before he had to meet again with the Federal City commissioners at Georgetown.

Writing to David Humphreys on July 20, Washington described his presidential tour of the South in three paragraphs which summed it up admirably:

"In my last I mentioned my intention of visiting the Southern states, which I have since accomplished, and have the pleasure to inform you that I performed a journey of 1887 miles without meeting with any interruption by sickness, bad weather, or any untoward accident. Indeed, so highly were we favored that we arrived at each place where I proposed to make any halt on the very day I fixed upon before we set out. The same horses performed the whole tour, and although much reduced in flesh, kept up their full spirits to the last day.

"I am much pleased that I have taken this journey, as it has enabled me to see with my own eyes the situation of the country through which we traveled, and to learn more accurately the disposition of the people than I could have done by an information.

388

"The country appears to be in a very improving state, and industry and frugality are becoming much more fashionable than they have hitherto been there. Tranquillity reigns among the people, with that disposition towards the general government which is likely to preserve it. They begin to feel the good effects of equal laws and equal protection. The farmer finds a ready market for his produce, and the merchant calculates with more certainty on his payments. Manufacturers have as yet made but little progress in that part of the country, and it will probably be a long time before they are brought to that state to which they have already arrived in the middle and eastern parts of the Union."

Except for those well-dressed and elegant ladies, no more was needed.

# Chapter 2

## Virginia Gentleman

What kind of man was this traveler, the gentleman from Virginia?

In the 153 years since he died, the answers have filled dozens of volumes, and the estimates have covered the whole range from idolatry to idol smashing. To Americans of this century, conditioned by nineteenth-century teaching and writing to regard Washington as a plaster saint, the noble picture on the schoolroom wall, the attempts of the twenties to make him more of a human being were shocking. People read these "debunking" biographies with the affronted fascination of a pious lady tracing dirty words scrawled on a sidewalk. The present generation (the minority, at least, who are interested) is only now beginning to absorb the more balanced picture that modern scholarship has enabled us to put together.

Still—what kind of man was he?

If John Adams' word were taken for it, he was an overrated hero, and in fact something of a fraud, to put the mildest construction on his estimates. These strictures have to be viewed in the light of Adams' overweening jealousy of Washington, which survived long after his rival had died. But they are nonetheless interesting when it is considered that Adams was not a disgruntled officer, a Jeffersonian democrat, or the proprietor of a republican newspaper.

"The history of our Revolution will be one continued lie from one end to the other," Adams wrote during his vice-presidency to his friend, the redoubtable Philadelphia physician, Dr. Benjamin Rush. "The essence of the whole will be that Dr. Franklin's electrical rod smote the earth and out sprang General Washington. That Franklin electrified him with his rod, and

*390*

thence forward these two conducted all the policy, negotiations, legislatures, and war."

The letters written in Adams' retirement, when he had time to consider the injustices, real and imaginary, of his life, were even more caustic. Answering a question from Dr. Rush about what talents he thought Washington possessed to gain such renown, Adams replied, on November 11, 1807, with an enumeration which told more of Adams than it did of Washington, because most of the "talents" he ascribed to the General were attributes he himself did not possess.

Washington had a handsome face and a tall stature, Adams said, "like the Hebrew sovereign chosen because he was taller by the head than the other Jews." Adams was neither handsome nor tall.

Washington was able to strike graceful attitudes, and he moved gracefully. No one would ever mistake Adams for one born to the drawing room.

Washington had a large fortune. Adams was far from being a poor man, and in some ways displayed his wealth more flamboyantly than the General, but no doubt he envied his rival all that real estate.

Washington was a Virginian, and as the world knew, Adams added ironically, "Virginia geese are all swans." That was the New Englander speaking, though in other respects he was not provincial.

Washington had the gift of silence. The loquacious Adams was not concerned as to whether the General's silence might ensue because his teeth hurt him or because he was not normally talkative.

There were other citations in a similar vein, and Adams concluded his letter: "Here, you see I have made out ten talents without saying a word about reading, thinking, or writing. . . ."

The older he grew, the more convinced Adams was that the world had been sold a bill of goods about Washington. "The Great Character was a Character of Convention," Adams told Rush in 1812 (in letters written March 19 and April 22). He made the astounding, and palpably untrue, disclosure that there had been an express agreement among statesmen and officers to "blow the trumpets of panegyric in concert, to cover and dissemble all faults and errors. . . ." In sum, he concluded, "That Washington was not a scholar is certain. That he was too illiterate, unlearned, unread for his station and reputation is equally past dispute." [1]

There are other such prejudiced opinions, but from sources not nearly so close to the subject. Among these is the English schoolmaster and divine, the Rev. Jonathan Boucher, one of those who struggled manfully to educate Jack Custis, who in turn manfully resisted the attempt. While this battle was going on in Boucher's school at Annapolis, he corresponded voluminously with Washington. When the Revolution came, however, he was an ardent Loyalist, and in that light one must read his portrait of Washington. After demolishing his family background, and dismissing his military record in one sentence of summary—"At Braddock's defeat, and every subsequent occasion throughout the war, he acquitted himself much in the same manner as in my judgment he has since done—i.e., decently but never greatly"—Boucher moved on to an equally condensed and unflattering summary of Washington's character:

" . . . Though occasion may call forth traits of character that never could have been discovered in the more sequestered scenes of life, I cannot conceive how he could, otherwise than through the interested representations of party, have ever been spoken of as a great man. He is shy, silent, stern, slow and cautious, but has no quickness of parts, extraordinary penetration, nor an elevated style of thinking. In his moral character he is regular, temperate, strictly just and honest (excepting that as a Virginian, he has lately found out that there is no moral turpitude in not paying what he confesses he owes to a British creditor), and as I always thought, religious, having heretofore been pretty constant and even exemplary in his attendance on public worship in the Church of England. But he seems to have nothing generous or affectionate in his nature. Just before the close of the last war he married the widow Custis, and thus came into possession of her large jointure. He never had any children and lived very much like a gentleman at Mount Vernon, in Fairfax County, where the most distinguished part of his character was that he was an admirable farmer." [2]

Washington would have said "amen" and "thank you" to that final sentence. After his youthful honor had been satisfied, he had no better desire in life than to be "an admirable farmer." His enemies, and even some of his old friends, did not believe his protestations against being in public life, but a thousand pieces of evidence lead the student of his career to take his protests at face value.

Having read Boucher and Adams on the subject of total character, and the contrary testimony of many other witnesses in previous chapters, it appears that Washington was very large or very small, depending on whose mirror did the reflecting.

That was even true of his physical appearance. There is considerable variation in Washington portraiture, as experts have pointed out at length, but whether any of them depicts him accurately in every respect is doubtful. George Washington Parke Custis wrote this critique of Washington art in 1839:

"The Head of Stuart is incomparably the best likeness of the Chief in his latter days, but in the person, that great Master of Portrait Painting failed entirely. Trumbull has painted the only correct portraiture of Washington as regards the person — for the person of Washington was unique, like that of no one else. Stuart has given a plumpness, or fleshiness, rounded off on the models of the Academy. Washington was never fleshy, as witness his weight. I placed the weights in the scale at the Mt. Vernon Mill, the very last time that the General was weighed, accompanied as he was by Governor Crawford of Canada. The Governor, not so tall by several inches, but compact and fleshy, outweighed the General by a good many pounds. Washington then observed that in his very best days, his weight never exceeded from 210 to 220 pounds. This weight for a man rising

393

six feet in height, of extraordinary breadth of frame, [he was twenty-one inches across the shoulders] and a matchless combination of bone and muscle, would indicate anything but fleshiness. That the Hero was a 'man of thews and sinews,' everybody knows, but of his hand and wrist, moderns have not even an idea." [3]

Enlarging on this appreciation in his *Recollections of Washington*, which is lamentably inaccurate considering the unrivaled opportunity Martha's grandson had to view the man intimately, Custis argues that the well-known Washington portraits show in his figure "a fullness that it did not possess," especially an "abdominal enlargement greater than in the life ...." Discussing Trumbull's equestrian portrait of 1790, a copy of which hangs in New York's City Hall, he asserts that this is one of two instances (the other an engraving by Loisler) in which "his matchless limbs have been faithfully portrayed ...."

When Colonel Benjamin Tallmadge, of Litchfield, heard about this remark, the General's former aide is said to have burst out laughing. The legs in Trumbull's portrait, he said, were his. Washington could not spare the time the painter required, he recalled, and since mutual friends had often remarked about how much alike their legs were (the fashions of the day made such comparisons natural), the General asked his aide to stand in for him. Trumbull examined Tallmadge's legs and, pronouncing them an exact match, gratefully accepted the substitution.

Few men in public life have ever been painted as often as Washington, and it is small wonder his patience sometimes gave out, particularly during the Revolution and his presidential years, when he had the weight of the nation on his shoulders. Once he summarized his career as a model in a letter to Francis Hopkinson:

"In for a penny, in for a pound is an old adage. I am so hackneyed to the touches of the painter's pencil that I am now altogether at their beck, and sit like patience on a monument whilst they are delineating the lines of my face.

"It is a proof among many others of what habit and custom can effect. At first I was as impatient at the request and as restive under the operation as a colt is of the saddle. The next time I submitted very reluctantly, but with less flouncing. Now no dray moves more readily to the thill than I do to the painter's chair. . . ."

When it came to describing in words what Washington looked like, there was the widest possible variation, as noted. One of the earliest descriptions remains the best, that written by his friend George Mercer in 1760, relating how Washington appeared to him the year before, when he took his seat in the House of Burgesses.

" . . . Straight as an Indian," Mercer said, "measuring six feet two inches in his stockings, and weighing 175 pounds . . . . His frame is padded with well-developed muscles, indicating great strength. His bones and joints are large, as are his feet and hands. He is wide-shouldered, but has not a deep or round chest, is neat-waisted, but is broad across the hips and has rather long legs and arms. His head is well shaped though not large, but is gracefully poised on a superb neck. A large and straight rather than prominent nose, blue-gray penetrating eyes which are widely separated and overhung by a heavy brow. His face is long rather than broad, with high, round cheekbones, and terminates in a good firm chin. He has a clear though rather a colorless pale skin, which burns with the sun. A pleasing, benevolent, though a commanding countenance, dark brown hair, which he wears in a queue. His mouth is large and generally firmly closed, but which from time to time discloses some defective teeth. His features are regular and placid, with all the muscles of his face under perfect control, though inflexible and expressive of deep feeling when moved by emotion. In conversation he looks you full in the face, is deliberate, deferential and engaging. His voice is agreeable rather than strong. His demeanor at all times composed and dignified. His movements and gestures are graceful, his walk majestic, and he is a splendid horseman."

As late as 1775, Silas Deane observed that the General had "a very young look and an easy soldier-like air and gesture." When he became President, a good many visitors remarked the "settled aspect of melancholy" which Maclay exaggerated, but Jefferson says of him, "His person, you know, was fine, his stature exactly what one would wish, his deportment easy, erect and noble." In the last years of his second term, William Sullivan wrote of his "strong, bony, muscular frame, without fullness of covering, well formed and straight. He was a man of most extraordinary strength. In his own house, his action was calm, deliberate and dignified, without pretension to gracefulness or peculiar manner, but merely natural, and such as one would think it should be in such a man. When walking in the street, his movement had not the soldierly air which might be expected . . . . At the age of sixty-five, time had done nothing towards bending him out of his natural erectness. His deportment was invariably grave; it was sobriety that stopped short of sadness."

One of the most remarkable descriptions, not alone because it varies so sharply from most others, is one the traveler Isaac Weld set down in 1797, when it seemed to him that Washington's chest was full and his limbs, though rather slender, were well shaped and muscular, but "his head is small, in which respect he resembles the make of a great number of his countrymen. His eyes are of a light gray color, and in proportion to the length of his face, his nose is long. Mr. Stewart [Stuart], the eminent portrait painter, told me that there were features in his face totally different from what he ever observed in that of any other human being; the sockets for the eyes, for instance, are larger than what he ever met with before, and the upper part of the nose broader. All his features, he observed, were indicative of the strongest and most ungovernable passions, and had he been born in the forests, it was his opinion that he would have been the fiercest man among the savage tribes."

That was the kind of man George Washington was physically, then, and you could take your choice from Stuart's fanciful view all the way to the ecstatic descriptions depicting him as a god. The net impression remains that he was a tall, well-built, fine-looking man, whose most unusual features were his large hands and long arms, and his long, muscular, superbly proportioned legs.

What else was he?

A man who slowly developed a continental point of view about his country, until he had in his mind what few Americans of his time possessed: a picture of the continent whole, even the vast stretches he had never seen. As a result of his absorbing interest in agriculture, he had a detailed mental map set in the large one, showing the Atlantic seaboard, its resources, appearance and potentialities.

Of the many evidences in his correspondence of this knowledge, the most striking are in the series of letters to Sir John Sinclair, the noted Scottish agricultural economist. Here, writing to one who shared his deep interest, he let himself go for pages in detailed analyses of climate, soil, crops and the American agricultural potential.

He knew, for example, that the cold New England climate consumed in winter a good part of what was produced in summer, but the fine grass crops were conducive to the raising of excellent horses, which were then an important American item of export to the West Indies. He knew that fish, not wheat, was the climate-determined future of New England agriculture, and he saw that the citizens of these states, expanding from the tight little insular civilization they had built, would soon be spreading out over the country, filling up particularly the Ohio country and western New York, as they were already doing.

Sometimes his prejudices affected his good judgment. Pennsylvania, he granted, was "a large state," but because of Philadelphia's fame in Europe, "has become the general receptacle of foreigners from all countries, and of all descriptions, many of whom soon take an active part in the politics of the state, and coming over full of prejudices against their own governments, some against all government, you will be enabled without any comment of mine to draw your own inference of their con-

*397*

duct." Here could be heard the echoings of those hard days of the wilderness campaigns, and of the Revolution, when the Pennsylvania farmers, the Quakers and the Loyalist Philadelphians seemed to him to be in an evil conspiracy.

He was inclined to promote whenever it was possible the idea he had held firmly from his youth, that the tidewater country, with its numerous rivers thrusting long fingers into the rich interior of the nation, was destined to be the center of American commerce, as soon as the vast network of inland waterways could be developed properly. Thus he wrote to Sinclair:

"But the western parts of the last-mentioned state [Delaware] and of Virginia, quite to the line of North Carolina, above tidewater, and more especially above the Blue Mountains are similar to those of Pennsylvania between the Susquehanna and Potomac Rivers in soil, climate and productions, and in my opinion will be considered, if it is not considered so already, as the Garden of America, forasmuch as it lies between the two extremes of heat and cold, partaking in a degree of the advantages of both without feeling much the inconveniences of either, and with truth it may be said, is among the most fertile lands in America, east of the Appalachian Mountains."

As for the rest of the South, he was disdainful of its prospects: "Towards the seaboard of all the Southern states (and further South the more so) the country is low, sandy and unhealthy, for which reason I shall say little concerning them, for as I should not choose to be an inhabitant of them myself, I ought not to say anything that would induce others to be so." [4] *

One of Washington's wisest observations on the state of agriculture was contained in a letter to Alexander Hamilton on No-

* In this letter, from which the above quotations are excerpts, Washington was in effect acting as a real estate salesman. Sir John, at that moment, was thinking of investing in American acres, and possibly coming to live in this country. In fairness, Washington described the whole eastern part of the United States, from the standpoint of a prospective estate owner, but then he did his best to sell his English correspondent on the "Garden of America." Specifically, he mentioned that George William Fairfax's old estate, Belvoir, was still up for sale. In this and other letters, he also offered sections of Mount Vernon itself, though not of course the main house and its surrounding acres.

vember 2, 1796, wherein he put his finger squarely on what is still in our time a national problem. He wrote:

"It must be obvious to every man who considers the agriculture of this country (even in the best improved parts of it) and compares the produce of our lands with those of other countries, no ways superior to them in natural fertility, how miserably defective we are in the management of them, and that if we do not fall on a better mode of treating them, how ruinous it will prove to the landed interest. Ages will not produce a systematic change without public attention and encouragement, but a few years more of increased sterility will drive the inhabitants of the Atlantic States westwardly for support, whereas if they were taught how to improve the old, instead of going in pursuit of new and productive soils, they would make those acres which now scarcely yield them anything turn out beneficial to themselves, to the mechanics, by supplying them with the staff of life on much cheaper terms; to the merchants, by increasing their commerce and exportation; and to the community generally, by the influx of wealth resulting therefrom."

Whenever he spoke of his own Virginia, even in the most casual way, Washington could not keep out a note of affection. He calls it "an infant woody country," but full of "the Virginia hospitality which is the most agreeable entertainment we can give." It was a territory he knew with the intimacy of one who had lived close to it all his life until war and public duties took him away temporarily. Even the vast wilderness of the Great Dismal Swamp was not strange to him. Once, examining it with his constant long view of what it would mean, reclaimed, in the inland navigation scheme, he lay on the ground at its border through the night, turning over its possibilities in his mind and planning its exploration.

He spent as much time as he could spare from a busy life promoting the grand project of linking the Ohio lands and the tidewater country. When the Revolution was over, he founded and became first president of the Potomac Navigation Company. One of his aides, John Fitzgerald, was on the board of directors, and the two men often made trips up and down the river, inspecting and planning. Sometimes they rode, at other times they navigated in sailboats or canoes between Georgetown and Harper's Ferry. However they traveled, one could be certain that these days were among the happiest Washington ever knew.

He lived to see land travel transformed remarkably in his own section of the nation, not realizing, apparently, that with every improvement the long-range prospects of the Potomac Navigation Company became dimmer. By 1785, for example, there was stage service three times a week from Norfolk through Hampton, Richmond, Fredericksburg and Alexandria, and from Alexandria, to the principal cities of every Eastern state, except Annapolis, which was off the post road to Baltimore. From any of these Southern points, a traveler could go by stage as far north as Portsmouth, New Hampshire, and not have to wait more than three days if he missed one departure. The journey from Richmond to Boston took, normally, ten or twelve days, during the "travel season," from April 1 to December 1. At other times, everyone was at the mercy of the weather and there was no such thing as a regular schedule. Southward to Charleston, there were no stages at this period, which accounts for the lack of good accommodation Washington found when he made his presidential tour. [5]

The travel was not all outward to Philadelphia, New York and Boston, by any means. Besides the normal traffic to such provincial towns as Baltimore, Annapolis, Richmond, Fredericksburg and Alexandria, there was a constant flow to such remote Western spots as the famed Warm Springs of Berkeley, or Bath. Today as Berkeley Springs, West Virginia, this thriving resort must certainly be the oldest watering place in America; it was already well known in 1748, when Washington first visited it.

As a resorter at these springs, whose efficacy he doubted, George saw the place grow from the most primitive accommodations to a cottage colony which had both its rich "summer people" and its poor "natives," who struggled to it at all seasons of the year, hoping for the cures they could not afford from medicine.

He had gone there first in 1748, as noted, to recover from one of his bouts with ill-health, but he returned in 1750 with his brother Lawrence, who was seeking relief from his lung ailment. George thought the springs in those days were situated badly, "on the east side of a steep mountain, and enclosed by hills on all sides, so that the afternoon's sun is hid by 4 o'clock and the fogs hang over us until 9 or 10, which occasion great damps, and the mornings and evenings to be cool."

The waters were taken inside and out, at a temperature of 72 to 74 degrees, making the bathing more pleasant than the drinking, although they did not have the medicinal taste of some springs. They could not, of course, help Lawrence's tuberculosis.

George was there again for his health in 1761, with Martha, and sent home an excellent description of what he saw: "We found of both sexes about 200 people at this place, full of all manner of diseases and complaints, some which are much benefited, while others find no relief from the waters. Two or three doctors are here, but whether attending as physicians or to drink of the waters I know not. It is thought the springs will soon begin to lose their virtues, and the weather get too cold for people not well provided to remain here . . .

"The place I am told, and indeed have found it so already, is supplied with provisions of all kinds; good beef and venison, fine veal, lambs, fowls, &c. &c., may be bought at almost any time, but lodgings can be had on no terms but building for them, and I am of opinion that numbers get more hurt by their manner of lying than the waters can do them good. Had we not succeeded in getting a tent and marquee from Winchester, we should have been in a most miserable situation here . . . . My fevers are a good deal abated, although my pains grow rather worse, and my sleep equally disturbed. What effect the waters may have upon me I can't say at present, but I expect nothing from the air — this certainly must be unwholesome. . . ."[6]

When he returned with Martha and the children six years later, in the summer of 1767, the visit was for pleasure as much as for health, and the character of the Springs was gradually changing to take in "resorters" as well as the ill. The Washingtons no longer had to live in a tent, but rented a cottage belonging to George Mercer. A baker had set up shop and provided the bread that formerly had to be baked by those who wanted it. A butcher was there, too, with veal, mutton, young pig and venison. There was chicken, and plenty of eggs and vegetables, and with these provisions the cook Washington had brought from home fared admirably. Probably he even had his evening glass of madeira. Except that the cottage was much too small, the Washington family lived well.

He had a fine time that summer. He met a comrade-in-arms from the days of the war with the French, Colonel John Armstrong, of the Pennsylvania troops, and presumably they talked of the old campaigns and of surveying, which Armstrong also practiced. The Pennsylvanian hoped the Springs would help his chronic rheumatism.

If anyone was bored, it was the children, who had no amusements whatever and must have found life exceedingly dull after the pleasures of Mount Vernon. Jack Custis was then nearly fourteen, an idle, easygoing, spoiled lad. Patsy was about twelve, studying music and beginning to be a young lady, but still a child.

It was Patsy who brought the family back to the Springs two years later, in hopes that the waters would improve her failing health; Jackie was by this time in school. They lived again in the Mercer cottage, entertaining the Fairfaxes and others, who were also summer residents that year, until the September chill drove them home, with poor Patsy's health still declining.

Washington visited the Springs now and again in later years, as thousands do in our own time. The waters today are bottled, a state park houses visitors, a sanatorium takes care of the ill, and the natives are engaged in light manufacturing.

There were more favored spots to visit nearer home. Often the family made excursions to Maryland, and in the years before the war it was the practice to go up to Annapolis for the races, where Washington failed to excel at the forerunner of the parimutuels. In one trip to the track, he lost fifteen pounds, and in the evening he did no better with the Maryland card players.

Fredericksburg was a place full of associations for George, as long as he lived. As a young man, he could usually find his friends at Hugh Mercer's drugstore; in those days, as now, the village sports were usually to be found at the neighborhood pharmacy, which was hampered in its role only by the lack of Coca-Cola. Later, Washington often stopped at the Rising Sun Inn, built by his brother Charles, whose landlord eventually became General George Weedon in the Revolution.

In Alexandria, Washington frequented Gadsby's Tavern, later the City Hotel, and in its ballroom he enjoyed many an assembly. Tradition says that he recruited his 1754 troops in a building adjoining it, and that he announced Virginia's adoption of the Constitution from its steps. Only a month before his death he had been invited to attend the winter season of dances, and sent this regretful note to the Gentlemen of the Alexandria Assemblies: "Mrs. Washington and myself have been honored by your polite invitation to the Assemblies at Alexandria this winter, and thank you for this mark of attention. But alas! our dancing days are no more. We wish, however, all those who have relish for so agreeable and innocent an amusement all the pleasures the season will afford."

Washington belonged to Masonic Lodge No. 39 in Alexandria, as he did to Fredericksburg Lodge No. 4. He interested himself in the affairs of the former town, leaving money in his will to Alexandria Academy, and paying pew rent to Christ Church.

He was a man, then, who knew the land, and understood both

403

its uses and pleasures, and in his own "country" was a constant traveler.

But what occupied his mind, when it was not filled with the details of military movements and the problems of the nation? There were those who said he did not possess what it is the present fashion to call "inner resources," that Adams was right when he charged that the President was too unlearned and unread for his station.

There was a measure of truth in this. Washington's reading and learning could not be compared with Jefferson's, for example, or with that of some of the other more polished minds about him. His spelling and grammar would not have passed muster with a nineteenth-century schoolteacher, when such matters were considered more important than they are today, but on the other hand, he was no worse than the majority of the gentlemen in his time and place. Few of his contemporaries could boast an impeccable syntax, and a good many of these had been educated abroad. Washington improved as he grew older; he suffered relapses only when he wrote in haste or anger. His early correspondence, so stiff and imitative, became in time a flow of adequately expressed, if not brilliant, letters.

He read a little, but not widely. His account books show how he acquired a library dealing with the things that interested him most — the lives of national leaders elsewhere in the world, books about the wars and military tactics, and agricultural treatises. Probably the first book he owned and enjoyed was The Young Man's Companion, a volume of little essays designed to guide aspiring youth from birth to death.

Of George's education, only a little is definitely known. It has never been established who instructed him, although traditions are abundant. The Rev. Mr. Boucher's assertion that his instructor was a convict servant named Hobby, whom his father brought over from Europe, was repeated by Parson Weems and has often been accepted as fact, but Hobby has never been positively identified by scholars. Another tradition, and one more likely to be true, is that George was educated principally at the Rev. James Marye's school in Fredericksburg, where it is said he was the colonial equivalent of the modern "grind" and attracted attention only by "romping with one of the largest girls." In any event, it appears that most of his schooling occurred between his seventh and eleventh years, and by instructors near home. His mother's overprotective concern for her first-born presumably kept him from getting the English education his two half brothers had enjoyed.[7]

Washington learned the things he had to know at first hand, and his natural abilities supplied the rest. Thus he was an extremely able but not a cultured man, like Jefferson and Franklin. His mind was an inventive one. In March of 1760 he invented a new kind of plow, and at that early date he began experiments with grafting. A tradition that is probably true says that he made the first pump used in Alexandria. At Mount Vernon, he introduced the best breeds of mule to America, and spent considerable time improving the breeds of sheep, hogs, horses, cattle and dogs.

His diaries show that he brought the same patient grasp of detail to his farming that he constantly applied to administering armies and the government. In 1788, for example, he counted the number of peas and beans in a pint measure for each one of six varieties, and from these figures estimated the area of ground he would need to prepare for planting, and the number of hills a bushel of each variety would plant.

He was a man, then, whose particular genius enabled him to make the most of his possibilities.

What were some of his lesser characteristics?

Well, he was a man who enjoyed his food and liked to have it on time. One of the most plaintive letters he ever wrote was his plea to Sally Fairfax, in November 1757, when he found himself, as a young bachelor, ordered by the doctor to go on a diet which omitted meats, "substituting jellies and such kinds of foods for a constancy. . . ." Evidently the larder was bare and the cooking inadequate, because he pleaded to Sally: ". . . as my sister is from home, I have no person that has been used to making these kind of things, and no directions, I find myself under a necessity of applying to you for your recipe book for a little while, and indeed for such materials to make jellies as you think I may not at the time have, for I can't get Hartshorn Shavings anywhere. I must also beg the favor of you to lend me a pound, or a smaller quantity if you can't spare that, of Hyson Tea. I am just out and cannot get a supply anywhere in these parts. Please also to lend me a bottle or two of Mountain or Canary wine. Mr. Green directs me to drink a glass or two of this every day mixed with water of Gum Arabic . . . ."

During the Revolution, when rations were short, Washington never complained to those around him, but in letters to old friends elsewhere he was, on occasion, quite frank. "We are debarred from the pleasure of good living," he wrote once, "which, sir . . . to one who has always been used to it, must go somewhat hard to be confined to a little salt provision and water."

He liked Indian hoecakes, honey and tea for breakfast, and as noted elsewhere, dined on one meat dish, although he ate heartily. Fish pleased him especially. Desserts he could do without if necessary, and seldom ate much of them, but he did like a bowl of fruit and a supply of nuts to finish off a meal. As for drinking, he was moderate; there is no reason to believe he was ever drunk. Following the English custom of the day, he consumed about four or five glasses of madeira with a meal, according to Custis. At other hours of the day he might drink a small glass of punch, or a draught of beer, and of course he was as regular a tea drinker as any born and bred Englishman.

His Sister Lewis knew his likings, perhaps better than anyone except Martha. She wrote to him in 1789: "When I last had the pleasure of seeing you, I observed your fondness for honey. I have got a large pot of very fine in the comb, which I shall send by the first opportunity."

Whatever he ate, he insisted that the meal be fitted into the schedule of his day, which moved from event to event with the regularity of a clock, and to which everyone was expected to conform. Ashbel Green recalls: "At his dinner parties he allowed five minutes for the variation of time pieces, and after they were expired, he would wait for no one. Some lagging members of Congress came in when not only dinner was begun, but considerably advanced. His only apology was, 'Sir, or gentlemen, we are too punctual for you'; or in pleasantry, 'Gentlemen, I have a cook who never asks whether the company has come, but whether the hour has come.'"

The Rev. Dr. Green was anxious in his reminiscences to dispel the idea that Washington was not religious. He recalls a dinner occasion when "the President's mind was probably occupied with some interesting concern, and on going to the table he began to ask a blessing himself. He uttered but a word or two, when bowing to me, he requested me to proceed, which I accordingly did. I mention this because it shows that President Washington always asked a blessing himself, when a chaplain was not present."

But was he really religious?

There were those who questioned it in his lifetime, long before the debunkers got to work. In the years immediately after his death, when it was not popular to question any part of the Washington legend, an Albany minister preached a sermon one Sunday in which he declared that the President always left the Episcopal church which he attended in Philadelphia as soon as the Sacrament was to be administered, and would come no more on communion days when the rector reprimanded him from the pulpit. An admirer of Washington's who heard the sermon wrote to Dr. James Abercrombie, who had been Bishop White's pastor at the church during the President's Philadelphia residence, and asked him whether this story was true. Dr. Abercrombie replied:

"... Observing that on Sacrament Sundays, General Washington, immediately after the desk and pulpit services, went out with the greater part of the congregation, always leaving Mrs. Washington with the communicants, she invariably being one, I considered it my duty, in a sermon on public worship, to state the unhappy tendency of example, particularly of those in elevated stations, who turned their backs upon the celebration of the Lord's Supper. I acknowledge the remark was intended for the President, and as such he received it.

"A few days after, in conversation with, I believe, a Senator of the United States, he told me he had dined the day before with the President, who, in the course of conversation at the table, said that on the preceding Sunday he had received a very just reproof from the pulpit for always leaving the church before the administration of the Sacrament; that he honored the preacher for his integrity and candor; that he had never considered the influence of his example; that he would never again give cause for the repetition of the reproof; and that, as he had never been a communicant, were he to become one then, it would be imputed to an ostentatious display of religious zeal, arising altogether from his elevated station. Accordingly, he afterwards never came on the morning of Sacrament Sunday, though at other times a constant attendant in the morning. . . .

"That Washington was a professing Christian is evident from his regular attendance in our church, but sir, I cannot consider any man as a real Christian who uniformly disregards an ordinance so solemnly enjoined by the divine Author of our holy religion, and considered as a channel of divine grace. This, sir, is all that I think it proper to state on paper. In a conversation, more latitude being allowed, more light might perhaps be thrown upon it. I trust, however, sir, you will not introduce my name in print. . . ." [8]

Dr. Abercrombie came as near to the truth as anyone can determine. Washington was certainly religious when it came to churchgoing, but it apparently was not fear of ostentation alone that prevented him from becoming a communicant. He seemed to be religious in a non-sectarian, unorganized, cosmic kind of manner. His avoidance of formal invocations of the Deity, except on state occasions, his vague references in letters to the "destiny" directing human affairs—all these and other pieces of evidence indicate that he observed the churchly aspects of religion because it was expected, but privately believed himself in the hands of a universal force which shaped his fate no matter what he did or did not do.

He was not as pious, then, as a good many patriots have imagined him.

Was he as cold and reserved as he appeared to most of those who saw him?

Again and again, in the writings of those who tried to describe his character, one encounters that Wilsonian aloofness; people did not feel at ease in his presence. His dignity was so monumental that no man could approach him closely.

Yet Jefferson says that "in the circle of his friends, where he might be unreserved with safety, he took a free share in conversation." According to James Madison, "in the company of two or three intimate friends, he was talkative, and when a little excited was sometimes fluent and even eloquent. . . . The story so often repeated of his never laughing . . . is wholly untrue; no man seemed more to enjoy gay conversation, though he took little part in it himself. He was particularly pleased with the jokes, good humor and hilarity of his companions."

Tradition offers several concrete instances of his hilarity, though it must be said they have more of the sound of legend than fact. More than a quarter century after Washington's death, a New York newspaper told of the day in the camp at Cambridge when a messenger brought the news that the British had sent out a large reconnoitering expedition from Boston. Instantly, so the story goes, headquarters was in turmoil as the officers who happened to be there made preparations to call out their troops. Some yelled for the horses, others for their arms, and in the midst of it the voice of General Greene was heard bellowing for his wig, shouting upstairs to the barber: "Bring my wig, you rascal, bring my wig."

"Your wig is behind the looking glass, sir," General Lee remarked.

Wheeling about, Greene saw himself in the mirror, with his wig reposing properly on his head. The story assures us that "Washington, in a fit of laughter, threw himself on the sofa"—a most unlikely occurrence.[9]

A Captain Blake reported that Washington even laughed at Valley Forge. An order had been issued that every officer or private found drunk would be punished by having to cut away one of the numerous stumps which had remained when the forest was cleared to make huts. One morning, on a regular tour of the camp, Washington observed a soldier attacking the only stump that remained and said to him: "Well, my good fellow, you have found the last stump."

The soldier did not look up, so it is said, or cease his chopping as he answered, "Yes, and now when an officer gets drunk there'll be no stump for him to cut!"

If Washington laughed as heartily at this sally as tradition relates, he must have been more easily amused than is commonly supposed.

At Trenton, he is supposed to have laughed when he overheard old General Scott tell his men that they had been shooting too high, and added, "For that reason, boys, whenever you see them fellows first begin to put their foot on this bridge, do you shin 'em."

Another unlikely tale is that General Lee refused to take the oath of allegiance, and when Washington demanded an explanation, replied, "As to King George, I am ready enough to absolve myself from all allegiance to him, but I have some scruples about the Prince of Wales." That, apparently, brought down the house.

But whether he laughed at one time or another—and it is established beyond doubt that he had no trouble laughing when something amused him—it is hard to believe that he was essentially a cold, reserved man when one recalls the emotional moments in his life. Nor does it seem that a man of such reserve would have written to Lafayette as he did. Disregarding the argument as to whether Lafayette exaggerated the warmth and intimacy of their friendship, Washington's letter to the General after they parted in November 1784 neatly sums up the affection of which he was capable, going hand in hand with the gloomy anticipation of death and disaster which runs through so many of his letters.

Lafayette had come down from Boston in the frigate *Nymphe* and, after landing at Yorktown, met his friend in Richmond on November 18, 1784, and went with him to Mount Vernon for a week. On December 5, Washington accompanied Lafayette as far as Annapolis, rode out a way with him in his own carriage toward Baltimore, then with a last embrace watched Lafayette's stage disappear. Three days later he wrote:

"In the moment of our separation upon the road as I traveled, and every hour since, I felt all that love, respect and attachment for you with which length of years, close connection and your merits have inspired me. I often asked myself, as our carriages distended, whether that was the last sight I ever should have of you? And though I wished to say no, fears answered yes. I called to mind the days of my youth, and found they had long since fled to return no more; that I was now descending the hill I had been 52 years climbing, and that though I was blessed with a good constitution, I was of a short-lived family, and might soon expect to be entombed in the dreary mansions of my fathers. These things darkened the shades and gave a gloom to the picture, consequently to my prospects of seeing you again: but I will not repine, I have had my day."

This curious fatalism of Washington's was expressed in a variety of ways. One was his absolute indifference to danger. During the war he often placed himself in an exposed position, apparently without thinking of it twice. It was not the reckless bravado of some extreme military types, but simply that by the time the Revolution occurred Washington had escaped death so often that he had apparently put it down to the "destiny" that guided him. If he was meant to be shot, he would be shot.

The stories of these escapes are innumerable. A British officer wrote to a friend in England that he once saw Washington's tall figure on a bay horse, and not knowing who it was, ordered three of his men to snipe at the target, then thought better of it. He called on Washington, who was only a hundred yards away, to stop. The General paused and looked in the British officer's direction, then went on again. The officer commanded once more and leveled his gun, but Washington cantered slowly away without looking back. Recalling the moment, the officer says he "could have lodged half a dozen balls in and about him before he was out of reach," but restrained himself because "it was not pleasant to fire at the back of an unoffending individual who was acquitting himself very coolly of his duty, so I let him alone." [10]

On another occasion, a certain British Major Ferguson, whose nephew was the Very Rev. Dr. Lee, once principal of the University of Edinburgh, saw three American officers walking on the opposite shore of a river, and when a small detachment of British soldiers near him raised their muskets to fire on the unsuspecting enemy, Ferguson struck down their guns and "reproved them sharply for their base conduct." The commotion attracted the attention of the American officers, one of whom raised his hat and bowed, acknowledging the courtesy. It was, of course, Washington himself, according to the tradition.[11]

Such were the amenities of war in Washington's day.

Some of the younger officers who observed the General's calm courage wondered why he scorned dueling even when provoked, as he was upon occasion.* It was because Washing-

* Thackeray, in *The Virginians*, has Washington as a young officer under Braddock fighting a duel. One of the sillier traditions asserts that George once fought Lord Fairfax over a young lady. At the time this alleged encounter took place, Lord Fairfax was fifty-four years old; Washington was thirteen.

ton regarded that variety of courage as brash, presumptuous and silly. After the incident at Monmouth, when the General and Lee had exchanged hot words as they met going in opposite directions from the battle, it was feared in some quarters that Lee, who loved dueling, would not hesitate to challenge Washington. The General's old friend, George Mason, was not worried. He wrote to Edmund Randolph on August 1, 1778: "You express a fear that General Lee will challenge our friend. Indulge no such apprehensions, for he too well knows the sentiments of General Washington on the subject of dueling. From his earliest manhood I have heard him express his contempt of the man who sends and the man who accepts a challenge, for he regards such acts as no proof of moral courage, and the practice he abhors as a relic of old barbarisms, repugnant alike to sound morality and Christian enlightenment."

He was a man of some sentiment and exceptional courage, then.

Was he rich? And how did he feel about money?

He was, and he liked it. His estate at the time of his death was said to be worth $530,000 not including Martha's property and Mount Vernon. Few Americans had more. His interest in the Dismal Swamp Company alone was valued at $20,000, and he owned thousands of acres of property besides.

Yet he was often compelled to borrow money. As the saying goes, he was always "crying poor" and with reason. His was the kind of wealth that produces little net income; consequently he was compelled to dip into capital to maintain himself, and often there was not enough liquid capital to warrant dipping. Except for an expense account, he took no money for his services as Commander-in-Chief and President. The presidential years were expensive in themselves, and of course Washington had to maintain appearances all his life—as the master of Mount Vernon, as the commander of the armies, as the President of the United States.

A letter he wrote to David Stuart on December 2, 1788, is

413

typical of his constant complaints about money: "The expensive manner in which I live (contrary to my wishes, but really unavoidable); the bad years of late, and my consequent short crops have occasioned me to run in debt and to feel more sensibly the want of money than I have ever done at any period of my whole life, and obliges me to look forward to every source from whence I have a right to expect relief. Under these circumstances I must ask you what prospect I have, and in what time (after it becomes due) I may expect to receive the present year's annuity from the estate of Mr. Custis?"

Washington did not want to live like a king, and he was not avaricious, but he wanted to live well, and the nature of his career compelled him to it. Only Martha's fortune saved him from real difficulties.

As a capitalist, then, what were Washington's views toward the proletariat?

It must be said they would not please a democrat, lower- or upper-case. To a present-day business executive, however, his management of Mount Vernon followed sound management practices, without the hampering effect of wages-and-hours legislation. In a series of instructions drawn up in 1789 for the benefit of his overseers and managers, he sets forth these basic principles:

"To request that my people may be at their work as soon as it is light, work till it is dark, and be diligent while they are at it, can hardly be necessary, because the propriety of it must strike every manager who attends to my interest or regards his own character, and who, on reflecting, must be convinced that lost labor is never to be regained, the presumption being that every laborer (male or female) does as much in the 24 hours as their strength without endangering the health, or constitution will allow of; but there is much more in what is called head work, that is in the manner of conducting business, than is generally imagined.

"For take two managers and give to each the same number of laborers, and let these laborers be equal in all respects. Let both these managers rise equally early, go equally late to rest, be equally active, sober and industrious, and yet in the course of the year, one of them, without pushing the hands that are under him more than the other, shall have performed infinitely more work. To what is this owing? Why, simply to contrivance resulting from that forethought and arrangement which will guard against the misapplication of labor, and doing it unseasonably. For in the affairs of farming or planting, more perhaps than in any other, it may justly be said there is a time for all things. . . ."

As for the working class in general, Washington held opinions that would have fastened on him in our time a wryly inappropriate label—Tory. Writing to the Rev. William Gordon on October 15, 1797, he declared:

"Workmen in most countries, I believe, are necessary plagues. In this [country], where entreaties as well as money must be used to obtain their work and keep them to their duty, they baffle all calculation in the accomplishment of any plan, or repairs they are engaged in, and require more attention to and looking after than can be well conceived. Numbers of these of all descriptions, having been employed by me ever since I came home . . . has allowed me little leisure for other occupations."

Did this hardheaded tycoon have the traditional softness of heart for women and children when he came home from the office?

The affirmative answer could hardly be exaggerated. There are even two poems extant which he committed as a youth, both quite normal. They are about love. One was an acrostic, apparently composed for a girl named Frances Alexander, but Washington stopped four letters from the end. Whether his muse had left him to go to the races at Annapolis, or whether he changed his mind about Frances, is not known. This was the acrostic:

> *From your bright sparkling Eyes, I was undone;*
> *Rays, you have more transparent than the sun,*
> *Amidst its glory in the rising Day,*
> *None can you equal in your bright array;*

> *Constant in your calm and unspotted Mind;*
> *Equal to all, but will to none Prove kind,*
> *So knowing, seldom one so Young, you'll Find*
> *Ah! Woe's me, that I should Love and conceal,*
> *Long have I wish'd, but never dare reveal,*
> *Even though severely Loves Pains I feel;*
> *Xerxes that great, was't free from Cupids Dart,*
> *And all the greatest Heroes, felt the smart.*

After getting past "Xerxes," it is surprising that young George felt himself unable to manage "nder."

To another lady, identity unknown, he composed this ode:

> *Oh Ye Gods why should my Poor Resistless Heart*
> *Stand to oppose thy might and Power*
> *At Last surrender to cupids feather'd Dart*
> *And now lays Bleeding every Hour*
> *For her that's Pityless of my grief and Woes*
> *And will not on me Pity take*
> *Ile sleep amongst my most Inveterate Foes*
> *And with gladness never wish to Wake*
> *In deluding sleepings let my Eyelids close*
> *That in an enraptured Dream I may*
> *In a soft lulling sleep and gentle repose*
> *Possess those joys denied by Day.* [12]

Tradition has it that Jane Souther, whose father's place adjoined Ferry Farm, was George's first love. Like Frances Alexander, she may have been one of those young ladies at whom the shy and awkward George, abashed in the company of females, gazed with natural longing and an excess of modesty.

Toward his secret love, Sally Fairfax, his manner was always carefully restrained, as the circumstances dictated, except for his one daring (and unanswered) letter. It appears that Martha was the only woman in his life with whom he ever enjoyed any intimacy, physical or otherwise. Somehow Martha has been no more able to emerge as a real woman from her portrait than her husband has been able to shake off the marble halo history has placed around his brow. Few Americans realize what a good-looking girl she was at twenty-six, when Washington met her. She had a small, well-rounded figure, dark hair, hazel eyes, and a vivacious charm. She also had a firm will, and in the opinion of some students, she fell far short of the intelligence and wit of women like Sally Fairfax, Elizabeth Schuyler and Catherine Greene.

But Washington did not weigh her defects and faults. He could never have Sally. Martha was young and pretty; she was also rich and a widow. Freeman rightly terms her "among the wealthiest and most desirable in Virginia." And if Washington was well aware of her worldly assets, in the realistic way of thinking in those supposedly romantic times, it was equally true that in picking a new husband after the death of her first, Martha Dandridge exercised her outstanding characteristic, common sense, and refused other eager suitors until the man with the proper qualifications came around.

The sentimental traditions of their courtship must be largely discounted, particularly Custis' recollection that they met for the first time when Washington paused in March 1758 on his way to Williamsburg, and was introduced to Martha by her neighbor, Major Chamberlayne, with whom the young Colonel had stopped to dine. Chamberlayne may have performed the introduction, but it probably took place the year before in Williamsburg, between April 27 and May 17, 1757, when the General Assembly was in session, Martha and her husband were there, and so was George; they could hardly have avoided meeting, perhaps saw each other several times, at the social events which occurred nearly every night of the session.

Later, one presumes, George heard of Custis' death in July 1757, and he must have resolved to call on Martha and assess the situation, as soon as his health permitted. (He was suffering from an indisposition in the winter and spring of 1758.) On his way to Williamsburg he stopped to see her, spending no more than a day (or a half day longer ) at the White House plantation. He returned the following week for a second visit. No proof exists that Martha promised to marry him after that second meeting; the actual engagement may not have been made until the following June. But Freeman presents most convincing proof that an understanding must have existed after their second March meeting: George ordered some new clothes from London — the best material for a suit, six pairs of shoes, and six pairs of gloves. Almost at the same time Martha sent an order to London—a nightgown to be dyed a "fashionable color," noting, "this gown is of good length for me."

Martha loved clothes and fashion. That was one of her weaknesses, and as Freeman remarks, it is the reason why no portrait of her conveys her charm and pleasant personality, since she would only pose wearing the enveloping cap that fashion demanded and her face is overshadowed by it. She had other primary faults: an anxiety about her children which led her into absurdities of overprotectiveness; and an almost pathologic fear of being alone. But to compensate she had a basic common sense, and she possessed one quality above all others which was necessary to the wife of a man in Washington's position — an absolute discretion. She never gossiped, never talked carelessly about her husband's affairs.

As First Lady, she presided over the President's social life with grace, tact and dignity. In a hundred small matters she stood helpfully at her husband's side, as on the occasion when she remarked, hearing the clock strike nine at a reception one New Year's Day, "The General always retires at nine, and I usually precede him."

Yet she was unhappy in official life. She wrote to a friend from New York: "I live a very dull life here and know nothing that passes in the town. I never go to any public place — indeed, I think I am more like a state prisoner than anything else; there is certain bounds set for me which I must not depart from — and as I cannot do as I like, I am obstinate and stay at home a great deal."

The more intimate side of her relationship with her husband we shall never know, since she carried discretion to the point of destroying all his letters to her, with a few exceptions. It is unlikely, however, that they would disclose anything except the fact that George loved his wife, if not with the passionate devotion he might have given to Sally Fairfax, if they had married, at least with constancy, kindness and respect.

Judging from his letters, Washington's attitude toward sex was conditioned by the necessities of public life and by his undeviating adherence to convention. He viewed the more exciting lives of other men with a certain wistfulness, as is evident in this letter to Theodorick Bland:

"By Colonel Fitzhugh I had the satisfaction to receive the humorous account you were pleased to give me of your nocturnal journey to Fredericksburg. I recollect very well the lady whom you mention to have had for a fellow traveler, and if you should chance to be in her company again, I should be much obliged by your presenting my compliments to her. The even tenor of my life (in which I can expect to meet with few extraordinary adventures) as well as my long seclusion in a great measure from the exhilarating scenes of mixed society, must be an apology for my not attempting (with such provocatives to gaiety) to say some more sprightly things in reply to the brilliancy of her dialogue, or the vivacity with which you have reported it. I commend you, however, for passing the time in as merry a manner as you possibly could; it is assuredly better to go laughing than crying through the rough journey of life."[13]

Sometimes, though rarely, Washington was capable of a heavy-handed double entendre. The following example, a letter to the Rev. William Gordon, dated December 20, 1784, is Washington in a most unusual vein—and to a clergyman at that:

"I am glad to hear that my old acquaintance Colonel Ward is yet under the influence of vigorous passions. I will not ascribe the intrepidity of his late enterprise to a mere *flash* of desires, because in his military career he would have learnt how to distinguish between false alarms and a serious movement. Charity therefore induces me to suppose that like a prudent general, he had reviewed his *strength*, his arms and ammunition before he got involved in an action. But if these have been neglected, and he has been precipitated into the measure, let me advise him to make the *first* onset upon his fair del Toboso with vigor, that the impression may be deep, if it cannot be lasting or frequently renewed."

Toward the marriage state itself, Washington expressed a certain ambivalence. To his friend the Marquis de Chastellux he struck a conventional, almost a coy note:

"In reading your very friendly and acceptable letter . . . I was, as you may well suppose, not less delighted than surprised to come across that plain American word, 'my wife.' A wife! Well, my dear Marquis, I can hardly refrain from smiling to find you are caught at last. I saw, by the eulogium you often made on the happiness of domestic life in America, that you had swallowed the bait and that you would as surely be taken (one day or another) as you was a philosopher and a soldier. So your day has, at length, come. I am glad of it with all my heart and soul. It is quite good enough for you. Now you are well served for coming to fight in favor of the American rebels, all the way across the Atlantic ocean, by catching that terrible contagion, domestic felicity, which like the smallpox or the plague, a man can have only once in his life, because it commonly lasts him (at least with us in America, I don't know how you manage these matters in France) for his whole lifetime. And yet after all the maledictions you so richly merit on the subject, the worst wish I can find in my heart to make against Madame de Chastellux and yourself is that you may neither of you ever get the better of this same domestic felicity during the entire course of your mortal existence."

When it came to advising someone in his own family, however, he was far more realistic, and even downright gloomy on the subject of matrimony. One may read as much as he chooses into these lines penned to Elizabeth Parke Custis, the oldest of

Jack Custis's three daughters, just before her marriage to Thomas Law in 1794:

"Do not, then, in contemplation of the marriage state, look for perfect felicity before you consent to wed. Nor conceive, from the fine tales the poets and lovers of old have told us, of the transports of mutual love, that heaven has taken its abode on earth. Nor do not deceive yourself in supposing that the only means by which these are to be obtained is to drink deep of the cup and revel in an ocean of love. Love is a mighty pretty thing, but like all other delicious things, it is cloying, and when the first transports of the passion begin to subside, which it assuredly will do, and yield, oftentimes too late, to more sober reflections, it serves to evince that love is too dainty a food to live upon *alone*, and ought not to be considered farther than as a necessary ingredient for that matrimonial happiness which results from a combination of causes, none of which are of greater importance than that the object on whom it is placed should possess good sense, good dispositions, and the means of supporting you in the way you have been brought up.

"Such qualifications cannot fail to attract (after marriage) your esteem and regard, into which or into disgust, sooner or later, love naturally resolves itself, and who at the same time has a claim to the respect and esteem of the circle he moves in. Without these, whatever may be your first impressions of the man, they will end in disappointment, for be assured, and experience will convince you, there there [sic] is no truth more certain than that all our enjoyments fall short of our expectations, and to none does it apply with more force than to the gratification of the passions. . . ."

To Elizabeth and the other children and grandchildren, Washington was always trying to be helpful. If they were uniformly spoiled and not cut to the sterner patterns of his own nature, it could be put down to Martha's influence. But he brought up her fatherless children, and Jack's fatherless children, in turn, as though they were his own, besides looking after his similarly bereft nieces and nephews. What this cost him he indicated in a letter to his Sister Lewis when he sent Harriet Washington to live with her.

"I shall continue to do for her what I have already done for seven years past," he wrote, "and that is to furnish her with such reasonable and proper necessaries as she may stand in need of, notwithstanding I have had both her brothers upon my hands, and I have been obliged to pay several hundred pounds out of my own pocket for their boards, schooling, clothing, &c, &c of them, for more than the period aforementioned; their father's estate being unable to discharge the executions as fast as they are issued against it."

Of all the children whose care he assumed in greater or less degree, his favorite perhaps was Eleanor, or "Nellie," Jack's youngest daughter, who with her brother George came to live with the Washingtons after Jack's death. Nellie was a lovely young girl, who grew into one of the beauties of the day. For her Washington imported a fine harpsichord which cost him a thousand dollars, and paid for the lessons Nellie dutifully took. He was always giving her little presents—"The Wayworn Traveler, a song for Miss Custis"; "a pair of gold eardrops," a watch. His account books are dotted with such items.

When she married his favorite nephew, Lawrence Lewis, he was highly pleased, and for a wedding gift he gave them that magnificent piece of colonial architecture, Woodlawn, across the way from Mount Vernon on a hill which commanded a superb view of the Potomac. William Thornton, one of the Capitol's architects, designed the splendid residence in the late Georgian style. The traveler today can visit this house, which has been restored and refurnished by the National Trust for Historic Preservation.[14]

Yes, Washington was a man who was good to his wife and adopted children. How did he get along with his mother?

With proper respect, but no overwhelming affection, as noted before. His sister must have been much closer to Mary Ball Washington, whose house in Fredericksburg did not adjoin the Lewis property, as is often mistakenly asserted, but was two streets and four rows of lots away.[15] Washington bought the house for her at the start of the Revolution, fearing for her safety at Ferry Farm, and reasoning that it would be best to have her near his sister. In this house, at the corner of Charles and Lewis streets in Fredericksburg, the General's mother lived during her indomitable old age. She no longer had any children to dominate, although she did her best even after they were grown, but in a sense she transferred this need to herself, refusing to permit the doctor to dress the breast cancer she developed, and maintaining a vigorous independence to the end. Her doctor reported that he had "a small battle" every day with "the old lady." Much of the time she sat in her garden, a spacious and sunlit place filled with boxwood and flowers and ornamental shrubs, and there she held court for anyone, including George, who paid her a visit.

There are numerous stories of distinguished men, friends of her son, who came to visit her, and of how she charmed and captivated them with her simple dignity, but there appears to be not the slightest element of truth in any of them, except that the visits were made, as a show of respect to Washington, and that his mother received people in her usual matter-of-fact way. That she ever said any such thing to Lafayette as, "Ah, Marquis, you see an old woman—but come, I can make you welcome to my poor dwelling without the parade of changing my dress," is certainly improbable. It is easier to believe she gave him spiced gingerbread and mint julep, as the story goes, but one hopes for Lafayette's sake that they were not served together.

What kind of a man was George Washington?

Some of the answers have been provided here, but it remains to this day, as in his own time, a matter of who does the assessing. He was less, surely, than his idolators have since proclaimed, but he was much more in a way they did not contemplate. Perhaps he was not even—a heretical idea—the original

Father of His Country. There is evidence to show that, of all people, George III was first given that designation. On page 183 of a book called *The Soldiers' Faithful Friend*, by one Hanway, printed at London in 1776, there is a vignette of the monarch, his head circled with a laurel wreath, and a legend beneath reading, "G. III, The Father of His Country."

Was Washington a great man, and how is the stature of greatness measured?

Historically every piece of evidence produced by scholars adds to his greatness, regardless of the questionings and doubts raised by some biographers of our time. If a great man is measured by the increase in his stature decade after decade, then Washington was great. He has been embalmed for years by the worshipers, but the recent disclosures of the full-bodied man, by Freeman and others, may in time provide him with some of the affection the American people have given largely to their "other" great President, Lincoln.

As for the physical dimensions of greatness, Tobias Lear tells us that Dr. Dick measured the general in his coffin. He was exactly six feet, three and a half inches of Virginia gentleman.

Chapter 3

Mount Vernon: The Traveler at Home


Always the road led home to Mount Vernon. And of the many times he traveled to its hospitable doors, there were two journeys he would never forget: the time he brought Martha there as a bride, and the last ride home from the war.


[1759]    It was an embarrassing moment, that first trip in the spring of 1759. After their marriage on January 6, and a honeymoon at the Custis plantation, they had gone to Williamsburg on George's twenty-seventh birthday while he began his service as a member of the House of Burgesses from Frederick County. But on April 2, the understanding House had given him a leave of absence so that he might get his new establishment in order.

The Colonel organized his expedition to Mount Vernon: wife, Martha; two children, Jackie and Patsy, four and two respectively; servants and luggage. As Freeman remarks, he "never before had been called upon to provide for the movement of so unusual a combination of humans and trunks and chests and boxes. . . ." [1]

On the way, it suddenly occurred to the new bridegroom that he was behaving like a bachelor. Mount Vernon had not been prepared at all for the coming of a family. He sat down and scrawled a hasty note to his manager, John Alton:

"I have sent Miles [a servant] on today to let you know that I expect to be up tomorrow, and to get the key from Colonel Fairfax's, which I desire you will take care of. You must have the house very well cleaned, and were you to make fires in the rooms below it would air them. You must get two of the best bedsteads put up, one in the hall room, and the other in the little dining room that used to be, and have beds made on them against we come. You must also get out the chairs and tables, and have them very well rubbed and cleaned; the staircase ought also to be polished in order to make it look well.

"Inquire about in the neighborhood and get some eggs and chickens, and prepare in the best manner you can for our coming; you need not, however, take out any more of the furniture than the beds and tables and chairs in order that they may be well rubbed and cleaned."

Martha had her own plans for Mount Vernon, which she had never seen until her new husband brought her there. There was the bedroom to be redecorated, with furnishings and draperies, blue and white; a tester bed, with curtains and canopy to match the window draperies and chair seats. Furniture was needed elsewhere in the house, and outside the lawn had to be reseeded.

It was the end of one journey and the beginning of another; George would not soon forget it.

[1783]     The journey he made in December 1783 was a race against time, to ride from New York to Mount Vernon with stops in Philadelphia, Baltimore and Annapolis, and still reach home in time to have Christmas dinner with Martha. To delay him there was the formal process of resigning his commission before Congress at Annapolis, and the inevitable dinners and addresses and ceremonies along the way.

As he left Philadelphia on the morning of December 15, he realized that the race would be a close one. By pressing the horses he was able to ride into Baltimore on the seventeenth, and there he had allowed himself a day for a public dinner he would have to attend at Fountain Inn. It is not known whether he also allowed for a ball at the inn, an affair so exuberant it lasted until two in the morning, or whether he stayed up to dance until that scandalous hour. In any event, he was out of his lodgings at Grant's Tavern and into the saddle only a few hours after the ball ended, riding down to Annapolis that day.

There he had to await the pleasure of Congress before he could proceed. The legislators told him they would receive him officially on the following Tuesday, the twenty-third. He had arrived on Friday. For three days, then, he had to submit to entertainments, and it appeared that everyone in Annapolis desired to honor him in some way.

On Saturday night it was a dinner given by General Mifflin. Sunday, after church, he spent in returning the visits of Saturday. Monday was the day of the grandest event, the ceremonial dinner given by Congress for the General and two hundred guests, followed by a ball in the State House, with the General Assembly of Maryland as host.

An observer of these events described them to a friend: "The feast on Monday was the most extraordinary I ever attended. Between two and three hundred gentlemen dined together in the ballroom. The number of cheerful voices, with the clangor of knives and forks, made a din of a very extraordinary nature and most delightful influence. Every man seemed to be in heaven or so absorbed in the pleasures of imagination as to neglect the more sordid appetites, for not a soul got drunk, though there was wine in plenty and the usual number of thirteen toasts drank, besides one given afterward by the General, which you ought to get acquainted with: it is as follows, 'Competent powers to Congress for general purposes.'

"In the evening of the same day, the Governor gave a ball at the State House. To light the rooms every window was illuminated. Here the company was equally numerous, and more brilliant, consisting of ladies and gentlemen. Such was my villainous awkwardness that I could not venture to dance on this occasion, you must therefore annex to it a cleverer idea than is to be expected from such a mortified whelp as I am. The General danced every set, that all the ladies might have the pleasure of dancing with him, or as it has since been handsomely expressed, 'get a touch of him.' " [2]

427

The first lady to get a touch was Mrs. James Maccubbin, described as one of the most beautiful women of her time, with whom the General opened the ball.

To expedite his departure on the following day, Washington had the horses ready and waiting at the State House, so that when he had finished his business with Congress he could jump into the saddle and ride off to Mount Vernon without delay.

He found Congress assembled in the Senate chamber, a large room decorated in the classic style, with Corinthian columns supporting a gallery and on the opposite side helping to frame the chair of the presiding officer, who was General Mifflin, then President of Congress. Promptly at twelve o'clock Washington appeared at the door, where he was met by the secretary of the Senate and conducted to his chair. He gazed up at the gallery, crowded with ladies, whose gentleman friends were jammed into the space at the rear of the hall. A throng filled the streets outside. The secretary called for silence, and the General rose and bowed to Congress. The members took off their hats, which they had been wearing until then, in formal salute, but they did not rise and return the bow, thus preserving the sovereignty of the states, and accurately forecasting the difficulties Washington would have as President. On that day, however, he accepted this piece of republican protocol as proper.

The General took his speech out of a side pocket and began to read. It was one of those moments of high emotion in his life, though perhaps he did not realize it until he came to the paragraph concerning his officers, from whom he had just parted in tears at New York. Speaking of their "peculiar services and distinguished merits," his voice and the paper shook, so that he had to use both hands to hold the pages steady. Again, as he came to the lines, "I consider it an indispensable duty to close this last solemn act of my official life, by commending the interests of our dearest country to the protection of Almighty God, and those who have the superintendence of them, to His holy keeping," his voice became rough and choked. At the end of the sentence he had to stop a moment to recover himself. In the silence there was the sound of quiet weeping from the ladies in the gallery, and later there were members of Congress who confessed they could hardly see Washington. Then, in command of himself once more, he read the final paragraph:

"Having now finished the work assigned me, I retire from the great theatre of action, and bidding an affectionate farewell to this august body, under whose orders I have so long acted, I here offer my commission, and take my leave of all the employments of public life."

Here he drew out his commission, and with a copy of his address, handed the documents to Mifflin, after which he stepped back and remained on his feet while the President of Congress replied in a speech of no more than 350 words. Jefferson had written the original of this reply, with the aid of an advance copy of Washington's speech, but others had made changes in it, including Elbridge Gerry and James McHenry.

A copy of the reply was handed to Washington, who bowed to the Congress. Again they took off their hats but did not bow, as G. Washington, plain citizen, left the Senate chamber with his former aides. He stayed in an anteroom while Congress was formally adjourned and the spectators were cleared from the room. Then he returned to shake hands with every member and bid them good-by. As he finished the circle near the door, he walked out to the steps and climbed at once into the saddle. It was nearly one o'clock of the twenty-third.

All the remaining part of that day and most of the next he rode, as fast as the horses could travel. As Freeman puts it so well, "Home was the magnet that drew him, home the haven he sought, home the years'-long dream that now was near fulfillment. Every delay was a vexation and every halt a denial. At last the cold, clear waters of the Potomac came in sight, then the ferry and after that the blusterous passage, the last swift stage of the ride, the beloved trees, the yard, the doorway, Martha's embrace and the shrill, excited voices of 'Jack' Custis's younger children—all this a richer reward than the addresses of cities, the salute of cannon and the approving words of the President of Congress." [3]

Washington was so glad to be home that he did not even note in his diary what time he arrived, or any of the details of his homecoming, except that it was Christmas Eve. At least he was in time for Christmas dinner; the promise to Martha was kept.

About his life at Mount Vernon, then and at other times, there are numerous contemporary accounts, written by the travelers who came from everywhere to see and talk with the great man. Anyone who came properly introduced had access to his hospitality, and so many took advantage of the fact that Washington occasionally complained that Mount Vernon had the appearance of a tavern. He wrote to George William Fairfax in 1786, urging him and Sally to visit, and added: "So many come here without proper introductions that it is a real satisfaction when I am able to discriminate. . . . My manner of living is plain. I do not mean to be put out of it. A glass of wine and a bit of mutton are always ready, and such as will be content to partake of them are welcome; those who expect more will be disappointed, but no change will be affected by it."

[1788]    One who apparently expected more of the master was Francis Adrian Vander Kemp, formerly a minister of the Mennonite congregation at Leyden, Holland, and a commander in that country's army. Fleeing the political troubles there in 1788, he came to America, and to Mount Vernon with an introduction from Lafayette. He recorded this impression in his journal:

"I arrived at last at Mount Vernon, where simplicity and order, unadorned grandeur and dignity had taken up their abode. There seemed to me to skulk somewhat of a repulsive coldness, not congenial with my mind, under a courteous demeanor; and I was infinitely better pleased by the unassuming modest gentleness of the Lady, than with the conscious superiority of her Consort. There was a chosen society—Col. Humphrey was there. I was charmed with his manners, his conversation; he knew how to please, he knew how to captivate, when he deemed it worth."

In spite of his first impression, Vander Kemp ultimately came to admire Washington. Settling finally as a minister at Oldenbarneveld (Trenton), he delivered a flowery eulogy on the "consciously superior" master of Mount Vernon when Washington died.

[1796]    Another visitor who came away with mixed impressions of the master and his house was the noted architect, Benjamin H. Latrobe. In his diary he describes a visit to Mount Vernon in July 1796 as follows:

"Having alighted . . . I sent in my letter of introduction [from his friend, Bushrod Washington] and walked into the portico, west of the river. In about ten minutes the President came to me. He wore a plain blue coat; his hair dressed and powdered. There was a reserve but no hauteur in his manner. He shook me by the hand, said he was glad to see a friend of his nephew's, drew a chair, and desired me to sit down.

"After conversing with me for more than two hours, he got up and said that 'we should meet again at dinner.' I then strolled about the lawn and took a few sketches of the house, &c. Upon my return I found Mrs. Washington and her granddaughter, Miss Custis, in the hall. I introduced myself to Mrs. Washington as the friend of her nephew, and she immediately entered into conversation upon the prospect from the lawn, and presently gave me an account of her family, in a goodhumored free manner that was extremely pleasing and flattering. She retains strong remains of considerable beauty, and seems to enjoy good health and as good humor. She has no affectation of superiority, but acts completely in the character of the mistress of the house of a respectable and opulent country gentleman. His granddaughter, Miss Eleanor Custis, has more perfection of form, of expression, of color, of softness and of firmness of mind than I have ever seen before. . . .

"... Dinner was served at about half-past three. ... He placed me at the left hand of Mrs. Washington, Miss Custis seated at her right, and himself next to her about the middle of the table. There was very little conversation during dinner. A few jokes passed between the President and young Lafayette [his old friend's son was then living with him], whom he treats more like a child than a guest. I felt a little embarrassed at the quiet, reserved air that prevailed. As I drink no wine, and the President drank only three glasses, the party soon returned to the portico. ... Coffee was brought about six o'clock. . . .

"Breakfast was served up in the usual Virginia style—tea, coffee and cold boiled meat—and for an hour afterwards he (Washington) stood on the steps of the west door talking to the company who were collected around him. His subject was principally the establishment of the university at the Federal City. He mentioned the offer he had made of giving to it all the interest he had in the city on condition that it should go on in a given time, and complained that though magnificent offers had been made by many speculators for the same purpose, there seemed to be no inclination to carry them into effect. He spoke as if he felt a little hurt upon the subject. . . ."

Trying to sum up his impression of Washington, Latrobe wrote: ". . . He was sometimes entirely silent for many minutes, during which time an awkwardness seemed to prevail in everyone present. His answers were sometimes short and approached to moroseness. He did not, at any time, speak with any remarkable fluency. Perhaps the extreme correctness of his language, which almost seemed studied, produced this effect. He appeared to enjoy a humorous observation and made several himself. He laughed heartily sometimes and in a very good-humored manner. On the morning of my departure, he treated me as if I had lived years in his house, with ease and attention. But in general I thought there was a slight air of moroseness about him, as if something had vexed him." [4]

[1798]     Another visitor, a Polish gentleman and scholar, Julian U. Niemcewicz, came to Mount Vernon for a fortnight's visit in 1798, only a year before his host's death, and described the routine Washington followed in these last years of his retirement, in which he pursued a "quiet and uniform life." The Polish gentleman reported:

". . . He rises at five in the morning and reads or writes until seven. He takes his breakfast—tea with a cake of Indian corn (because of his teeth), cutting it in slices, which he covers with butter and honey. He goes on his horse to see the work in the fields; sometimes he stops in the middle of a meadow in order to hold a consultation with Mr. Anderson (his superintendent). He comes back at two, changes his dress, and is ready for dinner. If there are guests, he likes to talk after dinner, with a glass of Madeira wine by his side. Afterward he reads very speedily the newspapers, of which he receives quite ten of different kinds, and answers letters. Tea is given at seven; he talks until nine, then he goes to bed.

"I was considered in this home not as a stranger, but rather as a member of the family. They cared about everything which concerned myself." *

[1783–1789]     That was the way Washington lived in his second period of retirement, after the presidency. It was not appreciably different from the manner of his living during the few years he had at Mount Vernon between the end of the war and his election, when he thought he had come home for good. He was chiefly occupied then with rehabilitating his estate, which was run down after eight years of comparative neglect.

It was his custom to mount his horse after breakfast and ride out to inspect the farms comprising the plantation. The trip might total as much as ten or fifteen miles before he got back in time to change his clothes for a three o'clock dinner, because

---

* When he left, Niemcewicz got a parting gift, a souvenir from Martha. It was a china cup, "bearing her initials and the names of the States of the Union."

these four farms of his totaled nearly 4500 acres of land and it was half a day's journey to circumnavigate them. They were called Union Farm, the Dogue Run Farm, the Muddy Hole Farm and the River Farm, besides the Mansion House Farm itself, where the main residence stood. The component parts operated as self-contained units, each with an overseer and its own tools and hands.

Washington accommodated his daily schedule of inspection to the visitors who might be at Mount Vernon, if they were people of importance or friends of long standing, otherwise the visitors had to fit themselves to the routine. In either case, their impressions seem to have been pleasant ones in the six years between public duty, perhaps more so than in the last three years of retirement, when age and the afflictions of public office accounted for much of the "moroseness" that Latrobe and others observed.

One of the best descriptions left by the postwar visitors was that of John Hunter, a London merchant who arrived at Mount Vernon on November 16, 1785, with Richard Henry Lee and his son, and Colonel Fitzgerald. They came to dinner and stayed for the night, and in his diary, Hunter wrote of the visit: ". . . When I was first introduced to him, he was neatly dressed in a plain blue coat, white cassimir waistcoat, and black breeches and boots, as he came from his farm. After having sat with us some time, he retired and sent in his lady, a most agreeable woman about 50, and Major Washington, his nephew, married about three weeks ago to a Miss Bassett. She is Mrs. Washington's niece and a most charming young woman. She is about 19. After chatting with them for half an hour, the General came in again with his hair neatly powdered, a clean shirt on, a new plain drab coat, white waistcoat and white silk stockings. At three, dinner was on the table and we were shown by the General into another room, where everything was set off with a peculiar taste, and at the same time very neat and plain. The General sent the bottle about pretty freely after dinner, and gave success to the navigation of the Potomac for his toasts, which he has very much at heart, and when finished will, I suppose, be the first river in the world. . . .

"After tea General Washington retired to his study and left us with the President [of Congress, who was Lee] his lady and the rest of the company. If he had not been anxious to hear the news of Congress from Mr. Lee, most probably he would not have returned to supper, but gone to bed at his usual hour, nine o'clock, for he seldom makes any ceremony. We had a very pleasant supper about that time. The General, with a few glasses of champagne, got quite merry, and being with his intimate friends, laughed and talked a good deal. Before strangers he is generally very reserved and seldom says a word. . . .

"I rose early and took a walk about the General's grounds, which are really beautifully laid out. He has about 4000 acres well cultivated and superintends the whole himself. Indeed his greatest pride now is to be thought the first farmer in America. He is quite a Cincinnatus, and often works with his men himself—strips off his coat and labors like a common man. The General has a great turn for mechanics. . . . It's astonishing with what niceness he directs everything in the building way, condescending even to measure the things himself, that all may be perfectly uniform. The style of his house is very elegant, something like the Prince de Condé's at Chantille, near Paris, only not quite so large; but it's a pity he did not build a new one at once, as it has cost him nearly as much repairing his old one. . . ."

Hunter also visited the stables, where he saw "his famous racehorse, Magnolia—a most beautiful creature," and "old Nelson, now 22 years of age, that carried the General almost always during the war; Blueskin, another fine old horse next to him, now and then had that honor. . . . Blueskin was not the favorite, on account of his not standing fire so well as venerable old Nelson." [5]

When he went fox hunting, Washington usually rode Blueskin, whom Custis tells us in his recollections was "of a dark iron-gray color, approaching to blue. This was a fine but fiery animal, and of great endurance in a long run." Recalling the days of the chase Custis wrote: "Breakfast was served on hunting mornings at candlelight, the general always breaking his fast with an Indian corncake and a bowl of milk, and ere the cock had 'done salutation to the morn,' the whole cavalcade would often have left the house, and the fox be frequently unkenneled before sunrise. . . . There were roads cut through the woods in various directions, by which aged and timid hunters and ladies could enjoy the exhilarating cry, without risk of life or limb, but Washington rode gaily up to his dogs, through all the difficulties and dangers of the ground on which he hunted, nor spared his generous steed, as the distended nostrils of Blueskin often would show. He was always in at the death, and yielded to no man the honor of the brush."

Custis, like everyone else who saw him in the saddle, was profoundly impressed with Washington's horsemanship. "One of the most accomplished of cavaliers," he put it, in his flowery way. "He rode as he did everything else, with ease, elegance, and with power. The vicious propensities of horses were of no moment to this skillful and daring rider! He always said that he required but one good quality in a horse, to go along, and ridiculed the idea of its being even possible that he should be unhorsed, provided the animal kept on his legs. Indeed the perfect and sinewy frame of the admirable man gave him such a surpassing grip with his knees that a horse might as soon disencumber itself of the saddle as of such a rider."

Washington loved the music of the chase, the baying of the hounds, the clear summons of the horn, and the subdued thunder of hoofs on turf. Some of that music he conveyed to the names he gave the dogs in the Mount Vernon pack: Jupiter, True Love, Truman (!), Juno, Ragman, Rover, Sweetlips and Vulcan.

With pleasures such as these, he was content on his plantation. Small wonder that his postwar mood was a mellow one.

A visitor* who had seen him before reported in 1786 that he was "more cheerful than he was in the army."

When Washington wrote of his home life in these years, he was inclined to view it in terms that today sound like resounding platitudes. He told De Chastellux on February 1, 1784: "I am at length become a private citizen of America, on the banks of the Potomac, where under my own vine and my own fig tree, free from the bustle of a camp and the intrigues of a court, I shall view the busy world 'in the calm light of mild philosophy,' and with that serenity of mind which the soldier in his pursuit of glory, and the statesman of fame, have not time to enjoy. I am not only retired from all public employments, but I am retiring within myself and shall tread the private walks of life with heartfelt satisfaction. . . ."

To Henry Knox a few days later he wrote in the same vein: "I feel now, however, as I conceive a wearied traveler must do, who after treading many a painful step, with a heavy burden on his shoulders, is eased of the latter, having reached the goal to which all the former were directed, and from his housetop is looking back and tracing with a grateful eye the meanders by which he escaped the quicksands and mires which lay in his way, and into which none but the all-powerful guide, and great disposer of human events, could have prevented his falling."

If anything disturbed his tranquillity, it was the burden of correspondence. Lear had not yet come back to his employment, and he found himself burdened with the same kind of self-seeking mail which afflicts men in public life today. It was not the letters of friends which he hated to see on his desk, he complained to McHenry, but "references of old matters with which I have nothing to do. Applications, which oftentimes cannot be complied with. Inquiries, which would employ the

---

* The visitor was Jedediah Morse, who incorporated his impressions of Washington's home life into an edition of his geography book which was published at Elizabethtown, New Jersey, in 1789. Morse's first edition of the book, the first American geography, was published at New Haven in 1784.

pen of a historian to satisfy. Letters of compliment, as unmeaning, perhaps, as they are troublesome, but which must be attended to. And the commonplace business which employs my pen and my time, often disagreeably."

To David Humphreys he further itemized this unwanted and burdensome mail which he had assured McHenry required "researches, consideration, recollection and the de--l knows what to prevent error. . . ." The letters included, he wrote to Humphreys, those "often of an unmeaning nature from foreigners. Inquiries after Dick, Tom and Harry who may have been in some part, or at sometime, in the Continental service. Letters, or certificates of service, for those who want to go out of their own state. Introductions, applications for copies of papers, references of a thousand old matters with which I ought not to be troubled, more than the Great Mogul, but which must receive an answer of some kind. . . ."

All these, he said, produced in him "heavy and painful oppressions of the head, and other disagreeable sensations," which, "if I do not change my course, I shall certainly sink under it."

Until he got help again, he could not hope to achieve that poetic serenity which he wrote of so often to friends. His dearest wish was "to glide gently down the stream of life in tranquil retirement till I shall arrive at the world of spirits."

Sometimes, as he rode about the estate, it seemed to him that he had glided all too fast down that stream, and the best days were gone. There was keen nostalgia in the letter he wrote to George Fairfax in 1785, begging him to bring Sally back from London and build a new home in Virginia. "I never look towards Belvoir without having this uppermost in my mind," he said. "But alas! Belvoir is no more! I took a ride there the other day to visit the ruins, and ruins indeed they are. . . . When I viewed them, when I considered that the happiest moments of my life had been spent there, when I could not trace a room in the house (now all rubbish) that did not bring to my mind the recollection of pleasing scenes, I was obliged to fly from them,

*438*

and came home with painful sensations, and sorrowing for the contrast."

The compensation for all his regrets and difficulties he found in the simple pleasure of farming. To one correspondent he wrote almost ecstatically: "I think with you that the life of a husbandman of all others is the most delectable. It is honorable. It is amusing, and with judicious management, it is profitable. To see plants rise from the earth and flourish by the superior skill and bounty of the laborer fills a contemplative mind with ideas which are more easy to be conceived than expressed." [6]

To those who invited him to leave his life of husbandman and visit in the cities of Europe, he returned an invitation to visit him instead. When Madame de Lafayette urged the Washingtons to come see her in 1784, he gave her the familiar answer, that he was happy beneath his own vine and fig tree, and expected to glide gently down the stream of life until he was entombed in the dreary mansions of his fathers.

As for Martha, she was "highly honored . . . and feels very sensibly the force of your polite invitation to Paris, but she is too far advanced in life, and is too much immersed in the care of her little progeny (her grandchildren) to cross the Atlantic." But Madame, Washington went on, was not burdened, and she "must have a curiosity to see the country, young, rude and uncultivated as it is, for the liberties of which your husband has fought, bled and acquired much glory, where everybody admires, everybody loves him. . . . You will see the plain manner in which we live, and meet the rustic civility, and you shall taste the simplicity of rural life. It will diversify the scene and may give you a higher relish for the gaieties of the court when you return to Versailles." [7]

Yet the "rustic civilities" of Mount Vernon sometimes did not seem so remote from the great world. Among the packs of letters which so distressed Washington there were often, embedded among the self-seeking epistles, requests which brought the remote parts of the earth into his library. In 1786, for example, Lafayette forwarded to him a request from Catherine the Great for a vocabulary of the languages of the Ohio Indians. Washington transmitted the Shawanese and Delaware languages, and with them his best wishes for the "attempt of that singular great character, the Empress of Russia, to form a universal dictionary."

[1797-1799]    With his retirement from the presidency, however, Washington made that withdrawal into himself which he had intended in his first period. He was preoccupied with the minute daily concerns of Mount Vernon, and spent less time in consideration of the cares of the nation and the world. He had found his buildings in need of repair, and in fact, the supports under one room had so decayed, he informed Bartholomew Dandridge, that "a company only moderately large would have sunk altogether into the cellar." He also had the immediate business of disposing of the contents of 97 boxes, 14 trunks, 43 casks, 13 packages, and " a large number of other things," which the sloop *Salem* brought down to him from Philadelphia—the accumulation of two presidential terms.

Of his life in this final retirement, he wrote modestly to James McHenry on May 29, 1797, that he had "nothing to say that could either inform or amuse a Secretary of War in Philadelphia. I might tell him that I begin my diurnal course with the sun; that if my hirelings are not in their places at that time, I send them messages expressive of my sorrow for their indisposition; then, having put these wheels in motion, I examine the state of things further, and the more they are probed, the deeper I find the wounds are which my buildings have sustained by an absence and neglect of eight years. By the time I have accomplished these matters, breakfast (a little after seven o'clock, about the time I presume you are taking leave of Mrs. McHenry) is ready. This over, I mount my horse and ride round my farms, which employs me until it is time to dress for dinner, at which I rarely miss seeing strange faces, come, as they say, out of respect to me. Pray, would not the word curiosity answer as well? And how different this, from having a few social friends at a cheerful board? The usual time of sitting at table, a walk, and tea, brings me within the dawn of candlelight, previous to which, if not prevented by company, I resolve that, as soon as the glimmering taper supplies the place of the great luminary, I retire to my writing table and acknowledge the letters I have received, but when the lights are brought, I feel tired, and disinclined to engage in this work, conceiving that the next night will do as well: the next comes and with it the same causes for postponement, and effect, and so on. . . .

"It may strike you that in this detail no mention is made of any portion of time allotted for reading. The remark would be just, for I have not looked into a book since I came home, nor shall I be able to do it until I have discharged my workmen—probably not before the nights grow longer, when possibly I may be looking in Doomsday Book. . . ."

One might have read some presentiment of approaching death in this remark, except that Washington had been viewing the approach since his youth with the same forebodings of imminent disaster.

The next to last year of his life, 1798, began with a winter which started earlier than most inhabitants could remember. There was hardly a moderate day after the first of November, with severe frost and heavy rains that damaged the winter grain. By December the creeks were ice-solid, and navigation on the Potomac nearly stopped, and the mercury was only a few degrees above zero. On the seventeenth of that December, Martha sat down to write a long letter, full of small gossip, to her Philadelphia friend, Mrs. Eliza Powel. In one paragraph she speaks of the General's state of mind, and discloses his bargain with death, which he failed to keep by less than a month:

"I am now, by desire of the General, to add a few words in his behalf [he had drafted the letter] which he desires may be expressed in the terms following: that is to say, that despairing of hearing what may be said of him, if he should really go on in an apoplectic or any other fit (for he thinks all fits that issue in death are worse than a love fit, a fit of laughter, and many other kinds which he could name), he is glad to hear before hand what will be said of him on that occasion, conceiving that nothing extra will happen between *this* and *then* to make a change in his character for better or for worse. And besides, as he has entered into an engagement with Mr. Morris and several other gentlemen not to quit the theatre of this world before the year 1800, it may be relied upon that no breach of contract shall be laid to him on that account, unless dire necessity should bring it about, maugre all his exertions to the contrary. In that case, he shall hope they would do by him as he would by them, excuse it. At present there seems to be no danger of his giving them the slip, as neither his health nor spirits were ever in greater flow, notwithstanding, he adds, he is descending, and has almost reached, the bottom of the hill, or in other words, the shades below."

Having heard George forecast his imminent demise so often, Martha probably considered it something of a family joke.

In this year, his diary recorded mostly the routine of Mount Vernon, but behind the bare words that the music master came and tuned Nellie's harpsichord, one can hear the unfortunate young lady tinkling away hour after hour, while Washington closed his ears to it or removed himself. "She would play and cry, and cry and play for long hours, under the immediate eye of her grandmother," her brother recalls. Washington, evidently, considered that his duties in managing children were at an end.

On February 12, the General went to Alexandria and celebrated his birthday.* In May he and Martha made a short trip, first to Hope Park, five miles northwest of Fairfax Court House, the home of Dr. David Stuart, and then to the Federal City. They were gone eight days on this journey. July 4 was

* In some old-fashioned parts of the country, people clung to the Old Style calendar. Alexandria ordinarily celebrated Washington's birthday on the eleventh, which fell on Sunday that year.

celebrated at Alexandria, too, where Washington appeared in full uniform and attended a dinner for five hundred people in nearby Spring Gardens. He spent Christmas with old friends: Dr. Craik, Judge Cushing and his wife, General Pinckney and his lady. "You may be sure it was a joyful meeting," the Judge's wife declared.

In May he had written a last letter to Sally Fairfax, with a letter containing one paragraph which must have said much to her, as she read it alone in England, her husband dead, the days of Belvoir and Mount Vernon a quarter century away. In that time, said Washington in his letter, "so many important events have occurred, and such changes in men and things have taken place as the compass of a letter would give you but an inadequate idea of. None of which events, however, nor all of them together, have been able to eradicate from my mind the recollection of those happy moments, the happiest in my life, which I have enjoyed in your company . . . ."

He wanted her to come home and live once more in the old surroundings, but even this late pleasure was denied him. It was too late, too late — Belvoir was in ruins, "those happy moments" in Sally's company were a part of the past. He would not see her again.

But Sally was the only part of the past he wanted to regain. He was heartily glad not to be in the presidential chair, and dealing with a Congress where Representative Leon Lyons, of Vermont, had spat in the face of another member, in an argument over the power of the President to deal with foreign nations.

As he entered 1799, Washington saw the last of his family obligations discharged. Nellie was married to Lawrence Lewis on his birthday. The ceremony took place at Mount Vernon. The bride wanted the newly created General of the Armies of the United States to appear in the splendidly embroidered uniform that had been designed for him by the War Department's board of general officers, but it turned out that the General had never ordered it made. He wore his Continental buff and blue to give away the bride, and presented her with the splendid white plumes given to him by General Pinckney. He wore his Continental cocked hat, with the plain black ribbon cockade.

It was a day of celebration and general rejoicing at Mount Vernon, that February 22, 1799, but no one would have known it by reading Washington's diary, where the entry stated simply: "Morning raining, Mer. at 30. Wind a little more to the Northward. Afterwards very strong from the No. Wt. and turning clear and cold. The Rev. Mr. Davis and Mr. Geo. Calvert came to dinner and Miss Custis was married abt. Candle light to Mr. Lawe. Lewis."

Whether moved by prudence or his usual forebodings, Washington made out his last will and testament on July 9, beginning: "I, George Washington of Mount Vernon, a citizen of the United States, and lately President of the same, do make, ordain and declare this instrument, which is written with my own hand and every page thereof subscribed with my name, to be my last will and testament, revoking all others . . . ."

It seemed that everyone else was ill or dying but Washington. Martha was in bed with ague and fever in September, and Dr. Craik had to be called at midnight. In the same month he was informed that his brother Charles had died, and remarked, "I was the first, and am now the last, of my father's children by the second marriage who remain. When I shall be called upon to follow them is known only to the giver of life. When the summons comes I shall endeavor to obey it with a good grace . . . ." [8]

One of the last of his old friends to see him alive that year was Richard Meade, who had been an aide during the Revolution. According to Custis' recollections, Meade rode up one morning and wanted to know where he would find the General. Custis told him, and added, "You will meet, sir, with an old gentleman, riding alone, in plain dark clothes, a broad-brimmed white hat, a hickory switch in his hand, an umbrella with a long staff which is attached to his saddle-bow; that personage, sir, is General Washington."

Meade smiled and said, "Thank you, thank you, young gentleman, I think if I fall in with the General, I shall be rather apt to know him."

Later, so the story goes, Meade found his ex-commander and rode with him a way over the fields, engaging in an amiable dispute as to whether Washington would alight and let down some cross-bars, or whether Meade would exercise the privileges of an aide and do it for him.

Perhaps the last of the visitors at Mount Vernon were Howell Lewis and his wife, who spent ten days there about the first part of December. Lewis tells of their parting as follows:

". . . We walked together about the grounds, and talked of various improvements he had in contemplation. The lawn was to be extended down to the river in the direction of the old vault, which was to be removed on account of the inroads made by the roots of the trees, with which it is crowned, which caused it to leak. 'I intend to place it there,' said he, pointing to the spot where the new vault stands. 'First of all, I shall make this change; for after all, I may require it before the rest.'

"When I parted from him, he stood on the steps of the front door, where he took leave of myself and another (probably Lawrence Lewis and Washington Custis), and wished us a pleasant journey, as I was going to Westmoreland on business. It was a bright frosty morning, he had taken his usual ride, and the clear healthy flush on his cheek, and his sprightly manner brought the remark from both of us that we had never seen the general look so well . . . ."

On Thursday morning, December 12, Washington rode out as usual to inspect his farms about ten o'clock. Soon after he left, the low, foreboding clouds began to let down a mixture of rain, hail and snow, blown along by a biting wind. It was after three before he came home, and when Lear brought in some letters to be franked, he remarked that they could be sent in the morning because the weather was too bad to send out a servant that night.

"I'm afraid you got wet, sir," Lear observed.

"No, my greatcoat has kept me dry," Washington replied.[9]
But Lear thought that his neck looked wet, and the snow
was still on his hair. Departing from his ordinary custom,
Washington came to dinner without changing his clothes, but
in the evening he appeared well.

Next day he wrote carefully in his diary: "December 13 —
Morning Snowing & about 3 inches deep. — Wind at northeast
and mercury at 30 — continued snowing till 1 o'clock — and
about 4 it became perfectly clear — wind in the same place but
not hard. — Mer. 28 at night."

These were the last words he wrote. The snow prevented
him from riding that day, but in the afternoon he walked down
the Mount Vernon lawns to mark some trees between the house
and the river he wanted cut down, as part of his improvement
program.

That night he complained of a sore throat and a cold. Between two and three o'clock in the morning (Saturday, December 14) he woke up in agony, his throat inflamed, scarcely
able to breathe. Lear summoned three physicians at once, because it took no medical knowledge to see that the illness was
serious. The faithful Dr. Craik came, and the others followed
as soon as they could ride there: Dr. Elisha Cullen Dick, of Alexandria, and Dr. Gustavus Brown, of Port Tobacco. They
held a consultation, and all but Dr. Dick wanted to bleed the
General. At Washington's own insistence, an overseer had already bled him of a half pint, since this senseless practice was
still considered a cure-all. In spite of Dr. Dick's remonstrance,
"He needs all his strength; bleeding will diminish it," the other
doctors took about a quart in "two pretty copious bleedings."

After these, Washington appeared to realize that he was dying, that the forebodings of the event which he had known all
his life were now a reality, and the reassurances he had always
given himself must satisfy him in truth. And they did. He had
not lied to himself. "I find I am going," he murmured, and
added, in Lear's words, that "as it was the debt which we must
all pay, he looked to the event with perfect resignation."

Lear did what little could be done to make him comfortable. When he appeared to be having great difficulty breathing. Lear says, "I lay upon the bed and endeavored to raise him, and turn him with as much ease as possible. He appeared penetrated with gratitude for my attentions, and often said, 'I am afraid I shall fatigue you too much,' . . . He would look upon me with eyes speaking gratitude, but unable to utter a word without great distress."

About half past four in the afternoon he asked for Martha, and when she came to his bedside, he directed her to go to his room and bring from his desk two wills she would find there. He looked at them and gave her one, remarking that it was useless because the other superseded it. He told her to burn the old one.

Toward evening, he was again in pain and told Dr. Craik, "I die hard, but I am not afraid to go." Then he said to the doctors: "I thank you for your attention, you had better not take any more trouble about me, but let me go off quietly."

A little after ten o'clock his breathing became easier, and he lay back quietly. He reached over with one long arm and took his own pulse — and must have felt the thin thread of life slip through his fingers. The hand fell away, and he died without so much as a sigh.

"I kissed the cold hand," Lear writes, "laid it down, and was . . . lost in profound grief."

Next day, when he had recovered a little, Lear wrote to the President of Congress the sad letter beginning, "Sir: It is with inexpressible grief that I have to announce to you the death of that great and good General Washington . . . ." He summarized the details briefly and closed with a paragraph which was a simple epitaph in itself:

"His last scene corresponded with the whole tenor of his life. Not a groan or a complaint escaped him in extreme distress. With perfect resignation, and in full possession of his reason, he closed his well-spent life."

The journeys were over. The traveler was home to stay.

447

# A Washington Chronology

February 22, 1732—Born in Westmoreland County, Virginia, at "Wakefield," eldest son of Augustine and Mary Ball Washington.

1748 —First journey to the wilderness, on a surveying trip with George William Fairfax.

1749 —Appointed county surveyor for Culpeper.

1751 —Only journey abroad, to Barbados Island, with his brother Lawrence.

1752 —Appointed by Governor Dinwiddie as district adjutant for the Southern District of Virginia, later transferred to the Northern Neck and Eastern Shore.

1753 —Carries Dinwiddie's message to Fort Le Boeuf.

1754 —Commissioned a Lieutenant Colonel of Virginia Militia, and (April 2) marches to meet the French at Fort DuQuesne. Defeats the French near Great Meadows, May 27, in a skirmish with a scouting party. French main force from DuQuesne defeats him at Fort Necessity. Resigns commission.

1755 —As aide to General Braddock, takes part in the British expedition against Fort DuQuesne, ending with the ambush and defeat of the army at the Monongahela.

Autumn, 1755—Appointed Colonel and Commander-in-Chief of all Virginia forces.

1756 —Travels to Boston on horseback, his longest such journey up to that time, to settle the question of command with Governor Shirley.

1758 —As a Brigadier, joins General John Forbes's expedition against Fort DuQuesne.

January 6, 1759—Marries Martha Dandridge Custis, widow of Daniel Parke Custis, and settles down at Mount Vernon. Takes his seat in the Virginia House of Burgesses, having been elected from Frederick in 1758.

1760–1774–Serves as a justice of Fairfax, holding court in Alexandria.

1770 –Surveys the bounty land of the Ohio basin by canoe.

1774 –Chosen a Virginia delegate to the First Continental Congress.

1775 –Elected a delegate to the Second Continental Congress. Elected (June 15) to command the Continental Army, and takes command at Cambridge, Massachusetts, on July 3.

March 17, 1776–British evacuate Boston.

August 27, 1776–Battle of Long Island.

September 15, 1776–Battle of Kip's Bay.

September 16, 1776–Battle of Harlem Heights.

October 28, 1776–Battle of White Plains.

November 16, 1776–British capture Fort Washington on the Hudson.

November 18, 1776–Americans evacuate Fort Lee, New Jersey, and begin the retreat to the Delaware.

December 8, 1776–Washington with the army crosses the Delaware into Pennsylvania.

December 25, 1776–Washington recrosses the Delaware, and next day defeats the British at Trenton.

January 3, 1777–Washington defeats the British again at Princeton, and goes into winter quarters at Morristown.

September 11, 1777–British defeat Washington at the Brandywine.

October 4, 1777–Americans repulsed at the Battle of Germantown.

December 18, 1777–Continental Army goes into winter quarters at Valley Forge.

June 18, 1778–British evacuate Philadelphia and move into New Jersey, followed by Washington and his army.

June 28, 1778–Washington defeats British at Monmouth Court House, N.J.

Winter, 1778–In quarters at Middlebrook.

*A Washington Chronology*

December, 1779—American army winters again at Morristown.

May 11, 1780—Washington Commander-in-Chief of the united forces of France and America.

September 22, 1780—Conference with Rochambeau at Hartford.

October 2, 1780—Execution of André, at Tappan, New York.

May 21-22, 1781—Second conference with Rochambeau, at Wethersfield.

August 25, 1781—Combined American and French armies start for Yorktown, from the Hudson River.

September 14, 1781—Washington and Rochambeau reach Williamsburg.

October 5-19, 1781—Siege of Yorktown. Cornwallis surrenders.

November 25, 1783—British evacuate New York City.

December 4, 1783—Washington bids farewell to his officers at Fraunces' Tavern.

December 23, 1783—Washington resigns his commission as Commander-in-Chief, at Annapolis, Maryland, and retires to Mount Vernon.

Autumn, 1784—Inspects his properties and land in Fayette County, Pennsylvania.

May–September, 1787—Acts as President of the Constitutional Convention.

April 30, 1789—Inaugurated as first President of the United States.

March 4, 1793—Takes the oath of office for his second term.

1797 —Retires to Mount Vernon.

December 14, 1799—Dies at Mount Vernon.

# Reference Notes

Part 1

1. His log, or diary, of this journey is printed by Fitzpatrick in the *Diaries*. It begins rather abruptly on October 4, ignoring earlier entries. In the original manuscript, the page containing November 3 and a portion of November 4, is missing. On the inside cover page of the *George Washington Atlas*, the ship's daily position on the voyage to Barbados is given. The account contained here is drawn largely from Freeman's narrative, which of course is exhaustive.
2. An interesting account of Ferry Farm today (1953) is in the Sunday travel section of the New York *Times*, July 12, 1953.
3. *Diaries*, I, 5. Also in Fitzpatrick's edition of Washington's *Writings*, I, 7.
4. Brother Gottschalk's *Journal* may be found in Vols. 11 and 12 of the *Virginia Magazine of History and Biography*.
5. *Writings*, I, 9.
6. *Writings*, I, 10. Subsequent quotations may be found et seq.
7. New York *Times*, July 5, 1953.
8. Washington to John Augustine Washington, June 28, 1755.
9. From biographical memoranda prepared in October 1783 for David Humphreys, who had submitted to him fourteen or more pages of a proposed biography. *Writings*, XXIX, 36–50.
10. Washington to John Augustine Washington, July 18, 1755.
11. Washington to Robert Dinwiddie, October 11, 1755.
12. Freeman summarizes everything that is known or may be reasonably inferred about this relationship, II 388n.
13. The text is in *Writings*, II, 287, and in *Freeman*, II, 336. For Freeman's extensive comments, see preceding reference (Note 12).
14. The complex reasons for this journey, and the expedition itself, are discussed in *Freeman*, III, 245-62. A full-scale treatment of the whole subject of Washington's land dealings in the West will be found in Roy Bird Cook's *Washington's Western Lands*.
15. This information about Charles Town, West Virginia, is derived from an article by Martha Pratt Haislip, in the New York *Times*, June 14, 1953.

## Reference Notes

16. These and subsequent observations on the journey are from Washington's diary of the trip, which he wrote of more fully than any other journey he undertook, even to the point of tedium. This record may be found in the *Diaries*, I, 400-52.
17. The journal of this trip is in the *Diaries*, but it will also be found, with valuable notes, in W. S. Baker's *Washington after the Revolution*, 10-17.
18. A contemporary account of the entire trip may be found in the *Pennsylvania Gazette*, July 17, 1782.
19. Those related here are taken from one of the best-known collections of such tales, in which fact and fancy are mixed indiscriminately, Jephtha R. Simms's *Frontiersmen of New York*, II, 624-25.
20. Thacher's *Military Journal*, reprinted in W. S. Baker's *Itinerary of General Washington*, 267.
21. From "Washington at Saratoga," by Ellin Hardin Walworth, in the *Magazine of American History*.
22. *New York Mirror*, August 15, 1835.
23. This story and the others relating to Washington's visit to Fort Plain and the Cherry Valley may be found in Simms's *Frontiersmen*, II, 656 et seq.


Part 2


*Chapter 1:*

1. The story of the trip is told in detail in *Freeman*, II, 157-67.
2. Freeman describes the journey in III, 460-82.
3. *Washington and His Aides-de-Camp*, by Emily Stone Whiteley, 6.
4. In the Connecticut Historical Collections, quoted in Baker's *Itinerary*, 2.
5. Washington to the President of Congress, July 10, 1775.
6. Washington to Samuel Washington, July 20, 1775.
7. *Constitutional Gazette*, August 23, 1775.
8. This story and others are told in Sawyer's *Washington*, I, 330 et seq.
9. Stephen Moylan to Washington, October 24, 1775.
10. Washington to Joseph Reed, November 8, 1775.
11. Washington to Lund Washington, November 26, 1775.
12. Washington to Joseph Reed, November 20, 1775.
13. Joseph Reed to Washington, November 26, 1775.
14. Washington to Joseph Reed, January 14, 1776.

15. *Works of John Adams* (Diary), II, 431.
16. Baker, *Engraved Portraits of Washington.*
17. Washington to Joseph Reed, January 31, 1776.
18. Washington to John Hancock, March 19, 1776.
19. *Pennsylvania Evening Post*, April 9, 1776.


*Chapter 2:*

1. A detailed account of the conference, although not an entirely accurate one, will be found in Stuart's *Life of Jonathan Trumbull*, 485 et seq.
2. The story of the stable and its modern predicament is told by Aline B. Louchheim in the New York *Times*, June 28, 1953.
3. Kilbourne's *Chronicles of Litchfield* contains details of this and other fascinating portions of Litchfield's remarkable history.
4. For further note of the strange drama which transpired at the Robinson house that day, see Part 2, Chapter 4, of this volume.
5. Washington to James Duane, October 4, 1780.
6. *Newport Illustrated*, 36.
7. *Diary of Claude Blanchard*, 93.
8. *Newport Illustrated*, 44.
9. Munro's *History of Bristol*, 242.
10. New York *Times*, March, 1953.
11. Washington to Elizabeth Washington Lewis, October 12, 1789.
12. Washington's journal of this trip is in the *Diaries*, but portions of it are printed, with valuable notes, in Baker's *Washington*, 150-60. Much incidental information is also contained in "Washington as President, 1789-90. New York City the Seat of Government," by Martha J. Lamb, in the *Magazine of American History*, February 1889, Vol. XXI, No. 2. The quotations in the narrative here are from the journal, unless otherwise noted.
13. Washington to John Hancock, October 22, 1789.
14. *Massachusetts Magazine*, October 1789.
15. Reprinted in the *Magazine of American History*, from the *Salem Gazette*, July 30, 1886.
16. This story first appeared in the *Massachusetts Centinel*, December 1789.
17. *Pennsylvania Packet*, August 28, 1790.
18. Ibid., August 31, 1790.

*Chapter 3:*

1. Washington to John Augustine Washington, July 4, 1778.
2. This anecdote, with the note on the Van Winkle family, is reprinted in the *Magazine of American History.*
3. *Pennsylvania Packet*, February 4, 1779.
4. Washington to Lafayette, March 8, 1779.
5. Andrew D. Mellick, in the *Magazine of American History.*
6. *WPA Guidebook to New Jersey.*
7. Smythe's *Journal*, 98.
8. Thacher's *Military Journal.*
9. This description of the Dey house is taken largely from "Washington's Headquarters at Preakness," by William Nelson, in the *Magazine of American History.*
10. De Chastellux, *Travels in North America*, I, 112. The whole account of this visit to Washington is one of the best parts of the book.
11. Ibid., 124.
12. Paraphrased from a manuscript memoranda kept by Major Woodbridge, dated August 26, 1780, reprinted in the *Magazine of American History.*
13. These stories, the reminiscences of Mrs. John M. Bowers, of Cooperstown, New York, are in the *Magazine of American History.*
14. Told in *Washington at Temple Hill*, by A. Elwood Corning, 101.

*Chapter 4:*

1. Washington's headquarters in Bucks County are discussed in more detail by W. H. H. Davis in the *Magazine of American History.*
2. Washington to the President of Congress, September 1, 1777.
3. Muhlenberg's *Journal*, September 19, 1777.
4. Washington to the President of Congress, September 23, 1777.
5. Ibid., October 4, 1777.
6. *Diary of Albigence Waldo.*
7. Dr. Waldo's *Diary*, quoted in *Freeman*, IV, 573.
8. *Journal of Elizabeth Drinker*, 93.
9. *Memoirs of Elkanah Watson*, 62.
10. Letter in the New York *Journal*, June 15, 1778, quoted anonymously, reprinted in Moore's *Diary of the American Revolution*, II, 49.

Reference Notes

Chapter 5:

1. A detailed description of the house and its associations is in "Smith's House at Haverstraw, New York," by Charles A. Campbell, in the *Magazine of American History*.
2. The best description of the march will be found in Washington's diaries. A less accurate but entertaining reconstruction is "The March from King's Ferry to Head of Elk," by John Austin Stevens, in the *Magazine of American History*, July 1880.
3. *Pennsylvania Packet*, September 1, 1781.
4. Certainly the finest and most accurate description of it is in *Freeman*, V, 386 et seq., one of the high points of descriptive writing in the first five volumes.
5. *Diary of John Conrad Doehla*, much quoted by Friedrich Kapp in his biography of Steuben.


Chapter 6:

1. *Ms.* letter from S. Hawke, in Moore's *Diary of the American Revolution*, 330.
2. Further details of it may be found in "The Miller House, Washington's Headquarters at the White Plains," by Wilson Cary Smith, in the *Magazine of American History*.
3. *Middlesex Journal*, December 3, 1776, reprinted in *Moore*, 330.
4. Smythe's *Diary*, 51, and in *Moore*, 399.
5. *Moore*, 442.
6. De Chastellux, *Travels*, I, 345.
7. An account of its history is in *Washington at Temple Hill*, 55-64.
8. Washington to Dr. John Cochran, August 16, 1779.
9. *New Jersey Gazette*, December 6, 1779, printed in the *London Chronicle*, July 22, 1780, reprinted in *Moore*, 300.
10. *Ms. Diary of Captain Joseph McClellan*.
11. Other traditions of the house will be found in "The De Wint House at Tappan, New York, Washington's Headquarters," by John Austin Stevens, in the *Magazine of American History*.
12. A detailed description of the Robinson house is in "Robinson's House in the Hudson Highlands," by Charles A. Campbell, in the *Magazine of American History*. The literature on Arnold's treachery is, of course, enormous, but the story as seen from the standpoint of Washington and his family is admirably told in *Washington and His Aides-de-Camp*.

13. *Diary of Claude Blanchard,* 115.
14. "Narrative of the Prince de Broglie," in the *Magazine of American History.*
15. Letter from a French officer to a friend, *Pennsylvania Packet,* October 24, 1782.
16. Schoonmaker's *History of Kingston,* 335.
17. *De Chastellux,* II, 301.


## Part 3

*Chapter 1:*

1. All nine verses of the song, and Gibbs's letter, are in *Moore,* 244-55.
2. The controversy over the peas was rehearsed in the *Magazine of American History.*
3. His career as aide is told with interesting detail in *Washington and His Aides-de-Camp.*
4. This description of the troops and other details of life in New York in August and September 1776 are derived in part from "General Grant's Resting Place, Its Historic Associations," by Martha J. Lamb, in the *Magazine of American History,* Vol. XIV, No. 3.
5. Freeman recommends that the great body of controversial writing about this battle can be avoided by going directly to what may well be the definitive work on the subject, Henry P. Johnston's *The Battle of Harlem Heights, September 16, 1776.*


*Chapter 2:*

1. Washington to General Knox, April 1, 1789.
2. *Pennsylvania Packet,* April 30, 1789.
3. Ibid., May 5, 1789.
4. *Pennsylvania Gazette,* April 22, 1789.
5. *Pennsylvania Packet,* May 1, 1789.
6. William S. Stryker, *Washington's Reception by the People of New Jersey in 1789.*
7. Jane Ewing to James Hunter, Jr., of Philadelphia, April 23, 1789. Quoted by Fitzpatrick, who says the original is in the Public Record Office, at Trenton.

Reference Notes

8. The details of this occasion, speculative and otherwise, are contained in "Washington's Historic Luncheon in Elizabeth," by Martha J. Lamb, in the *Magazine of American History*, May 1889.
9. Fisher Ames to George R. Minot, March 25, 1789.
10. Told in the article listed in Note 8, above.
11. Many of the details of the inauguration, the ball following it, and the New York scene at the time are derived from a paper read by Mrs. Martha J. Lamb before the New-York Historical Society at the opening meeting of the season, October 2, 1888, reprinted in the *Magazine of American History*, December 1888.
12. This and other quotations from Maclay are taken from his diary.
13. These and other details of the city at this period are in "Washington as President, 1789-90. New York City the Seat of Government," by Martha J. Lamb, *Magazine of American History*, February 1889.
14. Related by Stephen Jenkins in *The Greatest Street in the World*. Jenkins adds, "I had this story from Mr. Putnam himself."
15. Found, among other places, in Frank Moss's curious potpourri, *The American Metropolis*, I, 184.
16. Washington to David Stuart, June 15, 1790.

Part 4

*Chapter 1:*

1. These figures on manpower and population are quoted by *Freeman*, III, 439.
2. The artist's notebook is in the *Pennsylvania Magazine*, XIII, 359.
3. *Pennsylvania Packet*, December 6, 1781.
4. *Freeman's Journal*, December 19, 1781.
5. Bradley T. Johnson, *Life of General Washington*, 159.
6. *Autobiography of Charles Biddle*, 284.

*Chapter 2:*

1. Washington to Tobias Lear, September 5, 1790.
2. *Ibid.*, September 9, 1790.
3. These details and others may be found in William Sullivan, *Public Men of the Revolution*.
4. The theatre of Washington's presidency is discussed by Charles Durang in *History of the Philadelphia Stage*.

# Reference Notes

5. Rev. John Roth, in *Diary of the Moravian Congregation of Yorktown, Pennsylvania.*
6. *Travels in America and Italy*, published in 1828.
7. The scene has been described in several places, notably Richard Rush, *Washington in Domestic Life*, 65.
8. These letters and other pungent observations are in *Letters and Correspondence of Sir James Bland Burges, Bart., sometime Under-Secretary of State for Foreign Affairs*, edited by James Hutton (London, 1885).
9. Henry Wansey, *Excursion to the United States in 1794.*
10. The letters from Charlotte Chambers are in *Memoir of Charlotte Chambers, by her Grandson, Louis H. Garrard* (Philadelphia, 1856).
11. This is part of a pamphlet titled *A Prospect from the Congress-Gallery*, which Cobbett published in Philadelphia in 1796.
12. Isaac Weld, Jr., who described the day in his *Travels through the States of North America during the Years 1795, 1796, and 1797* (London, 1799).
13. Twining's diary, from which this excerpt is taken, was published in New York in 1894.
14. Related in *Memoir of the Life of Bishop White*, by Bird Wilson, D.D. (Philadelphia, 1839).

## Part 5

### Chapter 1:

1. Washington to the Secretary of the Treasury (private), June 13, 1791.
2. Unless otherwise identified, the quotations attributed to Washington in this chapter are from the *Diaries*.

### Chapter 2:

1. These quotations are in the admirable summary (in a fine book) of Adams' jealousy of Washington and Franklin, related by Zoltan Haraszti, *John Adams and the Prophets of Progress*, 3, and 305n.
2. Boucher's *Autobiography* was published in Boston in 1825, but as is obvious, was written some time before.

3. This critique was contained in a letter written April 7, 1839, to Thomas Carberry, of Washington, a member of the Washington National Monument Society.
4. The letter from which all these descriptions of land are taken is dated December 11, 1796, and marked "Private."
5. These travel details are contained in a letter from Washington to Sir Edward Newenham, March 20, 1785.
6. Washington to the Rev. Charles Green, August 26, 1761.
7. Freeman summarizes what is known about Washington's education in I, 64n.
8. In the *Magazine of American History.*
9. *New York Mirror*, January 11, 1834.
10. Related in Gilmore's *Rear-Guard of the American Revolution.*
11. Ascribed to Dr. Lee and printed in the *Magazine of American History.*
12. These poems, written about 1749–50, are in the memorandum book which contains Washington's first diary, "Journey Over the Mountains, 1748."
13. Washington to Theodorick Bland, August 15, 1786. Unfortunately, Bland's letter is not to be found in the Washington Papers.
14. A picture of the house and a brief description of it by Aline B. Louchheim is in the New York *Times*, June 28, 1953.
15. Freeman, III, 297n.

*Chapter 3:*

1. The journey is described in Freeman, III, 12–13.
2. James Tilton to Gunning Bedford, December 25, 1783.
3. Freeman, V, 469 et seq.
4. The original of this extract, according to Fitzpatrick, was given to President Hayes, in November 1879, and is in the Hayes Memorial Library, Fremont, Ohio.
5. Hunter's *Diary* is in Vol. 17 of the *Pennsylvania Magazine.*
6. Washington to Alexander Spotswood, February 13, 1788.
7. Washington to the Marchioness de Lafayette, April 4, 1784.
8. Washington to Burges Ball, September 22, 1799.
9. A direct paraphrase of Lear's indirect quotation in his description of the scene.

# Index

# Index

Coles, Col. Isaac, 387-88
Colfax, General, 135 *n.*
Collier, William, 231
Columbia, S.C., 386
Columbia College, 110, 267; as King's
College, 71
*Concorde,* French frigate, 104
Congress. *See* Continental Congress;
U.S. Government
Connecticut Valley, 81
Conshohocken (Matson's Ford), Pa.,
in war, 162
Constitutional Convention, 312-18
Continental Army, 143; volunteers of
1776, 235-36; on march through
Philadelphia in 1777, 306-8; in win-
ter of 1777-78 at Valley Forge, 168-
76; in 1779-80 at Morristown, 145-
48; after Yorktown, 215-17; concern
over final payment of, 219-20
Continental Congress, 258; commit-
tee investigations of condition of
army, 148, 173; first, 299-301; Wash-
ington elected commander-in-chief
by, 301-5; Washington's farewell
speech to, 426-29
Coolidge's, Widow, Watertown,
Mass., 123
Cooper, Dr. Samuel, 94
Cooperstown, N.Y., 59
Cornplanter, Seneca chief, 369
Cornwallis, Lord, 130, 131 *n.,* 167,
178-79, 189-91
Coryell's Ferry, Delaware River, N.J.,
136
Cotton textile industry, 119
Couenhoven's, Edward, Tarrytown,
N.Y., 223
Coulthard's, John, Williamsburg, Va.,
42
Cowley's Assembly Room, Mrs.,
Newport R.I., 100
Cox's Tavern, Bronx, N.Y., 80
Craigie-Longfellow house, Cambridge,
Mass., 85
Craik, Dr. James, 44, 272, 443, 466-47
Cranbury (Cranberry Brook), N.J., 68
Crawford, Capt. William, surveyor, 46
Cresap, Thomas, 26-28
Crompound, N.Y., on French line of
march, 179
Cromwell's Head Tavern, Boston, 71
Crow, Hyland, 347-48

Crown Point, Lake Champlain, N.Y.,
58
Culkins's Tavern, between New Lon-
don and Lyme, Conn., 94
Cumberland, Md., 353
Cumberland, Fort, Md., 41, 66
Curtis' tavern, Pompton, N.J., 134 *n.,*
35 *n.*
Cushing, William, 443
Custis, Eleanor (Nellie), 257, 272,
349, 422, 431-32, 443-44
Custis, Elizabeth Parke, 420-21
Custis, George Washington Parke,
257, 272, 349, 444-45; quoted, 393-
94, 435-36, 442
Custis, Jack, 87, 225, 233, 257, 299,
392, 402
Custis, Martha. *See* Washington
Custis, Nelly (Mrs. Jack), 87-88, 280,
299
Custis, Patsy, 402

Daggett's, Providence, R.I., 126
Dagworthy, Captain, 66, 73
Dalton, Tristram, 282
Danbury, Conn., in war, 138
Dandridge, Bartholomew, 351, 353
Daughters of the American Revolu-
tion, Connecticut, 97 *n.*
Davey, Martin L., 84
Dawes, Abraham, 165
Day's, Widow, Harlem, N.Y., 240
Deane, Silas, 81, 396
Dearborn, Lt. Col. Henry, quoted,
168 *n.*
Declaration of Independence, 234-35
Delaware, in war, 161
Delaware River, Washington's cross-
ing, 1776, 130, 158-59
Denny, William, Governor of Penn-
sylvania, 298
Dentistry, Washington's experiences
with, 278-80
Destouches, Admiral, 97-98, 101, 103
Deux Ponts, Count de, quoted, 185
De Wint house (Johannes), Tappan,
N.Y., 204-5, 221, 223
Dey house (Col. Theunis), Preakness,
N.J., 149-53
Dick, Dr. Elisha Cullen, 446

# Index

470

# Index

# Index

473

475

## Index

Woodbridge, N.J., 253
Woodlawn, Lawrence Lewis home on Potomac River, 422
Woolen industry, American, 111
Worcester, Mass., 82, 113-14
Worcester, Pa., army at, 165
Wormuth's, Peter, Palatine Bridge, N.Y., 59
Worthington, Conn., 124
Wright's Ferry, Pa., 355
Wynkoop, Henry, 260
Wynkoop's, Col. Cornelius, Marble-town, N.Y., 218
Wynkoop's, Judge Dirck, Kingston, N.Y., 218
Wythe house, Williamsburg, Va., 188

Yale University, 80-81

Yellow fever epidemic of 1793 in Philadelphia, 345-46
Yellow House (Old Yellow Cottage), Pompton, N.J., 134 *n.*– 35 *n.*
Yellow Springs, Pa., in war, 163
Yonkers, N.Y., 223
York, Ohio, 48
Yorktown, Pa., 328
Yorktown, Va., surrender of British at, 188-93
Yorkville, Ohio, 47
Youghiogheny River, Great Crossing of, 33
Young's, Oyster Bay, Long Island, 290

Zabriskie's, Peter, Hackensack, N.J., 128
Zelienople ((Murthering Town), Pa., 34, 36

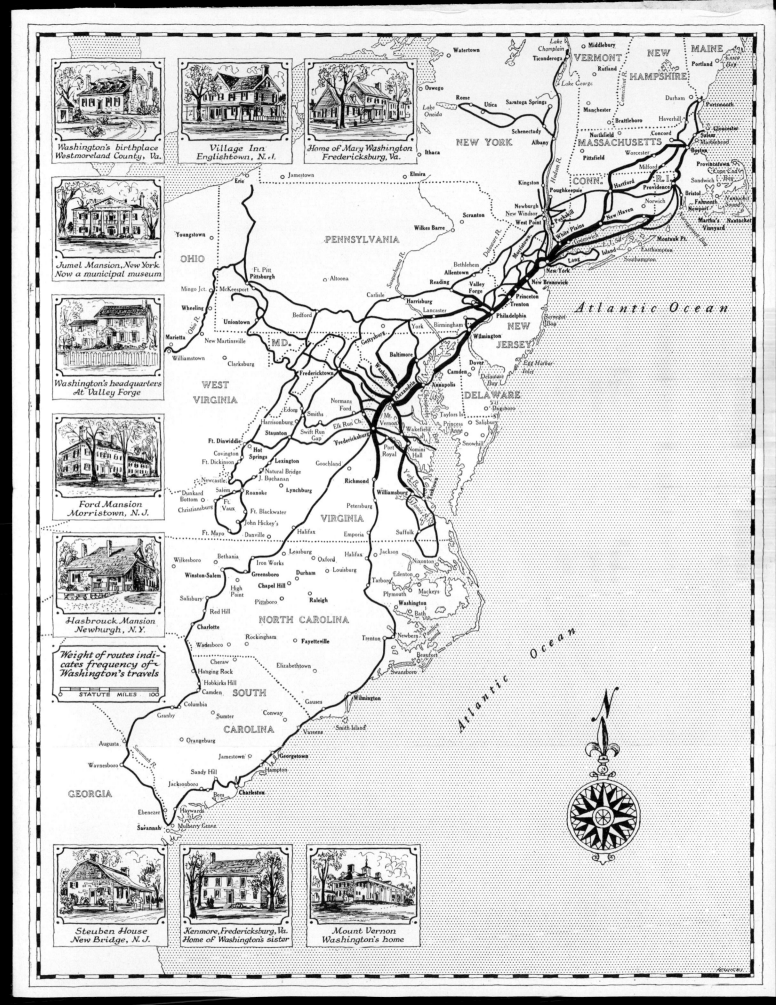

Washington's birthplace
Westmoreland County, Va.

Village Inn
Englishtown, N.J.

Home of Mary Washington
Fredericksburg, Va.

Jumel Mansion, New York
Now a municipal museum

Washington's headquarters
At Valley Forge

Ford Mansion
Morristown, N.J.

Hasbrouck Mansion
Newburgh, N.Y.

Weight of routes indicates frequency of Washington's travels

STATUTE MILES  100

Steuben House
New Bridge, N.J.

Kenmore, Fredericksburg, Va.
Home of Washington's sister

Mount Vernon
Washington's home

MAINE

NEW HAMPSHIRE

VERMONT

Lake Champlain
Middlebury
Ticonderoga
Rutland
Lake George
Watertown

NEW YORK

Oswego
Rome
Utica
Saratoga Springs
Schenectady
Albany
Lake Oneida
Ithaca

Portland
Casco Bay
Durham
Portsmouth
Gloucester
Concord
Salem
Manchester
Northfield
Brattleboro
Pittsfield
Worcester
Milford
Marblehead
Boston
Provincetown
Cape Cod Bay
Sandwich
Bristol
Falmouth
Nantucket Sound

MASSACHUSETTS

CONN.
Hartford
New Haven
Greenwich
Providence
Norwich
Newport
Martha's Vineyard
Nantucket

R.I.

Kingston
Hudson R.
Poughkeepsie
Newburgh
New Windsor
West Point
Peekskill
White Plains
Long Island
Montauk Pt.
Easthampton
Southampton

Jamestown
Elmira

Erie

PENNSYLVANIA

Scranton
Wilkes Barre

Youngstown

OHIO

Ft. Pitt
Pittsburgh
Altoona
Mingo Jct.
McKeesport

Wheeling
Ohio R.

Uniontown
Bedford

Marietta
New Martinsville
Williamstown
Clarksburg

MD.

Bethlehem
Allentown
Reading
Valley Forge
Carlisle
Harrisburg
Lancaster
York
Birmingham

Morristown
New Brunswick
New York
Princeton
Trenton
Philadelphia
Wilmington

NEW JERSEY

Barnegat Bay

Atlantic Ocean

WEST VIRGINIA

Fredericktown
Gettysburg

Washington
Baltimore
Alexandria
Annapolis

Dover
Camden

DELAWARE

Chesapeake
Taylors Is.
Salisbury
Snowhill

Delaware Bay
Egg Harbor Inlet
Dagsboro

Edom
Smiths
Normans Ford
Elk Run Ch.
Mt. Vernon
Wakefield
Princess Anne

Harrisonburg
Staunton
Swift Run Gap
Fredericksburg
Port Royal
Nomini Hall

Ft. Dinwiddie
Covington
Hot Springs
Lexington
Goochland

Ft. Dickinson
Natural Bridge
J. Buchanan
Richmond
Williamsburg

Newcastle
Salem
Roanoke
Lynchburg

Dunkard Bottom
Ft. Vaux
Christiansburg
Ft. Blackwater
John Hickey's

VIRGINIA
Petersburg

York R.
James R.

Ft. Mayo
Danville
Halifax
Emporia
Suffolk

Wilkesboro
Bethania
Iron Works
Leasburg
Oxford
Halifax
Jackson

Winston-Salem
Greensboro
Durham
Louisburg
Nixonton
Edenton

High Point
Chapel Hill
Pittsboro
Raleigh
Tarboro
Plymouth
Mackeys

Salisbury
Red Hill

NORTH CAROLINA

Washington
Bath

Charlotte
Wadesboro
Rockingham
Fayetteville
Trenton
Newbern
Pamlico Sound

Cheraw
Hanging Rock
Hobkirks Hill
Camden
Elizabethtown
Beaufort
Swansboro

SOUTH

Columbia
Granby
Sumter
Conway
Gauses
Wilmington

CAROLINA

Orangeburg
Jamestown
Vareens
Smith Island

Augusta
Waynesboro
Savannah R.
Sandy Hill
Georgetown
Hampton

GEORGIA

Jacksonboro
Bees
Charleston

Ebenezer
Haywards
Savannah
Mulberry Grove

Atlantic Ocean

N